# STAN MUSIAL

BALLANTINE BOOKS
NEW YORK

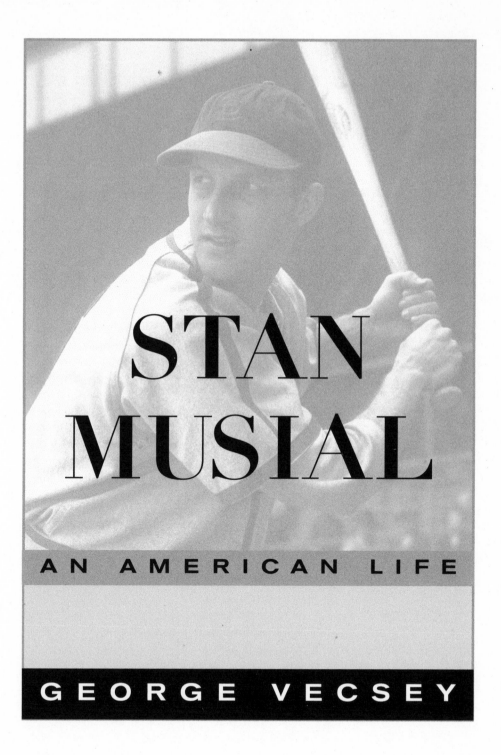

# STAN MUSIAL

## AN AMERICAN LIFE

## GEORGE VECSEY

Published in the United States by ESPN Books, an imprint of ESPN, Inc., New York,
and Ballantine Books, an imprint of The Random House Publishing Group,
a division of Random House, Inc., New York.

BALLANTINE and colophon are registered trademarks of Random House, Inc.
The ESPN Books name and logo are registered trademarks of ESPN, Inc.

Library of Congress Cataloging-in-Publication Data

Vecsey, George.
Stan Musial: an American life / George Vecsey.
p.   cm.
Includes bibliographical references and index.
ISBN 978-0-345-51706-7 (hardcover : alk. paper)
eBook ISBN 978-0-345-52644-1
1. Musial, Stan, 1920–   2. Baseball players—United States—Biography.
3. St. Louis Cardinals (Baseball team)—History.   I. Title.
GV865.M8V47 2011
796.357092—dc22   [B]   2011003271

Printed in the United States of America on acid-free paper

www.ballantinebooks.com
www.espnbooks.com

2  4  6  8  9  7  5  3  1

First Edition

*Book design by Jo Anne Metsch*

TO THE MUSIAL FAMILY

WITH ADMIRATION

# Contents

# STAN
# MUSIAL

# Prologue

## MORNING IN FLORIDA

W E DROVE straight through the night, married only a few months, on spring break, our first vacation together. Like Bonnie and Clyde, we had the feeling of putting something over on everybody. Every mile we traveled south of Baltimore was the farthest I had ever been from New York. We were twenty-one.

We arrived in St. Petersburg just after dawn on a Sunday, nothing much moving but the pelicans down by the bay. It was much too early to locate our friends, so we had a few hours to kill.

I happened to find the ballpark.

I had known about Al Lang Field since I was young, hearing Mel Allen describe DiMaggio and Henrich taking their first rips of the spring, the waves, and the sailboats on Tampa Bay.

The Yankees shared this homey little ballpark with the Cardinals, a team I had followed since I was seven years old, back in 1946. It was a wonderful year for the game, even though the Cardinals beat our beloved Brooklyn Dodgers in a playoff.

As that epic World Series began, my father, who worked at the Associated Press, brought home a full set of photographs—"glossies," they called them—of all the players: one head shot and one posed action shot of all thirty Cardinals and Red Sox. (The rosters were expanded that year to make room for the veterans—the rusty, the wounded, and the aged.)

Mesmerized by the glossies, I would make lineups out of them, scrutinize the faces of the hard-boiled players who had known war and the Depression and the struggle to get to the major leagues.

I can remember the studious glint of Boston's Dominic DiMaggio, who wore glasses, and the exuberance of the Cardinals' Joe Garagiola, who already had a reputation as a clubhouse character. But the player I liked best was Stan Musial, the lithe slugger of the Cardinals, just back from the war, who always seemed to be smiling as he went about his business of smiting terror in Brooklyn. Stan the Man, as we had named him, seemed to represent all the daily goodness of his sport—the workaday regularity, the possibilities, the joy.

Now, fourteen years later, I was a young sportswriter who had covered a few Yankee games, Casey and Mantle, the year before. I was old enough to be married, to be parked outside Al Lang Field, noticing a few cars arriving, men disappearing through the clubhouse door, with the quiet diligence of Depression-era workers grateful to be punching the time clock for another paycheck.

From the rearview mirror, I spotted two men strolling down the sidewalk, each carrying a bat. Why, it was Stan Musial and Red Schoendienst, old friends reunited after Schoendienst's four-year exile in New York and Milwaukee. They seemed as comfortable as matching salt and pepper shakers, wearing nice slacks and collared shirts, most likely just having come from church.

They walked past my car, not noticing the grimy clunker with New York plates that had gotten us out of the frozen North. Up close, I spotted Schoendienst's freckled catlike features and Musial's vaguely lopsided smile, straight off the glossies I had studied years earlier. They were strolling to another March Sunday at the ballpark.

My pretty, young wife professed not to mind when I woke her up to point out the two ballplayers. *Look,* I babbled, *it's Stan and Red.* I tried to explain about Musial's coiled batting stance, how he could run, how we had loved him in Brooklyn, how he was the most beloved man in his sport. She humored me. We had driven through the night and had found the heart of baseball.

# 1

## THE DO-OVER

**B**UD SELIG could see it coming. He did not know exactly which great player was going to be overlooked by the capricious impulses of baseball fans, but he was certain it was going to be somebody he loved.

The commissioner had brought this agony on himself by approving a commercial gimmick he suspected might backfire. A credit card company, a major sponsor, would arrange for fans to select the top twenty-five players of the twentieth century, using computerized punch cards. The winners would be announced during the World Series of 1999.

The drawback, and Selig knew it right away, was that this election could produce an injustice for some great players who had concluded their careers before the current generation of fans, before cable television began displaying endless loops of home runs by sluggers who were mysteriously growing burlier by the hour.

In addition to being the commissioner, with all the crass business decisions that post entails, Selig is a legitimate fan who grew up in Milwaukee, whose mother took him to Chicago and New York, giving him a lifelong appreciation for the game.

Knowing, just knowing, that some great players would be left out by mathematical inevitability, Selig did the prudent, fretting, consensual, quintessential Bud Selig thing: he arranged for an oversight committee that would add five players, making it a top-thirty team. He just knew.

Selig's premonition came true when voting closed on September 10, 1999. Pete Rose, who had been banned from baseball after blatantly denying he had gambled on games, was among the top nine outfielders on the all-century team; Stan Musial, with his perfect image, who ranked among the top ten hitters who ever played, was mired at eleventh. Stan the Man, an also-ran.

"Ughhhh," Selig groaned, a decade later, from deep in his innards. "How could they vote Pete Rose on that team before the great Stan Musial? You look at Musial's stats, oh, oh, I can't emphasize enough to you my regard for him, not only as a player, but when I got to know him in later years, when he came to Cooperstown. I can't begin to tell you what a wonderful human being he is."

His voice rising to an aggrieved squeal, Selig continued: "Did he deserve to be there? Are you kidding me? That to me was the biggest shock of the whole thing. I felt an incredible sadness. I said, 'This is impossible.'

"I love Stan Musial," Selig added. "He was just awesome. I watched him eleven, twelve times a year. I saw him in Ebbets Field, where they called him Stan the Man, because that's what he was."

"I'm seventy-four years old and I still say, in a kidlike way, wow!" Selig said, gaining steam. "And if you were trying to win a game in the eighth or ninth inning, you didn't want to see him up. In old Sportsman's Park, with that screen, he would pepper it. He was the man in every way."

It would have been easy enough for voters to look up Musial's statistics. Even in 1999, everybody had access to instant electronic information. And this is what Stan Musial accomplished: twenty-two seasons, a career batting average of .331, with 725 doubles, 177 triples, 1,951 runs batted in. Three times the National League's Most Valuable Player. Seven batting championships. He led the league in total bases and slugging percentage six times each, and he led the league in doubles eight times and triples five times.

Musial also hit 475 home runs and struck out only 696 times in his entire career—twenty-two seasons—an astounding ratio in contrast to the chemically enhanced worthies of recent vintage, who strike out 696 times per season, or so it seems.

Oh, yes, and Musial was also the most beloved great player of his time, was never thrown out of a game—and yet the fans of the Internet age, with all that information available to them, did not see fit to include him among the top twenty-five.

"He has not gotten the recognition he deserves," Selig said. "He is truly one of the great hitters. And believe me, I have great admiration for Ted Williams, but if you look at the stats, Stan Musial is right there. As far as I'm concerned, he's got to be on the all-time team. He's that great."

In the top twenty-five, the fans included not only Rose but four players active in 1999—Cal Ripken Jr., Ken Griffey Jr., Roger Clemens, and Mark McGwire.

Knowing what they know now—McGwire's extremely belated admission that he indeed used steroids that were illegal under the law of the land, though he still maintained he used them only for physical healing and never to gain extra power—fans of today might not vote for him.

But in 1999, given the choice, the fans voted for Bluto and stiffed Popeye the Sailor Man.

On further review, fans might not vote for the two Juniors a decade down the line, while Clemens's seedy image and rumors of his using illegal body-enhancing chemicals probably would keep him out of the top twenty-five just on general principle. But that was the way things looked to fans with a punch-out computer card in the summer of 1999, listening to the incessant now-now-now babble of the tube and the blare of the public-address system.

Fortunately, Bud Selig's oversight committee kicked in—the same panel that had come up with the original computer-card list of one hundred: Paul Beeston and Richard Levin from Major League Baseball, Gene Orza from the Players Association, Bob Costas and Jaime Jarrin, two experienced broadcasters, and four respected writers, Jerome Holtzman, Larry Whiteside, John Thorn, and Claire Smith. They did their work via conference call.

"The first thing we said was, 'We start here, we start with Musial,' " recalled Costas, the baseball buff who had lived much of his adult life in St. Louis. Costas loved Musial. Everybody in St. Louis loved Musial. Now it was time for Costas to do the right thing.

"We had to scurry to improvise a nudnik-cancelling measure," Thorn recalled. As Orza remembered it, the committee first added Musial and Christy Mathewson, then swiftly went to Warren Spahn, Honus Wagner, and Lefty Grove.

Even at that, to Selig's chagrin, Frank Robinson, one of the great clutch hitters of all time, was left off the top thirty, along with Roberto Clemente, the great right fielder who died in a humanitarian airlift mission. The top-thirty team did not include a single Latino star or Negro League star, not Satchel Paige, not Josh Gibson, which rendered the venture still something of a gimmick.

When you think about it, all lists are gimmicks. Top ten movies. Top hundred books. Five worst presidents. I once wrote a column saying I could pick a team of players who are not in the Hall of Fame and on any given day "my guys"—just off the top of my head, Roger Maris, Gil Hodges, Tony Oliva, Ron Santo, Maury Wills, Thurman Munson, Dick Allen, Jack Morris, Tommy John, Jim Kaat, Lee Smith (sure, I'd take Pete Rose the ballplayer on that team; I covered him from the day he was nick-named Charlie Hustle, and I believe he was clean as a player)—could give the Cooperstown guys a heckuva game. Somebody is always left off every list.

"It broke my heart to leave them off," Costas said of players like Robinson and Clemente. And he added, "There would have been hell to pay if Musial had been left off."

OTHER TOMFOOLERY was taking place in the closing months of 1999. People were obsessing that the world was going to fly out of orbit as computers spun from one digital millennium to another. People were hoarding gold bullion and plastic jugs of water and tins of tuna fish in their basements, getting weird over all kinds of apocalyptic nonsense. Maybe that explains why fans voted for Pete Rose over Stan Musial.

Through it all, Stan the Man remained Stan the Mensch—a Yiddish word for a human being, someone of high integrity, a major compliment where I come from. He handled the oversight with the same grace he had shown throughout his public life.

In July of that year, Musial was content to be a side man in the band of superstars that traveled to Boston for the All-Star Game. Ancient Fenway Park was one site of the ineffective World Series mano a mano between Musial and Ted Williams back in 1946, when both of them were young.

Now Williams was partially blind because of a stroke, unable to walk without a cane, no longer the postadolescent who could be goaded into a fury. The Kid was now the patron of the Jimmy Fund charity and a sage of hitting, probably the last .400 hitter ever, a charismatic storyteller, a beloved elder, dying in front of our eyes.

During the All-Star jamboree, the great players of past and present swarmed around Williams, giving him his due. This was his moment. The old storms were over, and the fans went crazy in their adoration for him; he had long since learned to accept this love. Henry Aaron and Junior Griffey helped him stand to throw out the first pitch, a haunting reminder for everybody hurtling toward old age and infirmity. Musial did not need the spotlight. In Ted's town, Musial was content to be the nice old guy playing "The Wabash Cannonball" on his harmonica.

MUSIAL'S MODEST pose in 1999 raises the question: why did he not strike a chord with the voters in that poll? Some players grow in stature over time, the way Williams did, while others dwindle, as Musial seems to have done with the general public. We all know that new trumps old just about every time, but was some other factor working in the general overlooking of Stan Musial?

The answer may have been that, in the celebrity-driven sizzle of the turn of the century, Musial was just not sexy enough. Once upon a time he had been sort of the American ideal, at least the white mainstream version of it, the *Life* cover boy. Friends and strangers semi-adopted him as the smiling brother, the amiable cousin, the father figure of his time, while Joe DiMaggio and Ted Williams, his counterparts, became known for their broken marriages, their moods, their absences.

Almost as if by will, DiMaggio and Williams became distant towering legends, the stormy Himalayas, whereas Stan the Man endured as the weathered old Appalachians, like the coal-laden hills behind his boyhood home in Donora, Pennsylvania.

DiMaggio would be remembered for the rose on Marilyn Monroe's grave.

Williams would be remembered for crash-landing his burning jet on an airfield in South Korea.

But Musial, a diligent businessman with a successful marriage, would be the nice old guy who mimicked his own batting stance in public. Was this a flaw on Musial's part—or ours?

Today, in Musial's chosen home of St. Louis, with its fine neighborhoods and hospitals and universities and industry, people refer to Musial as being forgotten or overlooked by coastal America.

"St. Louis thinks of itself as the best baseball town and resents both coasts," says Rick Wilber, a writer and journalism professor who grew up in the area and whose father, Del Wilber, was a friend and teammate of Musial's.

It is not hard to pick up on a form of blue-state/red-state resentment toward the two coasts. The issue surfaces on nearly a generational basis, going back to Musial's arrival late in 1941, when his predecessors, the Gashouse Gang, were regarded as Huns and Vandals let loose in the big eastern cities. The terrific Cardinal teams of the 1980s were easily annoyed by swarms of chattering New York media plus the celebrity of the under-achieving Mets players. And the flyover-neglect theory continues into the age of Albert Pujols.

*Ladies and gentlemen, on the right side of our airplane, you will see the famed St. Louis Gateway Arch alongside the Mississippi River. And ladies and gentlemen, a few blocks inland you may glimpse a large statue of Stan Musial, a local baseball player who used to be a big deal.*

The statue is just about the only lingering controversy in the generally tranquil public life of Stan Musial. Ever since it was unveiled in August 1968, Musial disliked it because it was too bulky and did not capture his coiled stance. Of course, the statue has been a landmark ever since, along with the Arch and the psychic presence of the man himself. As controversies go, the statue issue is pretty tame, as befitting the accepting mid-America region where it is based.

St. Louis is the Mound City, nicknamed for Native American burial mounds in the region, whereas New York is the Media Capital of the World and California is the Dream Capital of the World. New York is where Ruth and DiMaggio and Robinson and Mantle and Mays all gained sporting immortality, and the brainy harbor city of Boston is where Williams gained his twitchy fame, if not always adoration.

"May I tell you this?" said Marty Marion, known as Mr. Shortstop when the Cardinals won four pennants in the forties. Marion observed Musial as a weak-armed minor-league pitcher in spring training of 1941 and a few months later encountered him as the kid from nowhere who hit .426 in the last two weeks of a failed pennant drive—one of the most incredible leaps any player has ever made in one season.

"We always say, in baseball, if you play in New York, you get twice as much publicity, you become more popular," Marion said in 2000.

"It's just a known fact that everybody who plays in New York gets all the credit for being the best players or best whatever. Do you believe that? Well, I tell you, it's a fact. If Stan Musial played in New York City and was a member of the Giants or the Dodgers, he'd have gotten more publicity than he's gotten so far."

In that same end-of-millennium rush to quantify, ESPN came up with a series listing the top one hundred North American athletes of the twentieth century (Michael Jordan, Babe Ruth, Muhammad Ali, Jim Brown, and so on). Stan Musial finished sixty-first. Marion insisted that if Musial had played in New York, he would have been among the top twenty-five.

Musial did not complain publicly, but when ESPN began accumulating interviews with famous athletes, Musial would not cooperate, an act of quiet pique. He had his pride, and he had a long memory, as people would discover over the years. Musial let his friends do the speaking for him, and they did. Asked about Joe DiMaggio, Marion said, "I didn't see him make all these fantastic catches," meaning the regular season over the years. "I've seen guys catch as many things as he catches, but he wasn't the hitter that Stan was. Joe wasn't."

Marion added: "If Joe DiMaggio had of played in St. Louis and Stan Musial had of played with the Yankees, you'd see the difference in their ratings. I'm telling you. It's a fact. Either you can believe me or not. That's how ballplayers think."

But wait. Try reminding Cardinal fans that it was in Brooklyn where Musial was first called Stan the Man. Musial is a member of the Brooklyn

Dodger Hall of Fame, in loving tribute to all the dents he put in the score-board at Ebbets Field. But the complaint cuts deeper than that.

The perception of Musial's slighting is that he is too much a man of the heartland, a son of the Monongahela River valley of Pennsylvania who be-came a loyal resident of the Mound City, with no juicy scandals attached to him, a guy who played his harmonica in hospitals and for ladies who lunch in the suburbs.

No less an observer than Jim Murray, the Pulitzer Prize–winning sports columnist with the *Los Angeles Times,* once suggested that Musial was marginalized because he was a man of faith. Murray made this sug-gestion in January 1969, after 23 of 340 baseball writers somehow omitted Musial as he was overwhelmingly elected in the Hall of Fame in his first year of eligibility. (Musial's percentage was 93.24; by contrast, DiMaggio had needed three years to make the 75 percent needed for entry into the Hall.)

Days after the vote, Murray wrote a lovely column praising Musial, throwing in every apple-pie and peanut-butter-sandwich reference he could. Classic Jim Murray. Then there was this: "Oh, it wasn't unanimous. I guess that guy in New York with all the hair caught him coming out of church one day. A thing like that can hurt you in this gen-eration."

I couldn't resist. Knowing Murray from a few press boxes, admiring him greatly, I took the liberty of dropping him a note saying that not only was I a New Yorker but, as he knew, I had long hair (it was, after all, 1969) and sometimes I even went to church. I piled it on by reminding Jim that Brooklyn was where Musial had gotten his nickname. I have long since misplaced Jim's very nice reply, but it was something like, *Oh, geez, George, it was just one line in one column, and I was just trying to get through the day.* (Years later, as a columnist, I came to understand that level of desperation much more clearly.)

The oversight by the so-called fans in 1999 brought a response by guardians of the flame.

Dave Kindred felt much as Marty Marion did. Writing in the *Sporting News,* he said, "If they'd traded uniforms, DiMaggio in St. Louis and Stan Musial in New York, Musial today would be regarded as the second-best player of all time, raised to Babe Ruth's side by the Yankee mythology machine."

Kindred then submitted his starting lineup for what he called "One Game to Save All Civilization": Morgan, Wagner, Ruth, Mantle, Gehrig, Schmidt, Musial, Bench, Koufax.

No DiMaggio. No Williams.

# 2

---

# LUCKY STANLEY

TIM MCCARVER was called up in the summer of 1961, nineteen years old and filled with warnings from his father. One of them was: "You don't want to lose your money gambling."

Naturally, on his first road trip, McCarver gravitated to the lounge in the back of the old DC-6B the Cardinals used to charter, which had a card table for about eight players. A rookie could lose his four-dollar-a-day meal money very quickly.

Among the Cardinals who would slide into the semicircle of seats was Stan Musial, now forty-one years old.

"Stan was a horrible poker player," McCarver recalled. "He'd admit that today. Horrible."

If Stanley needed a six, and three of them had already been drawn, "most good players would have folded," McCarver said. "But not Stan. He would get the last six and he won money off it. Guys would laugh about it. That's just Stan."

"It always stood out that if you were against Stan, you were going to lose," McCarver added.

Musial could not explain his formula for poker just as he could never explain his corkscrew batting stance which set him off from almost every batter who ever lived. He just, ha-ha, did it.

"Jack Buck used to laugh about it," McCarver said. "I never played golf with Stan, but Jack said Stan would mishit the ball and the ball would hit the flag and fall next to the hole."

Just like Yogi, I said.

"Yeah, exactly," McCarver said. "God's chosen people. Just like that."

I remembered flying with the Yankees or Mets on charters in the early sixties, when the weather grew turbulent and we were slipping and sliding somewhere over a major American city, wondering how the pilot was going to find the airport. I would glance around the DC-6B and see the Mount Rushmore profile of Casey Stengel or the distinctive features of Yogi Berra and I would be reassured that nothing bad could ever happen to either of them, and therefore nothing bad could happen to anybody lucky enough to be in their company. Apparently, it was the same with Stan the Man.

"Anytime Stan Musial was around, you got the feeling that everything was gonna be all right," McCarver said. "And there are very few people that you run into in life that you can say that about. A man who can captivate a room without even anyone knowing that he's there, you could feel him in a room and, and a lot of great men I hear are like that. But with Musial it was very, very special."

One time the Cardinals played in Philadelphia on a Sunday and headed back to St. Louis after the game. With a day off Monday, Musial had permission to go to New York to be honored at a charity dinner.

"Guys were saying, 'Stan's not on the flight, uh, I'm not too sure I want to get on the flight.' And sure enough, we take off and you could look out the left wing and see the propeller. It's kind of a frightening sight when you're five thousand feet off the ground and your propeller's not going.

"Well, guys are saying, 'I knew I shouldn't have gotten on this flight, Musial wasn't on the flight.' We had to return to the airport, they repaired the plane or they got a new plane, I forget which, but the fact that Stan wasn't on it meant that things weren't all right with the Cardinals as a ball club."

McCarver thought about it some more and suggested that Musial's lucky touch stemmed from being a churchgoer.

"If you believe in the afterlife strongly, you know that he is one of God's chosen people," McCarver said. "And his whole life's been that way."

McCarver paused and added:

"Never underestimate Stan. As long as I've known him, I've learned. Never underestimate him. That's a serious mistake."

# 3

## THE OLD MASTER

$S$OMETHING WAS causing people to downsize Stanley. In 1986, Bill James wrote:

> The image of Musial seems to be fading quickly. Maybe I'm wrong, but it doesn't seem to me that you hear much about him anymore, compared to such comparable stars as Mantle, Williams, Mays and DiMaggio, and to the extent that you do hear of him it doesn't seem that the image is very sharp, that anybody really knows what it was that made him different. He was never colorful, never much of an interview. He makes a better statue. What he was was a ballplayer. He hustled. You look at his career totals of doubles and triples, and they'll remind you of something that was accepted while he was active, and has been largely forgotten since: Stan Musial was one player who always left the batter's box on a dead run.

The number crunchers, the baseball geeks, professional or amateur, put Musial much higher than the fans did. In the computer age, baseball surely has too many newfangled indices for measuring ballplayers. Stanley did not need printouts of pitchers' tendencies; he knew what they were going to throw. Billy Martin won a lot of games without computer printouts of statistics. Hell, Billy would say (no doubt flinging the printed report against his office wall), he knew all that damn stuff.

Still, sometimes it is helpful to walk on the wild side into the dense world of baseball stats. For example, Baseball-Reference.com came up with several new ways to compare hitters. One was the Black Ink test, first formulated by Bill James, which awards points for leading the league in major hitting categories. After the 2009 season, Musial was behind only Ty Cobb and Babe Ruth. Another comparison was through the so-called Gray Ink test, which ranks players by appearances in the top ten in various batting categories. In this one, Musial was third, behind Cobb and Henry Aaron.

James himself contributed to Musial's slippage. Once upon a time, James listed Musial as the best left fielder of all time, but in 2000 James somehow flipped Musial with Williams. Had Teddy Ballgame been working on his fielding? Had he suddenly begun hitting to left field?

James's revision came before Barry Bonds became the all-time leader in home runs in one season and in a career. It also came before Bonds became suspected of using steroids during the Balco scandals. Bonds was so good, with or without the juice, that he was competition for Stanley and Teddy, but his dirty image is going to hold him back for a long time.

In 2001, James ranked the top one hundred players in history, starting with Babe Ruth, Honus Wagner, Willie Mays, Oscar Charleston, Ty Cobb, Mickey Mantle, Ted Williams, Walter Johnson, Josh Gibson, and Musial.

By putting Musial in this company, James certainly rebutted the apocrypha that Musial is ignored because he was not all that interesting. All I can say is that the fans who saw Stan Musial play—*play* being the operative word—in New York are convinced he was one of the best players who ever wore a gray road uniform in Ebbets Field or the Polo Grounds. Or anywhere.

Fact was, in Musial's first full nineteen seasons, the Cardinals visited New York and Brooklyn for eleven games in each ballpark each summer, mostly day games, which created ample attention to number 6 in the next day's newspapers, of which there were nearly a dozen. Because of the great history of the Cardinals, the team itself was the subject of numerous articles during spring training, particularly since the Cards trained in the same sleepy town as the Yankees. New York–based columnists would take themselves over to Al Lang Field and interview that great player and most accommodating of superstars, Stan Musial. All season, every season, there was a forest's worth of articles.

Woody Allen, growing up in Brooklyn, loved the writing of Jimmy Cannon, the sports columnist with the good old *New York Post* back in the fifties. Decades later, Allen could recall Cannon raving about Musial's "serene dependability."

Many other odes to Musial were written by New Yorkers and printed in *Sport* magazine, based in New York:

- "Mr. Musial Marches On," by Arthur Daley (sports columnist, *New York Times*), 1947
- "The Man: Stan Musial Is Baseball's No. 1 Citizen," by Roger Kahn (later the author of *The Boys of Summer,* about the Brooklyn Dodgers), 1958
- "Stan Musial's Last Game," by Arnold Hano (New York– and California-based writer), 1964

The New York papers could not get enough of Musial. In 1951, Musial was hired by the *World-Telegram and Sun* to write a daily critique of the Dodgers-Giants playoff and the Yankees-Giants World Series. Under Musial's byline was his identification: "Baseball's Greatest Player."

Musial also "covered" the 1953 World Series for the Newspaper Enterprise Association and was identified in the *World-Telegram and Sun* as "Six Time Batting Champ." He was treated as visiting royalty by Joe Williams of the *Telly,* godded up by Red Smith of the *New York Herald Tribune,* lionized by Frank Graham of the *Journal American,* flattered by Jimmy Cannon (Woody Allen's favorite) of the *Journal American* and later the *Post,* and adulated by Joe Reichler of the Associated Press.

"Musial must come perilously close to being the best-liked ballplayer of his generation," wrote Arthur Daley of the *New York Times* in his August 16, 1962 piece, "Salute to a Man."

After coping with the moody DiMaggio and the irascible Williams, writers adored Musial as a player and accessible superstar. Sports columnists are easy. We love stars who talk to us. That simple. Of course, most fans in St. Louis did not know how much ink Stanley received in Big Town because, in those pre-Internet, pre-cable years (some of us call them the good old days), they were, most of the time, going about their business in St. Louis and did not know how well Musial was treated way out there on the East Coast. But Musial knew. All I'm saying is, don't blame us.

MUSIAL SHOWS up at the very core of his sport. Not long ago I was writing a short history of baseball, trying to jam nearly two hundred years of the American game into sixty thousand words, from the dubious myth of Abner Doubleday to the suspect muscles of Barry Bonds.

Somehow, the way writers do, I meandered into a prologue about teaching my grandson how to hit during an impromptu dusk lesson on his family's front lawn somewhere out there in America. Having coached youth baseball when my son was little, I always tried to turn youngsters into the coiled Musial stance. Start back there and then hit the ball. I realized Stanley knew exactly what he was doing.

After doing this little riff on Stanley's stance, I found myself coming back to Musial in the main narrative, not just because I had idolized him as a kid but because of his links to the past and the future.

Almost by accident, I postulated that Musial was the classic example of baseball's six degrees of separation. He was the heart of the game. He had personal connections backward to Branch Rickey and George Sisler and Dickie Kerr; he matched his contemporaries DiMaggio and Williams; when Jackie Robinson arrived in 1947, Musial let everybody know that he fully intended to show up for work; his batting stance was once used as a teaching tool for a young Japanese prospect named Sadaharu Oh.

He also met every president from Truman through Obama, except, for no particular reason, Dwight D. Eisenhower, for whom he apparently voted twice. Over time, Musial has come to be seen as the epitome of the Eisenhower years, from 1953 through 1960, a time now ridiculed for its—what? Complacency? Stability? Normalcy? In this age when yappers spout nuttiness over the airwaves and nihilists fly airplanes into buildings, normalcy is looking good.

In kinder times, Musial even united political opponents. For many years, Victor Gold, a prominent Republican, and Frank Mankiewicz, a prominent Democrat, ran the Stan Musial Society of Washington–Cardinal fans in the capital. Sometimes Musial showed up for the banquet, and played his bipartisan harmonica well into the night.

Musial is not the first or last public figure to suffer from the short attention span of the vox populi. Even presidents come and go in the power ratings.

With his deceptively transparent smile, Eisenhower—as in "I Like Ike"—won two elections handily, but after he was out of office Ike was often depicted as a mediocre fuddy-duddy.

Early in the twenty-first century, Ike began making a comeback. To demonstrate the contrast to a certain inarticulate president of more recent vintage, David Letterman displayed videos of Ike's clearheaded warning about the "military-industrial complex." Ike was looking better all the time. Maybe Stan the Man's time would come around again.

Artists are also susceptible to shifting tastes. I asked Michael Kimmelman, the arts correspondent of the *New York Times,* to name an artist whose career is comparable to that of Stan the Man in terms of losing critical or public acclaim after his peak. Kimmelman suggested Pierre Bonnard (1867–1947), the French painter of quotidian lunch and midday sunlight and his wife in her boudoir.

"It has taken a while, but the art world has come to its own 'a-ha' moment with Bonnard," Kimmelman wrote in 2006. "His self-effacement, his reticence, his inclination to see both sides of an issue and to let others perceive him as painting away in his little house, indifferent to the debates of his day, permitted critics after his death, especially those in Picasso's competitive and devouring orbit, to dismiss him without ever grasping what he had tried to accomplish."

Asked to name a performing artist who had been somewhat ignored and then rediscovered, Kimmelman—himself a concert pianist—came up with Dinu Lipatti (1917–1950), the Romanian pianist who died at thirty-three of Hodgkin's disease. I have heard a couple of Lipatti's clear, haunting performances on vinyl; they give the impression of a man who senses he does not have much time.

"He's the pianist's pianist and remains known to the pros and aficionados," Kimmelman wrote to me. "Both he and Bonnard are stylish, understated virtuosos of beauty."

Composers? I come up with Antonin Dvořák (1841–1904), so easy to stereotype with his love of Czech and American folk music, but as a dozen CDs in my collection confirm, Dvořák is layered, lush, diverse. He endures. Sam Cooke, Dave Brubeck, Nina Simone, Johnny Cash—every generation needs to discover, and rediscover, the old masters.

BUD SELIG worried how Musial would react to being so publicly tacked on to the original top twenty-five. The commissioner knew how some other superstars would have taken it. The world revolves around them; this is the nature of the superstar.

Baseball unveiled its all-century team during the 1999 World Series in Atlanta. Some of the top thirty, including Rose and Musial, had been at a collectors' show in Atlantic City. Banned from baseball, Pete now made his living signing autographs for money. He would show up in Cooperstown during the Hall of Fame weekend and sell his signature out of a storefront. It's a free country. He arrived in Atlanta as conspicuously as if he were wearing bells on clown shoes. It was his free pass to be back in the big tent.

Inevitably, Pete's presence became the central story. He had been a terrific player, the all-time hit leader, surely worthy of the Hall if he had not been caught lying about his gambling. Musial had always praised Pete, even when Pete chipped away at some of his records, but now he understood that Pete had cheapened their sport, so Stan backed off a bit.

Perhaps Pete's election to the top-thirty team had been an instinctive anti-establishment gesture by the fans, to express their view that gambling was not so bad, not in a society that encourages lotteries and casinos. Certainly fans could remember Rose diving headfirst into a base, his Prince Valiant haircut flopping as his helmet flew off. In a new age of reality shows and talk-show screamers, Pete fit right in.

Rose showed up in Atlanta, unrepentant, giving a bravura performance on national television, sticking out his jaw, asking what he had done that was so bad. Was he some kind of mass murderer, he asked, like Charles Manson?

While Rose strutted and preened, Musial arrived in the company of eternally charismatic figures like Williams and Gibson and Koufax. Stan the Man had his agendas; he knew what he wanted to show and what he wanted to keep private. Being the gracious old man came naturally to him, and it served him well on that October day when reporters asked him about having been an afterthought by committee.

"I'm happy to be on their team—added on, voted on, what's the other word?" Musial said. "It's good to be with this club. I competed against about ten of these guys—Ted Williams, Mays, Henry Aaron, DiMaggio, Warren Spahn, Koufax. I played in the '40s but I competed against guys who played in the '30s and I played in the '60s and competed against guys who played in the '70s."

Reminded of the method by which he was included, Musial said, "I wasn't upset. Not really. There are 100 million fans, and only 3 million of them voted.

"It's what the fans wanted, and I'm happy to be here. It's human nature to look at your own generation. It's hard to analyze what happened fifty, sixty years ago."

Fans would recognize Musial, call out "Stan the Man," and he would go into his crouch, wiggle his hips, waggle an imaginary bat. He was home, where he belonged, among his peers. He did not need to create a fuss.

"Never," Selig said. "Never. Never. Never."

# 4

## STANLEY HITS

JIM FREY'S big mistake in life was coming along in the Cardinals organization. Not much room for career advancement on a team that already had Stan Musial.

Finally invited to train with the Cardinals in 1958, Frey figured, what the heck, he might as well study the man who was keeping him out of the major leagues.

One sultry morning in St. Pete, hundreds of fans swarmed behind the dugout, squealing when they spotted the familiar number 6. Musial responded with his regular nonsense mantra, "Hey-hey, whaddayasay-whaddayasay," causing the fans to squeal some more.

Making the most of his opportunity, Frey asked this most approachable of stars if he wanted to play a little pepper—one man taps the ball with his bat and the others flip it around with their gloves until somebody flubs it.

Sure, Musial said.

Frey thought he might do the batting, but with a big grin on his face, Musial informed the farmhand: "When Stanley plays pepper, Stanley hits."

*Stanley hits.* Frey liked his style.

The fans cheered every time Musial tapped the ball. The public perception of Musial may have been of a humble superstar, but it was clear to Frey that Musial relished performing in front of the crowd.

"He's standing facing the stands, the crowd is going crazy," Frey recalled. "And he kind of ducks down into the dugout and he says, 'Lefty, they all come. They love to see Stanley hit.'"

"It was so funny. When he talked about himself, it was almost like he was talking about somebody else."

Frey would never play a major-league game. Years later, as the manager of the Royals and Cubs, he loved talking about the man who called himself Stanley.

"There are a few people in the world who love being themselves," Frey said. "And I think Stan Musial is one of them."

Most of all, he loved being Stanley. It was his stage name, self-perpetuated. To others he was Stan or Stash or Stan the Man. (A woman of a certain age on the Main Line in Philadelphia told me recently that as a teenager she thought of him as Stanley the Manly; she liked his, um, batting stance, the way he wiggled.) However, in his finest moments he referred to himself as Stanley.

Stanley the magician. Stanley the harmonica-playing virtuoso. Stanley the batting guru ("Aw, hell, Curt, just hit the ball"). Stanley the restaurateur. Stanley the guild greeter, shocking some rookie on the other team by welcoming him to the big leagues.

Later in life he would chat with a pope, refer to a president as "my buddy," travel overseas with a famous author. His nom de baseball allowed him to get past his modest beginnings as the poorest kid in town. With a bat in his hands, he became Stanley.

THOUSANDS OF people have their Stan Musial story, about his spontaneous generosity of heart and wallet. I call them Musial Sightings. He was a man of action rather than reflection, a man of anecdote rather than narrative. He had a way of appearing at some appropriate moment, making people laugh, followed by the clattering hooves as the Lone Ranger rode off into the sunset. Who was that masked man?

These sightings are not a string of miracles, to be used as documentation for canonization. He was not without ego. He smoked for a long time. He drank a bit. He could shatter pomposity with a timely obscenity. Late in life, he broke off at least one long friendship over a business disagreement.

He was no activist, no crusader, no saint, but twice, when baseball was being integrated, Musial was a benignly positive presence, a man who spoke little but who was there.

For the postwar generation, when baseball was still America's favorite sport, Stan Musial was its happy face. He was picked by *Life* magazine as the Player of the Decade from 1946 through 1955, ahead of Joe DiMaggio, Ted Williams, and Jackie Robinson. He exuded endless optimism, a one-man GI Bill, grateful to be working at his trade, which in his case was being one of the greatest hitters the game has ever known. And then, somehow, Stanley was obscured.

# 5

## THE STANCE

STANLEY WAS no fool. When he was out in public, he would move into that familiar batting position—twisting sideways to his left, peering over his right shoulder, addressing his right hip to an imaginary pitcher.

The stance was his signature, his trademark, and demonstrated why he was a successful entrepreneur. He knew how to brand himself.

In his later years, from his place in time in long-ago America, Musial knew innately that this was the best way to present himself to people who still remembered him—people who might order memorabilia from Stan the Man, Inc., or pay for his autograph at a collectors' show.

The crouch was his essence, the thing that made him Stanley Hits. He performed it in the Vatican, at the Colosseum, for throngs at the Kentucky Derby and Wimbledon, on the streets of Warsaw or Tokyo or Dublin.

Strangers would see an older gent contort himself halfway into a human pretzel, shake his rear end, flap his right elbow, and wonder, *Who is that man, and why is he coiled up like that?* Others would smile contentedly and say, *Stan the Man.*

As long as he could go out in public, this would be his ultimate way of being himself. The crouch became a self-caricature, a way of identifying himself without showing too much, without getting too deep into politics or social issues. The personal stuff he handled with a smile, all part of the package, but the crouch was for all seasons. Nonverbal was the way to go.

Perhaps he used the whaddayasay-whaddayasay to cover up the trace of stammer he had picked up in elementary school when teachers made the left-handed boy write with his right hand. His script would remain beautiful and his accent would remain somewhere between western Pennsylvania and Missouri.

The crouch was sui generis, not an act, not some mannerism he had picked up. It was who he was. It was the source of his .331 batting average, so he treated it with great respect and incorporated it into the act, defending it with great passion.

When Fay Vincent was commissioner, he loved to study the Hall of Fame ballplayers to try to discover the source of their greatness, what made them themselves—the whiteness of the whale, as Melville put it. One time Vincent engaged Musial in serious conversation.

"I said, 'My question is this, if you came along in high school or American Legion baseball, did anybody try to change that?' I thought that was a legitimate question, but he looked at me and said, 'Commissioner, why would anybody want to change my stance? I was always hitting .500.' I thought, from his point of view, he's absolutely right."

Musial probably always contorted himself into some version of the stance, from the first time he picked up a bat in Donora. He was blessed with a lithe body that had been trained in gymnastics classes at the Polish Falcons club.

When he morphed from sore-armed pitcher to desperate hitter in the low minor leagues, he naturally twisted into a defensive stance, probably because hitting was going to be his ultimate chance to be a professional ballplayer, or maybe to be anything. He could not afford to fail. Make contact or go home. So he waited back on the pitch, then struck, letting his reflexes take over. Power was incidental at first. The important thing was, *Don't let them send me home.*

The result was the Musial crouch—feet parallel, knees bent, right hip showing, bat back, eyes peering over his shoulder. Most hitting stances are personal expressions, and there are thousands of them. Bill James has called Musial's the Strangest Batting Stance.

Musial's stance actually became more pronounced after the war, but it always lent itself to jests, to description. Baseball is such a verbal sport, with its dugout full of drugstore cowboys, making observations on the passing scene.

Ted Lyons, an older pitcher, spotted Musial in his early years in the majors and quipped that he looked like "a small boy looking around a corner to see if the cops are coming."

And Buzzy Wares, a first-base coach for the Cardinals in those simpler times before designated hitting coaches, was impressed with Musial's selectivity at an early age and urged him to keep twisting into his unique stance, the prewar version.

"Musial reminds me of a housewife choosing tomatoes at a market," Wares was known to say. "She picks up one, feels it and puts it down. She squeezes another, pinches a third and then—ah!—here's the one she wants. That's the way Stan sorts out pitches."

How's this for discipline: in 1943, his second full season in the majors, Musial struck out only 18 times in 701 plate appearances. Our behemoths today would be ashamed of such a statistic, as an indicator of lack of manliness.

Musial was never a big man for his sport—six feet, 170 pounds. Nowadays he would be turned back at the tryout gates "unless you can"—*wink-wink*—"put on some weight, son." His ribs showed. He had a parlor trick of sucking in his stomach until it seemed to be touching his spine, but when he took off his shirt anybody could see he was blessed with powerful, rippling back muscles, the source of his strength.

"The only real good hitter I can think of with small hands was Stan Musial. Little bitty hands. But you couldn't find a better hitter," said Bob Gibson, who never pitched to Musial in a game but studied him to see what made him work.

"Stan Musial will twist around so he has to peek over his shoulder," Gibson said, but then he got to the main point about the Stanley Stance: "In the end, we're all fundamentally similar, even if we arrive at our release points by different routes."

Gibson figured out the secret of Stan Musial: he was an illusionist. In his early years, Musial had a friend named Claude Keefe, who taught him a few magic tricks, just enough to make him the Second Worst Magician in the Sporting World, behind only Muhammad Ali—not bad company when you think about it. Ali always said his faith demanded he explain his tricks, so he did; Musial kept the secrets, such as they were.

The stance was part of the act—an intermediate step, to make himself comfortable but also to confuse the rubes sixty feet away. By and by, the smart ones figured out what Musial was doing.

"I never thought his stance was that unusual," said Ralph Kiner, the Hall of Fame slugger, beloved broadcaster for the Mets, and great admirer of Musial.

"He did two things," Kiner said. "With that stance, he was coiled and back with his bat and his body, and he would push off and spring." In other words, what really mattered was what Musial did afterward.

"Every time I see Stan now at an autograph show or out to dinner, he says, 'I kicked your ass, didn't I?' and I say, 'Yes, you did, you wore me out,'" said Don Newcombe, the great Brooklyn pitcher who beat back alcoholism to became a valuable member of the Dodgers' front office.

"But ask him who won the games," added Newcombe, who had a 16–6 career record against the Cardinals, despite Musial's .366 average against him.

Newcombe insisted the Musial stance was just a charade: by the time the ball was pitched, Musial had already unlocked his hips and was in a forward motion, able to hit the ball to any part of the field.

No less an authority than Branch Rickey, the master builder of the Cardinal farm system, explained the Musial stance. "The preliminary movement he has is a fraud," Rickey boomed. "No batter's form is determined by his preliminary stance. When the ball leaves the pitcher's hand, that is the time when you take a picture of a batsman to get his form. Before the ball is pitched doesn't mean a thing. If you want to see a proper stride, a short stride, a level swing bat full back, a coin wouldn't drop off the top of the bat. He is ideal in form."

Musial agreed with Rickey.

"Stance is not so important," he once said, adding that he found his way into that stance because of his desire to meet the ball in his early years in the majors.

"At St. Louis, I always wanted to hit .300," he said, adding, "My stance is very comfortable." In one way, hitting is more complicated than people think, Musial said, in that a good hitter learns to adjust to the pitcher, the count, the situation, the weather, the field. The main thing is to have a good level swing, and to learn to hit to the opposite field.

In the same interview, he made himself sound like a lucky stiff to have played at Sportsman's Park, shared by the Cardinals and Browns for most of his career, a place whose lumpy infield was so baked by the sun and worn by constant usage that players called it "Hogan's Brickyard."

"I got a lot of hits through the infield," Lucky Stanley insisted.

BALLPLAYERS TRIED to analyze Musial, pin down his secrets.

Was it the bat itself?

In 1962, the Mets signed a brash teenager named Ed Kranepool, straight out of the Bronx. He was not in awe of anybody, not his manager, Casey Stengel, and not his esteemed opponent, forty-one-year-old Stan Musial. Around the batting cage one day, Kranepool picked up Musial's bat, the M159 model.

"I said, 'Stan, it's got a very thin handle,' " Kranepool recalled. "He said, 'Ed, I don't hit 'em with the handle.' "

Stanley honed the bat handles even thinner using sandpaper in the clubhouse, thereby validating the shop classes he took back at Donora High.

Or was it the stance?

Ed Mickelson, who was briefly a teammate of Musial's and later a prominent high school coach in the area, tried to break down what happened after the man went into that temporary crouch.

"I have a theory why Stan's bat showed ball marks only closely aligned in a small area on the sweet spot of his bat," Mickelson wrote. "No ball marks on the end or on the handle. I believe it had to do with the placement of his front foot as he would stride toward the ball."

Mickelson made a drawing of what Musial did with his feet. The marks looked like something out of an old-fashioned learn-to-waltz diagram.

For the outside pitch, Musial's front (right) foot would move toward the plate.

For the inside pitch, Musial's front foot would open up slightly, toward the outside of the batter's box.

For the pitch over the plate, Musial's front foot would move straight ahead.

This consistency of ball marks on the bat indicated excellent discipline, control, balance, eyesight, reflexes—a command of the body that probably went back to his days in the Falcons gymnastics drills.

Amateur prestidigitator that he was, Stanley seemed to be hiding his secrets. According to Joe Garagiola, Curt Flood, at the time buried deep on the Cardinals' bench, once asked Musial the secret of his hitting.

"Curt, all you can do is when you see the ball just hit the hell out of it," Musial said, thoroughly mystifying the young player.

The closest Musial ever came to explaining himself was to Roger Kahn, who had built a rapport with him over the years.

"Do you guess?" Kahn asked Musial in 1957.

"I don't guess. I know," Musial replied.

"You know?"

"I can always tell, as long as I'm concentrating."

Some hitters say they read the rotation of the ball, but Musial said his edge came even earlier.

"I pick the ball up right away. Know what I mean? I see it as soon as it leaves the pitcher's hand. That's when I got to concentrate real hard. If I do, I can tell what the pitch is going to be."

That meant, in the clubby days of the eight-team National League, that Musial had a feel for the repertoire of approximately seventy pitchers at a time.

"Every pitcher has a set of speeds," he told Kahn. "I mean, the curve goes one speed and the slider goes at something else. Well, if I concentrate real good, I can pick up the speed of the ball about the first thirty feet it travels."

Perfectionist that he was, Musial said that approximately twenty or thirty times a season he found himself not concentrating. Imagine what he could have hit if he'd paid attention.

Just consider the pitchers he victimized for the most home runs: Warren Spahn, 17; Preacher Roe, 12; Johnny Antonelli, 11 (all three of them lefties, thereby defying the general rule that lefty pitchers are tough on lefty hitters); Newcombe, 11; Murry Dickson, 11; Bob Rush, 10; Robin Roberts, 10. All these double-digit victims ranged from Hall of Fame level to very good starters. Of course, a pitcher would have to be pretty good to last long enough to give up that many homers to one man.

Stanley hit his homers without causing animosity. Roberts, who gave up

505 career home runs, remained socially friendly with Musial, often meeting him in Florida after they were retired. Roberts said he had exactly one photograph of an opposing player in his home—Stan the Man.

Everybody liked the way he referred to himself as Stanley, creating a character in his own personal video, much the way latter-day superstars refer to themselves in the third person—*Michael Jordan doesn't do garbage time,* or whatever.

But Stanley was not a showbiz celebrity. The television highlight show had not yet been invented, which is another reason some of us call them the good old days. Stanley just wanted to make contact. Nobody took it personally.

Newcombe respected Musial going back to when the league was being integrated and Musial was a symbol of moderation.

"He was one of the true professionals," Don Newcombe said. "That's what I say about Stan Musial. A true professional. In that era when Jackie came in and then Roy [Campanella] and then me, and Mays and all those others, Musial was a man who hit you hard but never showed you up. He hit the ball out of the ballpark, he wouldn't clown going into the dugout. He'd go in and shake hands with a few guys and get a drink of water. He would never show you up. You wouldn't have to knock him down."

That was important in the old days, when showboating was discouraged. If a hitter lost sight of that nicety, he might get his uniform dirty, fast.

"Today, if me and Drysdale and Gibson pitched like that, we'd wind up in jail because we'd be killing somebody," Newcombe said in 2009. "They're trying to show you up, going around the bases waving their hands and all that high-fiving when they get to the dugout. Our guys didn't do that. They hit the ball out of the ballpark and they ran around the bases. We watched 'em, you know, to see what they would do and how they would do it, and Stanley never showed you up."

The Dodgers did not hate Stanley, which was the highest respect possible in that harsh rivalry. Everybody recognized that the man with the unusual stance was a gentle man, a kind man.

# 6

---

# A HAND ON THE SHOULDER

JOHN HALL'S father died when the boy was seven. To bring some life back into the house, John's mother bought an RCA Victor radio and phonograph. One day John's uncle was doing some work around the house, and he turned on the radio and he told the boy, "I want you to listen to this."

It was a baseball game, emanating from St. Louis but coming over the local station in nearby Carthage, Missouri, one of eighty-four stations that carried Cardinals games all over Missouri, Illinois, Arkansas, Iowa, Kentucky, Mississippi, Oklahoma, and Tennessee.

The boy listened to Harry Caray blustering names like Slaughter and Marion and Musial, and from then on he was a Cardinals fan, like much of the American South and Southwest.

On July 2, 1950, when the boy was eleven, family friends drove him and his mother along Route 66 all the way up to Sportsman's Park in St. Louis, where George "Red" Munger outpitched Bill Werle of the Pirates, 2–1. Half a century later, Hall could remember the details.

After the game, there was only one choice for a restaurant—Stan Musial and Biggie's, where, legend had it, Musial himself appeared whenever he did not have a game.

During the meal, John set off in search of a men's room.

"Being a country boy, or at least one from a small town, I went outside to see if there might be an outhouse somewhere," Hall would recall. "When making a visual search for an outside privy, I observed something that I hadn't seen in my hometown—a parking lot full of Cadillacs." In his imagination, one of those Cadillacs belonged to Musial. However, he did not spot a restroom in the parking lot.

"When I came back in, I guess I looked lost," Hall said. "All of a sudden there were two hands on my shoulder, and a voice said, 'Son, can I help you?' and my heart stopped."

His heart stopped because it felt good to be called "son," particularly by Stan Musial, wearing a nice suit. The boy promptly forgot his other mission and darted back to his table to see if anybody had a paper and pencil.

"I had never asked for an autograph in my life, and when I went back he was seated with the guy that I later figured out was Amadee"—Amadee Wohlschlaeger, the renowned illustrator for the *St. Louis Post-Dispatch* and the *Sporting News,* known by his first name.

Eyeing the pencil and scrap of paper, Musial said, "Come here, bud," and he led the boy into his office, where he produced a photograph of himself and a fountain pen.

"I was surprised, he was writing with his right hand," Hall said years later, after learning the left-handed boy had been forced to write right-handed by his teachers.

"He signed it in green ink, 'To John Hall, from Stan Musial,' and he asked, 'How's this, is this better than a piece of paper?' " The boy said, "Yes, sir, it is. Thank you very much."

Nearly sixty years later, a historian of minor-league baseball, Hall had met Musial a time or two. He wanted it known that the man was just as decent as he had seemed on that evening back in 1950. John Hall still had the autographed photo, still cherished the memory of being called "son."

# 7

## LUKASZ AND MARY

HIS FAMILY lived down by the river, close to the mill. This was bottomland in every sense, where the newest immigrants lived, closest to the noise and the grime. The ground was barren, and people understood that was because of the smoke that flowed twenty-four hours a day; they had yet to learn just how much the smoke was damaging their bodies.

In the afternoon, the boy would sometimes wait for his father outside the mill. Lukasz Musial was not much more than five feet tall, and he spoke mostly Polish, calling the boy Stashu, the diminutive of Stanislaus.

At home there was Lukasz and Mary Musial and the girls, Ida, Victoria, Helen, and Rose, all born within six years, and then Stanislaus, born on November 21, 1920.

"They didn't even have enough money to baptize my father until his brother came along and they were baptized together. That was poor!" Musial's oldest daughter, Gerry Ashley, said. "I don't even think they had indoor plumbing for quite a long time," she added.

Just before Stashu's second birthday, he was joined by Edward, so the family arranged a bargain christening at the Polish church overlooking the steel mill. The church was the Holy Name of the Blessed Virgin Mary, popularly called St. Mary's.

When the boy was seven or eight, the family moved from 465 Sixth Street up the hill to 1139 Marelda Street—eight Musials plus Mary's mother in a two-bedroom house. Because the house was farther from the mill, Lukasz took more time getting home, stopping in the Polish social club and maybe the Russian social club or the Croatian social club or the Czech social club or any of the other ethnic clubs on the hillside.

The beer and the shot, or some variation, helped dissipate the metallic particles in the men's throats, took the pain from the fresh burns from the sparks and spattered drops of acid. Lukasz Musial was not healthy and did not always work, but even when he did work he made more stops than some of the men, trudging home without his full paycheck.

"As far as drinking, the guys in the steel mill worked hard," said Mark Pawelec, whose maternal grandfather was a prominent Donora gymnast named Frank Musial, no relation to Lukasz. In 2009, Pawelec was living high on the hill in a family home, commuting to Pittsburgh on a modern toll road a few miles to the west, and in his spare time he studied the history of the Poles of Donora.

"My grandfather, Frank Musial, was an alcoholic," Pawelec said. "He did drink. That's not something I tell people, but I know for a fact it was true." Pawelec would not speculate about Lukasz Musial but said he would not be surprised if anybody thought he needed a drink or three on the way back from that mill.

Stan Musial never talked much about Lukasz within his family; men of the thirties and forties did not say much about what they saw at work or at war, and they tended not to discuss destructive behaviors under the roof of their childhood home.

"I think he struggled with alcohol, that's what I would prefer to say, as reported from my grandmother," said Gerry Ashley, the second child of Stan and Lil, as she tried to reconstruct the life of her grandfather, whom she barely remembered.

Watching Lukasz struggle did not turn Stan into a teetotaler. He was loyal to his father and a proud son of Donora, but parts of his life were off-limits. His friend Bob Broeg discovered this reticence in 1963 when they were collaborating on Musial's autobiography, right after Musial's retirement.

Broeg was a writer, one of those curious types who always want to know more. He prevailed on Musial to drive to 1139 Marelda, where strangers now lived, and urged his friend to slow down, maybe even get out and walk around and dredge up a few memories.

Undoubtedly, Broeg was hoping his friend would knock on the door and say, *Hello, my name is Stan Musial, and I used to live here.* What a chapter that would have been—digging into Stanley's Rosebud, Stanley's madeleines—but Musial showed no interest in revisiting what had taken place inside that tiny house. Musial kept the car rolling, did not want to go there.

Family members told Broeg how in the old days, when nobody was watching, the young Stashu might take a swig of the sweet canned milk used for coffee. The father might get annoyed by this bit of mischief, but the women would say, *Look at that smile. Stashu is a good boy.*

Musial alluded to spankings, but Broeg, ever sensitive to his friend's mixed feelings about his childhood, added a modifier: "Not unkindly, either."

Lukasz remained a man of the old country, the perpetual outsider, the greenhorn, even among the large Polish community. He said he was born on a farm near Warsaw, but according to immigration records he was actually born in Galicia, then part of Austria-Hungary. Since Warsaw was the only city in Poland that most Americans knew, in some small way Lukasz may have been trying to fit in, to sound a bit more mainstream.

Either way, Lukasz left Hamburg, Germany, on January 24, 1910, sailing out of the massive Elbe River, arriving at Ellis Island in New York Harbor six days later. He was pointed directly to Donora and the American Steel and Wire Company, where he loaded wire into freight trains, becoming a small speck in the great mosaic of the new American factory class.

The family's name was pronounced MEW-shill, the Polish way. When Stan got to the major leagues, he pronounced his name for reporters and broadcasters, but they turned it into three syllables, MEWS-ee-al, and it has been that way ever since.

Musial's tone always softened when he spoke about his mother. Mary Lancos was born in New York City with a Hungarian name but of Czech origin, due to the blurring of borders back in Europe. She arrived in Donora when she was around eight years old and soon was rowing across the Monongahela River every day to deliver a hot lunch to her father, who was working in a coal mine. At fourteen she went to work at the wire mill.

They met at a dance—a tiny man who spoke mostly Polish and a large girl, five foot eight, who spoke Czech and English—and they were married

on April 14, 1913, when Lukasz was nearly twenty-three and Mary was sixteen, although the marriage certificate said she was twenty-one. In a hard
company town, the details on a marriage certificate were not scrutinized
too closely.

There was a pecking order among the town's fifteen thousand residents. The Spanish lived closest to the mill and the Italians lived farther up
the hill, with their gardens and their decorations. On the East Coast there
had been NINA signs—NO IRISH NEED APPLY—but in Donora the Irish were
virtually landed aristocracy. The East Europeans lived where they could;
for the most part, so did the African Americans.

For those who had jobs, the salaries were enough to make many people feel they were living better than they ever had in the old country.
Women dressed up to go shopping on McKean or Thompson, the main
drags. At one point there were three movie theaters downtown, including
the Harris, which Mary Musial swept out as one of her part-time jobs. She
also cleaned other people's homes.

"Mommy did a lot of housework," Ed Musial recalled for a documentary years later, "and we lived almost, might as well say, rent-free, because
we lived with my grandma, it was her house." Ed added, "Between my
grandma and my mother and that, we weathered the storm pretty good.
Well, them old-timers can stretch a dollar, boy, I'll tell you."

Bill Bottonari, who lived in the same part of town and would stay in
touch with Musial into old age, remembered watching Mary Musial, a tall,
powerful woman, carrying homemade bread to the church to be blessed
on Palm Sunday.

"My grandmother would tell me that she would go buy a sack of potatoes each week for the kids, and that's how she would feed them," Gerry
Ashley said. "She said she had to go work in the church just to make extra
money to feed her family."

For most meals, there was always cabbage, which could be stored all
winter in a cold room, as could potatoes. The meat was usually bologna,
known in Appalachia as coal miners' steak, but for holidays Mary learned
to make the Polish dishes her husband liked.

In later years, Musial would learn the best cuts of meat as the propri-
etor of a famous restaurant with his name on it. On the road, he would not
seek out the East European pockets in the big cities; major leaguers were

expected to patronize upscale restaurants. But when he talked about his childhood, he would grow weepy, never abandoning the Polish culture.

"I'll never forget the 'hunky' dishes Mom turned out, such as pierogi, halucki and kolatche," Musial wrote in his autobiography. "Kolatche is a kind of sweet roll, halucki the more familiar cabbage roll and pierogi a delicate combination of flour, potato and sugar folded into a thin turnover and baked."

He liked being called Stash by teammates and would go along with Polish jokes until later in life, when he'd had enough of them. His pride in carrying a Polish name would lead him to adventures and contacts that enriched his life.

He loved talking about Polish delicacies, but his childhood was not open to retrospection. After Musial had become a star, a New York writer named Ray Robinson, a subsequent biographer of Lou Gehrig and Christy Mathewson, was working on a children's book about Musial, and called Mary Musial on the telephone.

"She did not care to talk to me and I figured it was a lost cause, so I said, 'Mrs. Musial, you have a very young voice on the phone,'" Robinson recalled. "That made a difference because she suddenly became more animated, and kept talking for a while, very giving."

During the interview, Mary Musial gave Robinson the impression the father had sometimes struck the son.

"I didn't write it," Robinson said. "It was for a kid's book, and you didn't write things like that in those days." However, the memory stayed with Robinson for decades.

Mary had spoken sympathetically of her late husband, telling Robinson: "Mr. Musial never had an easy time of it. There wasn't much money."

The house was built into a rugged hillside, which had already been mined of its major veins of coal. The two Musial boys would scrunch into the seam to forage for chunks of coal to keep the family alive through the night.

"We had a shaft thirty foot deep, don't ask me how they dug it," Ed Musial said, describing a makeshift crank that lowered a rope with a barrel at the end, to haul the coal more easily.

One time an uncle came by with an old Appalachian solution for loosening coal from a stubborn vein—a stick of dynamite, more than a little dangerous in a derelict shaft. When the smoke cleared, the uncle and the two boys emerged with their booty, to the relief of their family. Decades later, Ed was still chuckling about the close call as the boys filled the coal bucket to satisfy Lukasz.

"He was tough," Ed said of his father. "He had these rules, regardless. I mean, we had to do our chores first, and then baseball, whatever, came second."

Lukasz was not interested in the games of the New World, but Mary understood they were important for boys growing up in this country. When Stan became an American celebrity, he would always tell how his mother had stitched rags into a makeshift baseball and played catch with him between chores. When he told that story he would weep, and so would she.

"But I was mostly busy working," Mrs. Musial would add.

Gerry Ashley thinks baseball liberated her father, helped him survive. "I can see how a kid like that would just be out playing all day long, just running. He would be outside so he wouldn't have to be concerned with troubles in the house."

Stashu was the star athlete even in grade school, but not the kind of jock who tossed his weight around in class or the hallways. For the rest of his public life he would remind people that he had not been a good student.

"He was always the nice boy he is now," Mary told Roger Kahn in 1958. "He never sasses anybody. Ask his teachers. But he has changed. His head is still the same. It's got no bigger. But now he speaks a whole lot better than he did."

The speech problem began in grade school, after teachers insisted he write with his right hand. Because the alphabet and numbers were essentially created for right-handed people—90 percent of the population, by most counts—teachers tried to make handwriting conform, to the inconvenience of natural left-handers. Lefties also had to deal with the tradition that left-handedness was something unusual or eccentric—perhaps even sinister, which comes from the Latin word *sinistra,* meaning "left hand."

Not all stutterers were left-handed, of course, but in a classic study, "Left-Handedness and Stuttering," in the *Journal of Heredity* in 1933, Bryng Bryngelson and Thomas J. Clark suggested: "The usual practice of shifting a left-handed child to the non-preferred right hand could be said to be responsible for the changing of inherent neurophysiological patterns in the brain." They added that stuttering or other traits could also be linked to subtle differences in left-brain/right-brain makeup.

These days, students are generally not forced to write right-handed—and in fact have profited from the fame of Sandy Koufax, Martina Navratilova, John McEnroe, and that left-handed basketball player who went into public service, Barack Obama.

Musial would retain a trace of a stammer into his adult life, sometimes speaking fast in the local accent of his childhood, sometimes using familiar mantras—*whaddayasay-whaddayasay, wunnerful-wunnerful*—as a defense mechanism, to soften having to speak seriously.

Teachers recalled Stan's pink complexion, his athlete's grace, his sweet smile. Katherine (Kappy) Hayes, the Donora school psychologist, remembered a junior high school discussion of the migrant workers in *The Grapes of Wrath*.

"I saw a group of women like that the other day," Musial had said. "They were camped right on the edge of town and they were dressed just like hoboes. They even wore pants." For whatever reason, giving that much detail about the clothing of these female vagabonds touched off a deep red flush on the boy's face.

"I think Stan blushed for the rest of the period," Hayes recalled. "He was sensitive and shy and a swell kid."

Stan was alert, observant, involved, bright-eyed, and looking for his main chance. He was also blessed to have the body, the reflexes, and ultimately the confidence of a superior athlete.

Lukasz did not go to his son's games, but he did make a mighty contribution to his son's athletic career by enrolling him in the Falcons, a club movement that began in Poland in 1867, honoring the ancient Latin phrase *mens sana in corpore sano*—sound mind in a sound body. The Donora branch, Nest 247 to be precise, featured gymnastics as well as track and field meets and social gatherings, and it supported charities and other causes back in Poland.

"Three times a week, from the time I was nine or 10, we went to the Falcons," Musial said in his autobiography. "We'd march and drill and then work out on the apparatus and mats. We'd swing on the parallel bars, leap over the 'horse' and do all the tumbling that helped me avoid injury in my playing career. In the spring our instructors took us outdoors to compete in track and field events with other towns. I can't say enough for the three body-building years I spent with the Falcons."

At least four athletes named Musial were prominent in Donora—Joseph, Chuck, Josephine, and Frank, none related to Lukasz. Frank was a national star in the Falcons, winning medals in track and field and in gymnastics, and sometimes he would show up at traveling carnivals and box against the resident strong man for prize money.

Upon Frank's death, years later, a column in the *Sokol Polski,* the publication of the Falcons, compared him to another Musial, who by that time was known nationally as Stan the Man. Ever gracious, Stan gave an interview saying he was never the athlete Frank Musial was.

As long as he played the American game of baseball, Stan remained an advocate for the skills he had learned in the Nest in Donora. He praised his father for steering him to the Falcons but was reticent about the hard times and his father's drinking, and he always would be.

"He doesn't like to think about it. He doesn't like to go there," his oldest daughter, Gerry, would say years later.

In many ways, Musial mirrored Ronald Reagan, the son of an alcoholic, who also, in his later years, praised his mother. Reagan's sunny, diverting personality was often said to be typical for the son of an alcoholic father. He wanted to smile, make everything turn out all right, not give much away.

In an essay in *Time* on January 2, 1981, naming the newly elected Reagan as Person of the Year, Roger Rosenblatt wrote:

One thing the children of alcoholics often have in common is an uncommon sense of control—control of themselves and control of their world, which they know from harsh experience can turn perilous at the click of a door latch. Not that Jack Reagan was known to be a mean drunk; but brutal or not, all alcoholics create states of alarm in their children. They learn a kind of easygoing formality early on, like the Secret Service, and they are often acutely alert to danger, for the very reason that the parent's binges are periodic. That receding look and sound of Reagan may be the hallmarks of such control. One cannot retain anger in the presence of such a man, and thus in a sense he makes fathers of us all.

In fact, Reagan seems ever to place himself in the position of being adopted. He has, in a sense, been adopted by a plethora of fathers over the years, wealthy patrons and protectors who recognized a hope for the country's future in their favorite son.

According to a recent study by the National Association for Children of Alcoholics (NACOA), more than twenty-eight million Americans are children of alcoholics:

Addicted parents often lack the ability to provide structure or discipline in family life, but simultaneously expect their children to be competent at a wide variety of tasks earlier than do non-substance-abusing parents.

The study added that children of alcoholics have a higher rate of various disorders and often perform less well in school than children of non-alcoholic parents.

However—and this is a giant however in the life of Stanislaus Musial—the study emphasizes the dependence on a non-alcoholic parent as well as "other supportive adults." The study also says that children who find mentors develop "increased autonomy and independence, stronger social skills" and better coping skills.

Stan Musial's childhood remained tucked away, perhaps even from himself, but it did teach him to laugh his way through life, to seek control, to dress nicely. He also demonstrated a tropism toward father figures, men who knew how to handle themselves, who had education, who knew how things worked. He found them, they found him; on both sides, their instincts were spectacular.

# 8

## INVITATION TO LUNCH

In the spring of 2002, Ulice Payne Jr. was the new president of the Milwaukee Brewers, the first African American ever to hold that high position with a major-league team.

A lawyer recruited out of the corporate world, Payne was looking forward to opening day, when the Brewers would open in St. Louis, because he was hoping to introduce himself to Stan Musial—another guy from Donora.

They had never met, but Musial had been a regular presence in Ulice Payne's childhood. The men in Payne's family would sit on the front porch after work, drinking Iron City beer and listening to the ball games. Whenever the Pirates played the Cardinals, Bob Prince would tell Musial stories.

"It was always about Donora," Payne said. "Everybody was so proud of him."

Stan Musial was a beacon to all the boys in town, who taught themselves to hit left-handed, in a coiled position—well, except for Ken Griffey, who batted left-handed naturally and did not need to borrow anybody else's stance.

"We used to flip baseball cards," Payne recalled, "but you'd never flip a Stan Musial card because that would mess up the corners."

When Payne was a child, legend had it that anybody with a Pennsylvania driver's license and a Donora address would eat on the house at Stan Musial and Biggie's.

"That's what we heard," Payne said. "But not many people could ever get to St. Louis."

There was also a legend among blacks in Donora that when some of the southerners on the Cardinals had started yapping about not wanting to play against Jackie Robinson in 1947, Musial's response had been, in effect: *I grew up with black guys, I played basketball with them.* That was no small thing.

PAYNE'S UNCLE, Roscoe Ross, had run in the same Donora High backfield as Deacon Dan Towler, who went on to star for the Los Angeles Rams. Their Donora team went undefeated two straight years in the midforties.

"The story was, my uncle was running on the field against Charleroi one day and a rabbit ran on the field," Payne said. "My uncle picked up the rabbit and kept on going into the end zone. That was the legend."

Donora sent steel and zinc downriver to Pittsburgh, and it also exported athletes into the world. Bimbo Cecconi played tailback at Pitt; Arnold Galiffa earned eleven varsity letters at West Point; Buddy Griffey, the football star at Donora High when Musial was the baseball star, produced a couple of pretty fair left-handed hitters, Ken senior and Ken junior. And Ulice Payne, six feet six inches tall, played basketball for Al McGuire at Marquette, where he got the feeling many blacks did not trust their white teammates, and vice versa. But Payne felt he had gotten that out of his system in Donora, years earlier.

"We were known as the Home of Champions," Payne said. "We were from a small town, but I grew up believing we could do anything. My teachers were white and black, men and women—you didn't have any choice, man. We were all steelworkers' kids."

He was talking about the sixties and early seventies, not the twenties and thirties, when Musial went to school in Donora. But the mix was the same—blacks living near whites, a basic fact that influenced Ulice Payne's life.

"People had houses," Payne said, years later. "Whether you rented them or not, people had houses. For the most part, everybody was employed. My best friend was Anthony Lazzari, an Italian kid. I grew up in the house my mother was raised in, and Anthony was raised in the house his mother was raised in.

"I eat more Italian food than anything because my best friend was Italian," Payne continued. "I wasn't Catholic but my best friend was, and I went to St. Philip Neri Church on Saturdays with him, so we could go fishing on Sundays."

Payne's family attended the St. Paul Baptist Church on McKean Avenue. He would hold back a dime from the collection plate so that he could slip into the grocery store on the same block, run by the Labash family. Stan the Man and his wife had moved away by then, but Payne got a thrill out of spending his dime for candy with Stan Musial's in-laws.

A FEW days before opening day in 2002, Ulice Payne received a phone call from St. Louis, saying Stan Musial wanted Payne to be his lunch guest at the stadium club.

"I'd have gone to the game and tried to find him," Payne recalled. "Honest to God, he asked me to lunch."

On opening day, Musial was wearing a red Cardinals blazer as he greeted Payne.

"He was proud of the fact that I was from Donora and I was president of a major-league baseball team," Payne said.

"Just to be in a restaurant with him was great," Payne continued. "He knew all about the Brewers, he knew all about his team. I will never forget it. For me to get to meet Stan Musial, that was big for me. Like meeting the president."

A few weeks later, Payne received a bat, a Stan Musial model, autographed by Stan the Man. Many other people tell similar tales about receiving a surprise souvenir from Musial, with his elegant script on the label.

Payne barely lasted two years with the Brewers, running into power struggles that convinced him to get right back into corporate law. When asked about his brief interlude in baseball, he starts with the luncheon with the man in the bright red jacket, the man from his hometown.

# 9

## HOW DONORA

## GOT ITS NAME

PEOPLE SAID Stan Musial put Donora on the map, but actually a young surveyor named George Washington did.

In 1753, working for the British in the French and Indian War, Washington made a historic map of the region. The Iroquois who fished and hunted along the river referred to the "high banks or bluffs" or "falling banks" in their language; on his map Washington turned it into the closest approximation in English, Monongahela.

As a result of Washington's explorations, a treaty signed in Baltimore on August 31, 1779, allocated the region to the fledgling state of Pennsylvania, and retained the Iroquois name for the river.

Twenty miles down from what would become Donora, the Carnegies and Fricks made steel in Pittsburgh, at the confluence of the Monongahela and the Allegheny, forming the Ohio. The factories moved up to Homestead, site of a bloody confrontation between imported Pinkertons and striking steelworkers in 1892.

In May 1899, the Mellon family purchased land farther upriver at a place first called Horseshoe Bottom and later West Columbia. A year later the Mellons broke ground for the American Steel and Wire Works, and engaged a businessman named W. H. Donner to organize a factory town.

Donner did such a good job that Andrew Mellon wanted to honor him. At first, the town was going to be called Meldon, but then Mellon fell in love.

While on a European vacation, he proposed to a woman of nineteen, half his age, from an Irish brewing family. She was resistant at first but he pursued her to her family's rented castle in Hertfordshire, England. She married him after his fifth visit to the castle.

Soon Mellon was escorting his young bride to his stolid brick mansion hard by the clattering trolley tracks and spewing smokestacks of unregulated, nineteenth-century boomtown Pittsburgh. According to legend, her reaction upon seeing her husband's home was "You live *here*?" or words to that effect.

Her name was McMullen, Nora McMullen.

In one of the more romantic gestures of his gloomy life, Mellon decided to honor his young wife by putting her name on the new town, although giving W. H. Donner first billing. There is no record of Nora McMullen Mellon ever visiting the town partially named after her. She was soon involved in a scandalous affair with an English rake that led to a divorce, leaving her two children, Ailsa and Paul, in the paid care of housekeepers and governesses. After a tempestuous life, Nora died in 1973, in leafy Greenwich, Connecticut.

W. H. Donner did not stick around Donora. In 1933, alarmed by the tax policies of the new Roosevelt administration, he moved to Switzerland.

Andrew Mellon later served as treasury secretary for three Republican administrations, favoring the reduction or even abolition of income taxes. He later donated his magnificent art collection to the National Gallery, and died on August 27, 1937, at the age of eighty-two, in Southampton, New York, far from the smokestacks of Pittsburgh.

Mellon's son, Paul Mellon, inherited much of the wealth, which became diversified as the steel industry went into decline. He became a patron of Yale University and a frequent visitor to London, a collector of Constables and Turners, Reynoldses and Gainsboroughs.

Paul Mellon was also the owner of thoroughbreds lodged at his estate in Upperville, Virginia. Familiar with the sports pages through racing, Mellon undoubtedly heard about Stan Musial from Donora. It is not known what Mellon thought about the fact that a great slugger came from the town named for Nora McMullen Mellon.

THE MON Valley needed people to work the mills. English and Scotch and Welsh and Irish came first, on train tracks that carried human cargo as well as freight. Belgians settled farther up the river and called their town Charleroi after the city they had left behind. Germans came from Essen, the city of the Krupps, and settled on the east bank of the river in a town that came to be called Monessen. There was talk of building a munitions factory there, although that never happened.

Donora received the zinc plant, forty acres alongside the river, smoke-stacks spewing, essentially as a reward for Donora's workers having opposed the Homestead strike and resisted unionization. At its peak, the zinc works employed about 1,500 workers—Italians and Spanish, African Americans, East Europeans. In 1910, Donora's population was 8,174; by 1920, when Lukasz and Mary Musial's first son was born, the count was up to 14,131. In 1940, when Stan and Lil Musial had their first child and Stan hurt his shoulder making a diving catch in the outfield, 13,180 people remained in Donora despite the Depression. By the 2000 census, the population would be 5,653.

In Musial's boyhood years, the steel mills and the zinc factory worked around the clock because the world had an insatiable need for American goods. If the fires were ever quenched, the furnaces would crack.

The factories were dangerous. In his epic book *Homestead,* William Serrin notes that 313 workers were killed in the Homestead Works alone between 1914 and 1980. Serrin writes:

The monstrous crucibles of molten iron and steel, the white-hot ingots, the great slabs and billets, the fast-moving cranes, the great cutting machines, the locomotives and railroad cars, the exploding furnaces, the splashing steel, the scalding water from bursting pipes, the high, dark walkways—all this made the mill a natural place for injury and death. Wives and children in their homes came to dread the sound of whistles, the screaming sirens that meant that an accident had occurred, the telephone call, particularly late at night, that could mean that a steel-worker, "the mister," was injured or perhaps dead.

Sometimes death happened fast. On January 20, 1920, Andrew Posey, a veteran of World War I, was engulfed by three-thousand-degree molten steel when a restraining wall cracked suddenly. There was no body to be removed, but his co-workers did bury a human-sized ingot just outside the mill, being unable to transport it uphill to the cemetery. During World War II, the chunk of steel was removed as part of the scrap metal drive. He would have wanted it that way, people said.

Working in the steel mills debilitated people. Serrin quotes John A. Fitch, a sociologist who worked in Homestead in the early twentieth century, as saying that around the age of thirty-five, workers "had begun to feel a perceptible decline in strength. The superintendent and foremen are alert to detecting weakness of any sort, and if a man fails appreciably, he expects discharge."

Lukasz Musial was already broken down by 1937, when the union finally made inroads. His son seemed to understand that improvements had taken place when workers organized. When some baseball players began to organize after the war, Musial was at least a moderate, which in ballplayer terms was like being a flaming liberal.

One athlete who saw the benefit of collective action was Lou "Bimbo" Cecconi, a star quarterback at Donora High and later a star tailback and beloved icon at the University of Pittsburgh. Cecconi spent a few summers working at the zinc plant, where workers still had to supply their own makeshift gear.

"That's why I appreciate the unions," Cecconi said. "They fought for all those things. You didn't have your own shower. You finally got a locker where you could carry your clothes. Guys came home dark and dirty."

In 2009, Cecconi drove me past the ghostly banks where the mills used to be. I could feel his old sense of fear rise as he described the dangerous chore of getting close to the sizzling ingot and whacking off the residue before it cooled: "You had to knock it off with a big steel bar. Shit, I didn't realize how heavy they were, those big steel bars. Slag, junk. You had to throw all this stuff in there."

And then a foreman would order sacks of chemicals to be thrown into the vat for the next round. "You'd throw that stuff in, sacks of magnesium. It would splash up, coming up at you from everywhere," he said with considerable feeling.

How did he protect your face? I asked.

"They'd give you glasses," Cecconi said, "but I would take one of those things the cowboys wear, what do you call them? Right, a bandana. I'd put it around my face, put my glasses on, protecting you from sparks and heat.

My dad had big scars on his face and neck and I'm sure a lot of other injuries.

"Their main concern was safety," Cecconi said. The foremen did not want to slow down production just because something unfortunate happened to one of the workers.

This was Stan Musial's world growing up. In his autobiography, Musial mentioned "the strong smell of sulphur from the zinc works" and described the view from near his house, with "the switch engines darting between the smoke stacks and the barges moving slowly along the river. Across the Monongahela, the hills were completely bare, vegetation killed by the smoke and chemical fumes carried over from Donora by the prevailing west wind."

People were just beginning to figure out what those chemicals were doing to their land, to themselves. In her powerful book *When Smoke Ran Like Water,* Dr. Devra Davis wrote about Donora, her childhood home:

> Fumes from the mills, coke ovens, coal stoves and zinc furnaces were often trapped in the valley by the surrounding hills. They gave us astonishingly beautiful sunsets and plenty of barren dirt fields and hills to play on.

Davis's family used to sit outdoors on camp chairs on a summer evening, the way families in other places watch the sunset or fireflies. In Donora, people watched the "fiery spray" from burning graphite spewing off the emerging steel ingots. Motorists driving on the other side of the Monongahela River would slow down to watch the sparks from the zinc mill, like fireworks on the Fourth of July.

In 1933, Davis wrote, Native American graves had been "washed out of the hillside downwind of the zinc plant's plumes." It was a hint, a warning.

Even backyard gardens were affected by the plumes from the mills. Davis's neighbor Mrs. LaMendola "told me she could never get tomatoes to grow in the path where the plume from the ovens ran. On the other side of her house, they did just fine."

The factories were just there, part of life. Davis said her mother used to tell her: "That's not coal dust, that's gold dust."

Ulice Payne's family lived on First Street, seventy yards from the gate of the steel mill. His dad worked across the river in Monessen, as many shifts as he could. During the war Payne's mother began working a regular shift at the mill, and she kept working after the men came home.

"There was always a store where guys got their lunch," Payne recalled. "And a hotel. I just knew it as a hotel. I got to college, I found out it was a house of ill repute, but to me it was a hotel."

The bad air was part of the deal of living in Donora.

"You breathed that air all the time," Payne said. "It was always dirty. My grandfather, who retired out of the mill, made a living washing cars. He passed at ninety-four. That's how I made my money for many summers, washing cars. The cars were always dirty. We lived right outside the gate, so especially paydays, Fridays and Saturdays, you would be busy. Guys come out of work, man, we'd wash their car, simonize their car, I'd make $3–4 a car. So I remember, it was an accepted way of life, I don't think anybody thought about the impact. And of course the mill was 24/7. Never stopped."

When Payne went away to play basketball at Marquette, he could not believe winters in Wisconsin. Clean snow. So beautiful.


THE TRADE-OFF was that in the boom days, Donora promised a better life. Devra Davis lovingly recalls some landmarks of her childhood—the Fraternal Order of Eagles, Masons, Polish Falcons, Sons of Croatia, bowling alley, Weiss's drugstore, Niccolanco's candy store. Time was measured by the mill whistles, which also called the volunteer fire department into action. The sign atop the factory gate read WORLD'S LARGEST NAIL MILL.

Davis also recalls how the men would come home and work on their houses, and the women would wash the windows and the curtains. When they had worked their way around the house, it was time to start all over again.

Old photographs suggest the gritty middle-class life of the main streets: awnings, women all dressed up to go shopping, trolley cars. In one photo of those bustling days, I count fourteen people near one intersection, waiting to cross—critical mass downtown.

Here is the Irondale Hotel at Sixth and McKean, one of four hotels in the center of town. There is the Polish church and rectory, rising proudly on a hillside, one of twenty-two churches, almost all of them ethnic. There is the mansion—that is what they called it—for the superintendent of the mill, a Colonial Revival building looming on a hillside above a dignified-looking trolley car. The building later became the Spanish Club, haven for hundreds of new laborers. There is the hulking American Steel and Wire Company with its twenty smokestacks, bordering the river for blocks and blocks. And there is Donora's own Penn Station, circa 1912, a major stop on the Mon Valley train line, down from South Side Station in Pittsburgh. At the peak of the railroad days, the station employed nineteen men.

In Musial's boyhood, the town had three movie theaters. "On the southern end of town, there was the Princess Theater, between Fourth and Fifth streets. That sort of specialized in western movies, and it was known as the Ranch House," said Dr. Charles Stacey, the former superintendent of schools, later the town historian.

The Liberty Theatre showed second-run movies, Stacey said, and the Harris Theatre, which Mary Musial swept out, showed most of the first-run movies.

"This tells how big Donora was but also how important movie theaters were," Stacey said. "We have a picture at the Historical Society of people lined up maybe half a block ready to buy their tickets to get into it. People seemed to have their Sunday best on. The Harris Theatre used to have some stage shows. One of the fellows who used to come up from Pittsburgh was Dick Powell. One time Tex Ritter performed on the stage. That was our entertainment, prior to TV."

Higher above the town was Palmer Park, where children played baseball. In the winter, the children would take their sleds to the top of the hill and barrel down toward the river, crossing the main streets, always an adventure. A child could manage only a couple of runs a day, because it was six or eight blocks to trudge up to the top again.

Musial went to the public schools, but some of the children whose families could afford the tuition went to Catholic grade schools. Sundays were segregated by race and ethnicity. Musial was baptized at St. Mary's but went to church at St. Michael's, an Orthodox Catholic church, with married priests.

"Their priests were very flamboyant, great speakers," Bimbo Cecconi said. "I got married in that church. Their priest was Father Chegin, who was like a singer at the opera."

Cecconi gave me a guided tour of where some of Donora's most famous sons and daughters lived. That empty plot used to contain the home of Deacon Dan Towler. There was the block where Arnold Galiffa, known as "Pope," lived. Cecconi's voice grew husky as he told how his teammate died young, of cancer.

There was the house where the Griffeys lived—first Buddy, then Ken senior, who moved back to town so his wife at the time could give birth to their oldest son, Ken, later known as Junior.

On these hills, Cecconi said, people continued the customs of the old country. This was no ethnic cliché: the Italians loved their gardens and their kitchens.

"My father worked at the mill. He was a crane man," Cecconi said. "When they needed him, they'd call for him." That freedom meant his father would be cooking in his spare time—sauces, chickens, groundhogs— or canning fruits and vegetables. The Romantinos, down the block, kept pigs, and Cecconi's father would help butcher them, help make sausage— "barter system," he said.

Some of the Italian families would cross the river to Webster Hall, climb the hills to the elderberry patches, spend the day picking, then go home and make white wine.

"At a certain time of year, a whole boxcar full of grapes would come to town and all these different families would get wheelbarrows and go down and fill them up, and for three weeks after that, if you had lit a match this town would have blown up," said Bill Bottonari, who was the same age as Musial.

"Whenever I brought over anybody Irish or English or Scotch, my house always smelled," Bottonari said. "Their houses were antiseptic, you couldn't smell a thing, and that embarrassed the hell out of me."

People were often judged by their father's job down at the mill. "Stan's father, not to be snobbish about it, but he was primarily a laborer," Bottonari said.

There was no major segregation into ethnic or racial neighborhoods.

"Our barber was black," Bottonari recalled. "Blacks were working when the whites were working." A photo in a Donora diamond jubilee book shows proud old lifers standing in front of the mill. Four or five of the old-timers are clearly African American. Bottonari said that all five blacks in his graduating class went on to college.

AND SOME Donorans went beyond. The Honorable Reggie B. Walton, the United States District Judge for the District of Columbia, grew up in the same neighborhood as the Cecconis and the Griffeys.

In 2007, Judge Walton presided over the trial of I. Lewis (Scooter) Libby Jr., the former chief of staff to Vice President Dick Cheney. Libby was convicted of leaking government secrets, including the identity of a covert agent of the Central Intelligence Agency.

Judge Walton is proud of not coddling youthful offenders. He often talks about how his father, a laid-off steelworker who held two jobs to keep the family together, monitored him when Reggie was heading toward serious trouble. Ultimately, Reggie went away to West Virginia State College on a football scholarship.

After law school, Walton was appointed to the district court by President Ronald Reagan and later was second in command of the Office of National Drug Control Policy under Presidents Reagan and George H. W. Bush.

Judge Walton never met Stan Musial, who had moved away by the time Walton was born early in 1949, but he did come under the sway of another great person from that town, Dr. Charles Stacey, the superintendent of schools. (When I said I would love to chat with Walton, the judge called me a few days later, letting me know that Stacey had told him to call. That is the way things work in Donora.)

"I think you had a really good core of people who had migrated to Donora because of the relative affluence of the steel industry," Judge Walton said, adding, "It had a good education system. I had excellent teachers, although I was not a stellar student."

Judge Walton, who is African American, added: "To be candid, race was not a non-issue. My mother could not get a job as a salesperson in a store downtown. Very few blacks in the steel mills had supervisory positions. But we intermingled in the town, especially when it came to education. I never feel slighted when I talk about my education.

"Sure, there were some restaurants where you wouldn't go. They didn't have a sign that said blacks were not served, but you knew you were not welcome.

"I never had a black teacher. But I never felt my teachers treated me any differently because of my race."

The judge concluded: "It was a tough city and it made you tough. I attribute all my success to my parents and coaches."

The judge's memories sounded familiar. He came out of that hard town with a lifelong bond with Stacey and other mentors who looked after him, much the way people had looked after young Stan Musial.

# 10

## MENTORS

IN HIS long public life, Musial seemed so spontaneous, so merry, that it was hard to imagine his having ulterior motives with the words he used so apparently casually. However, in at least one case, he may very well have created a parallel childhood, to match other boys' memories of that staple of American childhood—their dad taking them to their first game.

His possible mythmaking took place in 1969, for a documentary about his childhood. The trip was planned around the Cardinals' visit to Forbes Field, which would close in June 1970.

"We were standing near the batting cage and Musial says to me, 'Come on, Slim, let's take a walk,' " a journalist, Scott Dine, recalled. "He had started calling me Slim earlier in the day. And walk we did. Across the infield, then the outfield to the bleachers. Musial wasn't saying much. He opened a gate and we walked up several rows and sat down.

"After a long silence Musial explained that his dad would bring him to baseball games and his dad would get a pail of beer (pretty sure he said it was a pail—but I may be confusing it with another story). I sort of visualized him as a fledgling pitcher studying the guy on the mound or carefully sizing up a batter.

"So there we sat, in silence, on a gorgeous summer day. Then Musial said quietly, 'It was here that I figured that baseball was my way out of Donora.' He said nothing more and I was too stunned to respond. We quietly returned to the batting cage."

It is a lovely memory, connecting a boy and his father and his childhood dream. No doubt Dine recalled the conversation accurately, whether or not Musial said his father ordered a "pail" of beer or just a cup. But according to other Musial words on the subject, Lukasz never took his son to a game at Forbes Field, and Musial often said it was his mother who had played catch with him. The only revealing part is that Musial felt the need to place his dad in the old ballpark.

The trains ran regularly from Donora to downtown Pittsburgh and were not expensive. People from Donora went "up" to Pittsburgh on a daily basis for one thing or another. But Lukasz was not a baseball fan, and once he had made his way from Poland to the west bank of the Monongahela, his peregrinations may not have gone beyond factory and ethnic clubs and the trudge home up the hill.

Parents can loom large in their children's memories. Twenty years after his father's death, Musial may have been trying to portray Lukasz as a man with big dreams, the way Judy Collins did in her classic song "My Father," about a miner who promises his daughter that someday they would live in France.

Sitting in the bleachers in doomed Forbes Field, Musial may have been indulging in a touching bout of wishful thinking.


THE BOY'S journey began with the rudimentary baseballs Mary Musial manufactured with spare rags and strings, and the few minutes of catch she could muster just outside the house.

As the two Musial boys began to roam around Donora, other adults were often willing to act in loco parentis.

"We all had 'relations' in any part of town who would whip your ass if you were doing wrong, which you can't do today," Ed Musial said in 2000. "Anybody was allowed to take care if you was up to no good . . . so you had to be good, because somebody's going to see you."

There was no Little League in those days, so boys played ball wherever they could. Flat land is precious in Donora. The steel mills had priority, laid against the Monongahela River, sending their precious product downriver to Pittsburgh. A block or two from the river, the Appalachian hills rise steeply.

The boys played at Weed Field, an odd name for such a dusty flat patch on the hillside. Nothing grew there because of the plumes of smoke from the American Steel plants directly below.

Stash's training at the Polish Falcons' gymnastics classes had made him comfortable with his body, instantly adept in this most American of sports. He was a natural left-handed hitter who could hit the ball farther than anybody else, and his long drives to right field would go bouncing down the arid, rocky gully.

"You had to wait five minutes for the outfielder to get the ball," Musial recalled with a laugh many years later.

Right field was out of bounds, so the young man tried to hit the ball to center or left, where there was more space.

From his gymnast's training, he discovered a coiled stance—right hip facing the pitcher, head tucked down behind his right shoulder, weight back.

The young man also learned to pitch from watching the men. With the same superb timing and selectivity he would develop at bat, young Stash found his first mentor—Joe Barbao, who had played minor-league ball and now lived for baseball in his hours away from the mill.

Barbao allowed the Musial boys, both lefties, to play catch on the sideline while he was working out with his buddies, and he would teach them the game. Because Stan was two years older than his brother, he was first to serve as batboy for the team Barbao managed, the Donora Zincs. Stan was slender, in the manner of the Depression, when Americans visibly had ribs and sternums, but anybody could see the boy was an athlete, had a competitive drive.

One day the Zincs were playing Monessen and their pitcher ran out of gas early. Barbao asked the skinny batboy if he would like to pitch. According to Musial's memory, he pitched six innings and struck out thirteen, but even if his stint was a little less spectacular, he pitched well enough to retire grown men. He also managed to annoy some of the Zincs, who grumbled that he was not an employee of the mill and had not paid his club dues. Eventually Barbao smoothed it out and soon Musial was a regular with the Zincs, one time breaking Barbao's ankle with a hard foul to the coaching box at first base.

Ed also was a hitter and soon earned a spot on the Merchants team.

One story, told at many Musial family gatherings, dates back to when Stan lashed a drive that was rolling toward the outfield fence, a triple for sure, until Ed surreptitiously kicked the ball under the fence, turning the hit into a ground-rule double.

"When I came in, I told him," Ed said, still cackling about it after many retellings. "I says, 'You know, I beat you out of a triple.' First time up, he put one right between the shoulder blades. He was very competitive, very competitive," Ed added with a laugh.

Stan also found mentors at school. The head coach was James K. Russell, a Notre Dame man who had been recommended by the legendary Irish football coach Knute Rockne shortly before Rockne's death in 1931.

Russell became aware that Musial was a sandlot quarterback, probably good enough to play for his varsity, but Lukasz considered that sport too violent and would not give his permission. Lukasz won that battle, although he did not know his son continued to play informally, with minimal equipment and no supervision. Blocked from varsity football, Musial became a prominent member of Russell's basketball team as a sophomore.

Another adult keeping an eye on Musial was Michael Duda, who taught English composition and civics. Duda was known as Ki, short for Kaiser, not from any adult admiration for the former leader of Germany but because he had once portrayed the kaiser in childhood neighborhood war games. A local boy, Duda had gone to St. Vincent College in nearby Latrobe, returning in 1934 with a degree as well as a bride, Veronica (Verna), a classically trained violinist.

The young couple lived in a third-floor apartment above the Union National Bank downtown. They would later have a daughter, but in the mid-thirties they had time and energy to pay attention to the young Stan who may have needed it more than some of his teammates did. In the summer, Duda worked at a camp in Latrobe and brought along some Donora boys; Stanley was always included.

Donora High had not fielded a baseball team for a dozen years, so Musial pitched for the American Legion post. Word got around to the scouts, doggedly wearing out shoe leather and tire rubber to find talent.

Two miles away in Monessen, the St. Louis Cardinals fielded a team in the Class D Penn State League. Branch Rickey had built a farm system on the theory that he could make more money by owning entire teams rather than having to purchase single players at a premium. The crafty Rickey had lined up teams stacked with Depression-era youths, mostly southerners, competing with one another for a ragged uniform that had been worn, several incarnations earlier, by somebody higher in the organization.

The business manager at Monessen, Andrew J. French, invited Musial to a tryout at Page Park, with its flimsy wooden stands, and introduced him to the manager, Ollie Vanek, who had broken his index finger that spring while catching for Decatur. To amortize the vast amount they were undoubtedly paying him, the Cardinals sent Vanek to manage at Monessen, a steep fall from his own playing ambitions. As part of his job, he had to supervise tryouts.

"It was deep in the Depression, we didn't have any lights and we didn't start our games until four thirty in the afternoon," Vanek would recall. "That way we figured we might draw a few of the men who were lucky enough to be working in the few mills that weren't shut down."

The Musial boy crossed the river for a tryout on a Saturday. He weighed 135 pounds and wore a white T-shirt, blue jeans, and canvas sneakers. "He looked, as Ollie described him, like a grammar school kid with his pink cheeks and gangling arms," Jack Sher wrote. The boy pitched batting practice—"pretty fair curve," Vanek would recall—and could also hit pretty well, for a pitcher.

"He seemed to love to play ball but he was very shy, almost the sort of kid you'd forget if you didn't look twice at the way he slugged the ball. I watched the stuff he threw and recommended that Andy French sign him."

The scouting report of June 5, 1937, signed by French, called Musial a "green kid," but praised him for being aggressive with good habits.

Vanek kept up with Musial over the summer of 1937, as other teams, but not the Pirates, began showing an interest. In late August, French turned up at the Musial house, trying to sign Musial for the vast Cardinal system and touching off negotiations with as many variables as a World War II summit involving Roosevelt, Churchill, and Stalin.

Because he would not turn eighteen for another fifteen months, Musial could not legally sign a professional contract. Musial has always maintained his father balked at signing the Cardinals' contract because Lukasz wanted Stan to accept a basketball scholarship at the University of Pittsburgh.

This version is plausible at best. Musial was a very ordinary student, but in high school he had taken the somewhat humbling step of making up a necessary algebra credit at the junior high—a star athlete sitting in with children three years younger than he. More likely, Stash's real goal was to play professional baseball, while Lukasz wanted him to work in the zinc mills and play semipro ball on the weekend.

"His father wanted him to work and make money, because they were poor," Verna Duda said emphatically in her retirement apartment in Pennsylvania in 2009.

Asked about the parallel version that Lukasz wanted his son to go to college, Duda said with ironic inflection that there had been "mixed emotions," and she let it go at that.

One constant in the telling about this crisis is that Musial always gave credit to the high school librarian, Helen Kloz. While he never spent much time in the library, somehow Kloz recognized his torment and told him to follow his heart. (In 1961, long retired, Kloz came to see him play in Philadelphia and asked him to hit a home run for her, on the premise they might never see each other again. The wind was blowing in that day—but Stanley managed to hit one out, and he laughed for joy around the bases.)

Andrew French came back on September 24, 1937, contract in hand for $65 a month for the short minor-league season. Through the typewriter of his longtime friend and biographer, Bob Broeg, Musial described the meeting, starting with his mother's role:

> She's a big woman, taller than my father. In typical old-world custom, Pop wore the pants in the family, but now Mom spoke up to him quite sharply.
>
> "Lukasz," she asked, "why did you come to America?"
>
> "Why?" my father said, puzzled in his broken English. "Because it's a free country, that's why."
>
> My mother nodded triumphantly. "That's right, Lukasz," she said. "And in America, a boy is free NOT to go to college, too."

Pop grumbled, then paused. "All right, Stashu," he said with a sigh, "if you want baseball enough to pass up college, then I'll sign."

Somebody who has heard the Musial family variations on this meeting over the years says there is another detail to that summit: to make her husband more amenable to signing, Mary Musial plied him with a drink. Or two.

Lukasz signed the contract, but there was a social cost: father and son were not on good terms for several years after that, perhaps did not even speak. Good son that he is, Musial has never talked much about that time; sitting for the documentary in Forbes Field in 1969, he placed his father at the core of his youthful ambitions.

BECAUSE HE signed with the Cardinals after the 1937 season, Musial was still eligible to play basketball for Donora High as a junior that winter. He had grown to six feet by seventeen and became one of the stars as the Donora Dragons surprised the Mon Valley by winning eleven of twelve league games.

Just before the regional tournament in Pittsburgh, Musial came down with the flu. Fearing the boy would not recover quickly enough in his crowded home, Jimmy Russell and his wife took him in and got him well enough to play.

Donora upset Washington in the first game, and Russell later said, "We probably wouldn't have won it without Stan. But sick or not, he did what you'd expect. He played a wonderful game." Donora was then eliminated by Har-Brack in the next round.

The team was also tested off the court during the tournament, as the players were put in a side room at the hotel restaurant because of their two African American players, Grant Gray and Buddy Griffey. Musial and his teammates said they were willing to forfeit rather than be treated that way, which pleased Russell, who once had taken them out of a Donora restaurant after a similar incident.

Musial never gave long dissertations on race, but in later years he would cite this episode as crucial to his own tolerant vision of race.

Through his basketball ability, Musial gained another mentor—Frank

Pizzica, who owned a DeSoto-Plymouth dealership in Monongahela and sponsored a team called the Garagemen. The perks included a few dollars here and there, but, more important, Frank and Molly Pizzica often invited Musial to eat with their family.

Pizzica gave Musial an example of how to dress, carry himself, run his own business, be confident, get ahead in this world. He would tell the boy, "Keep your head high, look 'em in the eye and give 'em a warm, firm handshake, not a dead fish."

In later years, Musial would invite the couple to visit him in St. Louis or on the road and would consult Pizzica before making business decisions.

When Pizzica was quite old, Musial stopped off at the Pizzica household on Sunday with his grandson, Tommy Ashley. "Mr. Pizzica wore a coat and tie to watch the Steelers," the young man recalled. "He dressed up as if he were going to church." Pizzica's legacy was that in his adult life Musial rarely went out in public without a sport jacket.

In the spring of 1938, Ki Duda decided to start a baseball team. Whether or not he did this for the benefit of the young prodigy is unclear, but he even hired an assistant coach, Charles "Chuck" Schmidt from nearby Cement City, who knew the game far better than Duda did. Musial was the star of the new team, often striking out ten or more batters and hitting long home runs.

One of those shots became a legend. Long after Donora High was blended with Monongahela High and the old high school building was turned into an elementary school, Bimbo Cecconi took me to the old athletic field and pointed to a grove of trees in deep right field.

"We played baseball on the football field," said Cecconi, who was only eight years old and not present when Musial hit his most celebrated shot. But the old Pitt tailback had heard plenty about it from eyewitnesses. "Guys would come to school the next day and say, 'Bim, you should have seen the one Musial hit yesterday,' " Cecconi said.

Cecconi pointed to where Musial's shot lofted over the football field— 360 feet, including end zones—and over the running track, heading toward the trees, an inside-the-park grand slam. The distance used to be accepted as 388 feet; sometimes it reaches 450 feet, depending on the teller.

After hitting .455 as a junior, Musial was clearly a baseball prospect, but Jimmy Russell may have been trying to talk him into playing basketball in his senior year and then attending Pitt. Years later, Musial said he had been put in touch with Pitt by Jerry Wunderlich, a gym teacher at Donora High. But Ki Duda recommended that Musial play minor-league ball and attend college in the off-season. Nothing was totally settled yet.

At the same time, Musial became disenchanted with the Cardinals. Baseball commissioner Kenesaw Mountain Landis, angry after Branch Rickey tried to purchase several teams in the same league or even buy entire leagues, described Rickey as a "hypocritical Protestant bastard wrapped in those minister's robes," and accused Rickey of being in violation of fair trade laws.

Musial may have been influenced by Landis's hanging-judge rhetoric. He had a lifelong aversion to conflict, wanted things as stable as possible, and began to develop doubts about the Cardinal organization.

In March 1938, Landis cracked down on Rickey's domination of the Three-I League, releasing a number of the Cardinals' farmhands, alternatively counted as ninety-one and seventy-four. The most prominent of those players was Pete Reiser, a St. Louis boy who would become a star in Brooklyn but had the unfortunate habit of running into unpadded outfield walls.

"I honestly hoped I had been among them," Musial would say of the released players. "If the Cardinals really were as bad as Judge Landis said they were, I didn't want to be part of that organization."

In the spring of 1938, the sports editor of the *Donora Herald-American,* Johnny Bunardzya, invited Musial to drive up to Pittsburgh to see a game, getting him in on a press pass.

There are several reasons to believe this was Musial's first visit to Forbes Field. He sometimes told the story of saving up money to see Babe Ruth come to Pittsburgh during Ruth's brief run with the Boston Braves in 1935, after the Yankees had spurned him. But Musial lent the money to a friend and could not afford the carfare and the ticket, thereby missing seeing Ruth hit three home runs shortly before his retirement.

"Even though Donora is only twenty-eight miles from Pittsburgh, I had never seen my favorite team play," Musial wrote in his autobiography. "The distance was short, but the price was high for a kid who didn't have the money or, when he did, didn't have the time because of a summer job or ball game he was playing in himself."

Admittedly, this was Bob Broeg doing the typing, not Musial, but Broeg was as close to Musial as anybody and derived a good side income from presenting Musial in a positive way. Broeg would have known better than to describe a first trip to Forbes Field with a friend if Lukasz Musial had escorted Stashu at an earlier age.

"Bunardzya remembers that I was bug-eyed when, from the upper tier behind first base, I got my first glimpse of the field and the tree-shrouded backdrop of Schenley Park," Musial wrote.

In his account, Musial said he turned to his hometown friend and said, "John, I think I can hit big-league pitching." This memory also suggests Musial was thinking like a hitter more than a pitcher, even though he had signed as a pitching prospect.

There was another trip to Forbes Field that spring, courtesy of Irv Weiss, "a sports-minded Donora merchant and ardent Pirates' fan," as Broeg/Musial called him, who may have been trying to steer Musial to the Pirates.

The Pirates let Musial pitch batting practice, and the Pirates' manager, Pie Traynor, made some inquiries about his status. Always honest, Musial informed Traynor that he was under contract but suggested the Cardinals might have forgotten him. Traynor assured him that Branch Rickey never overlooked a signature on a piece of paper. Soon afterward, the Cardinals notified Musial that it was time to report to the minor leagues.

No matter what kind of loving revisionism Musial might present down the line, his words suggest that a sportswriter and then a businessman, rather than his father, escorted him on his first forays to Forbes Field. He did not lack for kindly father figures.

# 11

## LIL

H E WAS a familiar sight around Donora, a slender young man pulling a cart, lugging boxes of groceries to front doors.

People remembered his quirky left-handed hook shot for Jimmy Russell's Dragons. The Musial boy. Hadn't he signed with the Cardinals? Why was he delivering kielbasa and cheese?

In a town the size of Donora, most people soon came to know that Stan was going with Lillian Labash, whose family owned a grocery store on McKean.

Lil was fourteen when her dad took her to a Zincs game. Sam Labash (pronounced LAY-bash) had been born on this side, was American enough to have played baseball as a youngster, and had been good enough to think about pro ball, but there was more money in groceries than the minor leagues, so he wound up running the family business.

"My grandparents married so young," Musial's daughter Gerry Ashley has said, calling her maternal grandfather "a frustrated baseball player," which would work out to Stan Musial's advantage.

The Labash family had a good reputation in Donora, extending credit, trusting neighbors to settle up on payday. The family was regarded as middle-class, almost bourgeois; Sam was comfortable enough that he could take time off to watch a ball game.

One day in 1934, Sam took his fourth daughter, Lillian, to a Zincs game and told her to keep an eye on "that Polish kid" who was pitching. She liked the Polish kid even more the next winter when she saw him in the abbreviated basketball shorts of the time—shorts that actually displayed knees and thighs, not the baggy ones of today. Over the next seventy-five years, Lil would often tell Stan she had been attracted to him because of the way he looked in his satin shorts.

Lil was two months older than Musial, pretty and blond, a shade over five feet tall and thereby nicknamed "Shrimp." She may have carried herself with a touch of confidence because of her parents' relative stability. Lil's older sister Ann was dating Dick Ercius, Musial's lanky basketball teammate, and one day Lil went along with them to a skating rink, where they spotted Musial, and Ercius arranged a date.

"Always neat as a pin," Lil said of Stan, who managed to be presentable despite his family's limited finances. He had not dated much, or at all, but he was hardly a recluse.

"Stan was never idle," recalled Eddie Pado, the second pitcher on the Donora team. "After school, he worked at the Spur Gas Station. On several occasions, they'd have a dance at the Polish hall down by the church where Stan attended, and we'd go down and peek in the window and say, 'Boy, look at that Stash dance!' He could do the polka and was an outstanding dancer."

"Sometimes Stan would infuriate me by being late for dates," Lil said in 1958. "He'd watch ball games or other sports events while I'd be at home stewing. But other times he'd be late because he'd stopped to attend Sunday-afternoon benediction at the church—and how could I be mad at him then?"

She recounted this in an article in *Parade* magazine under the byline of Mrs. Stan Musial—her public identity. Those who knew her best asserted that Lil ran the family over the years, allowing Stanley to be Stanley.

"It's tough to be the wife of a superstar," Tom Ashley, her former son-in-law, said. "She is totally dedicated to Stan. She is the one who raised the kids. They are great kids. I'd give her ninety-five percent of the responsibility.

"She has a nose for smelling out phonies. She's a fighter for their privacy. We've had our ups and downs but I respect her."

People who met Lil at the ballpark, at parties in Cooperstown, or around town in St. Louis described her as a lot of fun, no pushover. Stanley probably knew that the day he met her.

LIL'S BALLPLAYER father was born in Pennsylvania, but his parents, Samuel and Susie, are both listed as born in Slovakia. Given the vagaries of shifting borders and ethnic fortunes, Sam was considered to be of Russian ancestry.

Lil's mother, Anna Mikula, arrived in New York on December 21, 1912, on the *President Lincoln,* after leaving Hamburg, Germany, on December 7. Her home country was listed as Hungary, but she herself was listed as Slovakian and the legal minimum age of sixteen. The 1920 census listed Anna as twenty-one, which would have made her thirteen at the time of her crossing, apparently unsupervised. When she arrived, she possessed $3, the legal minimum. She was sponsored by her sister's husband in Donora; somebody made sure she had a train ticket for Donora.

By the 1920 census, Anna was married to Sam Labash, also listed as twenty-one, and they already had three children five or under—Mary, Helen, and Annie. Lillian would come along that year, followed by two boys and then Dorothy. Another boy would be stillborn, what they called a "blue baby" in those days.

The parents, the two Labash brothers, Sam and John, and their growing families all lived under the same roof, along with a boarder from Croatia named Mike Brkvenac, age twenty-nine, who is listed in the 1920 census as a laborer in a blast furnace.

"I've been in that house and, believe me, it wasn't big!" Gerry Ashley said years later.

Many people who grew up in large families in small houses look backward and play the mental game of "who slept where." On any given night, where did all those adults put all those children?

Gerry tried to re-create the Labash family home above the store—kitchen and living room downstairs, three bedrooms upstairs. Gerry shook her head at the logistics of it, to say nothing of the boarder from Croatia. She had fond memories of visits to her mom's home, calling her grandparents by the East European nicknames Dido and Baba.

There was also the legend of how the Labash family had welcomed the shy boy from up the hill.

"Stan had enormous respect for her parents," Tom Ashley said. "They didn't have much money, but they had food."

Long after they were married, Lil would tease Stanley: "You know why you went out with me? Only because my father owned that grocery store and fed you so well."

He would giggle, never quite denying the charge. From the assortment of salami and liverwurst and cheeses at the store, he never would choose bologna. He had eaten enough of that at home to last a lifetime.

Musial understood he had been attracted to the family as well as the girl. He once told Roger Kahn: "I wasn't sure in the beginning, either, but the girl I was going to marry, Lillian, her father owned a grocery store. No matter what happened in baseball, I knew I could always get a job in the store."

The store gave Musial a sense of an ordered life, based on food. He worked around the store, delivered groceries in the neighborhood using the wagon, watched Sam Labash run a business. No wonder he took so quickly to the restaurant business when he met Biggie Garagnani a decade later. From his middle teens, Stanley had been, in some overt way, taking mental notes.

Gerry Ashley felt her grandfather was instrumental in the courtship and the marriage. "He pushed my mother to my father," she said, in the most positive way.

Perhaps Sam Labash saw something of himself in his daughter's young beau. He thought it was exciting that Stan was going off to the minors, even at the modest salary of $65 a month.

Even then, for an obscure young athlete without much experience out in the world, Musial displayed a personal gyroscope of what worked for him and what did not. The Cardinals wanted him to play his first season, 1938, at their farm team in Greensburg, Pennsylvania, about an hour from Donora, but he balked. Perhaps he sensed Greensburg was too close, that he would have family and friends looking over his shoulder; perhaps he was trying to put some distance between himself and his father after their dispute over his contract.

The Cardinals had roughly six hundred players in their system, and players generally did what they were told, but somehow or other, Stanley prevailed and was sent to Williamson, West Virginia, in the Class D Mountain State League.

Williamson was a coal town across from eastern Kentucky, approximately 250 miles away from home. It was a different world: people from the Mon Valley think of themselves as being from the Pittsburgh area and resist the suggestion of commonality with deepest Appalachia.

Very much an outsider, Musial rented a room, paid five dollars a week for a meal ticket at the Day and Night Lunch, and played pool at the Brunswick Pool Room. In his first season, 1938, he pitched 110 innings, struck out 66, walked 80 batters, and had a 6–6 won-lost record with a high 4.66 earned run average. He also hit .258 in 26 games, with a home run.

"I didn't have confidence in my pitching," he would say years later. "I had confidence in my hitting. Why they didn't sign me as a hitter, I'll never know."

In the winter of 1938–39 Musial worked at the Labash store and was also given a safe job at the zinc mill.

Sent back to Williamson in 1939, Musial missed his high school graduation, but Lillian stood in for him. He won 9 games and lost 1, struck out 86, but he walked 85 in 92 innings with a 4.30 ERA. His manager, Harrison Wickel, recommended that the Cardinals cut him loose because of wildness, but almost as an afterthought mentioned that he was a nice young man who could hit—.352 with a home run.

He also caused a stir late one night when he wandered into the identical house next door, after perhaps taking one beer too many. It could have been dangerous to ramble around the wrong house, looking for his room, but the Fiery family recognized the popular young ballplayer and escorted him home, making sure he was safe.

On Sunday mornings Musial would attend Mass, and Geneva Zando, a senior in high school, would observe how devout and handsome he was on the Communion line. Soon she would marry Howard Fiery, who lived in the house Musial had entered by mistake. Over the decades they would listen to Cardinal games on the radio and tell their son, Randolph, why they rooted so intensely for Stan the Man.

Back home in Donora, Lil was aware that her boyfriend was playing for pennies so far from home.

"She wanted him to get a job," Verna Duda, the widow of Musial's teacher-mentor, said in 2009. "Her family had money. They weren't wanting for anything."

With war looming, Lil's father told Musial to give it another year, so the young man went off to Daytona Beach, Florida, in the spring of 1940, a minimal upgrade. His manager was Richard Kerr, who already had an honorable place in baseball history.

In 1919, Kerr had been a rookie left-hander with the Chicago White Sox, ignored by some unscrupulous older teammates who were involved, to one degree or another, in a gambling scheme to lose the World Series. This scandal has been chronicled by Eliot Asinof in his book *Eight Men Out* and later by John Sayles in his movie of the same name. In both works, Dickie Kerr is a minor character, but an honest one.

Ostracized by the sharpies, Kerr pitched a three-hit shutout in the third game and a ten-inning victory in the sixth game, but the conspirators managed to lose the Series to the Reds. When the scandal was exposed after the 1920 season, all eight players were found not guilty of legal charges but were banished for life by the new commissioner, Kenesaw Mountain Landis.

Dickie Kerr suffered in the wake of the scandal. The symbol of incorruptible decency, he asked for a better contract after 1921 but was turned down by the same haughty owner, Charles Comiskey, whose cheapness—dirty uniforms, substandard salaries, broken promises—had emboldened Kerr's crooked teammates to blow the 1919 Series. Kerr quit the White Sox and pitched in independent leagues, returning to the majors only for a cameo in 1925.

The reward for his honesty was that in 1940 Kerr was still scuffling for a modest minor-league managing salary when the Cardinals sent him the wild left-hander from up north.

Stanley's poker luck came through at a crucial time. He could have been managed by a bully, a drunk, a liar, an incompetent, or some combination thereof. The wrong manager could have sent him rushing back to Donora. Instead, Musial drew another inside straight in the card game of life.

When Lil joined Stan in Florida early in the spring, she was visibly pregnant. They said they had been married in secret on Stan's birthday, November 21, 1939. Kerr and his wife, Cora, had no children, and they took the young couple into their home.

On May 25, 1940, Stan and Lil were married at St. Paul's Roman Catholic Church in Daytona Beach. For Lil, this involved a conversion from the Orthodox faith of her family to the Roman Catholicism of her husband. They would always celebrate their anniversary in conjunction with Stan's birthday; many years later, one family member was surprised to learn about the May wedding.

Far away from her own protective family, Lil now had two kind people looking after her. In early August 1940, Lil gave birth to a son, whom they named Richard Stanley Musial, in tribute to their host.

BECAUSE OF the small roster, Kerr began using Musial in the outfield. Later in August, Musial dove for a line drive, landing on his left shoulder. Pitching in pain the rest of the season, he managed to win 18 games and lose only 5, by far his best record as a pitcher, and his ERA was an excellent 2.62, but his wildness had gotten worse. Then again, he batted .311 in 113 games.

At the end of the season, Stan and Lil stayed in Daytona Beach, where he worked in the sporting goods department at Montgomery Ward for $25 a week, to supplement his salary, which had been $100 a month for essentially six months. Ki Duda wrote letters telling him to be patient, but Musial realized the Cardinals were not about to bring in a lower-echelon pitcher for medical treatment.

"I didn't even see a doctor," he said years later, recalling the legions of players in all those Cardinal camps. "You're mostly a number."

Musial realistically began to fear he was finished as a pitcher. At some point Lil went home to Donora to stay with her family.

"He called me one day and he was kind of despondent, and he said, 'I might have to come and work in the Donora mills,' " Lil recalled. "I got my father on the phone and he said, 'Now you just keep on playing baseball because I'll take care of Lil and Dick here. Don't worry about anything.' "

Dickie Kerr would not let him quit.

"You won't make it to the top as a pitcher, but you'll get there some way because you're a damn fine ballplayer and a big-league hitter," Kerr told him.

SKIP AHEAD nearly two decades to 1958, when the Cardinals stopped in Houston on their way north and Musial visited Cora and Dick Kerr. Dick was now turning sixty-five and working as a bookkeeper for a construction company. Musial told him to go out and buy himself a birthday present—a house.

"He had mentioned a house before but we had never taken it seriously," Kerr said when the secret came out. "This time he told us to get busy. So we did."

The Kerrs moved into a subdivision where homes cost between $10,000 and $20,000 in 1958 dollars. Over the years it has been widely written that the Musials gave the house to the Kerrs, but in fact they held title to it, which suggests the Musials also paid the taxes on it, and who knows what else. Either way, it was a generous act toward a couple who had kept them going in a shaky time.

The Kerrs and Lil's family helped Musial keep his confidence and hit his way out of obscurity. By that summer of changes, Stan and Lil had known each other for six years. Their long and stable marriage would be a beacon for everybody who knew them.

# 12

---

## TAKEOFF

I N A nation that professes to love underdogs, very few great American athletes have come as far as Stan Musial did from 1940 to 1941. That glorious year is one of the great sagas of sport—the slow, sputtering toy firecracker of a minor-league career suddenly turned into a rocket.

Musial had good reason to doubt himself as a pitcher, and he had only vague hopes he could make it as a hitter. In May 1940, Ollie Vanek, who had scouted Musial three years earlier back in Pennsylvania, was assigned to inspect the Daytona Beach club. His evaluation of Musial: "Good form and curve, fast ball a bit doubtful. Also a good hitter. May make an outfielder."

Bob Broeg once ruminated on how far his pal had traveled, noting how the 1940 All-Star Game had been held in St. Louis while Musial was mostly pitching in the low minor leagues.

"And he is sitting in a room in Daytona Beach, trying to keep score," Broeg said for a documentary. Pausing for effect, Broeg added, "I've seen this scorecard. Max West of the Braves hit a three-run homer to win the game, 4–0." Broeg noted that West was a right fielder—and that twelve months later Musial would be playing right field in Sportsman's Park.

"Now that's incredible," said Broeg, who had a bit of a stammer. "I mean, I think it's, uh, the most fantastic story you have."

It became even more fantastic after Musial injured his shoulder and faced the 1941 season fearing his career was over.

Nineteen forty-one is most remembered for the attack on Pearl Harbor and the growing global involvement in World War II. But in the narrow world of American baseball, that year is remembered for Ted Williams's .406 batting average, Joe DiMaggio's consecutive-game hitting streak of 56, and Bob Feller's 25 victories and 260 strikeouts.

It was also the year Stan Musial roared upward, from virtual reject to astounding rookie.

He began his fourth season at the Cardinals' minor-league camp in Hollywood, Florida, a sore-armed pitcher scheduled to pitch batting practice to top prospects and then perhaps be released. Fortunately for him, the Cardinals had a vast cadre of managers and instructors who could recognize talent and bring it along.

In the swarm at Hollywood, Musial came under the scrutiny of the manager of the Class AA farm team at Columbus, Ohio, an older gent named Burt "Barney" Shotton, who had once played the outfield for the Browns and Cardinals.

Shotton watched Musial try to pitch on the sidelines and said, "Son, there's something wrong with your arm. At least, I know you're not throwing hard enough to pitch here. I think you can make it as a hitter. I'm going to send you to another camp with the recommendation that you be tried as an outfielder."

Years later, Musial would honor Shotton as "a man who never seems to have received enough credit for the help he gave me," and would describe Shotton as "a dignified, bespectacled man best known for later managing the Brooklyn Dodgers to two pennants." This was in 1947 and 1949, when Shotton would manage Jackie Robinson against Musial's Cardinals.

One person Musial did not include in his memories of those trying days was the general manager of the Cardinals, Branch Rickey. However, as Musial became the best player ever to emerge from the Cardinals' farm system, Rickey placed himself near the center of the process.

Interviewed on camera nearly two decades later, Rickey gave his ornate version of the retooling of Stanley:

He was signed as a batting practice pitcher for the Columbus, Ohio, club in the spring of 1941, training in Hollywood, Florida. It was the first time I was impressed with his ability as a hitter. Barney Shotton was the manager of the Columbus club. That morning when I came to visit him, he said, "Do you know a batsman named Musial?" And I said, "I never heard of him, but I do know a pitcher named Musial and he was sent here to pitch to your hitters." And he said, "I want to show you where he hit the ball in this park out here," and when we got out there that morning, he showed me where he hit the ball over the bank of the railroad in right center, and I asked him, "Did you see him hit it?" and he said, "I did," and if he hadn't seen it, he wouldn't have believed it, and I said, "Well, I wouldn't, if you don't mind, I won't either."

After that long shot, Musial at least had some hope of making it as a hitter as he traveled from coastal Hollywood deep inland, first to Albany, Georgia, and then to Columbus, Georgia, where the Cardinals' lowest minor leaguers trained.

However, as often happens in large organizations, Shotton's observations about Musial's hitting did not make their way to Columbus. Clay Hopper, the manager of Columbus, noticed Musial was listed as a pitcher and asked him to pitch against the Cardinals' varsity as it headed north.

"I told Clay, 'I'm not a pitcher anymore,' " Musial said, but Hopper told him to pitch anyway. Terry Moore and Johnny Mize both hit home runs off him, and a few days later he pitched against the Phillies and was whacked again.

As he despairingly waited for the next step, Musial spotted a familiar, weathered face—Ollie Vanek. In a not overly friendly world, here was somebody Musial knew, somebody who had once trekked to the Musial house to help persuade Lukasz Musial to sign the contract, somebody who might understand the desperation in a young man's eyes.

"Mr. Vanek, remember me?" Musial asked.

Vanek, who had praised Musial as a hitter the year before while scouting in Daytona Beach, drew a momentary blank.

"I place the face, kid, but not the name."

"Stan Musial . . . Stan Musial of Donora, Pennsylvania."

"Oh, sure, I remember," Vanek said. "You're the kid whose father needed so much persuasion to let you play."

The decency of both of them was very much in play. Musial was not polished enough to know how to work on the guilt or sympathy of managers or farm directors; he needed a deus ex machina, somebody to swoop out of the sky and rescue him.

If the young man—still not twenty-one—had been a smart aleck or a whiner, the Shottons and Vaneks might have turned their backs on him. But people saw something decent in Musial as he virtually begged for a chance.

WHO WAS Ollie Vanek? He had grown up around St. Louis, where his father worked for a foundry, and had attended St. Procopius College, now Benedictine, outside Chicago. After college, Ollie went into the Cardinal system, playing the outfield or third base or catching, which is how he had taken a foul tip off his right pinky in 1937, bending it permanently at a forty-five-degree angle.

Years later, Vanek's son, Ben, a dentist near Denver, would recall how the father would point "over there" as he told his sons to perform a household chore—and the Vanek boys would ask Dad to be more specific since his catcher's fingers were pointing in various directions. That was catcher humor—what, you thought Joe Garagiola invented it?—typical for that miserable breed, whose handshake often resembles a sack of peanuts, bulging in odd shapes.

In 1941 Vanek was slated to be a player-manager at Springfield, Missouri, with moderate leeway in choosing his players. At a staff meeting in Georgia, conducted by Rickey, managers at the A and B levels passed on Musial.

Dib Williams, who had played for the 1930 and 1931 champion Philadelphia A's, was a player-manager with the Cardinals' Class C team in Decatur, Illinois, in 1941. Williams said he put in a bid for Musial but was rebuffed.

"Mr. Rickey, in a fairly loud voice, told me he didn't want to put the weakest outfield arm in the organization [Musial] in the largest professional ballpark [my ballpark] relaying throws to the weakest-throwing second baseman—ME!" However, the ballpark in Springfield, Missouri, had a short right-field fence, Williams said. In later years Musial and Vanek made it sound as if Vanek had been proactive in asking for the boy he had scouted.

The more Musial hit in the major leagues, the more Branch Rickey would assert that he had his eye on the lad all along, while Vanek would insist Rickey had merely gone along with his request. Vanek could remember the boy crying as his father balked at signing the contract, and Vanek felt that a boy who wanted to play that badly . . .

The relationship between Vanek and Rickey is complicated. In 1962, Rickey would resurface in St. Louis as the éminence grise of Gussie Busch, and would purge most of the front office staff, including the longtime scout Ollie Vanek. This cut Vanek's income and pension, leading to bitterness toward Rickey.

"The man was good for baseball," Ben Vanek said years later, praising Rickey's signing of Jackie Robinson and building farm systems.

"He was also a man who liked to take credit for things when he was on the periphery," Ben Vanek added. His father had put his own job on the line in 1941 by asking Rickey to let him take Musial.

"You have to remember that now Musial is like Willie Mays, but back then he was just another face in the crowd," Ben said.

In Ollie Vanek's obituary in 2000, Bob Broeg, the legendary Musial confidant, wrote: "Vanek spoke up. He liked Musial as an athlete. Ollie would take Stan." So Musial's career gained traction in Springfield, the Queen City of the Ozarks, in the southwest corner of the state, a hub of the Frisco and Missouri Pacific railroad.

Springfield's White City Park was located next door to the town sanitation disposal plant.

"On a warm humid night they couldn't draw any fans. The stench would just make you ill," said John Hall, an authority on old-time Missouri baseball.

In the fetid heat of the afternoon, Musial gravitated to the ballpark, where Vanek taught him to play the outfield. "He was the only ballplayer on the club who would come to me and ask me to put him through extra outfield practice," Vanek said. One night Musial chased a line drive, running smack into the right-field fence. He was shaken up but stayed in the game.

Minor-league fans understand that the best prospects do not stay long. You've gotta catch 'em fast, before they move on. Willie Mays played 81 games at Trenton in 1950 and 35 more at Minneapolis in 1951. Roberto

Clemente, under wraps by the Brooklyn Dodgers at Montreal in 1954, was allowed to play 87 games, enough for Pittsburgh (Branch Rickey!) to figure out the ruse and claim him. Now Musial began his rush up the ladder.

From that coiled stance, he began launching homers over the right-field fence, bouncing them off the houses across Boonville Avenue. The children of Springfield learned his name fast. Frank Hungerford, eleven years old, was allowed by his stepmother to take the bus to the ballpark. After the games, management let the children swarm onto the field to mingle with the home-team players.

More than half a century later, after a career as an army colonel including hitches in Korea and Vietnam, Hungerford could remember getting close to the new star of the Springfield Cardinals.

"I would pat him on the back. He was real friendly, very gracious," Hungerford said.

In his old age, Hungerford still had a newspaper clipping of his being given a Kiwanis Cardinals shirt by Musial, catcher Alvin Kluttz, and shortstop Dale Hackett. Another photo shows Stan and Lil Musial and their baby son, Dickie, surrounded by Kiwanis Leaguers.

Over the years there have been suggestions that Lil was running out of patience with her husband's choice of careers, but Musial has praised his wife for keeping him going, saying with a smile, "She was the one that rubbed my arm."

Stan and Lil and Dickie shared an apartment with the family of John "Fats" Dantonio, a catcher from New Orleans and Musial's best friend on the team. Years later, Lil would tell Tom Fox, a columnist in Philadelphia, how Dickie had come down with the whooping cough and Fats Dantonio caught it and the front office sent him home—without pay.

Laughing over it years later, Lil also told Fox how she and Fats's wife had gotten into an argument: "We were both cooking in the same kitchen and we almost came to blows over a slice of bread."

They were tense times. Nobody knew what was just ahead.

ONE SOURCE of diversion in the Springfield clubhouse was a personable fifteen-year-old catcher Rickey had spirited out of St. Louis, to hide him from the scouts until he reached the legal signing age—a common Rickey tactic. The young catcher performed odd jobs in the clubhouse, like an apprentice in some ancient guild, and he also caught batting practice and played in the local Kiwanis League.

Long before the kid, Joe Garagiola, became one of America's favorite television personalities, Musial relied on him for comic relief. They had no way of knowing the friendship would shatter, many years later, in one of the darker episodes for both men. Back then it was all chatter and good times.

Musial was tearing up the league. During one long bus ride to Topeka, Kansas, Vanek said, "You know what, Stan? I wouldn't be surprised to see you in the majors in a couple of years." Musial laughed politely.

Back in Springfield, eleven-year-old Frank Hungerford read rumors in the papers that Rickey was coming down to inspect Musial. Apparently unaware of Rickey's presence, Musial hit a homer and a single.

Late in the game, as Vanek and Musial jogged to the outfield, Vanek said, "Goodbye, Stan."

The younger man was taken aback. "What do you mean, goodbye?" he asked.

"Just goodbye. You'll see," Vanek said.

The next morning Musial went fishing on the White River with Fats Dantonio and pitcher Blix Donnelly. The front office had a difficult time finding him to inform him he was being sent to Rochester.

In later years, Rickey would assure everybody he had been keeping an eye on the prodigy, but Sam Breadon, the owner of the Cardinals, suggested otherwise.

"I'll let you in on a secret," Breadon told the writer, Jack Sher, after the 1948 season. "Few know it, but when Stan Musial began hitting at Springfield, the Giants offered us $40,000 for him. And a certain party wanted to sell him. I couldn't see the idea of selling Stan. I felt a hitter like that belonged on the Cards." St. Louis fans, who feel that Musial was underrated in the East, can only shudder at the prospect of his being lionized for his hitting exploits in the oddly shaped Polo Grounds.

Musial departed Springfield with a batting average of .379 in 87 games, 26 homers, and 94 RBIs. Before he left town, Musial stopped off to thank Vanek, twice.

Stan and Lil took the train to Rochester. Lil remembered her pragmatic husband saying to her, "It looks now like all our baseball ambitions are coming true." He probably meant the high minors. He had no idea.

As luck would have it, Stanley had a friend in Rochester. Chuck Schmidt, the peppy assistant coach from Musial's one year of high school ball in Donora, was now working in Rochester, and appeared at the train station when Musial arrived, carrying his clothes in a paper bag.

Lil and Dick joined Stan in a rented apartment not far from the ballpark, and Chuck and Betty Jane Schmidt were a daily presence in their lives.

Manager Tony Kaufman immediately put Musial into the lineup and discovered he was an apt pupil, with unusual hand-eye coordination. When Kaufman suggested Musial keep the third baseman honest by choking up on the bat and slashing a ground ball past him—Casey Stengel called it "the butcher boy"—Musial performed it perfectly twice. Kaufman asked if he had ever tried it, and Musial said, "Naw—it's easy." Kaufman, who had been at this game a while, knew it was not easy at all.

Musial, who had missed Babe Ruth's epic three-homer explosion in his final days with the Boston Braves in 1935, did get to see the Babe up close in Rochester six years later. Making a personal appearance, the Babe was sitting on the bench before a game, and Musial thought about going over to say hello—until he spotted the Babe taking a swig from a hip flask.

Sticking to business, Musial hit .326 in 54 games for the Red Wings, who then played the Newark Bears in the International League playoffs. Meanwhile, the parent team was engaged in one of those old-fashioned all-or-nothing pennant races with the Dodgers—none of this modern wild-card business. Enos Slaughter, Johnny Mize, and Terry Moore were all injured, and Jimmy Ripple, the ranking left-handed hitter at Rochester, was out with a broken finger.

With the rosters expanding on September 1, Rickey went to New Jersey to watch Musial hit against the top Yankee farmhands. The Red Wings were eliminated in six games and Musial, assuming his season was over, said goodbye to the Schmidts. "Well, guess I'll be seeing you next year," Musial told Schmidt before he headed home to Pittsburgh, taking the night train to save a few dollars.

Lil met him in Pittsburgh and drove him down to Donora, where he attended Sunday Mass. Then he came home and lay down for a nap. In a few months he had gone from batting-practice fodder to promising slugger in the high minor leagues, and now he assumed his season, his breakthrough season, was over.

# 13

## PENNANT RACE

LIL INTERRUPTED his nap. He had just received a telegram ordering him to report to St. Louis because the Cardinals needed him for the final two weeks of the pennant race. The Labashes drove him up to Pittsburgh, where he missed the train, but he did arrive in St. Louis and signed a major-league contract for $400 a month. Even prorated for the couple of weeks he would be there, the contract gave him a nice little bonus to his $150-per-month salary in the minors.

When Musial arrived at Sportsman's Park, there was none of the bloggery and tweets that accompany every coming and going during a contemporary pennant race. No columns, no sidebar articles, no profiles on the kid who had hit .379 and .326 on his rapid rise up from the bushes. They were simpler times.

Butch Yatkeman, the tiny sparrow of a clubhouse man, gave the kid uniform number 6, not because anybody thought Musial merited a single-digit number but because that uniform was available.

The low number did not help him when Musial tried to grab a few swings during batting practice. In the custom of the times, Walker Cooper, the crusty old catcher, barked, "Get your ass out of there."

The Cardinals had earned the nickname "Gashouse Gang" for their bumptious pranks and hard-edged excellence in the thirties, and they still had a solid core of competitors in 1941. Cooper was not indulging in fraternity-boy rites when he ran the kid out of the cage; that was how things were in those days, on that team. But the manager made the lineup, and Billy Southworth needed Musial.

Musial made his major-league debut on September 17, in the second game of a doubleheader. The Braves were en route to another seventh-place finish but, since the Cardinals had a shot at the pennant, Braves manager Casey Stengel played it straight with his best lineup. For his first view of major-league pitching, Musial got to track knuckleballs from Jim Tobin, a veteran who would win 105 games in his career and was some-times called "Abba Dabba"—magician language. Never having seen a knuckler—released from the fingertips, not the knuckles—Musial popped up the first time.

"This is strange," he recalled thinking. "I never saw anything like that."

He was a fast learner. The second time up, he calibrated the Abba Dabba floater and rapped a double.

Stengel watched the kid adjust to Tobin's hocus-pocus. Sometimes Casey let himself look like a clown to make up for his bad teams, but he was serious about the game. When the Braves played the Dodgers a few days later, Casey told the Brooklyn writers, "You fellas will win it, but those Cardinals got a young kid in left field who you guys are gonna write about for twenty years."

There is another version from Bob Broeg, who in 1941 was a rookie re-porter far from home, in Boston. Stengel, who had a magnificent memory for details, spotted Broeg shortly after his first sighting of Musial.

"Your club has got a guy with an unusual name," Casey rasped at Broeg, acknowledging Broeg's hometown. Stengel then described how Tobin had slipped the kid the knuckler. "Popped it up," Stengel narrated. "So he threw that dead fish again, and he popped one"—a reference to Musial's double. According to Broeg, Stengel paused for effect before adding, "He's gonna be a great player."

Then there is a third version I have heard over the years, maybe from Casey himself. In that one, Casey told reporters, "They got another one," which makes him sound a trifle jealous of the depth of the Cardi-nal system. Having been around Stengel during his days managing the Mets, I know the Old Man could be scintillatingly terse when he wanted to be.

However Casey said it, he and Musial developed a lifelong affection. Whenever Stengel's team came to town, he would take a party of "my writ-ers" to Musial's restaurant, where Musial would bustle over, calling him

"Case," and making sure the New Yorkers got the best cuts of beef, and laughing at every salty observation from the Old Man.

In 1941, however, Musial could not have imagined ever owning a restaurant. He just wanted to last the two weeks of the season without embarrassing himself.

In the St. Louis *Globe-Democrat* the next day, sports editor Martin J. Haley noted that the young hitter had two of the Cardinals' six hits. Haley did not indulge in any rhetoric about "Who is this pheenom?" or "A star is born," or even explain who Musial was. The kid just suddenly appeared and started swinging.

Not everybody was impressed. Among the spectators in those dwindling days of 1941 was Boris "Babe" Martin (real name Martinovich), a St. Louis–based catcher who had just led his league in hitting with .353 at Paragould, Arkansas, while Musial was slugging at nearby Springfield. Martin was sitting in the stands at Sportsman's Park with a couple of scouts as they scrutinized Musial's semi-defensive crouch.

"When I saw him up there with that batting stance of his, I said, 'He'll never make it,' " recalled Martin, who would have a modest career of 69 major-league games.

With all the injuries, manager Southworth kept using Musial. The proud franchise had not won a pennant since 1934, and the team was desperate to catch up with the Dodgers.

On September 20, the *Globe-Democrat* praised Musial in a subhead, "Terry Moore and Musial Star at Bat," after Musial went three for three with a walk.

In a doubleheader on September 21, Musial batted ten times, made six hits and scored six runs, and also made three excellent catches, but his chief contribution was an alert romp on the bases. With two outs, Musial was on second base when Coaker Triplett beat out a feeble swinging roller equidistant from the pitcher, catcher, and third baseman.

James P. Dawson of the *New York Times,* in town covering the race, referred to Musial as "the 20-year-old rookie sensation" who was "racing madly from second, rounded third on high, thundering right on over the plate before the Cubs woke up." Dawson noted that "the amazing rookie from Rochester" had scored the winning run.

The Cardinals were off the next day, which gave Robert L. Burnes some space to address this phenomenon in the *Globe-Democrat*. "Musial is really the answer to someone's prayer. His terrific hitting since joining the club last week has insured at least two triumphs. He can just about do everything." Burnes added: "The only thing that one could still want to know is whether or not he can cook. And Southworth is willing to wait to find out about that."

In the manic days of late September, the Cardinals were delighted to get help from a stranger. There was no all-sports television or radio in those days, no Internet, no glut of information, no great maw to be filled. More than sixty years later, when the Cardinals' Rick Ankiel morphed from a wild failed pitcher into a powerful center fielder, he was a national sensation. In 1941, people hardly knew who Musial was.

As the team embarked by train on its final road trip of the season, Terry Moore, one of the most respected captains of any era, chatted with the young player in the parlor car, just to get to know him.

Musial politely noted they had actually met in Georgia in March, from a distance of sixty feet six inches.

"It can't be," Moore blurted. "You're not that kid left-hander."

Moore called to Mize, the big soft-spoken Georgian known as the "Big Cat," and said, "Hey, John, you won't believe this! Musial is the left-hander who threw up those long home-run balls at Columbus this spring."

Looking back at Musial's debut, Moore would say: "Well, when I saw him in a Cardinal uniform, I just couldn't believe it. At the start of the season, he is a humpty-dumpty, bum-armed kid pitcher who I tag for a home run, a guy who is almost as low in the pro leagues as you can get. And at the end of the same year, he is a big-league outfielder!"

The first opponent on the road was the Pirates, Musial's hometown team, which had ignored him until after he had signed. On September 23, he hit his first major-league home run in Forbes Field, and after the game he brought his father into the clubhouse. Lukasz and his son had grown close again, and Musial joyously introduced him to his new teammates.

"Pop and I may have been shy, but we were two happy, proud Poles that evening," Musial wrote in his autobiography. Two nights later, neighbors from Donora gave him gifts before the Cardinals-Pirates game.

The Cardinals did not catch the Dodgers. When Southworth rested his regulars in the meaningless final game, Bob Burnes led off his story by writing: "A group of unidentified citizens, vaguely resembling in makeup and uniform the Cardinals of 1941 . . ." One of those "unidentified citizens" had just hit .426 in twelve games.

Think about it, Broeg bubbled years later: if Rochester had been knocked out earlier, Stanley might have had time to help the Cardinals win the pennant.

# 14

## MEET ME AT THE FAIR

S T. LOUIS was the perfect place for Musial—a grand old American city with status, with history, with shoe factories and breweries and railroads and river traffic, and with two baseball teams, the Cardinals and the Browns. It was a baseball town that would appreciate his talents. Fans knew how to idolize their heroes in St. Louis, did not drive them away with expectations and disillusionment.

"It's where he played, where he moved, where he lived, and he's still there," said William O. DeWitt Jr., the principal owner of the Cardinals since 1996, whose father was involved in St. Louis baseball as an official and owner going back to 1916.

DeWitt is a Yale graduate with an MBA from Harvard, just like his former oil partner, George W. Bush. He knew the town; he chose to buy the Cardinals, to invest in St. Louis.

"It has that that midwestern culture, family orientation, general respect for people," DeWitt said, adding that it has culture, art, medicine, schools—and "the feel of a smaller city, the perfect size."

The Cardinals were a major force in the city, DeWitt added, because of their "generational continuity" from the 1920s into the twenty-first century. And, DeWitt said, Musial was the great icon of perhaps the most visible institution of the city.

"As I travel around, people from New York tell me they are Cardinal fans because their father was a Stan Musial fan," DeWitt said. He told of baseball fans who visited the Cardinals' spring base in Jupiter, Florida, and flocked around the aging Musial, the symbol of the sport and the city.

As he did throughout his life, Musial recognized when he was well off and resisted trade opportunities later in his career.

"I was able to make my home, educate my kids, good schools, nice city. Got involved in civic duties, charities. Great people. Great fans. My wife and I love St. Louis."

THE CITY still had an air of entitlement when Musial arrived. The area had been explored by the French in the seventeenth century, shunted from the Spanish Empire to Napoleon Bonaparte, then sold to the United States in 1803 as part of the Louisiana Purchase. Known as the "Gateway to the West," St. Louis was the starting point for wagon trains, the link for river trade near the confluence of the Missouri and the Mississippi.

At the start of the twentieth century, St. Louis was the fourth-largest city in the United States, with 575,238 residents, behind New York, Chicago, and Philadelphia, just ahead of Boston. In succeeding decades, it would be fourth, sixth, and in 1940, just before Musial arrived, seventh.

By 2000, St. Louis would be fifty-third among American cities, with a population of 348,189, and by 2010 its population would fall to 319,294, a drop of 8 percent.

But in Musial's early seasons, the city still had an aura of glamour, the outer edge of eastern civilization. In 1944, Americans would be charmed by the movie *Meet Me in St. Louis*, with Judy Garland and other elegantly clad passengers riding the handsome trolley out to the 1904 World's Fair. Everybody knew this song:

> *Meet me in St. Louis, Louis,*
> *Meet me at the fair,*
> *Don't tell me the lights are shining*
> *Any place but there;*
> *We will dance the Hoochee Koochee,*
> *I will be your tootsie wootsie.*
> *If you will meet me in St. Louis, Louis,*
> *Meet me at the fair.*

The 1904 fair was still vivid when Musial came along. It had commemorated the one hundredth anniversary of the Louisiana Purchase—with an added attraction. Chicago had been picked to hold the third version of the modern Summer Olympic Games in 1904, but the deal fell through, so the Games were moved to St. Louis. The Games were a makeshift event, with athletes just showing up and competing, nothing like today's highly professional extravaganza, but they were the Olympics, all the same, on the fairgrounds in St. Louis. To this day, St. Louis is one of three American cities to have held the Summer Games, with Los Angeles having hosted them twice, in 1932 and 1984, and Atlanta in 1996.

The fair created an image for St. Louis that would last half a century and longer. Musial was in the right place at the right time, as he often was.

If the Pirates had discovered him ahead of the Cardinals, or if he had been able to renege on Lukasz's hard-gained signature, he would always have been the kid from the Mon Valley. The fate of the Pirate franchise—the fate of the entire steel industry, the entire region—would have somehow rested on his shoulders.

Or suppose Musial had played for one of the New York teams—three of them back then. He would have been celebrated at first for his smile and his base hits, but I know my hometown, and eventually the crowd would have demanded something more from him—more power, more championships, more quotes, more public visibility, some scandal, some controversy, something extra.

He would have been scorned for not having Willie Mays's perceived glee (one of the great misconceptions of the sport), Joe DiMaggio's inscrutable hauteur, Mickey Mantle's self-destructiveness (the red rising on Mantle's neck when he struck out), or Duke Snider's brash sizzle. New York would have wanted more out of Musial. Not sure what—just more.

Sometimes athletes find their proper karma in their first city. Joe Namath, from the Pittsburgh area, was destined to become Broadway Joe in New York. Earvin Johnson from Michigan was born to perform showtime magic in Los Angeles. Ted Williams, from San Diego, probably needed Boston's biting damp wind—and its biting damp "knights of the keyboard" as Williams called the city's sportswriters—to heighten his inner churl.

When Musial arrived at the end of the 1941 season, St. Louis was a crossroads, a jumping-off point, the Last Chance Saloon. The population was resting momentarily, not even halfway across the continent, ready to rip, like the mighty Mississippi about to go over the levees. The city was a worthy subject for American writers.

Thomas Wolfe almost surely never heard of Stan Musial, inasmuch as Wolfe died at the age of thirty-seven, of pneumonia and tuberculosis of the brain, on September 15, 1938, when Musial was still a wild and anonymous left-hander in Class D ball. But in his autobiographical novel, *Look Home-ward Angel,* whose title still resounds in the American soul, Wolfe cap-tured the essence of Musial's sport and Musial's adopted home.

St. Louis had a pull on Wolfe, a weight of sorrow, a tinge of glamour. One of his brothers, Grover Cleveland Wolfe, had died in an epidemic during the 1904 World's Fair and Olympics, while the Wolfe family was running a boardinghouse there. Wolfe would always remember the bustle and clang of St. Louis.

In his novel, Wolfe depicted a young writer named George Webber— known as "Monk," for his simian appearance—returning from New York to his home in the hills of North Carolina for the funeral of his aunt Maw. On the train he runs into a boyhood friend, Nebraska Crane, part Cherokee, who now plays baseball for an unnamed team in the Bronx. Crane tells his friend he is beginning to feel old at thirty-one, and when Webber ex-presses incredulity, Crane goes into a soliloquy about the brutal competi-tion of baseball, the ravages of time, and the draining climate of St. Louis:

> "Monkus," he said quietly, turning to his companion, and now his face was serious and he had his black Indian look—"you ever been in St. Looie in July?"
>
> "No."
>
> "All right, then," he said very softly and scornfully. "An' you ain't played ball there in July. You come up to bat with sweat bustin' from your ears. You step up an' look out there to where the pitcher ought to be, an' you see four of him. The crowd in the bleachers is out there roastin' in their shirt-sleeves, an' when the pitcher throws the ball it comes from nowheres—it comes right out of all them shirt-sleeves in the bleachers. It's on top of you before you know it. Well, anyway, you dig in an' git a toehold, take your cut, an' maybe you connect. You straighten out a fast one. It's good fer two bases if you hustle. In the old

days you could've made it standin' up. But now—boy!" He shook his head slowly. "You can't tell me nothin' about that ballpark in St. Looie in July! They got it all growed out in grass in April, but after July first"—he gave a short laugh—"hell!—it's paved with concrete! An' when you git to first, them dogs is sayin', 'Boy, let's stay here!' But you gotta keep on goin'—you know the manager is watchin' you—you're gonna ketch hell if you don't take that extra base, it may mean the game. And the boys in the press box, they got their eyes glued on you, too—they've begun to say old Crane is playin' on a dime—an' you're thinkin' about next year an' maybe gittin' in another Serious—an' you hope to God you don't git traded to St. Looie. So you take it on the lam, you slide into second like the Twentieth Century comin' into the Chicago yards—an' when you git up an' feel yourself all over to see if any of your parts is missin', you gotta listen to one of their second base-man's wisecracks: 'What's the hurry, Bras? Afraid you'll be late for the Veterans' Reunion?' "

"I begin to see what you mean, all right," said George.

Other writers took their measure of St. Louis, but from a distance. Kate Chopin, T. S. Eliot, Tennessee Williams, and William S. Burroughs had all lived in the Central West End, but as writers will do, they departed, putting their youthful grievances in print.

Asked why he did not remain in his hometown, Eliot said: "I didn't like being dead that much."

Williams wrote the play *The Glass Menagerie* from the viewpoint of a man who writes poems on boxes at the shoe factory, dreaming of leaving the family tenement and his beloved, wounded sister:

I left St. Louis. I descended the steps of this fire escape for a last time and followed, from then on, in my father's footsteps, attempting to find in motion what was lost in space.

Williams put himself in motion, but he did come back, to be buried in Calvary Cemetery in St. Louis.

Josephine Baker left. She was celebrated in Paris and given a state funeral there, buried in Monaco.

Maya Angelou left. She won a Pulitzer Prize and split her time between Harlem and North Carolina.

Chuck Berry traveled far and wide but he always came back, and once in a while he would give a late-night concert in his hometown.

Musial arrived with no expectations. He was a Donora boy who at first went home every winter, but he understood right away that St. Louis loved him, accepted him, adopted him, reassured him, defended him, protected him. St. Louis was loyal and highly undemanding psychologically. He did not have to fulfill everybody's psychic needs. All he had to do was just hit the ball. Run out of the batter's box. Smile when he slid into second. Sign autographs. Just say *whaddayasay-whaddayasay* and the people were charmed.

# 15

## THE MAHATMA

## OF THE MIDWEST

T HE CITY was also associated with one of the great builders of that sport, or any sport: Branch Rickey. If not an American original, Rickey was an American prototype—a Bible-quoting, money-loving lawyer and teacher and lay preacher. But most of all he was a baseball man—athlete, coach, manager, builder, intellectual inventor at the peak of his career.

Nineteen hundred and forty-two would turn out to be the only full season in which Rickey and Musial would overlap as general manager and player. (Rickey would return twenty years later in a highly divisive role as advisor.)

In 1942, Rickey was already acknowledged as one of a kind. He had started with the Browns in 1913 when they were the top team in St. Louis, but then he switched to the Cardinals and turned them into champions.

One of Rickey's most famous sayings was "Luck is the residue of design." Musial was, in his own Stanley way, the epitome of Rickey's design.

Rickey's take over the years was that he had always been there for Musial, a cigar-chomping fairy godfather, shepherding the lad through the less imaginative dunderheads in the organization.

"I went down to see him two different times," Rickey recounted years later. "He went to Rochester in the International League. He had led the Springfield league. Now he led the International League. I was so intrigued with his kaleidoscopic advance—extra-base hits galore—I brought him into St. Louis at the end of the season, and he led that league, too."

Actually, Stanley had stood in the batter's box all by himself. Rickey would give him that. But that was the point of the Rickey farm system: put an infinite number of lads (hungry) in an infinite number of uniforms (frayed) and, Judas Priest (Rickey's favorite declaration), you get Stan Musial.

By coming along when he did, Musial got to size up Rickey in his prime.

"He was very diplomatic in a way, and then he had a . . . terminology of his words that was very impressive," Musial once said with a laugh. "He was a pretty impressive guy."

Asked to elaborate, Musial added, "Well, he was very nice, knowledgeable baseball man, and he was a hard worker and he was always involved in baseball. Loved baseball. He worked hard at it.

"I would say that he could have probably gone ahead in any profession because he was a brilliant man."

Could have been a senator. Could have been a corporate founder. Could have been a college president. Rickey did better. First he built the St. Louis Cardinals. Then, he would have you believe, he flicked his magic cigar in the air, and presto—he produced Stan Musial.


WESLEY BRANCH Rickey was a farm boy raised in rural southeast Ohio, whose family dressed up and drove buggies to church in town every Sunday morning, singing hymns above the clatter of the hooves. The Rickeys were settlers, farmers, pioneers, but hardly primitives: they made sure their son went to college at Ohio Wesleyan.

Rickey played ball well enough to work his way up to the major leagues early in the century. A sore-armed catcher with the Highlanders, the predecessors of the Yankees, he had eleven bases stolen against him in one game, still a record. Then he because a lawyer and coached baseball at the University of Michigan, where he developed a young player named George Sisler, who would move on to the Browns and become their greatest star. Rickey soon followed, as Sisler's manager.

Sisler was baseball's perfect knight before Commissioner Ford Frick laid that term on Musial. In fact, if Musial had not come along, St. Louis would still be celebrating the dignified Sisler, who could pitch as well as hit.

Rickey was never much of a manager, perhaps because his mind was usually a step beyond the immediate action, but the Browns were a better franchise than the Cardinals, the other team in town.

Often insolvent, with few prospects for relocation, the Cardinals did have the first female owner of a major-league team, Helen Robison Britton, who had inherited the team from her uncle in 1911. Known as "Lady Bee," she was hamstrung by financial problems and a failing marriage, and the Cardinals stagnated. In 1917, the Cardinals' new ownership persuaded the Browns' owner, Philip Ball, to allow Rickey to move a few feet from the Browns' office to the Cardinals' office.

After serving in World War I, Rickey began developing a farm system that would control players, an idea that nineteenth-century pioneers like Harry Wright and Albert Spalding had tried. In 1926, the Cardinals won their first pennant, with Rogers Hornsby and Grover Cleveland Alexander beating the Yankees.

Sam Breadon, the Cards' new owner, persuaded the Browns that it would be to their advantage if the Cardinals were tenants in shabby Sportsman's Park, the last major-league stadium to get a public-address system. (Until it did, a man with a megaphone announced the starting lineups and subsequent changes.) While many fans remained loyal to the Browns, the Cardinals won five pennants and three world championships from 1926 through 1934, but their best attendance was only 778,000 in 1928, just before the Depression.

"You know he was a man who never took a drink. And he never came to the office on Sunday, and when he managed the Browns, later the Cardinals, he never managed on a Sunday," said William O. DeWitt, who began his career selling soda in the ballpark and later became general manager under Rickey.

(In the St. Louis flow of things, DeWitt moved to the Browns and eventually bought them. His son, William O. DeWitt Jr., would later own the Cardinals in the age of Pujols.)

Rickey had promised his mother never to work on the Sabbath, and he kept his word via a classic Rickey stratagem: by taking a room at the YMCA across the street from Sportsman's Park and no doubt counting the crowds flowing through the turnstiles.

Despite close monitoring by Judge Landis, Rickey managed to stockpile hungry players from the Depression. Dizzy Dean, the great pitcher who broke down too soon, knew the alternative for uneducated southerners was to bend in the hot Delta sun, picking cotton. Pepper Martin and Leo Durocher had come from other hard corners of the country and would raise their spikes into anybody's knees to avoid having to go home.

Martin and Joe Medwick provoked the Detroit Tigers during the World Series of 1934, with Medwick's hard slides causing fans to heave fruit at his head. With the Cardinals far ahead, Landis persuaded Medwick to leave the game to calm the fans, as the Cardinals wrapped up the Series.

The Gashouse Gang was known for pranks like disrupting ladies' luncheons in a hotel dining room by arriving with scaffolding and painters' costumes. Some of them were masters at throwing water balloons out hotel windows. In an age before headsets and clubhouse boom boxes, they made their own music.

"Pepper played the banjo-guitar," Terry Moore recalled in 1957. "And Lonny Warneke played the guitar. Fiddler Bill McGee played the fiddle. He held it down low, in the crook of his arm. I never did see him put it under his chin. He'd sit there straight as a board, real serious holding the fiddle down low and sawing away on it. Bob Weiland played the jug. Boomp, boomp. Boomp, boomp. And Frenchy Bordagaray played the washboard. You know, running a stick up and down on it. Damn, they practiced all the time. They drove Frank Frisch crazy. Their favorite song was 'Buffalo Gal.' I heard 'Buffalo Gal' so often I used to dream it at night: 'Buffalo Gal, ain't you comin' out tonight, comin' out tonight, comin' out tonight.' "

Moore recalled the anger of Frisch, the playing manager who had never seen a clubhouse band on his first team, John McGraw's more conservative Giants.

"Frisch couldn't stand it," Moore chortled to sportswriter Robert Creamer. "He used to say he was going to trade McGee and send Weiland down to the minors just to break up the Mudcats. We sure had a lot of fun."

That Gashouse Gang had pretty well dissipated when Musial arrived. The mainstays were Moore; Cooper; Enos Slaughter, the hard-driving right fielder; and Marty Marion, the elegant and lanky shortstop. Medwick, the scowling son of New Jersey, was helpful to Musial, perhaps because Medwick saw him as a fellow easterner.

Musial caught the tail end of Mize's time with the Cardinals in 1941. Rickey had a theory, often expressed, that it was better to unload a player a year too soon than a year too late. That theory was reinforced by the little detail of Rickey's receiving a percentage of the profit every time he unloaded a player. After the 1941 season, Rickey traded Mize, still only twenty-eight, to the Giants.

"That one really got to him," Tom Ashley, Musial's ex–son-in-law, said. "He thought they were shortsighted. He would talk about all the games they would have won if they had Mize in the lineup."

Musial did not seem to be under extreme pressure to replace the output of Mize, who had led the league with .349 in 1939 and hit 43 homers in 1940 before getting hurt in 1941. The Cardinals really did not know what they had in Musial, who seemed to spring straight out of Branch Rickey's fevered prayers.


THE 1942 season began on a somber note with the world at war following Pearl Harbor on December 7, 1941. Williams, Feller, and Hank Greenberg had either enlisted or been drafted, but Musial was deferred because he was a father and the main support of his own parents, and also because the Donora area had enough eligible men to fill the quota. So he headed for spring training, unsure he actually belonged.

The breezy Stanley-hits persona had not yet emerged. For all he knew, Walker Cooper would still run him out of the batting cage. But the good side was that on this veteran team, Musial did not have to take responsibility for anybody but himself. He could be the kid, let the veterans show him how it was done.

Half convinced he would be back in Donora by opening day, Musial started out slowly in Florida, possibly because his roommate, Ray Sanders, a rookie first baseman, was keeping late hours. Also, this was the first time Musial had ever trained with the big club, and he had trouble seeing the ball with the bright sun shining on the water and the wind fluttering in the palm trees of St. Pete.

"I didn't do well. In my low crouch, I was always looking up at the palm trees. We had a terrible background. I never did well in spring training."

If Musial had come along as an untested rookie in March of 1942, the club might have been seen him flailing and been tempted to send him back for more seasoning. With the war coming on, he could have gotten lost in the minors, been called up sooner by his draft board, who knows? But we are talking here about Stanley, always in the right place at the right time. Rickey and the rest had seen him for two weeks at the end of 1941. Musial changed roommates, started to get more sleep, and manager Southworth reassured him he had the job.

When the Cardinals reached St. Louis for opening day, Rickey summoned Musial into his office, known years later in Brooklyn as the "Cave of the Winds."

The cigar-chewing preacher could quote Scripture or the Bill of Rights with equal fervor, making baseball seem like the finest way to serve God and country, preferably at minimal pay. Joe Garagiola once described a similar visit to the man everybody called Mr. Rickey: "He was big. I noticed his eyebrows first because they were so thick, almost as if they need a haircut as they drooped over his horn-rimmed glasses. His hair was just as thick and might have been combed that morning, but looked like he had been running his hands through it all day."

Musial had never spent much time around Rickey until this moment in April 1942. Rickey told him he had been monitoring the lad's progress from stop to stop in the minors. He then alluded to the prorated salary of $400 a month he had paid Musial for his two weeks with the Cards at the end of 1941.

"I'm tearing it up, my boy," Rickey said. (Players sensed it was dangerous when Rickey referred to them as "my boy." That paternal affection usually came at a price.) "We're going to pay you $700 a month," he announced, meaning Musial would make a total of $4,250 for 1942. "We expect you to be our regular left fielder," Rickey added.

Stanley promptly called Lil in Donora and told her to come to St. Louis.

Not everybody was convinced Musial was here to stay. Harry Walker, who was competing with Musial for the left-field job, remembered how Don Padgett, one of the Cardinals' spare catchers, had questioned

Musial's odd stance in 1941. Musial turned to his left, wiggled his hips, and waited on the pitch rather defensively.

"Don Padgett told me I had nothing to worry about," Walker said in 1957, recalling Padgett saying, "This guy has a real crazy stance. The league's pitchers will get on to him the second time around because there is one pitch that bothers him." That pitch, Walker said, was the changeup.

Marty Marion also observed the odd posture. "Everybody started laughing when they saw him walk into the batting cage, you know, and take a few swings with that unique stance, I'd call it. We said, 'Kid, you'll never make it to the big leagues with that kind of stance.'" The lanky shortstop added that until Musial retired after the 1963 season, "I'll bet they was still talking about that funny stance."

The older players figured out that Musial was going to be around a while, and they began teaching him how to play left field. Musial was well aware of his one weakness, and would refer to it long after his playing days were over: "I didn't have my good arm," he once said. Without that shoulder injury? "I'd have been a good complete ballplayer," he said. He had fine instincts as an outfielder, kept strengthening his arm, and listened to everything Terry Moore said.

"Whenever the center fielder would say 'I got a ball,' we'd say 'Take it,'" Enos Slaughter recalled, adding: "We listened to Terry Moore, Musial and I both. I know in St. Louis, myself, every time a ball was hit up against a screen, I'd go to the wall and when I heard 'careful,' I knew I was close and when I heard 'plenty room,' I knew I could go all out. And that's one thing about Terry Moore. To me I think he's one of the greatest defensive center fielders I ever played with, bar none. And I think Musial listened to him a lot in playing left field."

Musial missed a week early in the season with an ankle injury, and the Cards fell ten games behind the Dodgers, the defending league champions, a cocky bunch managed by the old Gashouse Gang shortstop Leo Durocher. The hard feelings had begun in 1940, when Bob Bowman of the Dodgers beaned Medwick, and by now there was a long list of grievances on both sides.

Leo would put one foot up on the top dugout step, point to his own ear, and shout "Stick it in his ear" so loudly he could be heard over any crowd. Les Webber, a nondescript right-hander who did Durocher's dirty work, threw at Musial in 1942, and Musial tried to charge the mound, but the catcher and umpire got in the way. Tellingly, he was not ejected from the game, an indication the umpires knew Durocher had instigated it. This was the only time in his career that Musial would go after a pitcher; from then on he held an open contempt for Durocher, one of the few people in the game he did not like.

After the quiet young man went after Leo's pitcher, Cardinal fans understood: Musial could have played for the Gashouse Gang.

In August, Harry Walker became enamored with a Spike Jones recording of "Pass the Biscuits, Mirandy"—a goofus ditty about obstinate hillbillies. The Cardinals played "Mirandy" after every victory, punctuating it with music of their own. Trainer Harrison "Doc" Weaver, a big man who had played tackle for Rickey at Ohio Wesleyan, could strum the mandolin between stints of ankle taping. Walker and Musial beat time with coat hangers; Johnny Beazley thought he could sing a bit.

The Cardinals were hot, and Southworth could do no wrong. Musial was hitting well over .300, but one day the manager replaced him with the right-handed Coaker Triplett, who drove in the winning run. They won the pennant on the final day, beating the Cubs twice, with Musial finishing third in batting at .315 with 10 homers and 72 runs batted in.

Now they would play the Yankees in the World Series, the Cardinals' first since the fruit bombardment in Detroit in 1934.


THE YANKEES won the first game of the 1942 Series in St. Louis, with Musial going hitless, but the Cards won the second as he made a hit. Now he and Lil had to decide if she would come to New York for the next three games. With money tight and wartime travel difficult, they reasoned she could go home to Donora and then catch the final game or two in St. Louis.

Instead, Lukasz and Mary came to New York. Emaciated and shy, all dressed up, Lukasz could not stop beaming as his son took him around the clubhouse in Yankee Stadium.

This was probably the only World Series ever influenced by a trainer. Doc Weaver came up with a hex gesture called the double whammy— "crossed wrists, hands back to back, then closed the second and third fingers of each hand so that the first and fourth fingers protruded like horns," Musial recalled.

The Yankees were not used to such loosey-goosey behavior in the more staid American League, although that was probably not the reason they lost three straight games in their awe-inspiring stadium in the Bronx. Yankee management had to blame somebody: it promptly fired the trainer, Earle "Doc" Painter, apparently because he was not as good as Doc Weaver at the mandolin or the double whammy.

Musial batted only .222 in his first World Series, but that was not the reason he was upset as the Cardinals celebrated in the Yankees' home park.

"Stan was having a terrible time trying to decide whether to go back or go home to his family in Donora," Marty Marion recalled. "He finally decided it would be better if he went home."

Marion described the scene in the train station as the giddy Cardinals piled into their special car, heading for a raucous celebration in St. Louis: "He went around shaking hands with all of us and then the guy busted right out and began to bawl like a kid. As he walked away, so did some of the others."

Musial would always insist that this was the best Cardinals team he'd played on. The winners' share was $6,192.50—nearly 50 percent more than his salary—which made it a happy winter in Donora.

The Rickey era ended after the World Series. Breadon had become unhappy with Rickey's contract, which called for him to receive a percentage for every player he sold, and let him move on to the rival Dodgers. It was impossible to predict the impact Rickey would have within a few years, but for now, Musial was the great product of the Rickey farm system and the Cardinals were back on top.

NOW THAT Rickey was gone, the team would be dominated by the longtime owner, Sam Breadon, a former automobile mechanic with a gravelly accent that revealed his New York roots. Breadon had worked on Pierce-Arrows and later on Fords before buying his own agency. He was a salesman, but with an approach different from Rickey's.

"They were entirely opposites," said William O. DeWitt, who worked across the hallway with the Browns, and later owned them. "Rickey never took a drink," DeWitt added, whereas Breadon "belonged to a little club at the Jefferson Motel. And he'd go down and have two or three drinks at lunch, and then he'd drink at night. And after he'd drink a while he wanted to sing."

Now that he was handling the payroll, Breadon negotiated with Musial directly. He did not call Musial "my boy," as Rickey had done, but he did find a way to work on him, offering Musial a $1,000 raise to just over $5,000. Musial asked for $10,000 at first and later dropped his request to $7,500, but he also made a crucial negotiating mistake: with Moore and Slaughter going into the service, Musial told Breadon he would have to play "even harder" in their absence, which was just the opening the master auto salesman needed. He said he was disappointed in Musial, which, of course, was translated into dollars.

Musial held off for a while, taking advice from his friend Frank Pizzica, himself an auto dealer, who theoretically might have had insight into Breadon's tactics. Breadon dispatched Eddie Dyer, the Cardinals' farm director, to Donora to talk Musial into signing. With Pizzica out of town, Musial listened to the fatherly Dyer and signed for $6,250.

Because of wartime restrictions on travel, the Cards trained in Cairo, Illinois, in 1943. Musial was moved to right field after Slaughter went into the service, and he felt comfortable there because he did not have to throw across his body so often. Mostly he played wherever the manager put him.

The Cardinals were somewhat more divided than has been generally thought. Marty Marion has talked about cliques developing between the beer-drinking, card-playing teammates and the family-man teammates like himself, Walker, Howie Pollet, and Musial. Walker Cooper, his brother Mort, and some of the other older players referred to them as the "college kids," which possibly alluded to Danny Litwhiler, who actually had a degree in science and social science from Bloomsburg State in Pennsylvania.


LITWHILER BECAME Musial's first good friend on the team, arriving from the Phillies early in 1943 because Southworth liked the way he hustled. From a Pennsylvania Dutch area in anthracite country, Litwhiler was a disciplined family man, and he began hanging out with Musial, bringing their families to a little lake in nearby Illinois, where Litwhiler had the key to a friend's cabin.

The lake was pleasant in the evening after a day game, and on days off ten or fifteen Cardinal families might congregate at the retreat.

"We'd cook corn on the cob and hot dogs and sometimes we'd gig frogs and cook them right there," Litwhiler recalled with great fondness in 2010. Gigging frogs, a regional pastime, required a long stick with prongs at the end; major-league hands helped considerably. Once Litwhiler brought a bag of live frogs home with him from an evening excursion with Musial, planning to ask the hotel chef to cook up the legs for lunch. He deposited the sack in the hotel bathroom, forgetting that his wife, Dot, was an early riser and would not be amused by the frogs that squirmed loose.

Many of the Cardinals stayed in the Fairgrounds Hotel because it was close to the ballpark and the players could walk to work, not having enough money for cars under the Breadon-Rickey payroll. Dickie Musial thought the Litwhilers were rich because Danny and Dot had an automobile.

"We named our son after Dickie," Litwhiler said.

Most of the Cardinals rented rooms on the top floor, which tended to heat up nicely on long sunny days. After a few seasons, Musial was given a cool corner room on a lower floor because he was a star, recalled Freddy Schmidt, a useful pitcher on those teams. Schmidt had no complaints. The Cardinals were fast becoming Musial's team, and they did not begrudge him the favor he had not sought.

"We had a young club," Litwhiler recalled of the 1943–44 Cardinals. "Pepper Martin and the Gashouse Gang were pretty hard-nosed. Stan was as nice a guy as I've ever met. He set the pace. Such a nice guy."

Musial and Litwhiler hung around together on the road as well. One time, on a day off in Philadelphia, Litwhiler invited Musial to his hometown, Ringtown. One woman in a modest restaurant heard that Musial was a ballplayer and said, "You keep trying hard and you'll get there. I know you will."

"I ran into Pappy Kleckner at the gas station, on the porch," Litwhiler recalled in 2010. Relishing dusting off an old Pennsylvania accent, Litwhiler mimicked the old-timer asking Litwhiler, "Who is dis?" When Litwhiler told him, Pappy asked, "And vat are you doing here?" Litwhiler said they had an off day, which must have grated on the Pennsylvania Dutch work ethic.

"Vat is this off day?" Pappy asked.

"I told him about baseball, and he wished Stan luck," Litwhiler said. "Stan told me, 'I'm never coming back here with you. Nobody knows who I am.'"

By now, most of the country knew who Stan Musial was. He made the All-Star team for the first time in 1943, won his first batting title with .357, and was voted Most Valuable Player, and the Cardinals won their second straight pennant.

Stanley also showed his inner Gashouse Gang in August against his old pal Les Webber, who had thrown at him in 1942. With first base open, Durocher was heard to order Webber to walk Musial.

Webber was steaming because earlier in the season Musial had hit a line drive that broke the hand of Hugh Casey, who was Webber's drinking buddy. What's worse, Musial broke Casey's drinking hand, the Dodgers' catcher, Mickey Owen, joked.

"Musial came up next time," Owen recalled. "Four straight times, right by his ears." Rather than charge the mound this time, Musial turned to Owen and said, "That SOB can't hit me if he throws all day." Owen was awed by Musial's coolly evading Webber's beanballs: "That's how agile that man is."

Players had their own ways of handling these matters. The Cards' next batter was Walker Cooper, who had run Musial out of the batting cage back in 1941 but had since figured out that Musial was a vital part of the team. Cooper slapped a grounder to second base and then planted his left foot high on the calf of first baseman Augie Galan, which could have seriously injured Galan. Owen then tackled Cooper, and they rolled around for a while—just a normal day at the ballyard between the Cardinals and Dodgers.

The two teams battled on the field, but Rickey's stockpiled players on the Dodgers were no match for Rickey's wartime work-in-progress with the Cardinals. The Cardinals won the pennant by 18 games over Cincinnati, as Musial led the league in batting with .357 and 48 doubles and 20 triples.

Because of wartime travel restrictions, the teams were able to make only one trip, so the Series began with three games in the Bronx, with the Yanks winning the first and third. Mort Cooper won the second game, pitching to his brother, although their father had died earlier in the day. The Yanks then won two straight in St. Louis to close out the Series, getting by with one Tuck Stainback playing center field in place of DiMaggio, who had enlisted under pressure from fans and press. Musial batted .278 in the Series with no extra-base hits, and had to settle for the losing share of $4,321.99.

In 1944, still deferred, Musial signed a three-year contract worth $10,000, $12,500, and $13,500. The Cardinals won their third straight pennant as Musial hit .347 against increasingly depleted wartime pitching.

The Yankees were so decimated by the draft that the Browns actually won the pennant, something they had never done with George Sisler or their few other stars. The Browns were beneficiaries of wartime baseball, having thirteen of their prewar players disqualified from military service for one impediment or another.

Lil made an amazing discovery during the first and only all–St. Louis World Series. She and Stan rented a modest apartment near the ballpark because they did not have a car. As the city heated up for the trolley-car World Series, she noticed that although the Cardinals had won three straight pennants, St. Louis was, as she put it, a "Brownie town."

It was true. The old loyalties to the Browns came pouring out, but the Cardinals won in six games as Musial hit what would be his only World Series homer and batted .304. Because of low wartime ticket prices in small Sportsman's Park, the Cardinals' winning share was $4,626.01. Musial had now played three full seasons and had won three pennants and two championships, but he knew that streak was about to end.

# 16

## OLD NAVY BUDDIES

JOHN HERNANDEZ considered himself lucky. Here he was, a professional ballplayer getting to play his sport on Pearl Harbor in the middle of the war, on the same team as Stan Musial.

A pretty fair hitter himself, Hernandez had been beaned in the minors—no batting helmets in those days—and was having trouble seeing the ball at night in the rickety minor-league parks. He pretty much knew he was never going to make it to the majors.

However, at Pearl Harbor in the spring of 1945, the sun was always out, and life was fairly peaceful three and a half years after the horrific attack on December 7, 1941.

In the mornings, Hernandez helped repair the *Yorktown* and the *Lexington,* some of the behemoths that had played a role in the United States regaining control of the Pacific. In the afternoons, he played ball. The commanding officer loved the sport and had set up an eight-team league comprised mostly of professionals. Sometimes there were parties, luaus, on the beach in front of the Royal Hawaiian Hotel.

One day Hernandez was pitching batting practice and decided to fire his best fastball down the middle, just to see what Musial could do with it. Big mistake.

Musial was known to hit a ball exactly where it was pitched. Middle of the plate? Back at you. With no malice, Musial drilled a line drive a few inches past the head of John Hernandez, straight out to center field, making Hernandez decide that from here on he would keep the ball on the corners.

They were not teammates for long. Musial was shipped home later in 1945 because his father was gravely ill, but the men kept in touch after the war. Hernandez wound up in the St. Louis farm system and in 1947 helped win the Dixie Series for the Houston Buffs, managed by Johnny Keane. Not long afterward, Hernandez went home to San Francisco and became a fireman.

Then it was 1960, and Hernandez told his seven-year-old son that an old navy friend was leaving tickets for them at Candlestick Park.

"I remember the old Cardinal uniform, the baby blue caps," the son would recall. "We'd sit right over the third-base dugout and I could see that batting stance. I could see that swing. My dad told me Stan coiled like a cobra."

After the game, father and son visited the clubhouse and chatted with Musial, Ken Boyer, and some of the other Cardinals, just enough for the young man to gain an insight into the minds of major leaguers. Even the great Musial could suffer a slump or an injury or an impatient manager.

Musial offered to leave tickets for every game the Cards played in San Francisco, "but my father did not want to go overboard," the son said.

The boy, Keith Hernandez, would become an excellent left-handed hitter and one of the best defensive first basemen ever to play the game, and would help both the Cardinals and Mets win a World Series. (The son would also receive copious amounts of late-night telephone batting instruction from his very Americanized dad, whom he referred to, rather darkly, as Juan.) Long after his dad had passed, Keith Hernandez treasured the memories of the two former sailors talking over the old days.

# 17

## THE WAR

MUSIAL WAS the last of the superstars to go into active service. He did everything properly, registering with his draft board in Donora, reporting his whereabouts—the sports pages tended to confirm that—and never appearing to lobby for special treatment.

"I was fortunate just to miss one season," Musial once said. " 'Course, I was married and had a couple youngsters, and they weren't drafting married men from our area at that time, until later on."

There is no record of anybody in Donora or St. Louis complaining because the baseball player got a lucky break. He was married, and a second child, Geraldine, would be born on January 23, 1945. Lukasz had had a stroke in 1943, and Musial was the primary support of his parents.

The people of Donora could not have considered him a draft-dodger inasmuch as they held a celebration on October 18, 1943, chipping in to give him war bonds and other presents. The event was sponsored by the Donora Zinc Works, where Musial worked that off-season—in the office—which qualified as essential service.

Musial was not called up sooner because Donora had a large supply of single men of military age. Bimbo Cecconi recalled how either his football teammates would volunteer or their number would be called. "They were called into the service their junior, senior year. They would just disappear. You might have 'em for football and they were gone."

Musial was playing by the rules set at the highest levels of government. Early in the war, President Franklin Delano Roosevelt had issued what was later called the "Green Light Letter," saying organized baseball should continue but asserting that major-league players were subject to the draft, just like anybody else. The fans in St. Louis, who would have smoked out a slacker, were happy to have their young star as long as they could.

Musial signed up to visit the troops for six weeks in the winter of 1943–44, going to Alaska and the Aleutian islands along with his Cardinal pal Danny Litwhiler, Hank Borowy of the Cubs, and Dixie Walker of the Dodgers, along with Frankie Frisch, the crusty old manager. The players found the weather and conditions far worse than they could have imagined. Walker had to leave when several members of his family took ill back home, and Frisch departed after a two-day storm rocked the ship and sent five inches of water sloshing on the deck. Back on land, the three remaining players were booked for a boat trip that would take them to a plane heading home.

"A storm came out and we got marooned up there," Litwhiler recalled, referring to the strong and sudden winds, called williwaws, that kick up in that part of the world. Jeeps were not able to get up the hill, so the three players decided to hike a mile downhill to the harbor, in a foot of snow.

"The blizzard was blowing," Litwhiler said. "You'd walk down at a forty-five-degree angle against the wind. We just pulled our knit caps over our eyes. You had an idea where you were going though you weren't too sure. But we were able to get down in time to get the ship out."

The return flight grew even more perilous. As Litwhiler told it many years later, the military pilot welcomed the ballplayers and invited them into the cockpit. Litwhiler accepted and the pilot showed him how to maneuver the plane, using both hands and feet, while the co-pilot actually commanded the plane, at least theoretically.

"The pilot gave me a seat while he took a break," Litwhiler recalled, suspecting that the pilot had taken a quick nap.

"When he came back, he said, 'Let me in there,'" Litwhiler said, recalling a vast amount of urgency on the pilot's part. "It was night and we were flying through the mountains," Litwhiler said. The plane had drifted down to eight thousand feet, with mountains several thousand feet taller on both sides of them in the wintry night. The pilot raised the plane out of danger as Litwhiler tiptoed back to his seat. Musial was aware of the danger, although he never mentioned that flight in his autobiography.

That trip to Alaska made Musial realize how lucky he was. He always praised the other stars who went into the service earlier than he did.

Bob Feller could have requested a deferment because his father had terminal cancer, but Feller joined up right after Pearl Harbor and sought active duty with an anti-aircraft gun crew on the USS *Alabama* in the South Pacific. Hank Greenberg was drafted early in the 1941 service, was released on a technicality on December 5, 1941, and voluntarily went right back into uniform after Pearl Harbor.

A star athlete from the University of California at Los Angeles, Jack Roosevelt Robinson, became an army officer and entertained the quaint impression that wearing the uniform of his country and facing the distinct possibility of being killed entitled him to the right to sit anywhere in a public bus in Texas. He did just that and wound up being court-martialed, although not convicted, and he left the military.

Cardinal fans who claim Musial did not—does not—receive the adulation of the national press might want to study the way two great East Coast idols were pursued in matters of salary demands, private lives, and military service. New York and Boston papers definitely took an independent and critical tone toward Joe DiMaggio and Ted Williams.

From the first day he reported from San Diego, Williams had been impulsive and immature—"the Kid" was a perfect nickname. When war broke out, Williams was classified as 3-A because he was the sole support of his mother; then he was reclassified as 1-A, but upon review he was moved back to 3-A. Williams said he would enlist as soon as he had made his mother secure.

"If I hadn't done it, I wouldn't have been doing right by my mother," Williams said. "If I wasn't sure of that, I couldn't steel myself to face all the abuse."

Oddly enough, sportswriter Dave Egan, one of Williams's most caustic critics (he called himself "Col. Egan" but was a colonel only in his own fevered imagination), actually defended Williams, saying, "The patrioteers should examine their own consciences."

Ultimately, Williams responded to the pressure and signed up with a naval reserve unit in Massachusetts, where he quickly became such a good pilot that he was used as an instructor rather than in combat, which was not his choice. At one point, he said, when the ruckus was over, he might consider a full-time career as a pilot, which may have been his way of expressing disdain for baseball, Boston, the press, or all of the above. This was a cranky dance that would continue virtually to his retirement.

Williams was shipped to Pearl Harbor in August 1945 and was headed for China when the war ended. He proudly kept his commission in the Marines and was hounded back into active duty in Korea, where he flew as a wingman for John Glenn. He was flying an F-9 jet over Korea when his plane was hit, his radio went out, and Williams did not hear the instructions to bail out. He landed at 200 miles per hour, and his plane exploded; he probably would have been killed except that he had only a minute's supply of fuel left. Williams dove for safety and lived to bat again. For the rest of his long and colorful life, the fiery crash in Korea would define Williams.

DiMaggio was married with a son and was entitled to a deferment under the draft rules. But the Yankees, in their charming way, managed to equate his salary demands with a lack of patriotism.

"Doesn't he know there's a war on?" Ed Barrow, the general manager, asked.

Having been labeled ungrateful in an earlier salary impasse, DiMaggio understood that many New York writers took the side of Yankee management. When DiMaggio rejected the first contract offer of $37,500 for 1942, Dan Daniel wrote in the *World-Telegram:* "People just don't like to hear a ballplayer grumbling over being asked for a paltry $37,500 a year when the base pay for privates is twenty-one clackers per month."

This criticism of DiMaggio played on public suspicion of Italian Americans, since Italy had been led into being an ally of Nazi Germany. Joe D. was no fool. He signed his contract, publicly placed $5,000 into war bonds, and then played the 1942 season, including the World Series against Musial.

Joe D. had other trouble: his wife, Dorothy Arnold, an actress, had gone to Nevada to begin divorce proceedings. She also advised him to push up his active duty, on the theory that he would not have to serve in combat. DiMaggio may have thought going into the military would somehow save the marriage. Without notifying the Yankees—nuts to them—he enlisted in San Francisco on February 17, 1943, and a week later reported for duty.

Arnold was right. DiMaggio would receive a pretty good deal in the service, playing ball and making appearances, but his enlisting did not save the marriage. Arnold filed for divorce in 1944 and Joe D. wound up in Honolulu, where he played ball. In February 1945 he showed signs of duodenal ulcers and was transferred to Atlantic City. He was released in September 1945.

The question can be asked, why did Musial not push up his service just to be part of the war effort? Some of his contemporaries saw the threat and signed up for action; others sought units that seemed eager, at least at first, to give a major leaguer a break.

"I remember that very well because Pete Reiser always wanted me to join the Fort Riley team out here, in the Army," Musial would recall of the Dodger from St. Louis. "And I said no, Pete, my mind's set up to go in the Navy when I go in, but he said, no, we had a great ball club and the general watched baseball."

Musial added, "Before long, they were in the Battle of the Bulge over in Germany."

Was this another example of Stanley always picking the right card? Somebody who knows Musial very well calls him a "pacifist," not in the conscientious-objector sense but in the conflict-avoidance sense. Musial had every right to claim his status as provider for his family, with a lot of obligations. And when his number came up, he went.

On April 22, 1944, Musial was contacted by his draft board. On May 16, he was examined at the Jefferson Barracks in St. Louis and accepted for navy duty. On June 23, the Donora *Herald-American* reported he would have more time to play for the Cardinals.

"It depends on how well we can fill our quota," one member of the local draft board said. "We are calling single men ahead of the married registrants."

In January 1945, Musial was called up by the navy and was sent for basic training at Bainbridge, Maryland, where his head was shaved by a zealous navy barber.

"Why didn't you tell me who you were?" the barber said after the fact. "I wouldn't have cut it so short."

"Thanks," Musial said, "but now I know how a guy feels when he's going to the electric chair."

Playing first base for the base team at Bainbridge, Musial quickly learned the unique responsibility of a major leaguer. The sailors—and the admirals—did not want to see a single chipped to left field. From a man who had just played in three consecutive World Series, they wanted the real thing, the big bang, the long ball.

"I altered my batting stance a bit," Musial said. "I moved up closer to the plate. This proved to be an important step in my evolution as a hitter."

He was soon assigned to Treasure Island in San Francisco and then to Pearl Harbor. Men who were training there could soon be dying out in the Pacific, but Musial was scheduled for other duties.

The navy's league in Hawaii contained good minor-league players like John Hernandez as well as major leaguers like Cookie Lavagetto, Billy Herman, Bob Scheffing, Johnny Pesky, and Williams himself. Bill Dickey, the old Yankee catcher, was the commissioner of the league, and Dan Topping, part owner of the Yankees, ran two marine teams.

Musial worked on a launch in the morning, ferrying sailors out to the giant ships they were repairing.

"After bouncing around in that launch for three hours . . . God, my legs were like rubber," Musial said. "So I told him, 'Sir, I'm either going to play baseball on a regular basis or run the launch, because I can't be doing what I'm doing and do a good job playing baseball.' "

The brass kept him mostly on solid ground after that, playing three or four games a week.

"One thing about the Navy," Musial said years later, "if you're a ballplayer, they let you play ball. If you were . . . you know, had some form of talent, why they let you do that sort of talent, but . . . as compared to the Army . . . know a lot of the Army guys didn't have a chance to play ball."

Eager to please the brass with home runs, Stanley moved closer to home plate, again exaggerating his stance. That October, playing in the Service World Series at Furlong Field in front of crowds of over forty thousand he hit four doubles in one game, all within two feet of one another.

He was also persuaded to pitch one game in August, beating an army all-star team with a four-hitter, without further damage to his shoulder.

He knew just how blessed he was, and would find out even more when the war ended. The only criticism he ever discussed came via a letter from home. Dickie Musial had been teased by a boy in his neighborhood about Musial's soft duty, and the boy had knocked Dickie to the floor.

"My five-year-old picked himself up and hit the boy back, right in the nose," Musial wrote in his autobiography.

Late in October, Lukasz came down with pneumonia, and Mary asked the Red Cross if her son could come home to take care of his father. Musial was sent east and rushed straight to his father's bedside (where he was photographed in a navy uniform, administering a spoonful of medicine), and Lukasz bounced back. Musial was then assigned to a navy yard in Philadelphia.

He told the story himself: "The day before I was scheduled to work, I walked over to watch men already at work, wearing goggles and heavy gloves and carrying blowtorches. I realized that a green pea like me could wind up maiming himself or someone else. I went to the athletic officer and said: 'Sir, I'm a ship repairman who has never repaired a ship. For my sake and the Navy's, can't you please have my orders changed?' "

The officer recognized a chance to help the war movement—addition by subtraction, as Branch Rickey often said—and gave Musial duty away from the blowtorches.

Early in 1946, after fourteen months of duty, Musial was released, hitchhiking across the state in uniform. He caught a lift from a member of the state legislature, heading home from Harrisburg. Recognizing the man in the navy uniform, the legislator made a detour and drove Musial right to his door in Donora.


MUSIAL WAS no doubt grateful to be home in one piece, particularly when he learned what some of his colleagues had gone through.

Baseball struggled through the war with older players and younger players, including fifteen-year-old Joe Nuxhall, whom Musial encountered in 1944, swatting a hit off the kid in his first major-league appearance. While Musial was gone in 1945, the Browns had used Pete Gray, an outfielder who had lost an arm in a childhood farming accident.

Bert Shepard, a minor-league pitcher, was shot down over Germany while flying for the Air Corps in 1944 and had his right leg amputated below the knee. In 1945, as an outpatient from Walter Reed Hospital, Shepard pitched five and a third innings for the Senators against the Red

Sox, giving up one run and three hits in what turned out to be his only major-league appearance, but he did pitch in the minors after that.

DiMaggio, Williams, and Musial had not been sent to the beaches of Normandy like more anonymous ballplayers such as Yogi Berra, or the woods of Germany, like Harry Walker, or the atolls of the Pacific, like Gil Hodges.

More than five hundred players served during the war, including thirty-one Cardinals. Most of them spent the winter of 1945–46 getting discharged, going home to their families, and resting up. Then came spring training of 1946, when they would try to get back in shape and also catch up on what their teammates had been through.

Musial was reminded of his decision not to join Pete Reiser's unit. "They sent the whole unit over there," Musial said, referring to Europe. "Everybody. Harry Walker, Murry Dickson, all those guys. They were in some battles, I'll tell you! And I think Harry killed twenty-two guys or something like that. Al Brazle captured a division that was surrendering. I often think of that—that I could have gone with those guys."

War veterans generally do not speak of these things. Harry Walker was one of the more loquacious men ever to wear a uniform—he was known to fans as "Harry the Hat" because of the way he fidgeted with his cap at the plate, but to reporters he was "Walker the Talker."

As a coach and manager, Walker would hold forth on hitting or just about anything else, but I never heard him so much as allude to military service, much less his personal role. However, in 1979 Walker did discuss the Battle of the Bulge with the writer Richard Goldstein.

"It happened right near the end," Walker said. "You realized the war couldn't last much longer and it scared the hell out of you. You've always read about how many people were killed after the war was over because nobody knew it. I thought, 'My God, why don't they just go ahead and quit. The last bunch we captured were boys fifteen to eighteen years old.' "

Walker described being in a reconnaissance outfit near Passeau, looking for bridges in the sleet and rain, and how he tried to get three German soldiers to surrender.

"Well, one guy pulled his gun up in my face. I had a .45 revolver that I'd bought in the States. That little thing saved my life. The guy that pulled the gun, I shot him in the chest and then I shot the others. Killed the first two and wounded the third guy. It was so damned quick, it was almost like a machine gun went off. It was just one of those deals that you didn't want to happen, but your reaction was to live and that's about it."

The next day, Walker was the point man with a .50-caliber machine gun "when we ran into a bunch that were trying to get across the bridge. I shot a few with that. It would tear up most anything. And we captured a bunch of soldiers and some big guns, 88s."

"First I got hit in the hand with a piece of artillery, shrapnel from an 88. Later, I got hit in the rump with a piece of our own. I took a rifle grenade and threw it. It hit this building before we could get out. But it wasn't too bad. I was real lucky."

Near the end of the war, Walker was ordered to construct a baseball field on crushed brick in the stadium in Nuremberg where Hitler had staged his rallies.

"All the guys wanted to play ball all day long," Walker said. "They didn't understand it was no toy to me—it was my livelihood."

Walker received the Bronze Star and Purple Heart. A year later he would help the Cardinals win the World Series.

Other Cardinals came back wounded. Howie Krist, a useful pitcher before the war, had been injured carrying ammunition in France and was never the same.

Johnny Grodzicki, a pitcher, had taken shrapnel in the right thigh five weeks before V-E Day as his paratroop unit tried to scale a wall near Berlin. He came to camp in 1946 wearing a steel brace on his leg, but despite the ministrations of Doc Weaver, he was never the same.

"Some of the guys told war stories. But Johnny never talked about the war. He kept everything inside," Walker said.

Terry Moore played ball in Latin America in the three years he missed; Enos Slaughter was an instructor in the Army Air Corps, keeping fit by playing ball in the South Pacific during his three years away. And Musial served where he was sent—Hawaii.

"He stands in awe of Ted Williams and Bob Feller for missing those years," Tom Ashley said of his father-in-law. "Whenever he refers to them, he says Williams would have hit over forty home runs for five years, maybe two hundred more home runs. He had great respect for them."

By collating Williams's statistics directly before and after his hitch, I come up with a total of 99 homers and 558 hits for his three missing years. By averaging DiMaggio's best seasons before and after his service, I come up with 84 homers and 531 hits. By averaging Musial's seasons around the war, I come up with 18 homers and 201 hits for that one missing season of 1945.

"If it hadn't been for missing those years, the fellas I mentioned would have set all kinds of hitting records in baseball," Musial said. "They were just unfortunate to miss that time during the war."

They did not yap about it. They all knew others who had given more.

# 18

## CHECKS ALL OVER

## THE BED

STAN AND Lil stared as a stranger signed five checks, each worth $10,000, and laid them on the hotel bed that was serving as a desk.

This was just the bonus, the man said. The majority would come later, if Stan would cross the border and play ball in Mexico. The stranger was Alfonso Pasquel, one of five brothers who ran the Mexican League.

The date was June 6, 1946—two years after D-Day. All of St. Louis quivered, knowing that Alfonso Pasquel was visiting the Musials in their room at the Fairgrounds Hotel, presumably carrying suitcases crammed with money.

The Pasquels had already siphoned off some useful players from the majors. When they went after Pistol Pete Reiser, Branch Rickey ran them out of camp in Florida, shouting, "Assassins of careers! Assassins of careers!" and other language considerably more profane than his normal "Judas Priest."

The Pasquels also made overtures to Jackie Robinson, the Negro League player who was in camp with the Dodgers' Montreal farm team, but Robinson was not interested.

Robinson surely knew the Mexican League was on the level of AAA ball in the United States, partially because it was a haven for outstanding African American players like Cool Papa Bell and Satchel Paige and Latinos like Santos Amaro of Cuba, whose skin was too dark to allow him to play in the United States.

Willie Wells, an African American, once said about playing in Mexico:

"I am not faced by the racial problem. . . . I've found freedom and democracy here, something I never found in the United States. . . . In Mexico I am a man."

In the spring of 1946, Ray Dandridge, playing third base in Mexico because of segregation in El Norte, spotted two new faces in the clubhouse—Sal Maglie and Danny Gardella from the New York Giants. Dandridge gave them a show by swatting drives all over the ballpark and picking hot grounders off the pebbly field.

After the workout, the two Americans asked him where in the world he'd come from.

"Same country you did," Dandridge replied.

Everybody knew that Gardella and Maglie were mere appetizers for the ambitious Pasquel brothers. An American advance man, who may have exaggerated his contact with Musial, was claiming that Musial was willing to drive his family to Mexico if the Pasquels would furnish a new car. The agent clearly did not know much about Stanley the loyalist, Stanley the homebody.

On May 31, 1946, Musial told the St. Louis *Star-Times:* "I don't think I will go, but I haven't told [the Pasquels] yes or no."

Musial had a lifelong affinity for the established process, for management, even when negotiating for money. Now, with the Pasquels wooing him, Musial sought out the new manager, Eddie Dyer, who had replaced Billy Southworth over the winter. He liked Dyer, who as farm director had once journeyed to Donora to urge Musial to sign his contract.

The two men stepped into an equipment room off the clubhouse, and Dyer told him, "Stan, you've got two children. Do you want them to hear someone say, 'There are the kids of a guy who broke his contract'?"

Perhaps Dyer was playing Musial pretty well, or perhaps he was being honest and fatherly. Either way, Musial was probably inclined to turn down the offer, but the Pasquels were persistent, sending Mickey Owen, who had jumped from the Dodgers to Veracruz in the Mexican League, to meet with Musial.

Owen, who was from Missouri, had remained friendly with Musial despite the rivalry between the Cardinals and Dodgers. Given permission to slip home to pick up his son, Owen visited Musial at the hotel.

"Musial was smoking a big cigar, and playing real cool, so I said, 'Stan, have you talked to the Mexicans?' " Owen said. "He said, 'No, no, I haven't talked to the Mexicans.' "

With the war over, the Musials were feeling secure enough to rent a house in St. Louis for the first time. While the Cardinals were on a home stand, Stan and Lil were packing their goods as reporters staked out the hotel on Pasquel watch.

This might have been the best poker game Stanley ever played. Alfonso came around with a briefcase and, concerned the Cardinals might have hired security to keep him from Musial, asked Owen to accompany him.

"Alfonso threw out those checks for $10,000 apiece, and he signed them," Owen recalled with a chuckle in 1989. "And I thought Musial would just swallow that cigar when he seen all that money on that table.

"Of course, that's peanuts to him now," Owen said decades later, "but then, that looked like all the money than they had in Donora, Pennsylvania. . . . He wouldn't say much, and he just kind of held back and looked at it, and bit on that cigar some more, and blew smoke all over the place."

While Stanley was blowing smoke, he was also doing the math.

"As I recall, Alfonso plunked five cashier's checks for $10,000 each onto a bed and said I could consider them a bonus," Musial said, recalling that Pasquel told him the actual contract would be for an additional $125,000 for five years.

"My eyes bugged out at the sight of so much money. I was getting only $13,500. How long would I have to play to be assured of $175,000?" (Something like thirteen years.)

Then came the big scare. Around midday, reporters spotted Musial and Litwhiler lugging suitcases and boxes and clothes to Litwhiler's car. Somebody asked Dickie Musial, going on six, what the family was doing, and Dickie tersely replied, "Packing," thereby touching off a modest nervous breakdown in the greater St. Louis metropolitan area.

What Dickie neglected to tell the reporters was that his family was merely moving to Mardel Avenue in southwest St. Louis rather than Mexico City.

Somewhere in the middle of packing, while St. Louis fretted, Musial informed Alfonso Pasquel he would not be accepting the checks.

"I told 'em that I wasn't interested in going to Mexico," Musial said in 1990. "That was about the gist of the conversation," he added.

Owen left that meeting convinced that Stanley the poker player had an extra card hidden away somewhere. He later claimed he asked Musial if he had a contract that forbade him from going to the Mexican League, and Musial told him he couldn't talk about it. Musial would forever remain coy about why he turned down the offer.

That night St. Louis fans—and Cardinal management—were thrilled to see Stanley reporting for work, putting on his familiar number 6 uniform, having his typical two-for-five game, to raise his batting average to .337, third in the league.

That same June 6, the Associated Press reported that Pasquel and Owen "boldly came to town today" and solicited Musial but "failed to sign" him.

Musial meandered around the subject in a mid-June interview, saying, "All that money makes a fellow do a lot of thinking before he says no." He added, "I'm still young. I should be able to make a lot of money for a long time here in the United States. Let's consider this Mexican thing a closed matter for the present. Let's say no more."

Breadon, the onetime auto mechanic from New York, had enough street smarts to recognize the Pasquels were serious—and to take them on. After losing Lou Klein, Fred Martin, and Max Lanier, a pitching mainstay of the 1944 Cardinals, Breadon flew to Mexico City to talk to the Pasquels.

"Breadon said, 'I want to see eyeball to eyeball a man who could steal my players,' " Bob Broeg said.

This expedition annoyed Albert "Happy" Chandler, the former governor of Kentucky who had been named commissioner after the death of Landis. Chandler promptly fined Breadon $5,000, although he may have rescinded it privately later on.

The American players quickly became restive in Mexico. Vernon Stephens, a powerful shortstop from the Browns, lasted only four days before heading for the border. Owen would fly the coop. Gardella, a fringe outfielder from the Giants, distinguished himself in Mexico by toying with a pistol he'd discovered in the Pasquels' office and firing a bullet harmlessly through an open window. Gardella ultimately returned to the United States and sued to be reinstated by the Giants, but his career never went far.

The players who jumped were eventually reinstated, but the only American who really helped his career by going to Mexico was Maglie, a pitcher from the Giants. Maglie had the immense good fortune to have as his pitching tutor the old New York Giants star Adolfo Luque, who had learned his craft from Christy Mathewson. (In the wonderful six-degrees-of-separation world of baseball, Maglie later tutored a young pitcher named Don Drysdale when they overlapped on the Brooklyn Dodgers in 1956–57, making a direct half-century line of Hall of Fame pitchers from Mathewson to Drysdale.)

After watching his colleagues trek back from Mexico, Musial was glad he had never budged. "A little later on we found out the conditions were pretty terrible," he said. "You know, roads and traveling and ballparks . . . It wasn't major league conditions."

He added, "I just had confidence in myself. I just loved baseball in this country, and I just didn't . . . give it any second thoughts about ever going down there."

"And Stan made a great decision," Marty Marion said. "I guess they were trying to get Stan more than anybody else, and I understand, although I didn't see the money, but they said they brought suitcases of money for Stan to look at, you know, but Stan made a wise decision to stay here with American sports."

LATER IN life, Owen remained convinced Musial had received a sweetener from Sam Breadon.

"I'm sure that he had signed not only for that year, but the following year," Owen said in 1989. "I seen that he didn't want to go, and his wife didn't want him to go, and he didn't want to talk about it too much."

Owen had his theory about what went down: "I imagine the wife might have called them and said, 'Look, they've contacted my husband, and we don't want to go . . . , but it's a lot of money.' " Owen guessed a wife would suggest to the ball club, "Well, you just come up with it."

He concluded with a chuckle, "I'm sure that something like that happened. And I think if it did, he better go home and kiss his wife and say, 'Honey, you're the best wife a man ever had.' "

While Lil had no desire to take her two children to Mexico, there is no evidence she ever lobbied Breadon. But that does not mean she did not make a suggestion or two to her husband that he get something tangible for his loyalty. What spouse would not?

Stanley always insisted he had not been offered a raise or bonus not to jump, but in his autobiography he added, "Later, Dyer did go to bat with Sam Breadon for a few of us who had turned our backs on Mexican offers."

Was it a total surprise that in August Breadon summoned Musial and said he was giving him a $5,000 raise for the season?

"I was nearly floored," Musial said.

Mickey Owen was not floored.

"Oh yeah, that was the greatest thing that ever happened for him, that he didn't go," Owen said. "The ball clubs then thought they was going to start having to pay the ballplayers some money. And I think that that was probably about the turning point of it, when they said, 'Well, wait a minute, we're going to be losing these outstanding ballplayers,' and I'm sure that there was some contracts with Musial. I'm sure the club owners got together and said, 'Wait, let's stop this now before it goes any further.' "

The company line was always that the Cardinals would never expand their salary structure in response to the Mexican challenge. But if Musial had not pressured Breadon for a little present for sticking around, he would have been a fool. And over the years, Stanley would prove he was no fool.

# 19

## JUBILEE

SAYING NO to the Pasquels was a relief to Stanley. He was able to get back to the business he enjoyed so much—being a major-league ballplayer, and a very good one at that.

The war was over. The Cardinals were glad to be in this uniform, glad to be alive, after what some of them had gone through. They kept it light, although they could see the damage in some of them that would never be repaired.

In spring training Musial went around camp introducing himself to players he had never met, including freckle-faced Albert (Red) Schoendienst, who had come up in 1945 and played whatever position was open.

Schoendienst had even worn Musial's number 6 because that thrifty organization did not like good flannel sitting in mothballs. Now that Musial was back, number 6 was returned to him, and Schoendienst was wearing number 2. Nobody would ever wear those numbers after them.

But first Stan and Red had to get to know each other. Red always liked to describe their first meeting.

"He'd shake hands solemnly during introductions and then roar as you suddenly drew back your hand—still grasping a false thumb."

War injury, Musial would explain, before giggling. The loose thumb was a staple of his magician's repertoire.

They had a lot in common, Stan and Red, including lean times in childhood. Schoendienst, from southern Illinois, had joined the Civilian Conservation Corps as a teenager, nearly losing an eye when a nail flew into it while he was repairing a fence. The damaged eye kept him out of the service, but he learned to work around it as a ballplayer.

After catching a ride to St. Louis for a tryout, he found himself pitching batting practice to two young catchers from the Hill, an Italian neighborhood in St. Louis—Larry (not yet called Yogi) Berra and Joe Garagiola, who had finally reached minimum age to sign a contract. Berra would swing at anything, Red remembered, and often would drill the ball off the right-field screen.

The mass tryout over, Branch Rickey corralled the three of them for a further workout in Forest Park. "He scared me to death," Schoendienst said. "I think he was the worst driver I've ever seen." Rickey was also a bad judge of catchers: he signed Schoendienst for minimal money and induced Garagiola for a $500 bonus but did not offer Berra a bonus, which sent the lumpy little catcher elsewhere. Imagine the Cardinals with Yogi behind the plate from the late forties into the early sixties.

By 1946, Berra was a Yankee, having survived the invasion at Normandy. Red and Stan were meeting for the first time at St. Pete. Musial went back to left field, and Marion was healthy again at shortstop, so Schoendienst slid over to second base.

Stan and Red became the quintessential baseball roommates, who would go everywhere together—church, dinner, the ballpark, and eventually the Hall of Fame.

"I'm no mental giant. Frankly, Musial isn't either," Red would say. But woe to anybody who judged them as bumpkins, on or off the field.

The Cardinals had missed a World Series in 1945, when the war threw the league so far out of balance that the Cubs won the pennant. Now the Cardinals were back and more than a trifle testy because Max Lanier, Lou Klein, and Fred Martin had all jumped to Mexico, spurred by Breadon's lowball contracts.

"We win the pennant easily if those three guys had stayed," Musial said. "It would have been a runaway."

He was also factoring in three teammates Breadon had sold over the winter: Walker Cooper to the Giants for $175,000, Jimmy Brown to the Pirates for $30,000, and Johnny Hopp to the Braves for $40,000 and a throw-in.

The Cardinals' surly mood at the owner's deals was compounded by watching Rickey's efforts starting to pay off in Brooklyn. The spiritual heirs to the Gashouse Gang wanted to put a stop to that incursion as quickly as possible.

The first time the two teams met in 1946, Enos Slaughter sidled up to Eddie Stanky, an annoying little second baseman who had prospered with the Dodgers during the war.

"So you're the little SOB who's been acting so big while the men were away," Slaughter said.

That's me, Stanky proudly admitted.

"Well, look out for me," Slaughter warned him.

I'll be around, Stanky promised.

It took Slaughter until July before he could dump the little SOB at second. In the minor leagues, Slaughter had trudged back to the dugout after making an out, and Eddie Dyer, his manager, scolded him for not hustling. After that, Slaughter never let up, a trait that would serve the Cardinals well in early October.

Now Dyer was the manager, with Billy Southworth having moved to Boston. The Cardinals were rusty at the start, particularly Terry Moore. "He had a bad knee and he was out four years and some of the older fellas had a harder time," Musial said.

Dyer was patient with the veterans, but he was not afraid to make changes. Dick Sisler, the son of the legendary George, was not hitting, so in early June Musial found a first baseman's glove in his locker. He began taking throws at first during infield practice and soon was starting there.

"I didn't like first base," Musial added. "It was a lot of work around there." He recalled Dyer's telling him that first base was only a temporary move, but Musial found out it was not: "Every year, I'd come to spring training, I'd start in the outfield and we had different first basemen and every year I'd wind up at first. So I stayed ten years there."

The night Musial went to first base, Red Barrett broke a slump to beat the Phillies on a one-hitter and then cornball music returned to the clubhouse. Doc Weaver could not locate the 1942 good-luck anthem, the Spike Jones recording of "Pass the Biscuits, Mirandy," but Robert F. Hyland, the team doctor, had a radio station cut a copy.

The Cardinals knew how to have fun; they also knew how to police themselves. Early in the season, Walker failed to hustle from first to third base, and Moore let him know about it.

"Terry would chew you out in a nice way," Walker said. "He'd say, 'Don't fraternize with the other team. What are you gonna do if you've got to break up the double play and it's your buddy out there?' Heck, Terry wouldn't let me talk to my own brother."

But Harry did talk with his brother, Dixie, the Dodger right fielder who was so popular in Brooklyn that he was known as "the Peepul's Cherce." (Some Brooklynites really did talk like that.) Dyer tried to make Harry, a left-handed hitter, pull the ball to right field for power; Dixie advised Harry not to alter his natural stroke to left-center. This fraternal advice would prove to be invaluable one afternoon in October, much to the dismay of Durocher, who shared Moore's low opinion of fraternizing—even between actual brothers.

Slaughter got the festivities going in 1946 by trying to run down Musial's old pal, Les Webber, near first base. Then he made two great catches in right field in a 1–0 victory. The Cardinals began to catch up to the Dodgers, sweeping a series in St. Louis.


THE NEXT time they visited Brooklyn, Musial blasted hits all over intimate Ebbets Field.

He had long since figured out there was no point trying to pull the ball down the short 297-foot right-field line to the wall and fence, since the left- and center-field stands were just as inviting.

While Musial was terrorizing the Dodgers, Bob Broeg, up in the press box, detected some kind of Brooklynese chant—hard for the midwestern ear to decipher. That night at dinner, Broeg asked Leo Ward, the road secretary, if he had heard something.

"Every time Stan came up, they chanted, 'Here comes the man!'" Ward said.

Broeg thought the fans were shouting "that man."

"*The* man," Ward insisted.

Broeg wrote it in the paper: Stan the Man. A nickname for life, given him by respectful fans—in Brooklyn.

(As if to justify the growing honor of his nickname from his most for-

midable opponent, in the Cardinals' 23 games in Ebbets Field in 1948 and
1949, Stan the Man would make 47 hits in 90 at-bats, good for 96 bases and
a batting average of .522.)

THE CARDINALS were a work in progress early in 1946. On June 9, three
days after helping the Musials move, Litwhiler was sold to Boston to be reunited with Southworth. The mainstay players still resented Rickey's sale
of Mize after 1941. Now the players resented the departure of Cooper,
who did not get along with Eddie Dyer. When other catchers did not work
out, the Cardinals called up Garagiola, the ebullient catcher from the Hill.
Now twenty, Garagiola was a much better player than he would ever admit
in his later career as broadcaster and celebrity, when he portrayed himself
as a hapless, hitless backstop.

"Oh, man, we were fearless," Garagiola said of the 1946 Cardinals—all
players, really, but certainly the Cardinals. "Anything you did, you felt you
were ahead of the game. Not that you'd been in the trenches necessarily.
But you were so glad to be back."

Garagiola was outwardly brash, but he also felt like an outsider. When
he was called up in May, Garagiola was told to room with Marion, but he
arrived late at night and was too timid to knock. Rather than disturb Mr.
Shortstop, he spent the night sleeping in the hallway.

The Cardinals trailed the Dodgers by five games at the All-Star break
when Musial and four teammates got a sample of Fenway Park and Ted
Williams, both imposing. Musial was hitless in two at-bats as the American
League pounded the Nationals, 12–0. Williams merely hit two home runs
and two singles and drove in five runs.

DESPISING DUROCHER just might have been worth a game here or
there.

"Durocher would say anything, like, 'Hit him in the head, knock him
down.' He was always trying to intimidate you," Musial said.

Musial added: "We had some tough guys. You know, you had to fight
back, and when they'd knock us down, we'd knock them down. You know,
there was something happening out at second base, why, next time, you

know, one of our guys were there, they'd do it, or vice versa. So, it was, it was a common thing but good tough action."

Durocher's voice had that chalk-on-the-blackboard screech that cut through other ballpark noise. Usually he was obnoxious. Once in a while he was funny.

"I remember one time Leo came out here and said, 'You couldn't get a pint of blood from your whole infield,' " Marty Marion said, referring to Musial, Schoendienst, Marion, and Whitey Kurowski. Durocher's remark made Marion laugh in the retelling, four decades later.

The Cardinals caught the Dodgers by the final day of the season, touching off the first playoff of the century. Under the best-of-three format, Durocher opted to open the series in St. Louis and then play two at home, rather than open with one game at home, a decision debated at the time by Dodger fans—still debated by aging Brooklyn fans, to be honest.

The night before the first game, the Cardinals held a team dinner in Ruggeri's, the popular Italian restaurant on the Hill. J. Roy Stockton, the powerful columnist at the *Post-Dispatch,* twitted Breadon about getting rid of Mize and Cooper: "Sam, you've always liked to slice the baloney thin, but this year you may have sliced it a little too thin."

On October 1, in hot, sunny weather, Garagiola kept up a running dialogue with the home-plate umpire, Beans Reardon, until Reardon snarled, "Shut up, dago. You're lucky you're not pushing a damn wheelbarrow selling bananas." That ethnic insult, common at the time, spurred Garagiola, who went three for four and drove in two runs as the Cardinals won, 4–2.

The Cardinals took the train east, with Moore working the lounge, going from player to player, encouraging, goading, teaching. They don't make captains like that anymore, but then again, teams don't ride the trains; players are isolated on charter planes, lost in their headsets and their video games. Those Cardinals talked baseball, made music, watched the country go past their windows.

Two days later, Murry Dickson, with relief from Harry "the Cat" Brecheen, beat the Dodgers, 6–4, to win the pennant—the Cardinals' fourth in five seasons.

As his team celebrated a few feet down the hall from the Dodgers' morose clubhouse, Dyer, always gracious, reminded reporters that both teams in this historic playoff had been built by the same man, Branch Rickey.

Once the Cardinals' farm director and a Rickey man, Dyer understood that systems won pennants in those days; he also knew his old boss was stockpiling Jackie Robinson and other talent for the next decade. But the fans were not fretting over the future at the moment, and neither were the players. They rushed to Penn Station to catch the overnight train to St. Louis, for their date with the Red Sox and Ted Williams.

# 20

## A VISITOR ON THE TRAIN

BIMBO CECCONI was about to make his first start at tailback for the University of Pittsburgh.

A nice easy debut.

At Notre Dame.

He was a freshman, small and handsome, looking more like an artisan than a football player. He had thought of going to Notre Dame, but the Irish had the pick of the national litter with Johnny Lujack, so Cecconi enrolled at Pitt, not that far from Donora.

On the night of October 3, 1946, the Pitt team was settling into the sleeper car for the run out to Indiana when one of the players rustled the curtains of Cecconi's lower bunk and said somebody was looking for him, but not just somebody. It was Stan Musial.

When he was younger, Cecconi had trailed after Musial in the streets of Donora, asking for an autograph, while Musial was delivering sacks of groceries for the Labash family store.

Later, when Cecconi was a star athlete up at the high school, Musial used to come around during the winter and use the gym, always asking permission even though the principal said, *For goodness' sakes, Stan, use it anytime you want.* But Musial would always ask.

"I'd look into the gym and said, 'God almighty, there he is, he's playing with the St. Louis Cardinals, he's in the prime of his life, and he's supposed to be somebody special, but he's a regular person,'" Cecconi said.

Now Musial was perched on the edge of a lower bunk, chatting with the Pitt players.

That afternoon, in Brooklyn, the Cardinals had won the playoff against the Dodgers, and now they were en route to their appointment with the Red Sox.

Years later, Cecconi would wish he could remember what they talked about that evening as the train rumbled across Ohio. Maybe they talked about Leon Hart, the western Pennsylvania behemoth who on Saturday afternoon would toss Cecconi around like a sack of rags during a 33–0 victory by the Irish.

The only thing Cecconi really remembered from that night was the humility of the man, talking to a homeboy about football, about the college life he might have had under other circumstances.


THEY WOULD meet many times over the years, at sports banquets, at weddings, at reunions, and increasingly at funerals. After playing football and basketball at Pitt, Cecconi would have two terms as offensive coordinator—"got fired by my alma mater, twice," as he put it. A cultivated man who cooked and read, Cecconi also would have a long run as a high school principal.

Whenever he and Musial would wind up under the same roof, the crowds would swarm around Musial, but Stanley would wave and say, "Geez, Bim, come over here and talk to me." In old age, they were just a couple of guys from Donora, just as Musial had made it seem on that train ride so long ago.

# 21

## BEST SERIES EVER

THEY PLAYED the World Series in the daylight back then, in early October—unlike the damp and gloomy late-night afterthought it has become. In those simpler times, the Series ranked with heavyweight boxing matches, the Kentucky Derby, and the Rose Bowl. Pro football? Pro basketball? Hockey? Soccer? Auto racing? Filler items.

And this was more than a World Series. It was a celebration of baseball's being back. Just the caliber of the players, the familiarity of their names, made this a national reunion. Nothing against the participants in the 1945 World Series between the Tigers and Cubs, but more than half of those players didn't even make it back to the major leagues in 1946.

Europe and Asia were still smoldering and the world was just beginning to comprehend the horrors of the war, but the United States had some semblance of normalcy—no ruined cities, no lines of refugees. Now baseball offered up the prospect of not just a revived World Series but an epic one.

Maybe because I had recently turned seven and was just discovering baseball and Musial and Williams, maybe because of where the world had been, maybe because of the events of the seventh game—but the World Series of 1946 still ranks in my mind as the best ever.

I've rooted for my Brooklyn Dodgers in their generally traumatic ventures against the Yankees; I've seen Mantle win a game with a line drive into the upper deck, seen Gibson and Bench and Reggie and Jeter and Big Papi, seen Mookie Wilson's grounder slither through Bill Buckner's legs at first base. But 1946 still resonates.

Part of the attraction came from the presence of the tempestuous Williams and the accommodating Musial, both products of their teams and their cities. Both had come back from the service and won a pennant. They were young, attractive, in their prime. Nobody needed much imagination to know this was great stuff.

"The big individual duel was expected to be between Williams and me," Musial said afterward.

Musial led his league with a .365 average and he also drove in 103 runs and 16 homers, all personal bests. After trying to hit for power to please the admirals, he displayed a little more power in 1946—three homers more than 1943—although his stance did not seem all that different.

Williams batted .342 with 123 RBIs and 38 homers. He wanted to be called the best hitter who ever lived, and he had a case.

In those rudimentary days, before free agency and interleague play, American Leaguers and National Leaguers did not know each other very well. Williams had taken his first look at Musial on September 20 when he happened to be in Boston while the Cardinals played at Braves Field. Musial went five for five and drove in the winning run that day, and Williams was quoted as saying, "Musial has shown me more than anybody else with the stick."

The contrast between the two sluggers was only part of the appeal of this first full-cast World Series since 1941.

Both teams were loaded. Boston had Rudy York, hard-living but savvy—"part Cherokee, part first baseman," as somebody had labeled him; Dominic DiMaggio, the smooth center fielder; Bobby Doerr, the powerful second baseman; and Johnny Pesky, the peppery shortstop. The Cardinals had Slaughter, Moore, Kurowski, Marion, and Musial's new roomie, Red. Both had deep pitching staffs and veteran benches—thirty players per team, to guarantee jobs after the war.

The Red Sox came into the Series at a disadvantage: Williams was hurt. To keep in shape while the Cardinals and Dodgers were holding their play-off, the Red Sox had played three exhibitions against American League All-Stars, but Mickey Haefner, a left-hander with Washington, inadvertently plunked Williams on his right elbow.

Williams did not discuss the elbow much, but there is no doubt it was stiff as he headed into the Series. *I'm fine,* the Kid roared at the people he called the "Knights of the Keyboard." Williams got off the train in St. Louis and had to answer questions about a rumor floated by Dave Egan that the Sox were looking to trade him for either Joe DiMaggio or Hal Newhouser, the star pitcher of the Tigers, before the next season—probably not totally unfounded, as it turned out.

This flap was a perfect example of the difference between the environments of Musial and Williams. When rumors surfaced in St. Louis, they were usually checked out through Musial's pal Bob Broeg. Fans had a protective civic impulse and, generally, so did the press. Then again, with Musial, what was there to criticize? In Boston, Williams was friendly with clubhouse attendants and his fishing buddies but was distant toward the public. The accepting tone of St. Louis meant Musial could go into the World Series with a calm mind; the cranky questioning from Boston meant Williams would go into the Series with a few more darts planted in his sensitive hide.

Another difference between the two clubs: Red Sox owner Tom Yawkey broke out cushy new uniforms for his players, while Breadon merely paid to have the Cardinals' threadbare uniforms dry-cleaned.

A note of defiance at the first game: Breadon, still smarting over being chastised for going to Mexico to address the Pasquels, entertained one of the brothers, Gerardo, in his personal box, much to the annoyance of Commissioner Chandler.

Another subplot involved the Cardinals' defense against Williams. During the season, the Indians' player-manager, Lou Boudreau, had shifted his infielders, leaving only one on the left side of the diamond, daring Williams to give up his power and stroke the ball to the opposite field. The hardheaded Kid refused, on the theory that he was not going to let some genius mess with his wonderful swing.

"Me, I'd have hit a ton against that kind of defense, but Ted chose to challenge it," Musial said later.

Dyer feinted in the press that he would not use the Boudreau shift, but he told his players that the dogged third baseman, Kurowski, would play the left side by himself. Marion and Kurowski suggested that the more mobile Mr. Shortstop patrol the left side, and Dyer agreed.

The Cardinals had another strategy for the Kid. Freddy Schmidt, a spare Cardinal pitcher out in the bullpen, said that when Williams batted in the first game, some players in the Cardinal dugout began pointing imaginary rifles at the sky, going *bang-bang-bang*, as if shooting imaginary pigeons. This was a reference to Williams's pastime of ridding Fenway Park of pigeons by blasting them with a shotgun in the morning hours— long before the fans arrived, a minor stipulation by the owner. (Once Williams had shot out some lights on the scoreboard, because he was in a bad mood. That was Teddy. Mostly he just shot pigeons.)

"Ted! Ted! They're up there!" the Cardinals shouted.

"Ted didn't like that," Schmidt said. Williams cussed at them, told them what they could do.

Joe Garagiola did not notice the commotion. He was crouching behind the batter's box, too much in awe of Williams to hear any racket from the bench.

"Twenty years old," Garagiola recalled. "I was afraid I was going to ask for his autograph."

Williams watched the pitch right into Garagiola's glove.

"That was inside," Williams boomed.

"I said, 'Yes, sir, yes, sir,' " Garagiola claimed.

Williams then grounded out to Schoendienst, stationed perfectly halfway into right field—a portent of what was to come.

The Sox won the first game, 3–2, on Rudy York's homer in the tenth inning off Howard Pollet. But the Cardinals tied the Series the next day as the left-handed Brecheen allowed four singles in a 3–0 victory.

Facing good left-handers, with a sore right elbow, Williams was over-compensating.

"Once he missed a third-strike screwball with such a violent swing that his bat flew like a javelin into the visitors' dugout," Musial wrote.

The series moved to Boston on October 9, and Williams broke his refusal to acknowledge the Boudreau shift by plopping the ball down the third-base line and beating it out. The headline in one Boston newspaper said, "Williams Bunts." That annoyed the Kid, too.

In the same game, Musial wandered off second base and was promptly picked off. He had no excuse, just lost his concentration. The Sox won, 4–0, as York belted a three-run homer and Boo Ferriss pitched a complete game.

The Cardinals won the fourth game, 12–3, tying a Series record with 20 hits, four each by Slaughter, Garagiola, and Kurowski.

But Boston went ahead again on October 11 as Joe Dobson beat the Cardinals, 6–3, and hit Slaughter on the elbow. Doc Weaver soaked the elbow in Epsom salts on the train ride home, but Dr. Hyland warned Slaughter against playing, for fear of doing permanent damage to the elbow.

"If I'm breathing, I'm all right to play," Slaughter said.

Before the sixth game, Slaughter tested his elbow with a few tosses as the Sox watched attentively. "I thought I had him out of there," Dobson said later, respectfully. Slaughter played, and the Cardinals drew even with a 4–1 victory behind Brecheen.

After a day off, the teams took the field for an epic seventh game that is still being dissected, more than six decades later.

Still hurt, still stubborn, Williams was trying to crank the ball over the short porch at Sportsman's Park. He hit two long flies early, but they were chased down by Moore and Walker. Dickson retired eighteen of nineteen Red Sox from the second to the seventh inning.

In the eighth inning, Dickson gave up two hits and was replaced by Brecheen, who was feeling sick as he sat on the bench, but told nobody.

DiMaggio hit a double to drive in two runs to tie the game, but injured his hamstring racing to second and had to come out.

Brecheen now had to face Williams, with two outs and DiMaggio's pinch runner on second base. This was a chance for the Kid to make his statement, a chance to live up to his self-image as the greatest hitter in history. Williams tipped a Brecheen screwball, splitting a bare finger on the right hand of Garagiola, who had to come out of the game. Then Williams popped up to Schoendienst to end the rally, with the game still tied.

In the bottom of the eighth, the Boston manager, Joe Cronin, sent in thirty-six-year-old Bob Klinger, who had not pitched since September 19. Years later, some of the Sox would reveal they had been lobbying Cronin not to use Klinger, but it was too late. He was in the game.

Slaughter, playing with an injury, just like Williams, then hit a single to center. The next two batters made outs without advancing Slaughter from first.

That brought up Harry Walker, who had fought his way through the

killing fields of Germany and organized rudimentary baseball games on
Hitler's tainted marching grounds in Nuremberg. Back in civilian life,
Walker—counseled by his rival and brother, Dixie—had ignored orders
from Dyer to pull the ball for more power. *Be true to your stroke,* the
Dodger had told his Cardinal brother.

Klinger, a righty with a sinkerball, got a 2–1 count on Walker, who followed his brother's advice and stroked a hit over the shortstop into left-
center field.

Slaughter, running on the pitch, raced around second as DiMaggio's re-
placement, Leon Culberson, chased the ball from straightaway center
field. (Only after Culberson's death in 1989 did the gentlemanly DiMaggio
admit he had been agonizing on the bench, watching his substitute far out
of position for Walker. DiMaggio had feared what would happen next.)

Slaughter's dash had a history to it: in the first game of the Series,
Slaughter had been held up by coach Mike Gonzalez and had vowed he
would not be held up again. Thus, when Culberson bobbled the ball momentarily and then threw toward Pesky, the cutoff man, Slaughter was prepared.

"That gave me the first inkling of scoring," Slaughter said years later. "I
knew John would not be expecting it and I knew I had to slow up just
enough to decoy him into relaxing as I headed for third."

"My God, I thought he was crazy," Gonzalez said. "Who knows—
maybe he is. But who cares?"

"Gonzalez couldn't have stopped Enos with a gun," Garagiola said. And
neither could Pesky.

As Pesky received the ball, Slaughter barreled around third base and
headed home. First reports said Pesky double-pumped as he turned
toward home, but these were naked-eye impressions without modern television replays. Films showed minimal hesitation on Pesky's part.

Country Slaughter ran—and ran—and slid home as catcher Roy Partee
dove ten feet up the line chasing Pesky's hurried throw. The run was the
doing of Slaughter and Walker, but every World Series game has to have a
goat as well as a hero, so Pesky was elected. Forever.

"I've looked at those films a thousand times," Pesky said later. "They
said I took a snooze, but I can't see where I hesitated. Slaughter was at second when the ball was hit. He was twenty feet from home plate when I

turned. I can't blame anybody. Those things have happened to better ballplayers than me. I guess you have to live with it."

The official scorer took some of the romance out of Slaughter's dash by calling Walker's hit a double. The play would look better in posterity if the box score said Slaughter scored on a single, which essentially he did, with Walker taking second on the throw.

Either way, Slaughter scored—"the run heard 'round the world," Musial called it, pre-dating the immortal phrase for Bobby Thomson's pennant-winning homer in 1951.

In the ninth inning, the bloodless infield Leo Durocher had belittled held off the Red Sox. The wobbly Brecheen gave up two hits, but Kurowski and Marion collaborated on a force at second. Musial caught a foul pop near the dugout for the second out. Then Schoendienst, the man with the bad eye from the CCC accident in his teens, controlled a tricky grounder that threatened to roll up his forearm, and backhanded the ball to Mr. Shortstop for the final out.

The great game in the great Series in the great season was over. Not many people in St. Louis were thinking about the war as horns honked and bells chimed and men threw fedoras in the air.

In the rollicking clubhouse, Garagiola, the class clown, his split finger in bandages, was chirping: "I'm out for the season! I'm out for the season!" In the middle of the joy, Musial was surrounded by equals, by normalcy, just one of the gang.


LESS THAN two hours later, ten Nazi leaders were hanged, after trials for war crimes, in Nuremberg, where Harry Walker had been. The Nazis walked up thirteen steps to dual scaffolds "in an old gymnasium, used the previous weekend by American security guards for a basketball game," as journalist John McGuire wrote fifty years later. "The bodies were removed at 10:34 p.m., St. Louis time, as wild celebrations raged throughout the city over the world championship."


WHEN THE Sox arrived in Union Station, Williams stumbled to the private car and slumped into a seat, but forgot to pull the blinds. Hundreds of fans were standing on the platform, separated by glass, a few inches away, gaping at one of the great hitters in baseball as he sobbed.

Williams had no way of knowing he would never get back to the Series. All he knew was that he'd gotten five singles in twenty-five at-bats and driven in one run. The injured elbow? He was fine, dammit.

The self-styled Colonel Egan would devise a list of Williams's alleged failures in "the ten biggest games of his career." Everything the Kid did was larger than life.

Stanley had six hits in twenty-seven at-bats in the Series, but they included four doubles, a triple, and four runs batted in—and that one embarrassing pickoff in the third game. That gave him a highly ordinary batting average of .256 with one home run in twenty-three World Series games. The Cardinals had won three of four World Series in Musial's first four full seasons. As far as he could see, he would have more chances to do better.

Yet nobody in his adopted city, nobody in the great breadth of Cardinals radio, ever devised a list of Stanley's failures. Nobody would ever write or shout that he was not a clutch hitter or a team man.

"I hadn't contributed much, batting just .222, but in my head-to-head test against Williams, I had the edge," he would say about that series.

Because both parks were unusually small, the gate receipts were correspondingly low. Williams, known for his generosity to friends, would sign over his losing share of $2,141 to Johnny Orlando, the clubhouse attendant.

Full shares for the winning Cardinals would be $3,742, enough for a down payment on a postwar house for the Musials—and just low enough to draw a rare flash of sarcasm from Stanley, the good citizen.

# 22

## BOAT-ROCKER

AFTER THE last out of the 1946 Series, Musial did not have much time to celebrate. He rushed out to California, where Bob Feller had organized a barnstorming tour between white major-leaguers and the Satchel Paige all-stars from the Negro League. To Feller's credit, he was paying everybody the same, $100 per game, and treating the players well, chartering two DC-3s to transport them around California.

The World Series ended on the afternoon of October 15 (that classic seventh game, injuries and pitching changes and all, took exactly two hours and seventeen minutes). The next day Musial was in Los Angeles, in front of 22,577 fans, going hitless in two at-bats. (It was not the first time Musial had faced Paige: he'd hammered a home run off him in a similar barnstorming game in Sportsman's Park right after his meteoric 1941 season, on a day when blacks were allowed to sit anywhere for a rare breakdown in the normally segregated seating.)

After the 1946 season, the public got a glimpse of the inner Mother Jones in Stanley: making a speech at the Dapper Dan Dinner in Pittsburgh over the winter, Musial said he loved barnstorming for Feller because he made three times more money with Rapid Robert than he did in the World Series. Musial may have been exaggerating, but he managed to annoy some of the owners, who began pressuring Feller to cut down on the barnstorming. The idea of players making money from their baseball skills outside the season made the owners very nervous. They were operating on the assumption that they owned the players in perpetuity—and that included the off-season.

However, the players were getting restive, even Musial, who was not known as a radical in any form. He certainly knew about labor strife from growing up in Donora, one of the last steel towns to accept unions long after the 1892 Homestead Strike. His associations with businessmen in Pennsylvania and St. Louis had conditioned him to think of himself as an individual entrepreneur, but he also saw himself as part of the trade or profession of major-league ballplayer. And 1946 had been a landmark year in labor relations.

The end of the war had caused players to question their contracts with the owners. Returning service veterans were legally entitled to their old jobs, but players were still bound to their clubs by the so-called reserve clause, which had been approved in 1922 by the United States Supreme Court. The Court had declined to change the decision by lower courts that clubs operated as individual local businesses and that baseball was not an interstate business, despite being the national pastime. That non-ruling by the highest court was still in effect when the players came home from the service.

One of the great curiosities about baseball is that its players mostly came from the working class, like Musial, yet when they got to the major leagues they fell prey to something like the Stockholm syndrome, in which hostages identify with their captors. After having fought to save their country, however, some players began asking questions.

"I think a lot of these ballplayers, after they came back from the service . . . had to check the contracts they'd played with years ago, and all this came to a boiling point," Musial said.

The players hired a Harvard-educated lawyer, Robert Francis Murphy, who proposed a players union—he called it the American Baseball Guild—that would demand a minimum salary of $6,500, arbitration of all salary disputes, and a player's right to half the price in the event he was sold to another club.

Murphy's efforts were blocked by the owners, who worked on the players' fears and their patriotism. As Rickey told the writer Arthur Mann: "You couldn't get enough ballplayers to agree on any one thing to pull a strike. It's bogey-man stuff."

Murphy did not make significant inroads with the Cardinals, but in Pittsburgh, one of the stronger union towns, players scheduled a vote about ratifying the guild. On June 7, 1946, the Pirates' manager, Frankie Frisch, made out an alternative lineup with himself and coach Honus Wagner ready to be activated for a game against the Giants. In the clubhouse, Rip Sewell and Jimmy Brown, both from southern mill towns, urged teammates to take the field.

Ralph Kiner, later a Hall of Fame slugger and venerated broadcaster for the Mets, was a rookie on the Pirates. Kiner recalled Al Lopez, then finishing up his catching career, advising Kiner, "You don't know enough about this, so don't get wound up in this thing."

The players voted 20–16 in favor of striking, but short of the two-thirds needed for it to pass. The game was on and the public was spared the spectacle of Frisch and Wagner back in action.

After the game, Brown was roughed up by two men as he walked outside Forbes Field. Was he pushed around because of his anti-strike posture in the clubhouse? "Oh, positively," said William O. DeWitt, the owner of the St. Louis Browns.

Although the guild faded, Murphy did make some progress. In August, the owners gave bonuses to players making under $5,000, guaranteed major-league salaries to players sent down to the minors, and agreed to pay $35–50 per week for meal money the next spring training. To this day, spring meal payments are known as "Murphy money."

"If it hadn't been for the guild, if it hadn't been for the Mexican League, we would probably never got anything," Marty Marion said.

The players were not through. Each league nominated three representatives to meet during the 1946 World Series.

"Marty was kinda our leader," Musial said, referring to business matters. "He was always talking about trying to improve the conditions for the ballplayers, you know, and trying to set up a pension plan."

Meeting in a hotel in Boston, the representatives proposed setting up a pension plan with a portion of the radio receipts from the World Series, there being no income from television at that time.

Five marginal Red Sox players did not want to give up their shares of the radio rights, approximately $300 each. They feared that when the rosters were returned to twenty-five in 1947 they would be out of the major leagues without enough tenure for a pension.

Marion recalled: "I had to go into their clubhouse and convince the Red Sox that, you know, after all, boys, here we're only giving but a hundred thousand dollars, and we're starting a pension plan here. And some of you guys won't be around, you know, very long and you better take this when you can get it."

One of the leaders of the pension plan was Doc Weaver, the Cardinals' trainer better known for his cheerleading and mandolin playing (as well as inventing devices like a nasal filter to keep out the coal smoke on the long train rides). Doc also had a head for figures.

"I think our main idea at the beginning was a pension plan," Musial said, alluding anonymously to players they all knew who were said to be destitute.

On October 13, as the Series returned to St. Louis, the National League president, Ford C. Frick, announced that the Cardinal and Red Sox players had agreed to put $175,000 from radio rights into escrow to set up a pension fund that would be worth $4 million at first. The owners would also come up with a $5,000 minimum wage but did not budge on the reserve clause.

"We wanted some representation, but in those days, I don't think we wanted to be organized as such," Musial said in 1990. He called the pension plan "a great thing for baseball and baseball players. But it wasn't easy."

Musial would serve as a player representative in the future and supported the Players Association when it was founded. But in salary negotiations, players were still the property of their clubs.

After that 1946 season, Musial soon had another reason to doubt the saintly kindness of owners. He had batted .365 and won the Most Valuable Player award in 1946—while moving from the outfield to first base—and figured he might be due some real money in 1947. Instead, Breadon offered him a contract for $21,000. Musial pointed out this was a raise of only $2,500 from what he had been paid in 1946.

No, no, Breadon explained, it was a raise of $7,500. That other $5,000 that Musial had been given late in the season had been a gift between pals. Weren't they pals?

"Mr. Breadon, I don't care what you call it," Musial said, "but I know two things—I had to sign a new contract and I had to pay income tax on the money."

With the intercession of Eddie Dyer, Musial eventually signed for $31,000 for 1947. The reserve clause was still operative. And by then the Pasquels had stopped coming around with satchels of money.

# 23

## STANLEY THE SCOUT

STAN THE Man was telling this story about himself. He was back in Brooklyn in April 1997 for a conference at Long Island University, observing the fiftieth anniversary of Jackie Robinson's debut.

The Dodgers had long since moved west, but Musial was an enthusiastic member of the Brooklyn Dodgers Baseball Hall of Fame, still revered by aging Brooklynites. They remembered that by the time the Dodgers moved to California after the 1957 season, Musial had played 163 games (over a full year's worth by today's standards) in 15 seasons at Ebbets Field and batted .359 with 222 hits, 48 doubles, 13 triples, and 38 homers while driving in 127 runs and scoring 141 runs—all with a smile on his face.

"I'd be less than honest if I didn't admit liking it," Musial once said. "And liking Brooklyn, Ebbets Field, Flatbush fans and, especially, Dodger pitching."

On a more serious note, some fans and reporters at the conference questioned Country Slaughter and Bob Feller about their attitudes toward Robinson. Marty Adler, the assistant principal at Jackie Robinson Intermediate School and the leader of the Dodgers Hall of Fame, had to defuse some of the crankier questions.

But Musial charmed the crowd as he recalled seeing Robinson for the first time in the fall of 1946 during the Feller barnstorming tour.

"He was coming up the next year and I was anxious to see just how he fielded," Musial said. "I watched him take infield practice. He wasn't graceful on the infield.

"He had these short arms and short choppy swing, so when I got back to St. Louis, I was talking to the ballplayers and I said, 'I think Robinson might have a hard time in major-league baseball because he has that short choppy swing and all that.' "

The fans waited for Musial's punch line.

"So you know I·wouldn't have made a good scout at all," Musial added with the familiar Musial giggle, to laughter and applause.

Half a century later, Brooklyn still loved Stan the Man.

# 24

## THE STRIKE THAT NEVER
## HAPPENED

MUSIAL HAD doubts about Jackie Robinson's ability—at first glance—but he never wavered about Robinson's right to play.

Some of his teammates, not all of them southerners, will forever be branded as having talked about striking rather than play against the first African American major-leaguer of the century. There is not the slightest suggestion that Musial opposed Robinson, yet he rarely addressed the events of 1947, referring to them only obliquely.

Over the decades, he observed the baseball version of *omertà,* the Italian concept of "keep it in the family." He declined to reveal what he saw and heard in the clubhouse, hotel lobbies, or team trains. But the evidence is that he saw and heard something, and that his pragmatism negated some of the red-hots in the clubhouse.

Having grown up in anti-union Donora, Musial had heard stories about what happens to troublemakers of one kind or another. He had seen his share of disagreements in his family's crowded house, and he grew up with a tropism toward the safe and the secure. He had not turned down the Pasquels' money; why destabilize his profession so soon afterward? In the matter of Jack Roosevelt Robinson, Stanley kept his head down, which, it could be argued, was itself a stand.

His first exposure to Robinson came in California right after the 1946 Series. One of the Paige all-stars was Robinson, a former four-sport athlete from the University of California at Los Angeles, who had just completed a highly successful year in Montreal, the top farm team of the Dodgers.

Everybody knew that Rickey and Durocher expected him to play for the Dodgers in 1947.

All the attention to Robinson may have touched off the competitor, or the inner crank, in Feller. On October 21 in Sacramento, Rapid Robert was dressing fast after a game so he could take a personal excursion across the country for a lavish speaker's fee.

When asked by a reporter from the *Sporting News* if he had seen any Negro players who could make the majors, Feller blurted: "I haven't seen one—not one." He would hear about that remark until his death in 2010.

Feller's comment only added to the excitement of the next three games against a black team with Robinson on it. On October 23, a small crowd in San Francisco saw Feller pitch a two-hitter and beat Robinson's team, 6–0. The next day in San Diego, Feller's team won, 4–2, as Musial singled to start a winning rally in the eighth. And the third day, Feller's team won despite a late rally by Robinson's team.

"He didn't impress me too much when I saw him at the end of '46, in the fall," Musial said years later. "I figured this guy wouldn't . . . do well in the big leagues, and I can't recall if he got any hits against us out there or not."

This was classic Musial, not remembering much, not making waves. Having just hit .365, he did not have to fret about black players taking his job, as some white players feared. He was clearly the premier player of his league, and the Cardinals intended to ride him for a decade or more. He and his fellow Cardinals could not have fully imagined the changes that Branch Rickey was about to produce in Brooklyn.

Rickey has been depicted as everything from a sainted social visionary to a crass businessman, or all of the above. While he was running the Cardinals, they were as white as every other team, and Rickey did not protest or predict change down the road. However, late in the war, as President Truman pressed for more integration in the military and civilian life, Rickey found a way to take a positive public step while building the Dodgers at the same time.

Once he signed Robinson to a minor-league contract, Rickey began telling the story about his Ohio Wesleyan baseball team going to South Bend, Indiana, to play Notre Dame many years earlier, and how the hotel manager refused to rent a room to a black player, Charles Thomas. As

Rickey told it, he prevailed on the manager to allow Thomas to room with him, and Thomas began clawing at his hands, wishing he could scratch away the color.

For those who wondered if Rickey was indulging in a bit of self-serving apocrypha, Thomas, who had become a dentist in Albuquerque, backed up Rickey's hotel-room story in 1947. He told writer Mark Harris about visiting Rickey at Sportsman's Park in the mid-thirties and how Rickey considerately entertained him in his office rather than force him to sit in the segregated section of the outfield stands.

Robinson proved himself in 1946 in Montreal, a place Rickey had chosen because it was a Francophone city in Canada, with a more worldly racial attitude than most or all American cities had. The new man had helpful teammates at Montreal, including Al Campanis, a Greek-Italian immigrant who helped Robinson make the shift from shortstop to second base, and George Shuba, of Slavic ancestry, out of Youngstown, Ohio, who waited at home plate after Robinson's first homer for Montreal—"the first interracial handshake in baseball history," Shuba would call it years later. But these details were pretty much off the radar in the majors, back in the States.

"You know, he wasn't with the Dodgers at the time of the spring training; they probably didn't think he was coming up as quick as he did," Musial said. "And I think the general feeling at that time was, the atmosphere was not quite ready for a colored—well, we used to call 'em colored—ballplayers."

William Marshall, the very able interviewer for the University of Kentucky oral history series, pointed out that Robinson might have been discounted by major leaguers simply because they had never seen a black player in the majors.

"Well, that was probably true, I guess," Musial said.

In spring training of 1947, Rickey took the Dodgers and their Montreal team to Cuba, essentially because Cubans were used to blacks and whites playing ball together.

Some of the Dodgers, not all of them southerners, did not want to play with a black man, either because of their own strong racial convictions or out of fear how integration would be taken back home. One of the

Dodgers who opposed Robinson at first was Dixie Walker, the Alabaman who was highly popular in Brooklyn.

One night while the Dodgers were on a road trip to Panama, a few players held a meeting and perhaps even wrote up a petition for a strike if Robinson was brought up to the big club.

"I wasn't in that meeting," said Ralph Branca, the Dodgers' ace pitcher, who had grown up in an integrated New York suburb. "They never offered it to me because they knew I wouldn't sign."

Hearing of the meeting, an angry Leo Durocher burst in on the players, vowing to bust them if they acted against Robinson. Witnesses said the dapper Leo was wearing silk pajamas and a silk robe.

"I'll play an elephant if he can do the job, and to make room for him I'll send my own brother home," Durocher later quoted himself as saying, his language undoubtedly modified.

Leo, who personified burning ambition, warned the knuckleheads that some Negro players had more desire than they did, and maybe more talent, too.

"They're going to come, boys, and . . . unless you fellows look out and wake up, they're going to run you right out of the ballpark," Durocher said.

And speaking of Robinson, Durocher added: "He's going to win pennants for us. He's going to put money in your pockets and money in mine."

Some Dodgers may have been prejudiced, but most were not stupid. They could see Robinson was an athlete and a competitor—choppy swing, musclebound throw, bad fundamentals at first base, and all. And if the new man was going to put money in the Dodgers' pockets, that meant he was going to take money out of other players' pockets.

Fairly or unfairly, the Cardinals of 1947 have been characterized as the team that plotted to strike rather than compete with Jackie Robinson. The Cardinals were essentially, to use a modern concept, a red-state team—Terry Moore from Alabama, Enos Slaughter from North Carolina, Marty Marion from South Carolina, and Harry Walker from Alabama.

The white players were products of their time, reacting no differently than many politicians, businesspeople, clergy, or, for that matter, journalists.

IN APRIL 1947, Robinson was elevated to the Brooklyn roster. Some of his teammates were still muttering, but Robinson could count on a few Dodgers, including Branca and Harold "Pee Wee" Reese, the shortstop and captain from Louisville, Kentucky, who sent a message to the South with his visceral support of Robinson.

Rumors of a strike came out of St. Louis in late April when a reporter for the *New York Herald Tribune,* Rud Rennie, accompanied the Yankees on a trip to play the Browns. Rennie was a friend of Dr. Robert Hyland, the Cardinals' physician, and whenever they got together they would go out drinking and singing at a piano bar. (God bless day baseball; people used to have more fun back in those more civilized hours.)

At some point in an otherwise jolly evening, Dr. Hyland apparently told Rennie of his concerns that some Cardinals were planning not to play when they were due to visit Brooklyn, on May 6, 7, and 8. Rennie did not want to name his friend as a source, so he called his boss, Stanley Woodward, and told him the rumor. One of the most respected sports editors in New York, Woodward called the National League president, Ford C. Frick.

The strike rumors of 1947 have many versions, some of them conflicting. In Frick's version, he had heard "rumblings of discontent" six weeks before the Cardinals were due in Brooklyn, but he also claimed Sam Breadon called him before the season opened on April 15. Broeg, who covered the club, said he would not have been surprised if Breadon had warned the league office and New York newspapermen in order to get some backup against his restive players.

"Sam was one of their own," Broeg said, referring to Breadon's roots in Noo Yawk. "He had skinny-dipped into the East River as a young bank cashier and . . . he wined and dined the New York writers. So they were buddy-buddy."

Frick quoted Breadon as saying: "I don't know how far they'll go, but I've got to do something now. They are talking on the bench and in the clubhouse, and if it continues we might have some serious trouble. What do you think I should tell them?"

"Tell them this is America," Frick claimed he told the owner, "and baseball is America's game. Tell them that if they go on strike, for racial

reasons, or refuse to play a scheduled game they will be barred from baseball even though it means the disruption of a club or a whole league."

However it came about, Frick sent a letter to the Cardinals that said:

If you do strike, you will be suspended from the League. You will find
that you will be outcasts. I do not care if half the league strikes. Those
who do will encounter quick retribution. All will be suspended and I
don't care if it wrecks the National League for five years. This is the
United States of America and one citizen has as much right to play as
another.

The National League will go down the line with Robinson whatever
the consequences. You will find if you go through with your intention
that you have been guilty of complete madness.

Frick said Breadon called his office a day or two later to say the matter
was under control. Breadon later told Jerome Holtzman of Chicago, one of
the most plugged-in baseball writers of the time, "You know baseball players.
They're like anybody else. They pop off. Sitting around the table with a drink
or two they commit many acts of great courage but they don't follow through.
My feeling was that it was over and done with. We had no more trouble."

Most of the Cardinals, true to their code, would deny that anything was
ever discussed. However, Freddy Schmidt, who had pitched for them
since 1944, remembered a letter, something going around the clubhouse,
urging the players not to take the field in Brooklyn.

In those pivotal days, Musial may have been a bit more of an activist
than he ever let on. Frick once said that a "prominent player" on the Cardinals told people he did not care whether Jackie Robinson was white or
black or green or yellow. On the Cardinals, there was only one truly prominent player.

With a loquacious teammate like Harry Walker, Musial had to have
known something was brewing. In 1988, Walker reminisced about growing
up congenially with blacks in the rural South, fishing and eating and talking with them.

When asked about 1947, Walker said: "Nothing was ever concrete on
it. There was a rumor spread through the whole thing. And everybody was
involved to a point, but that was never done."

Walker continued his monologue: "All of these things have been blown out of proportion. People didn't understand. I think the war changed a lot really. It brought people from one part of the country to another part of the country, who had only heard and read negative things about each other. And in doing so I think you put a fear in people that was not there normally. That you just . . . if you don't know about something . . . it's like a little green door, you're scared to open that thing 'cause you don't know what's going to come out. It might be great. But you'll always think the negative side a minute."

Walker recognized the unfairness that some great black ballplayers never got a chance to play in the majors, but he noted that many white players, despite exposure from barnstorming, had assumed in 1947 that Negro Leaguers played an inferior brand of ball, or just a different brand.

"I'll bet you for every great one, there were four or five that were very, very mediocre AA, AAA players," Walker said. "But they had Josh Gibson and guys like that were super. And that was a misfortune that came along. But that was corrected. But as I say again, I think every ballplayer was worried about what would happen, what would be his future, how it would affect the game."

Then Walker got around to admitting the strike rumors were legitimate. "It was talked about when he first came in that if he first walked on the field that they might not do it. But the Dodgers did and everybody else went along with the whole situation."

Frick always insisted that strike talk had already been quashed by the time the *Herald Tribune* ran the story.

Breadon labeled Woodward's original article "ridiculous." By the time the Cardinals played the Dodgers, Harry Walker was elsewhere. The man who delivered the hit that sent Country Slaughter on his way home the previous October was traded on May 3, along with Freddy Schmidt, to the Phillies. There they would get to play for southerner Ben Chapman, who spouted vicious racial epithets in the dugout and was not too high on northerners, either, calling them "carpetbaggers."

Right after the trade, the Cardinals came into Brooklyn with a 3–11 record and won two of three.

"We never had a meeting. We never talked about having any organized boycott," Musial said in 1997. "We were having problems winning and getting started. Enos will tell you. Marty Marion. Kurowski. We'll all tell you we never had any thoughts in that direction, whatsoever."

Musial added that New Yorkers had preconceptions about St. Louis and southerners on the Cardinals. "I think they felt that we were, you know, we're a Southern town in a way," he said, "but as far as the players were concerned, you mighta heard some mumbles before that about playing against Robinson, but when the time came to play, why, everybody played, and it was really nothing. We didn't have any special meeting or anybody give us any special talk."

However, in a separate interview with Roger Kahn, Musial seemed more forthright: "I heard talk. It was rough and racial and I can tell you a few things about that. First of all, everybody has racial feelings. We don't admit it. We aren't proud of it. But it's there. And this is big-league baseball, not English tea, and ballplayers make noise. So I heard the words and I knew there was some feelings behind the words, but I didn't take it seriously. That was baseball."

In the same interview, Musial seemed to give credence to the rumors: "For me at the time—I was twenty-six—saying all that would have been a speech and I didn't know how to make speeches. Saying it to older players, that was beyond me. Besides, I thought the racial talk was just hot air."

In 1997, Musial told a reporter with the *Pittsburgh Post-Gazette:* "I didn't give it a second thought. I played against blacks in high school, played with Buddy Griffey." And he added, "You'd have thought fifty years ago we'd be a lot farther along in race relations in this country."

All this adds up to a man who, whether or not he made speeches, was not going to be stampeded into a racially motivated walkout.

Besides, Musial was dealing with something else on that trip to Brooklyn. He had not felt well the previous winter and doctors had suggested appendix and tonsil problems, but he shrugged it off. In early May he was confined to his room in the New Yorker Hotel while rumors circulated that Slaughter had punched him in the stomach during an argument over whether to strike.

The hotel doctor confirmed that Musial was suffering from acute appendicitis and recommended an appendectomy right away.

"I was in a hotel room with him the day the doctor came up," Broeg said in an interview in 1948. "Stan looked terrible. His face was drawn and thin, his ribs were sticking out and he was deathly pale."

Broeg, in his triple role as journalist, friend, and collaborator, said Musial had been naked from the waist up in the hotel, and that Broeg had seen no marks on his midsection. In subsequent photos of Musial being tended by nurses in St. Louis, his slender midsection is unmarked.

Dr. Hyland proposed that Musial fly home, which he did, accompanied by Del Wilber, a third-string catcher and friend of his. Dr. Hyland examined Musial at one in the morning and treated both the appendix and tonsils; Musial called the process "freezing" his appendix. He missed five games, then went twenty-two at-bats without a hit, and played the rest of the season in a weakened condition.

Strike talk pretty much vanished. By the time the Dodgers visited St. Louis on June 12, several Cardinals made a point of welcoming Robinson as the Dodgers took the shortcut from their clubhouse to the field through the Cardinals' dugout.

"Dyer says, 'Hiya, pal,' " Broeg recalled, and Robinson said hello back. After Robinson had moved away, Broeg teased Dyer, saying, "Consorting with the enemy?" Dyer then compared Robinson to Frankie Frisch, the crusty old competitor: "You get him mad, he'll beat you by himself. So, I told my players to take it easy. This is a great, great competitor."

The Cardinals were on their best behavior for a while. Marion expressed visible concern after spiking Robinson in a normal collision at second base. Joe Medwick—back with the Cardinals after a seven-year absence—sidled up to Robinson at the batting cage and told him he was going to be a terrific player but needed to relax his muscular hitting and throwing techniques.

Interviewed by the *Pittsburgh Courier*'s Wendell Smith, one of the giants of sportswriting, Robinson praised Musial, Garagiola, and the rest as "a swell bunch of fellows. They treated me so nice I was actually surprised."

Musial had reason to feel a little more friendly toward the Dodgers because the annoying Leo Durocher was suspended for a year by Happy Chandler for associating with known gamblers. Leo the Lip was replaced by Musial's old friend from the shaky spring of 1941, Burt Shotton, who wore civilian clothing in the dugout, à la Connie Mack.

But things never remained benign for long between the Dodgers and the Cardinals.

IN AN August series at Ebbets Field, Medwick landed on Robinson's left foot at first base, which was attributed to Robinson's raw footwork at that unfamiliar position. Because Medwick had already welcomed Robinson to the majors, nothing was made of this collision. But a few days later, Enos Slaughter stepped on Robinson, and that was a totally different case.

The spiking happened in the eleventh inning, with Hugh Casey pitching in relief with Musial on first base. Slaughter hit a grounder to Robinson, who decided not to try to force Musial at second but instead stepped on first base for the sure out. However, as Robinson turned to check on Musial at second, Slaughter's spikes raked down against the back of his right leg, just above the heel.

Robinson jumped around in pain before seeking treatment from the trainer, Harold Wendler, who later said, "Jackie was lucky he wasn't maimed. I can't understand how one ballplayer can deliberately do that to another one. He might have severed Robinson's Achilles' tendon and finished his baseball career."

Robinson did not doubt Slaughter had tried to spike him. "What else could it have been?" Robinson asked.

Different people remember it different ways. Branca, who had gone into the seventh inning with a no-hitter, was out of the game during the spiking. Branca was in the dugout by then and can describe Slaughter swerving to his left to plant his foot on Robinson's calf.

"How he didn't go tumbling, I'll never know," Branca said of Robinson.

Another close spectator was Joe McDonald, a high school kid who was working as visiting batboy that night. Later a general manager for the Mets and Cardinals, and a friend of Musial's, McDonald said he was on the field outside the Cardinals' dugout when Slaughter raced down the baseline. As a batboy, McDonald had a better look at the play than anybody sitting in the dugout. The dugout is a notoriously bad site for watching action on the

crowded field. When a manager says "I couldn't see the play," he is probably telling the truth.

"I see it developing," McDonald narrated sixty years later. "I really
thought Robinson was not the greatest first baseman; he hadn't played
there much."

McDonald continued: "When you're reaching for the ball, you don't
put your foot on the bag. I thought his foot was not straddling the bag but
that it was indeed on top of the bag. Slaughter spiked him but I came to
the conclusion that he didn't mean it.

"I'm not defending him in any way. I thought it was accidental,"
McDonald said.

McDonald recalled Slaughter trotting past the mound after being
called out, and Dodger relief pitcher Hugh Casey taking a step toward
Slaughter, as if to challenge him. "Two southerners were going to go at it,
one of them in defense of Jackie."

Musial soon became embroiled in the hard feelings. He was playing
first base that year, a position he did not like except that it allowed him to
get to know opponents. Not long after the spiking incident, Robinson
reached first base. Like many other incidents that year, this casual encounter has several versions.

"He said something to me like 'Well, I'll step on you, too,' or something
like that," Musial once said. "I said something to him too, in a way, but it
was such a thing that happened so quickly." Musial recalled how he was
"kinda keyed up, in a way, too, but it was nothing."

Everybody knew that Rickey had instructed Robinson to hold in his
competitive nature—"which was probably good," Musial said. "Rickey was
a good influence there, you know. And I think it kinda helped the situation." But Musial understood Robinson's temptations: "I think about that
time, he was about fed up with all of this that was going on, you know, but
he'd lose his temper every once in a while."

In another version of that first-base meeting, Roger Kahn quoted
Robinson telling Musial, "I wish I could punch the son of a bitch in the
mouth," the SOB being Slaughter. In a third version, Musial replied, "I
don't blame you." There is also a version that somebody—perhaps even a
Dodger—heard Musial's alleged response and relayed it to Slaughter, who
then beat up Musial in the clubhouse.

The fight version is bogus. The SOB remark, if it happened at all, took place in August, whereas the purported fight took place, or did not take place, in May. And if appendicitis was a cover story for a Musial-Slaughter fight, why did Dr. Hyland perform an appendectomy in October? This was after the weakened Musial had struggled through the season with a mere .312 average, down from .365, but he did hit 19 homers, a new personal high.

The real statistic is that the Cardinals finished five games behind the Dodgers. Robinson and Rickey had changed the order of the National League.

One detail that sounds realistic is that Robinson called Slaughter an SOB. The old war horse was sure that his identification with the rumored strike and the actual spiking kept him from being voted into the Hall of Fame until 1985, twenty-six years after his retirement. By that time, Musial was a power on the veterans committee that finally accepted Slaughter into the Hall—making it hard to work up a fight scenario after Musial's proactive support of Slaughter.

In 1997, Slaughter returned to Brooklyn for the Robinson anniversary and found himself questioned sharply about the incident at first base.

"I'm glad you asked that question," Slaughter said, off and running as if it were still 1946. "I was there. I did not intentionally step on Jackie. It was a low throw and he reached for it, he did step off the base, and I did step on his ankle."

Slaughter was in full stride now. "I can straighten out a lot of things. I played the game the way it's supposed to be played. I came up with the Gashouse Gang back in '38. We asked a lot and gave none. Jackie was the same type of ballplayer. He would run right over you. He was out to win."

Up to his death on October 28, 2005, Bob Broeg conceded that some of the 1947 Cardinals "beat their gums" about a strike but insisted this was a natural reaction to living in a world grown more complicated. Broeg also noted that Slaughter spiked a lot of people.

Years later, Musial said: "You have to admire a guy like Robinson going through what he did. He was pointed out, you know, as different, and 'course I'm sure a lot of the players and pitchers worked harder to try to not let him succeed against them, you know, and so, you know, you kinda gotta admire him in a way."

Then he added, "So what I am trying to say is that I was glad Jackie came along. He was a great ballplayer. He made a big difference with our way of life in our society, and he opened up a lot of doors. And I am sure Robinson took more abuse than we really, really know about."

No amount of political correctness can sugarcoat the rivalry. Robinson was just another reason the Cardinals despised and resented the Dodgers, more than ever once the Dodgers carried the mantle as good guys, progressives doing the right thing.

"They were making such a big deal out of it, and we thought, really, they showed partiality to Robinson," Marion said of the eastern media. "We thought he got the better of the deal, and we didn't think that was quite right because we were baseball players, too."

Marion added, "He was a heck of a ballplayer, and everybody didn't like him, really. But he was a heck of a ballplayer, one of the best ballplayers I ever played against. And a great competitor."

Asked if he ever chatted with Robinson, Marion said: "No. I tell you, the Brooklyn Dodgers and the Cardinals were kind of enemies, to tell you the truth." He added, "We didn't like anybody. Pee Wee Reese. We was always fighting. Me and Pee Wee were always fighting. And we just didn't like each other at all, and we were great competitors and I don't think we had any personal love for anybody in the whole club, and I'm sure they didn't for us.

"Well, the only time you would talk to the people, when you pass in the infield, you know, you say something nasty to 'em," Marion added, chuckling at the memory. "Yeah, you would. You know, you'd give a blast of something. It was very difficult times when the Dodgers had a great ball club and we did. We were always battling."

Long afterward, Harry Walker always praised Robinson, calling him "one of the classiest guys, a college graduate, one of the great athletes of all time. And why Rickey picked him was that reason. The man had the fight in him to fight back. Not let them hammer him down. And he was a superstar doing it. He went to bat quite a few times before he got a hit. But when he opened up, he just was a superstar same as Babe and the other guys."

In his mellow years as a manager, Harry Walker noted that taunting Robinson had proved extremely counterproductive.

"Well, it seemed to just rally him up. It didn't do much damage and so . . . the more you throwed at him, it seemed the harder he fought back at you. But he and Chapman had a row going on all the time. And Jackie would throw it back at him. You know he didn't back up."

In 1967, while managing the Pirates, Walker started eight players of color, blacks and Latinos. He would have started nine except that it was Dennis Ribant's turn to pitch. After working as a hitting coach with the Cardinals, Walker became hunting buddies with Bill White, the outspoken African American first baseman of the Cardinals. He'd come a long way.

THEN THERE was the question of what Robinson thought about Musial.

Julius Hunter, a broadcaster and writer in St. Louis who is African American and a friend of Musial's, recalled:

> Robinson had said that while he was catching the nastiest worst hell of his life, with catcalls and objects being hurled onto the field in a very racist St. Louis at the time, Stan was one of only a couple of the Cardinals who stayed above it all. Robinson often noted that Stan never said a discouraging word in front of, or behind Jackie's back. Some thought that Musial was too much of a superstar to lower himself to racial mudslinging with players or fans who had much less talent of any sort to offer the world. Stan had taken to the field in high school with black baseball players at Donora, but I had always given Stan extra props for not joining the rampant mistreatment leveled at the Black trailblazer on his first visits to the old Sportsmen's Park in good old racist St. Louis.

However, Roger Kahn, who had the ear of both men, said Robinson believed Musial was too passive in those vital years.

"He was like Gil Hodges," Kahn quoted Robinson as saying. "A nice guy, but when it came to what I had to do, neither one hurt me and neither one helped."

Hodges was the southern Indiana miner and former Marine who kept his thoughts to himself and was beloved in Brooklyn in somewhat the same way Musial was in St. Louis. There was never a trace of prejudice in Hodges. As everybody knew, Jackie Robinson had a mind of his own.

AND THEN there was the story Joe Black told.

It was June 9, 1952, and Black was a rookie pitcher with the Dodgers, a college man who had played in the Negro Leagues and heard some racial stuff in his first two months in the major leagues. On his first appearance in St. Louis, Black did not know what to expect.

When Black was called in from the bullpen, the first batter was Musial.

"After I warmed up and looked at Campy for the sign, out of their dugout come words like, 'Hey, Stan, you shouldn't have any trouble hitting the baseball with that big black background.' "

Black stepped off the mound, tempted to smile at the crude remark. Then he saw Robinson running over.

"That was sorta funny, wasn't it?" Robinson said.

"Yeah," Black said.

"Forget that son of a bitch," Robinson said of the heckler. "Go get 'em."

Black gathered his intensity for the man in the crouch, who popped up, although not out of kindness.

The next day, Black was taking the shortcut through the Cardinals' dugout. Stan Musial was waiting for him.

"He pulled me over to the side and he said, 'Forget those guys who call you names like that. You're a good pitcher, you're going to do okay.' "

Black went on to become Rookie of the Year and the first African American pitcher to win a World Series game.

After his pitching days, Black became an executive with Greyhound and was active in good causes until his death in 2002. In many of his speeches, Black would tell about the man who waited for him in the runway.

# 25

## STANLEY AND THE KID

THE WAY Ted Williams told it, the incident took place in 1960, after he had hit his 521st and last home run, the subject of the classic John Updike story in the *New Yorker.* Williams abruptly retired before the final road trip but returned to the ballpark to cover the World Series for *Life* magazine.

Rather than put Williams in the press box with his old friends, the knights of the keyboard, the magazine arranged for him to watch the game from a box seat.

Before one of the first games in Pittsburgh, a woman leaned over from the adjacent box and asked Williams to sign her souvenir program.

"You know, you're one of my favorite players," she said while he signed.

"Oh, is that right?" Williams replied.

"Yes," she said. And then she added, "I'm Stan Musial's mother."

According to Williams, he told her he ought to be asking for *her* autograph.

IN MUSIAL'S version, it happened at the 1959 All-Star Game in Pittsburgh, when he and Williams were both having subpar years.

Mary Musial was in a box seat before the game, asking for autographs, just another lady fan in the crowd. Williams came by and politely signed her program.

"And that is Stan Musial's mother," somebody told Williams.

Over the years, Musial always added that Williams sought him out at the batting cage to needle him about who really counted. Musial insisted that Williams was his mother's second-favorite player—next to her son.

But whenever he told the story, Stanley made himself sound not quite sure he was really ahead of the Kid in his mother's estimation.

# 26

## THE BIG THREE

THEY BECAME a trio after the war—the two distant stars of the American League and the approachable man-next-door of the National League. Welcome to the club, Stanley.

From 1946, when all three came back from the war, until 1951, when DiMaggio retired, Musial was every bit their equal—some would say maybe even better. They remained linked into old age, refugees from a time when baseball was king, but somehow DiMaggio and Williams excited the public with their air of mystery and inaccessibility, whereas Musial grew more familiar and somehow smaller.

DiMaggio became known for what was perceived as dignity, or maybe it was hauteur. He performed in a city that believed it was the center of the universe, and DiMaggio had the ego to encourage that adoration. In retirement, he brokered a guarantee that he would always be introduced last at every Old-Timers' Day in Yankee Stadium—the greatest living Yankee, after Ruth died in 1948—and he accepted all the booty and perks that went with it.

Williams was known for his edgy perfectionism, for ducking his long red neck when crossing home plate, for spitting in the direction of the fans or the press box. In his retirement he became a guru with a booming voice, John Wayne with batting theories.

Ever since that seething, handsome head was preserved in fluids in some nut-case regeneration laboratory, Williams has become a punch line for late-night comedians. Teddy Ballgame deserved better.

Musial had his own façade. It just happened to be a wall of good humor, a plastic bubble of harmonica solos and magic tricks. By the strange standards of today, if a man stood in a parking lot and signed autographs for urchins, how great could he have been?

Musial was a very different kind of superstar from the Kid and the Clipper. The latter two both arrived from California with expectations, which made their debuts and their moods and their demands all the more dramatic; Stanley came from inland, remained inland, and stroked his way into the formation of the Big Three.

Look at the photographs of the three greatest sluggers of the forties. They all had Depression physiques. Even in the bunchy flannel uniform of the time, DiMaggio is slim-waisted, slim-hipped, a gazelle who gracefully roamed the vast steppes of Yankee Stadium. In a classic photo, wearing only long white underpants, known as sanitaries, and waving a bat in the cramped Red Sox clubhouse, Williams is elongated, like a figure in an El Greco painting. Until late in his career, Musial's ribs were clearly visible, the torso of a boy who never had enough to eat.

Bob Feller, the great pitcher of that era, always said he developed his back muscles carrying buckets of water from the Raccoon River on the family farm in Van Meter, Iowa. He turned rural life into an asset, which it was, for him, but the three great sluggers of midcentury were more urban than Feller. DiMaggio was from San Francisco, Williams from San Diego, and Musial from a steel town near Pittsburgh; Stanley had never been hunting until Red Schoendienst took him.

Whatever it means, the three sluggers were also "ethnic" in the American way, meaning they had fairly recent roots in other countries. Did this give them a drive to excel, to fit in? A lot of successful Americans have recent ties to some other place.

Giuseppe DiMaggio came to the States in 1898 and four years later sent for his wife, the former Rosalie Mercurio, and their daughter, Nellie, who had been born shortly after Giuseppe departed. The family settled first in Martinez, California, and later worked at Fisherman's Wharf in San Francisco, with eight more children born in California, Joe arriving in 1914. The family spoke a Sicilian dialect around the house.

The Clipper's childhood was certainly the most stable of the three stars, with his older brothers and sisters bringing in money, supporting one another. The culture was secure—large Sunday dinners, a glass of home-made *vino*. In his early years as a Yankee, DiMaggio allowed photographers into his family life, and he was depicted perfectly attired in shirt and tie, admiring the long strands of Mamma's spaghetti dangling from a fork. The al dente photojournalism stopped after he settled in New York and became a steak guy.

In the clubhouse, sometimes even in print, his nickname was "the Dago" or "the Big Dago" or "the Daig." He married two actresses, neither Italian.

His family's hard work around the wharf strengthened DiMaggio's feeling that a man had to stand up for himself in this America. He adapted an immigrant suspicion—don't let the bastards rip you off—toward Yankee management, as well he should have.

Williams was more ethnic than people imagined. He somehow managed to obscure the fact that his mother, a Salvation Army activist in downtown San Diego, was of Mexican descent. May Venzer (alternately spelled Venzor) Williams was out of the house most of the time, doing the Lord's work, and the Kid, when he was actually a kid, went off to school without breakfast or lunch money. His father, a photographer, was pretty much out and about, so Williams, just like Musial, sought mentors in park supervisors and school coaches.

Sometimes young Teddy's mom made him march with the Salvation Army band. "I never wore a uniform or anything but I was right at that age when a kid starts worrying about what other kids might think, especially a gawky introverted kid like me, and I was just so ashamed. Today I'd be proud to walk with those people, because they are truly motivated," Williams would say years later.

In the public eye, Williams came off as a flinty Anglo curmudgeon, more Welsh and English on his father's side than Latino on his mother's. Amazingly, in a time of blatant stereotypes, Williams's teammates never called him "Mex" (as players would call the thoroughly gringo Keith Hernandez) and Williams's good chums in the press never hooked his smoldering temper to stereotypical hot Latin blood.

The mother's activism may have rubbed off on him, since Williams became the most politically outspoken of the Big Three, a Nixon Republican. He would also use the occasion of his Hall of Fame induction to speak out for the inclusion of Negro League stars. Was his advocacy connected to his Mexican ancestry? He never said.

In this land of immigrants, it was not cool to be too ethnic, but Musial was the most comfortable with his ancestry. Known in the clubhouse as Stash, he told and laughed at Polish jokes for a long time and bragged about his mother's East European specialties. At social gatherings he would demonstrate the polka steps he had learned at Falcon meetings back in Donora.

DIMAGGIO ARRIVED in the majors first, in 1936, at twenty-one, missing Ruth but playing with Gehrig. In 1941 he hit in fifty-six consecutive games, a feat that may never be broken in a sport that now values the dinger, the long ball, at the expense of consistency.

Frank Robinson, perhaps the second most underrated player in history, right behind Musial, cites DiMaggio's career totals of 361 home runs and 369 strikeouts as perhaps even more impressive than the streak—proof of DiMaggio's stunning discipline mixed with power. DiMaggio hit .325 in his career, his right-handed power sometimes negated by the long veldt in left-center at Yankee Stadium, known as Death Valley. He was clearly the best fielder of the three, a graceful center fielder and base runner who almost never made a mistake.

Williams arrived in 1939 at the age of twenty—the Kid. In 1941 he hit .406—making him the last .400 hitter of the century and maybe forever. He would retire with 521 home runs and that stunning .344 average, tarnished only by the .200 in his sole World Series.

Was it Williams's fault that the Sox won only one pennant in his time? In his retirement, he often boomed, "We'd have won a lot more pennants if we'd had that little SOB at shortstop," meaning Phil Rizzuto. Sometimes Williams would even say that in the company of Johnny Pesky, one of his best friends, who happened to be the shortstop in three of those seasons. That was Teddy.

Musial measured up statistically with Williams and DiMaggio, with his .331 average and 475 home runs and his speed. He scored plenty of manager points for his willingness to move between first base, which was hard work, and left field, where he compensated for his weak arm. He became the first Hall of Famer to play more than 1,000 games at each of two positions—1,896 in the outfield and 1,016 at first base. (Robin Yount, Ernie Banks, and Rod Carew all did it later.)

Williams and DiMaggio were strictly one-position guys, although Williams did pitch one inning for laughs, and DiMaggio did play one game at first base, decidedly not for laughs, when Casey Stengel tinkered with him in 1950.

All three were one-city guys, in the days before free agency, when players did not change teams voluntarily. The big three were rarely in the same place at the same time—five All-Star Games from 1946 through 1950, one World Series between Musial and DiMaggio, and one World Series between Musial and Williams. Stanley won both Series, if that means anything.

The leagues were more separate back then, so not many players could take the measure of the Big Three firsthand, but Ned Garver, a stylish right-hander who played for the Browns from 1948 into 1952, got to know all of them. In 2009, Garver was a very active eighty-four-year-old, splitting his time between Florida and his native Ohio.

"For some reason, Ted Williams kind of adopted me," Garver said. "One of the first times I pitched against the Red Sox, Williams was on third base. I was a rookie, and he acted like he was going to steal home. I mean, he danced up the line."

The sight of Ted Williams making like Jackie Robinson down the third-base line would be priceless on video today, but Williams refrained from taking a mad dash home.

"I didn't balk, but maybe I stopped off the mound," Garver said. "He looked back at me and smiled. That made me feel great. And all through his career, you look at the interviews, he says I could throw my glove out there and get him out; he couldn't pick up the spin off my slider." Williams did hit 10 homers off Garver, the most by any hitter except Gus Zernial, who also hit 10.

One time Garver caused Williams to break his bat lunging at a slider; somehow the bat came into Garver's possession, glued together—a memento of his duels with the Splinter.

Long into retirement, Garver brought the bat to a winter baseball gathering in Florida and asked his colleague to autograph it.

"Just don't let John Henry know I signed it," Williams whispered to Garver, referring to his son, who controlled Ted's autographs like a farmer with his cash cow.

For DiMaggio, Garver used the word "majestic," just like the stadium in which Joe D. played. "When he was taking batting practice at Yankee Stadium, a couple of us Browns, we'd just stop and watch. He was that way. But, by the same token, he did not communicate," Garver added.

"I don't remember ever saying anything to Joe on the field," Garver added. "Joe was aloof."

In 1951, Garver was selected to start the All-Star Game in Detroit and went to the park early "because I was so tickled being there." One of the other early birds was DiMaggio, who was injured and would not play, and was therefore a bit more sociable than usual.

"He said to me, 'I didn't know you were going in the service,'" Garver said, "and I said, 'I'm not going in the service,' and he said, 'You sure got a GI haircut,'" which was true, Garver said.

That was one of the rare times Garver saw DiMaggio unwind. Years later, he appeared at a card show and went out to dinner with DiMaggio and a few other players. A fan asked DiMaggio for his autograph, but the Clipper iced him.

"He didn't let that guy interrupt him," Garver recalled. "He just ran the show, you understand. He stayed in control."

DiMaggio did not talk much to opponents, Garver said, which was normal in those days. "I watch TV, everybody talks to everybody else at first base and second base, holy crap. We didn't do anything of that.

"We were taught, whoever was in the other uniform was your enemy. We were told not to talk to Yogi Berra, and if the mask was on the ground, you kicked dirt in it. It was an altogether different atmosphere. But Stan was a nice guy. I'm sure he communicated with guys in his league."

Garver loved Stanley. On the rare occasion the Browns happened to be in town while the Cardinals had a game, Garver went out to inspect the Musial stance up close.

"I thought it was a handicap," Garver said with a laugh. "I mean, to get down in that crouch, you've got to get into that coil. To me, it seems like you're in too much of a position."

Garver never really got to test himself against Musial. The only time they ever met was in 1951, when Garver started the All-Star Game.

"Jackie Robinson was next. Richie Ashburn was already on third base with one out and I didn't want to mess with Musial. I didn't have much confidence in striking him out. I pitched around him," Garver recalled.

Ashburn scored the only run Garver would give up in three innings. Musial got his chance to hit in the fourth inning against Ed Lopat, a lefty with tantalizing stuff, and hit a home run.

Garver often wondered how he would have done against Musial.

"He was just a guy with no weakness. He would hit the ball where it was pitched, and you just hate to pitch to people like that."

The friendship carried over after Garver moved on to the Tigers. After an exhibition against the Yankees in St. Pete, Garver was standing in the parking lot talking with some relatives when the Cardinals' bus returned from their exhibition elsewhere.

"Stan saw me and walked over through the parking lot, through the crowd, to say hello to me," Garver recalled. "I introduced him to my cousins, and he was so gracious to them that they never forgot it for the rest of their lives."


PERSONALITIES ASIDE, there was plenty of room to debate who was the best player of the big three.

Tyrus Raymond Cobb once declared that the game was better in his day—of course it was, bless his heart—but he did praise two players of 1949: Musial and Phil Rizzuto. Both of them, in Cobb's eyes, had the bat control and discipline from when baseball was baseball, before World War I.

"I don't want to say anything that may distress Cobb, but I simply can't go along with him," Musial told the *World-Telegram and Sun*'s Joe Williams, a great admirer of his. "I don't know when he ever saw me play and I must wonder how often he saw DiMaggio play.

"I'd take DiMaggio. He's a whole ballplayer," Musial continued. "I mean he can do everything. He can run, throw, field and hit. Williams is interested mostly in hitting. At least he was until this spring. I notice now that he is working on his fielding. I think he wants to be known as a whole ballplayer, too."

Joe Williams said DiMaggio had more power than Musial early in their careers, and clearly DiMaggio was superb on defense, but he rated Musial ahead of Ted Williams.

Musial met Cobb once. A few years after Cobb's kind words to Joe Williams, Cobb called Musial at the team hotel in New York and invited him for breakfast. They mostly talked hitting, but Cobb's biggest contribution was to change Musial's diet. "Cobb said, 'I see you use cream and sugar in your coffee. It would be better if you just used one or the other.' So Stan gave up sugar," said Musial's former son-in-law, Tom Ashley.

The debate over the three players continued into their retirement. Bill White, a teammate in Musial's later seasons, maintained that Musial was the best hitter he ever saw from the time he arrived in the majors in 1956—and remember that Willie Mays, in his prime, was a teammate.

White was a National League guy who wound up broadcasting for the Yankees, spending dizzying hours in the booth with Rizzuto, emphatically an American League guy.

In their long and loopy dialogues, White would praise Stan the Man, whereas Rizzuto would praise DiMaggio (presumably for the six World Series winners' checks they earned together). Rizzuto also praised Williams, who had terrorized the Yankees in that era.

Freddy Schmidt, who was a teammate and remained a friend of Musial, saw Williams in the 1946 World Series and saw DiMaggio in spring training a few years. At the age of ninety-two and clearheaded, Schmidt picked DiMaggio.

"I only faced him in spring training, but you could see he was polished. And the other players knew it," Schmidt said in 2008.

Income was not an easy indicator of their abilities because DiMaggio came along three years before Williams, who came along three years before Musial. As of 1949, the Clipper and the Kid were both making around $100,000, while Musial was making half that.

"Well, St. Louis isn't New York and I guess it isn't Boston, either," Musial said that year, probably knowing that his six-figure salary would arrive eventually. And if not, he was a businessman. He would catch up.

ONE THING the Big Three had in common was that all three were subject to itchy trade impulses. Musial blew up a proposed trade for Robin Roberts in 1956. And nine years earlier, in April 1947, Tom Yawkey, the owner of the Red Sox, woke up with the vague recollection of having traded Williams for DiMaggio a few hours earlier in Toots Shor's. Yawkey rang up Dan Topping of the Yankees, and they agreed to forget all about it. Alka-Seltzers all around.

That late-night trade would have given fans a laboratory experiment, since both DiMaggio and Williams would have moved to parks ideally structured for them.

"If we had traded Williams for DiMaggio, do you have any doubt at all that the Yankees still would have won those pennants and we still would have finished second?" asked Joe Cronin, the Red Sox' manager through 1947 and general manager through 1958.

Given the proximity of Athens and Sparta, Williams and DiMaggio could not help being in contention with each other—the kind of personal comparison Musial hardly had to deal with in far-off St. Louis.

The relationship between Williams and DiMaggio was respectful, with the occasional zinger dropped into the conversation.

"Sure, he can hit. But he never won a thing," DiMaggio once said.

In 1948, DiMaggio said: "He may out-homer me, but I will out-percentage him, I can out-throw him, I can out-run him, and out-think him."

DiMaggio thought of Williams as Teddy Tantrum. And one time Joe D. said: "He throws like a broad, and he runs like a ruptured duck."

Williams was more circumspect toward DiMaggio. In 1941, when DiMaggio was voted Most Valuable Player despite Williams's .406 batting average, Williams said, "Yeah, awright. But it took the Big Guy to beat me!"


ALL THREE had brothers.

DiMaggio's brothers were fishermen or major leaguers: Vince hit 125 homers in parts of ten seasons in the National League, while Dommy—as

Williams called the bespectacled DiMaggio—roamed far into left field, saving Williams's legs for his true calling, hitting. The Clipper sometimes seemed a trifle frosted when his little brother took away doubles and triples from him. Williams and Dommy would remain loyal friends, and Dominic would have a stable marriage and business success, able to function out in the real world.

Williams's brother, Danny, did a little time in San Quentin, then straightened out, and after that Ted conscientiously kept him solvent.

Musial's brother, Ed, made a decent life for himself after his minor-league career faltered; their lives mostly went separate ways.

Even in matrimony, Musial was the boring one—no divorces, no scandals, no notoriety. If he stayed out of the limelight, that was fine with him.

WILLIAMS PRAISED Musial as a peer, as a hitter. The Kid loved his calling so much he opened a museum in Florida dedicated only to hitters. As far as Teddy was concerned, pitchers could open their own freaking museum.

"He once told me about a time when he and Musial were at some old-timers' event," said Jim Prime, who collaborated with Williams on a book about hitting. "Ted's young son, John Henry, was with him, and Williams pointed to Musial and said, 'There's Stan Musial over there, John Henry. He was one hell of a hitter.' John Henry was skeptical and asked if Musial really was as good as his dad. Ted said he replied, 'Yes, I really think he was.'"

Williams went on to say that their hitting styles were vastly different and that he had more power than Musial. In fact, Williams said, if he had been blessed with Musial's speed, "there wouldn't have been that much comparing," Prime added. But speed, versatility, and reflexes happened to be part of Musial's arsenal, and he used them admirably.

Williams ranked Musial seventh among all-time hitters, comparing him to Shoeless Joe Jackson, the Black Sox' banned star whom Williams constantly pushed for the Hall of Fame despite his murky role in the Black Sox scandal.

"Musial was a slashing, all-around-the-ballpark hitter but he also hit to left-center and certainly to right center quite a bit," Williams said. "That's where he could pull the ball more—and Musial was definitely a guy who learned how to pull the ball. When he first came up he was hitting like he had two strikes all the time. Then he got to where he was taking a pitch and waiting for a certain pitch, and finally he reached the point where he was a lot more selective. Then they didn't know how to pitch him, so they'd try him inside and he'd rip the ball to right. I'm making an educated guess when I make that comparison with Jackson. It's a theory of mine."

Williams also said of Musial: "He was a better all-round hitter than Hank Aaron." And he added, "He was a quiet leader on the field and in the clubhouse and was one of the most universally respected ballplayers of our generation. He wasn't the biggest guy in the world but he was a lithe six-one and 175 pounds, and he was whippy."

Musial, always the first to admit DiMaggio and Williams had been held back by their longer military hitches, once said of Williams: "All he ever wants to do is talk about hitting. I don't say he doesn't know about anything else, but that is always the first thing he always wants to talk about." He also said: "Ted was a great student of baseball. He was the greatest hitter of our era."

But was Williams better than Stan the Man?

"When I get asked about Ted Williams, I always say, 'He was good, too,'" Musial said.


THEY WERE all good. Joe Cronin, who was Williams's manager in the 1946 World Series and the Red Sox' general manager from 1948 through 1958, was one of the voters in the *Sporting News* poll that chose Musial as the Player of the Decade from 1946 through 1955.

Cronin did not vote for his own man. He voted for Stan Musial.

# 27

---

# BAD AIR

JIMMY RUSSELL could not see his players at the other end of the
football field. Donora was known for its fogs, thick and brown and
vile-smelling, but this was like nothing they had ever seen or inhaled.
When Russell realized he could not keep track of his players, he sent them
home.

The air kept getting worse on Friday evening, October 29, 1948.

Verna Duda, the vivacious wife of Musial's high school mentor, Ki
Duda, was serving as Miss Halloween on a parade down McKean Avenue,
tossing apples and candy to the townspeople. The air was bad, but then
again, it was usually bad, so the parade continued.

By Saturday morning, nine people had died.

In the middle of the football game on Saturday afternoon, one player
was urgently instructed by the public-address announcer to rush home.
According to legend, the player's father was dead by the time he got home,
but historians say that part is apocryphal.

The game went to its conclusion, a 27–7 victory for Monongahela City,
and then people went home and discovered Donora had suddenly, in the
middle of a football game, become infamous.

"I was a senior in high school," said Dr. Charles Stacey, who would become the superintendent of schools. "I heard Walter Winchell talk about the
killer smog in Donora, and I said that must have been a different Donora."

Winchell was the radio predecessor to the shock jocks and cable
screamers of the next century. He was likewise known to exaggerate, but in

this case he was entirely accurate. By Saturday night eighteen people were dead.

Devra Davis, author of *When Smoke Ran Like Water,* was an infant in 1948. Years later, as an internationally known scientist and writer, she acknowledged that Donora's industry, thick air and all, had drawn her family to Donora.

"My *zadie* said, 'It smells like money,' " Davis said, using the Yiddish word for grandfather. Her grandfather was a big, strong man who lived to be ninety-seven, but her *bubbe,* her grandmother, was already infirm, from bearing children in the foul air of the Mon Valley.

"When I was very young, I simply assumed that all blue-haired grannies stayed in bed, tethered to oxygen tanks," Davis wrote.

LUKAZS AND Mary Musial were home on Halloween weekend. He had retired in 1943, after a stroke, and had suffered several others after the war.

People collapsing in the street, funerals up and down the main streets, made bad publicity for the steel industry. Once Walter Winchell's rat-a-tat-tat news had ricocheted into the consciousness of America, Roger Blough, the chief counsel for American Steel and Wire, called Michael Neale, the superintendent of the zinc works, at three o'clock on Sunday morning and told him to dead-fire the furnaces—turn them down halfway.

They both knew the situation: A coke oven, or battery, runs above 2,000 degrees Fahrenheit. If it goes below 800 degrees, the bricks will crack. "Once cooled, it can never be restarted," Davis would write. The halfway step would protect the furnace but temporarily reduce the plant's emissions.

Neale took three hours to follow Blough's instructions; only after company officials arrived at his plant did he finally turn down the fires. Fortunately, rain began on Sunday, cutting the thick air, and by Monday, November 2, the mill was able to resume full production. But at least eighteen funerals had been held or planned.

Lukasz Musial grew weaker and was moved to St. Louis, where he was given Dickie's room.

KILLER SMOGS in cities like London were regarded as local. Dozens of people had died in the steel city of Liège, Belgium, during an inversion in 1930, but a world war had rolled through the Meuse Valley since then, and nobody had time to study the cause of the smog.

The Public Health Service labeled the deaths in Donora as "a one-time atmospheric freak." In the age before computers, before the Internet, before curiosity, before outrage, the concepts of "pollution" and "environmental health" had not yet been articulated. Nobody linked Donora to its sister city in death until many years later.

"Zinc is one of those elements that the body needs in very small doses in certain forms, but zinc can be poisonous in larger amounts and other forms," Davis wrote in 2002.

Another material used in the zinc mill is fluorspar, "a rock made of crystals of fluorine tied with calcium," Davis wrote. One sign of excess fluorspar in the air is mottled teeth. "My father had teeth like that," Davis wrote. "We figured he simply hadn't brushed enough as a kid." Many years later, a chemist would find twelve to twenty-five times the normal levels of fluoride in the residents of Donora.

Scientists would learn that large amounts of sulfur leave "distinct marks on the linings of the lungs, but fluoride gases do not," Davis wrote. "They pass right into the bloodstream and attack the heart and other organs, without marring the nasal passages, throat, or lungs. The lungs of those who died in Liège were clean. Nobody noticed."

It would take science half a century to link fluoride gases with what had happened in Donora in 1948.

"Where there are valleys, the colder air from the hills can create an inversion layer that keeps warmer air from rising," Davis would write, describing the "massive, still blanket of cold air over the entire Mon Valley. All the gases from Donora's mills, furnaces, and stoves were unable to rise above the hilltops and began to fill the homes and streets of the town with a blinding fog of coal, coke, and metal fumes."

Davis took a topographical map of her hometown and marked where the eighteen deaths had taken place. "Most of the deaths occurred in the parts of town that sat just under the plume that spewed within a half-mile circle of the zinc mill." The Musial home was well within that circle.

"The fifty people who died in the month following the smog are nowhere counted," Davis wrote. "The thousands who died over the following decade are nowhere counted. And there is no counting of the thousands whom Clarence Mills called the non-killed—all those who went on to suffer in various poorly understood ways."

LYING IN his grandson's bed, Lukasz began to go downhill.

"Our grandfather Musial spoke very little English," Gerry Ashley said. "Dick had to give up his bedroom for our dying grandfather, who died right before Christmas. We knew when he died because Grandmother Musial screamed. We opened our gifts early because we were going back to Donora for Christmas."

Lukasz died on December 19 and the funeral was held at St. Mary's on December 24. Lukasz Musial was buried on the hill above Donora, where the air is relatively good.

# 28

---

# FAMILY LIFE

B Y COINCIDENCE, in the fall of 1948, Stan had agreed to be interviewed by Jack Sher, a writer for *Sport* magazine in New York.
When Sher arrived in mid-December, Musial apologized for having no
time because his father was dying inside the house.

"Every time my dad is with me he gets sick," Musial said, as if somehow
he were more to blame than the toxic air of Donora.

Sher later described the sadness in the house, how Lukasz had left
Donora because of "the smog disaster," but for many years the family did
not link the dying man with his occupation or the Halloween calamity in
Donora.

When the writer from New York showed up at the door, Musial did
something extraordinary for any athlete, any celebrity, then or now: he did
not turn him away. Jack Sher had a job to do, a paycheck to earn. Musial
seemed to honor that.

The Stan Musial of December 1948 was an example of instinctive
grace under pressure. In a moment of crisis, the Musials opened their lives
to the stranger. And while Stan apologized for not having time, Lil, who
rarely gave an interview, sat in the living room and told how she had been
introduced to Stan by his basketball teammate, and her long-standing suspicion that Stan had gravitated to the family store more for cold cuts than
a date.

Sher's article came out in the March 1949 edition of *Sport*, depicting
Musial as a homebody, an ordinary man, but also a great player, destined
to be underappreciated. More than six decades later, Sher's article remains

one of the best glimpses of this very private family. For a writer, it is encouraging to know that something written in the winter of 1948–49 still informs, still touches the heart. It might be the nicest thing ever written about them, because they were so open, so decent.

Somewhat to my surprise, Gerry Ashley had never seen the article, despite the large collection of clippings Lil has apparently kept in the house. I sent Gerry a copy, and it touched off memories, like her grandmother screaming when Lukasz died in Dickie's bed. The sadness of a family endures in print to this day.

During Sher's visit, Lil also introduced their two children to him. "Dickie, who is eight years old, was wearing a bright-red, wee-size Chicago Cardinals football sweater. He is a handsome kid with the fine, dark eyes and hair of his father. Geraldine, the little girl, age four, is small, pert and blonde, like her mother."

Sher described how Mary Musial entered the room, crying, and how her son comforted her. When the doctor arrived, the writer realized it was time to leave, but Musial said, "You'll never get a cab out here this time of night. I'll drive you to Biggie's. He'll get you a cab and take care of you."

Biggie was Julius Garagnani, the restaurateur, who was in the process of taking in Musial as a partner. Biggie invited Sher to sit in a booth, and he described what a nice man Musial was—how his telephone was still listed seven years after coming to the majors, how he took calls from fans at all hours. Biggie was gracious, a surrogate family member, but the writer went back to his hotel room that night convinced he could not possibly do his story while Musial's father was dying.

The next morning, the phone rang and the booming voice of Bob Broeg told Sher not to leave town. A lot of Musial's friends were going to be available.

It was a few days before Christmas. Cardinals were playing with their children and shopping, resting their weary bodies and also working at second jobs, the way ballplayers did back then.

Nevertheless, friends spent time with the writer from out of town: Red Schoendienst, Marty Marion, Terry Moore, Sam Breadon, Ollie Vanek, the clubhouse man Butch Yatkeman, and Ed and Sue Carson, two neighbors who had become close friends.

ONE VISION of Musial came from Robert E. Hannegan, the former post-master general of the United States, who briefly owned a share of the Cardinals. Hannegan had visited the Musials in the home they had purchased that fall, at 5447 Childress Avenue.

Hannegan told how he had paid a courtesy call and found Musial as fully involved as any new home owner.

"He showed me through every room in the house, as though I were his next-door neighbor. He told me all the plans for the house, the color scheme, what sort of curtains his wife was going to put up, how the kids' rooms would look, everything, right down to the rugs. I never felt so much at home in a house."

Musial had expressed some ambivalence about committing to St. Louis, perhaps because he felt he should be living closer to his parents.

"Frankly, I would just as soon have returned to Donora, or, at least, the Pittsburgh area close by our people," Musial said in his autobiography, "but our son Dick was eight and we didn't like him to have to miss or change schools. We had met many fine people in St. Louis. When Dick told Lil he wished we could live there year-round, that clinched it."

Hannegan told Sher about his salary negotiations with Musial right after the 1948 season, when Musial dug in for a base of $50,000 a year for two years, with a $5,000 bonus per year if the Cardinals surpassed an attendance of 900,000 (which they did, both years).

"All I'll tell you is that in all my years of experience in business deals I never talked to a man who was so humble but firm, so honest and definite in his opinions of his ability. There wasn't an unpleasant moment," Hannegan said, not bothering to note that Musial's pay was far below that of Williams and DiMaggio.

Hannegan also did not volunteer that he had been toying with selling Musial to the Pirates for $250,000 to ease his own finances. That detail did not fit into the narrative of the great loyalty between the Cardinals ownership and its greatest player.

But Hannegan did tell Sher how proud Lukasz had been of his son. Whenever the father was around the ballpark, Hannegan had directed autograph-seeking fans to the modest little man.

"That's Stan Musial's dad. There's an autograph you should get," Hannegan would say. And the fans would fuss over the older man, who never, in his days at the zinc mill, could have imagined signing his name for strangers.

"And now," Hannegan told Sher, "I'll have to leave you. I'm going to catch a plane to Donora to the funeral of a friend of mine, Lukasz Musial."

ANOTHER OF Sher's stops was at the Carsons'. Ed was "a large, soft-spoken, round-faced man who works for a machinery manufacturing concern," and Sue was a "pretty, blue-eyed brunette, vivacious and genuine. They are a typical American family with a modest home."

Ed Carson had recognized Musial at the lunch counter of the Fair-grounds Hotel when Musial first came up in 1941, and they had gotten along—"talking, friendly, like a couple of ordinary guys would."

He described the private Stan Musial: "Whenever he wants to get Lil laughing, he'll do his strip. This consists of removing his shirt, sucking in his stomach until it touches his backbone and then holding his breath. It doesn't sound funny to tell, but it's quite a sight and it always breaks Lillian up."

Sue said she had seen Stan eat seven sandwiches or eight ears of corn, and praised Lil as "a marvelous cook, does all the cooking herself, making complicated Russian and Polish dishes." She recalled, "One night last year, when it was 110 degrees in the shade, Lil had a party of fifteen people and their kids at her house. She did all the cooking for the entire gang and it was the best food I've ever tasted. Stan's sister comes to visit them often and spends all her time baking cakes for her brother. I've never seen any-one bake so many cakes."

Sue described how Stan was shy but would warm up at parties, a trait that would follow him forever: in a corner, hands in pockets, until later in the evening when he would pull out his harmonica.

She also described the banter that went on between Stan and Lil. Not known to be demonstrative toward his wife in public, Stan once gave her a compliment during a small party: "Lil, you're the most gorgeous wife a ballplayer ever had."

Sue then teased him: "Stan, why don't you give your wife a rose?"

Lil responded, "If Stan did give me a rose, it'd probably have a bug in it."

Sue Carson, in December 1948, defined Musial to the writer: "I've got a title for your story. You ought to call it, 'He Doesn't Know It.' I mean by this that Stanley doesn't realize what a famous person he is. He is exactly the same as the day we met him when he was almost unknown."

On his way to the airport to fly to the funeral, Musial called Biggie and asked him to convey his apologies to Sher for not having more time for him.

"You ought to get to know what kind of a guy he is," Biggie told the writer.

The last paragraph of the article goes like this: " 'I got to know him,' I said. 'I got to know what sort of a guy Stan Musial is.' "

The title of Sher's article: "The Stan Musial Nobody Knows."


STAN MUSIAL and Biggie's would link the two men forever, like Martin and Lewis, like Sonny and Cher. The name still resonates in St. Louis the way Toots Shor does in New York—a memory from another age, never been anything like it since.

Julius Garagnani was a St. Louis character, straight off the Hill, the Italian part of town. Even today, some old-time St. Louisans can imitate his rough-hewn "dems" and "doses."

Biggie was the son of a miner but a city boy. There are suggestions he worked for bootleggers as a teenager in the late days of Prohibition, which would not have been that unusual. Later he moved into patronage jobs stemming from his Democrat contacts, serving as a delegate at two Democratic conventions and helping get at least one friend appointed to a judgeship. He developed a close friendship with Warren E. Hearnes, who in 1965 would become the first Missouri governor to serve two full terms, with Biggie raising over $80,000 in campaign donations.

Perhaps inevitably, given his Italian name, there were suggestions that Biggie had connections to the mob. But Musial had influential friends watching his back at all times; one well-connected pal said recently that Biggie had been checked out in every important way.

"If he hadn't, we'd have pulled Stan's coat," the friend said not long ago. "Biggie was a restaurant guy."

Garagnani was thirty-four when he met Musial around 1947—"larger than life," was the way Tom Ashley, Musial's former son-in-law, described him. "He had total control of the operation. A lot of his relatives were working there, so you never saw funny business at the bar. He was a true character."

"A bit rough around the edges," Gerry Ashley said about Biggie, quickly adding, "To me, he was always nice."

Biggie and Stanley met somewhere—the ballpark, the golf course, maybe in St. Pete. Before long, Stan and Lil were welcome in Biggie's restaurant on Chippewa. The men began playing golf, and somewhere on a fairway or in the clubhouse one of them brought up the restaurant business. Perhaps because of his Donora mentor, Frank Pizzica, Musial already had an image of himself as an entrepreneur, not just a front man.

"I had a moderate amount of capital to invest," Musial said in his autobiography. "My principal asset was my baseball name."

"Biggie said, 'You get an accountant and I'll get an accountant,' " Tom Ashley said. "They met the next day at lunch time and the two accountants agreed on how much the business was worth, and how much 50 percent would be worth. Biggie said, 'You don't have to pay anything down. You'll pay me back in profits.' They made it back in a year."

The partnership was formed in January 1949, with Musial's share coming to $25,000.

"Biggie and my dad worked with a handshake all those years. They never had a contract," Gerry Ashley said, adding, "My dad always told this story: 'You know how to make a small fortune in the restaurant business? You start with a big one.' "

The truth was, Stan and Biggie's, as it was popularly known, soon rivaled the famous Italian restaurants on the Hill, serving that major St. Louis culinary invention, toasted ravioli, which had become popular around 1943 or 1944 at Oldani's and then at Ruggeri's.

The restaurant caught on. Fans could drive hundreds of miles for a ball game and hope for a glimpse of Musial at mealtime. The place became something of a hangout for St. Louis athletes.

The young catcher from the Hill, Larry Berra, spurned by Branch Rickey, came home after the 1948 season with the Yankees and chatted up a part-time waitress at Stan and Biggie's named Carmen Short. Carmen would always remember that Yogi clumped into the restaurant, still wearing his golf spikes. Well, Yogi would rumble, he and the guys had just finished a round of golf; what else was he supposed to be wearing? This rather clattery first meeting led to a wedding early in 1949, and one of the most enduring baseball marriages ever.

A lot of epic encounters took place at Stan and Biggie's.

"I had my first sour cream and chives on a baked potato at the old place," Tim McCarver recalled with obvious enthusiasm. Bob Grim, an older pitcher passing through the Cardinals, invited McCarver to dinner— "fall of 1959. I was seventeen years old and didn't have a clue about life or anything," McCarver said.

"Stan put a lot of time in the restaurant," McCarver continued. "They weren't open on a Sunday, but it was common in those days to play day games on Saturday and Stan was there after the game. The food was terrific."

Everybody agreed the relationship between Biggie and Stanley was fair and equal.

"Biggie just loved Stan," McCarver said.

Another view of Biggie comes from a strange article in *Sport* in July 1950: "My Partner Stan Musial," by Biggie Garagnani, as told to J. Roy Stockton. A prominent columnist in St. Louis, Stockton employed the exaggerated malapropisms that Ring Lardner and other celebrated American writers used for ethnic characters of America. New York columnists were always writing about Greek diner countermen using exaggerated accents, and some of the syntax attributed to African Americans in midcentury is beyond parody and into racial stereotyping.

Within Stockton's Lardneresque language is the dead-serious, mother-wit, tired-and-poor ambition of Julius Garagnani. No angel, probably, but no fool, either, in talking about his partner:

I don't charge him nothing for good will because I'm smart enough to know he'll have more good will than I got.

He is very conscious-stricken about answering all mail.

The only things he don't pay any attention to is unanimous letters. He just throws them in the wastebasket.

The real Biggie was not far from the ghosted Biggie. For a while, Jack Buck was the host of a talk show emanating from the restaurant, often using guests in town for baseball or the famed Muny Opera in nearby Forest Park. One night Arthur Godfrey was a little late, so Buck grabbed Biggie to help fill time. One old-timer remembered it this way:

"Say, Big, have you been over to the new planetarium in Forest Park? It's been open for two weeks now."

After a long pause, Biggie replied in stentorian tones, "No, Jack, I never cared much for all those fishes and whales and stuff!"

There was a quick cut to a commercial, until Godfrey blessedly arrived.

By all accounts, Musial was a hands-on presence who wanted to know how the business worked, wanted to know cuts of meat in the freezer. His expertise would pay off when he would direct teammates to the best steaks all over the league.

The restaurant became Stanley's other place of business, as important to him in its way as the ballpark was. He knew he might have a long life ahead of him, and wanted to have control of it. He and Biggie branched out to other restaurants as well as hotels in St. Louis, Miami, and Clearwater, Florida.

"Stan lifted himself up," Tom Ashley said. A friend, Clarence Diehl, who had a construction business, would meet at the restaurant and talk business. Diehl, who would eventually build the second version of Stan and Biggie's, understood Stan's conservative streak, his desire not to be greedy or get caught up in wild schemes.

EVEN THOUGH he lived only a few blocks from the restaurant, Musial was not around much to help with homework or discipline the children. Lil sometimes blamed Biggie for her husband's absences.

"He and my mom didn't get along," Gerry said. "Biggie wanted my dad to go to the restaurant and my dad would go at lunchtime and for an hour and a half in the evening, so that meant he wasn't home."

Musial insisted he would always get home "so I could say good night to the kids."

Gerry has fond memories of toasted ravioli and spumoni in the form of a baseball at the restaurant, but she also learned she had to share her father with the public.

"He'd be there for the lunch crowd and the evening crowd because he knew it increased his earning," she said.

The family soon moved from their first tiny house on Childress to a four-bedroom house on Westway Road, a few blocks up the hill, making sure to stay in the same parish. The house was not ostentatious, with its kitchen, breakfast room, and family room all blended into one, and a small dining room they rarely used.

Two more children followed: Janet, five years younger than Gerry, and Jeanne, nine years younger than Janet. Dick was already on his way to Notre Dame when Jeanne was born, meaning there was rarely a time when all four were living full-time under the same roof. This could produce a *Rashomon* effect—everybody might have a different version of childhood. Lil's theory was that every one of her children was an only child, special, unique.

Since Lil had grown up in a large family, and so had Stan, four children, spaced well apart, seemed quite modest by the standards of 1920s Donora. Lil had grown up in a household where her father was a presence, even when he was working long hours downstairs in the store. She had to adjust to life with a husband who was mobbed for his autograph at the ballpark, who chatted up customers at the restaurant, who went on road trips for a week or two at a time. Gerry Ashley and her former husband both praise Lil for running the family.

In a rare interview, Lil once talked a bit about her husband, saying he was pretty even-tempered but a useful disciplinarian when he was around. "Sometimes if they do something wrong and he raises his voice just a little, they stand there with their mouths open, as if to say 'Look at Daddy. What's the matter with Daddy?' "

Lil continued, "Stan takes a personal interest in everything about our children. . . . Stan never loses his temper, although sometimes he gets a little impatient when I'm late. Early in our marriage I'd get annoyed when Stan had to leave home for banquets—but I soon realized I must accept that as part of his life."

Gerry learned to live with a father who was not always home. "In those days, men were away a lot and the mother had to be the disciplinarian. My father was like the backup disciplinarian: 'If you don't go to bed, I'm taking my belt off.' He'd take his belt off and swing it on the ground. I think everybody is afraid of their own father. You don't cross your father."

Gerry did not say Stan used the belt. He just displayed it, Mr. Deep Voice, the theoretical enforcer for Lil, who did the heavy lifting.

"My father was a smart businessman," Gerry said. "My mom, she could run a company. She could be a CEO. She knows when things are missing around the house. He was a great driving force. It was tough to be a baseball wife. The players were always on trains. The wives had to do everything for themselves."

The telephone had been invented, of course, but cell phones, personal computers, and other gadgets were unimaginable, meaning that when ballplayers were on the road, the wives "were on their own," as Gerry put it.

Stan did have his useful side at home. Lil praised him for taking care of the shrubbery and being able to panel a room, and she said he dabbled with a camera and could play a piano by ear.

The Musials' lives seem straight out of *Life, Reader's Digest,* or the official handbook of the Eisenhower years. Gerry would become sentimental about life on Westway: her young and energetic parents, friendly neighbors, common backyards, picnics in the summer—"really nice, some of our best memories," she said.

Gerry recalled how one of her friends reached sixteen and was able to drive into the countryside and load up on fireworks for the Fourth of July. The children would set off firecrackers all day and then Daddy would come home from work—in this case the ballpark—and set off the big stuff after dark.

"Rockets, in a bottle," Gerry recalled, giggling. "It was kind of dangerous if you think of it—a talented ballplayer setting off rockets."

At Christmas, Stanley would climb up on the roof and install figures of Santa Claus and the reindeer, plus lights. "One time he won third prize in St. Louis Hills," Gerry proudly recalled.

"It was a nice neighborhood," Tom Ashley said. "No fences. Upper-middle-class, not fancy. Stan was just one of the guys."

The Musials were friendly with their neighbors, had friends who were neither celebrities nor ballplayers. Claude Keefe, an insurance salesman from Minnesota, was a good friend who taught Musial his first magic tricks.

Clarence Diehl and his wife, Gerry, plus George and Mary Strode, would sometimes keep the Musial children when Stan and Lil were on a trip.

"I think the Diehls and Strodes were a good respite from some of the more glamorous people they took trips with after my father's career was over," Gerry Ashley said.

Stan was a regular at the early Mass on Sunday and religious holidays. The children went to parochial school, observed the sacraments, dressed well for school and church and any public outing.

Musial had learned from his mentors, had developed an old-fashioned guildsman's view of his craft, an ideal of how he should look and act. His wife and his children were part of his self-image.

"Until very recently I dressed up to go to the ballpark," Gerry said. "That was our station in life."

Stan smoked sometimes; so did a lot of people in those days. He took a drink or two—social drinking by the standards of the time. He was known to tell a bawdy story, spoke the vernacular of the clubhouse.

"My father isn't perfect," Gerry said. "I mean, what father is?"

An example of imperfection? Musial performed in a driver safety video, but Gerry said, "That was funny because he was such a wild driver. I remember as a little girl, they didn't have the highways the way they do now. They only had two-lane highways. I'm still terrified to this day.

"We used to drive down to spring training, you know how far that is, how long it takes, St. Louis to St. Petersburg.

"When I was old enough to drive, my mom would say, 'Please take your father to the airport,' and he would leave at the last minute. Oh my God, it was a wild ride. *Mr. Toad's Wild Ride.* Now in the last few years, he doesn't drive anymore so he says, 'Hey, you're driving too fast.' Done a complete turnaround."


IN OTHER ways, Stan and Lil were not the prototypical suburban family.

"My parents were so glamorous," Gerry said, recalling Stan and Lil all dressed up, going out.

"It was so normal for him to be my father, for him to do great things," Gerry said. "We'd wait for him after the games and all these people would wait, just to get his autograph, and then he comes, just running out of the clubhouse, and we would take off with him, running, because he was our ride home. The crowd would shove us out of the way because they thought we were autograph seekers, but then you would get in the car, and they would surround the car and you could barely drive off.

"In those days, there was no secret passage the way they might have now. He was across the street from Sportsman's Park and, you know, we could barely drive. He just signed and signed and he would say, 'What do they do with all of those? We must have signed a million of them by now.'

"I remember one day, we were in a convertible," she continued. "This kid just kept hanging on the side and I said, 'We're going to drive off, you'd better get off,' and he said, 'I can't, my finger's stuck in the door.'" Fortunately, Stan got the message before he gunned the car.

Gerry said she did not feel resentment about sharing her father's time with the crowds. That was the deal. "You knew you had to share him, and that was okay, and once you got home he was Dad. You learned how to share, you had to."

There is a famous story about Lil pushing a fan who had knocked her down, and Stan telling Lil not to shove his fans. Gerry has heard Lil's more complete version.

"It was during World War II and she had silk stockings and they were really hard to get in those days," Gerry said, alluding to the wartime shortages of luxuries like nylons. "The fans were running after him and one of them knocked her down. She got up and she had ripped her stockings, and she said, 'You made me rip my stockings.'" Apparently Lil did give the fan a shove. What woman wouldn't have?

STAN AND Lil were very much part of the gang, according to teammates like Hank Sauer, an older slugger who played for the Cardinals in 1956.

"He'd always be holding open house," Sauer told Roger Kahn. "He has a tremendous family. I mean, they're the nicest family and home and wife you've ever seen."

Sauer added that if somebody's child broke something, the parent would start to scold, but Musial would say, "Never mind what they do. Just let them alone."

This was a man whose first childhood plaything had been a homemade rag ball from his mother. Given some of the less pleasant moments between Lukasz and Stashu, Musial now had a chance to run a house where children could enjoy themselves.

"There are kids all over the place," Sauer told Kahn. "You go to his house and you step on kids everywhere. 'That's what my home is for,' Stan says. 'It's for kids, yours and mine.' "

The neighborhood was a projection of their home—comfortable, accessible. Boys would ride their bicycles up and down Westway, hoping to spot Stan Musial mowing his lawn.

When Gerry met her brother, Dick, in St. Louis in 2008, they took what she called "a nostalgia drive" to the old neighborhood of St. Louis Hills and were thrilled to see the Ted Drewes frozen custard stand, a landmark of their youth, still open on Chippewa. The brother and sister, close in age and experience, felt reinforced about what a nice childhood they had had.

FOR ROMAN Catholics, the town was divided into parishes. While they lived on Childress, Dick and Gerry remained at St. Gabriel the Archangel, but after St. Raphael the Archangel opened in 1950, closer to their home, the family transferred there.

"You would say, 'Where do you go?' " said Ben Vanek, the son of Ollie Vanek.

The Vaneks attended Mary Magdalen, within walking distance of the Musials' parish, but the two families had different lives.

"My dad was interested in his territory, his bird-dog scouts, where he was going, who he could sign," Ben Vanek said. "It's a day-to-day job."

Fans would get hysterical, could jab out somebody's eye with a pen in the rush to get Stan the Man's signature, but Ben Vanek felt insulated from hero worship.

"I hate to get on my soapbox, but we have elevated professional athletes much higher than it used to be," Ben said. "I mean, if you saw Musial's house, it was not a mansion, it was a house among other houses. Neighbors right next to him. No security fence out front. You probably could walk up, paperboy or something, walk right up to the door, get paid, give him change, stuff like that. Fact was, a couple of scouts lived in the area.

"Most ballplayers were not excessively paid," Vanek continued. "The average guy was making $50,000, now it's $1–2 million, $10–15 million. There wasn't that discrepancy. They were making good money, but not twenty, thirty, forty times what the average fellow was making."

The son of the scout and the son of the superstar played football against each other for rival high schools—Dick at Christian Brothers, Ben at St. Louis University High.

"Dick and I were not close," Vanek said, making it sound like a result of attending different schools, nothing personal. "Dick hung around with his group at mixers and stuff like that. We'd say hello and talk for a little bit, but that's just the way it was.

"Nobody was looking at him as the son of the fantastic first baseman of the St. Louis Cardinals. He was just another kid. At that time, St. Louis was full of all-girls schools and all-boys schools. During social season, there were mixers, dances, guys from St. Mary's, guys from SLU and CBC, everybody was cordial. You were a rival on the field but not a rival on the street."

If harsh words were exchanged, Vanek said, "it was more like 'Your grandma wears combat boots.' It wasn't a big deal then. He was a ballplayer and my father was a scout. They did their jobs. Everyday life. I don't think anybody made a big deal of being Stan Musial's son.

"When you put your shoulder pads on or your baseball uniform, you wanted to beat those guys because they were your rival, but at the end of the game you could just as soon go out and have a hamburger. You didn't give 'em the finger or anything, although it got to that. You wanted bragging rights. Once you got past it, there wasn't anything. It wasn't an issue. . . . I can honestly say I can't remember a fight breaking out. It was a kinder, gentler time."

———

IT WAS not easy being Richard Stanley Musial, first name from a heroic pitcher and family benefactor, second name from a celebrity father. Dick's early childhood was spent in Daytona Beach, Springfield, Rochester, and shuttling between Donora and St. Louis. He was always going to have a ticklish relationship with baseball.

Was he going to hit like his daddy? Who could? Multigenerational baseball families were rare in that day, although Donora did produce a lineage of Griffeys from the thwarted Buddy to the very fine Ken to the excellent Junior. Recently there have been Bells and Boones and Hairstons all over the major leagues, but not in those days.

"Dick isn't interested in baseball, and in a way I'm glad," Musial told a reporter in 1958. "I knew George Sisler and he was a fine baseball player. His father, George, though, was a finer baseball player."

Back in 1946, Musial had been a teammate of Dick Sisler, the younger son of George senior. Dick was a lovely man who did not hit enough, which meant Stan had to move to first base. Later, Sisler had a fine career, hitting a pennant-winning homer for the Phillies in 1950 and managing the Reds, but it was a fact of life that he could not hit like his daddy; neither could Dick Musial.

"And this fact Dick never could live down, or live up to. It hurt him," Musial said of his son. "Besides, Mrs. Musial and myself have always believed in letting our children lead their own lives. The boy is a fine student and he earnestly desires to be a doctor. I think it's wonderful."

Dick did not become a doctor, but he was an athlete and did go to college, fulfilling the dream that Stan had been maintaining for twenty years. Given Lil's short stature, Dick turned out to be an inch or two shorter than Stan but very much an athlete, running track at Notre Dame.

The star quarterback at Christian Brothers was a rugged, rangy kid named Mike Shannon—now a gravel-voiced broadcaster for the hometown team, earlier a regular with the Cardinals in the sixties before an injury cut short his career. The Cardinals called him "Moon" because he was a bit spacey.

In high school, Mike Shannon was a star. During one game he heard fans from St. Louis University mocking his backfield teammate.

"Those kids used to try to kill Stan Musial's kid," Shannon recalled.

"And Dick was very talented. They kept saying, 'Give it to Musial, give it to Musial,' and I said, 'Okay, you guys want Musial?' "

Down near the goal line, Shannon called the money play, handing the ball to his teammate.

Touchdown, Musial.

"And I said, 'You guys want any more of that Musial?' "

# 29

## DAY OFF IN CHICAGO

JOHN BISKUPSKI was running a Little League on the North Side of Chicago in the mid-fifties. Most of the boys in the league were of Polish descent, and their hero was Stanislaus Musial, perhaps the most visible Polish American in the twentieth century, unless you wanted to count Liberace. However, the pianist with the wavy hair could not hit like Musial.

In a surge of ethnic pride, John Biskupski and his brother, Joseph, sent a note to Musial, saying they ran a league not far from Wrigley Field and would be honored to meet him sometime. They would have settled for shaking his hand at Wrigley, telling him how much it meant to them to read his frequent references to the polka and pierogis.

What the brothers did not expect was that one day, while they were hitting grounders to their young players, Stan Musial would materialize. The Cardinals had a day off in Chicago, and there he was.

"The kids were all thrilled to have a famous ballplayer there," John Biskupski's son, M. B. B. Biskupski, said years later.

Musial inquired if the kids had uniforms, and the brothers said no. Then Musial asked if they had bats and balls and the brothers again said no. At that point, Musial took out his checkbook and started writing.

M. B. B. Biskupski does not know the amount of the check—he was living elsewhere, since his parents were separated—but he often heard his father and uncle tell the story.

"Musial was spoken of with great respect for what he symbolized for all of us," said Biskupski, now the holder of the Stanislaus A. Blejwas Endowed Chair in Polish and Polish American Studies at Central Connecticut State University. He grew up hearing Polish spoken at home and also endured Polish jokes on the street and in the media. Musial had been an answer to the stereotypes. "In addition to being a fine ballplayer, he had the reputation for being a fine gentleman, somebody the people could admire," Biskupski said.

The professor added that his own young son is named Stanislaus—partially after an uncle and a dear friend, he said, but also after the man who once showed up at the Little League field on the North Side of Chicago on a day off.

# 30

## PRIME TIME

H E HAD always been a hitter. In 1948, Musial became a slugger.
Baseball has had similar transformations in more recent times, with hitters suddenly discovering their inner Babe, their latent Henry, in their late twenties. If Musial had staged his metamorphosis in the steroid generation, there would have been demands that he be tested on a daily basis—*get this man a Dixie cup!* Except he never bulked up.

Suddenly Stan Musial could hit home runs. He had come up to the majors as an insecure stripling, slapping at the ball to avoid being exposed and shipped back to Donora. Then during the war, to satisfy the admirals and the sailors in Pearl Harbor, he had exaggerated his crouch, stayed in it longer, and swung for the fences. Now, after Dr. Hyland removed his appendix and tonsils in October 1947, Musial began hitting the ball farther, more often.

"Stash seemed to stand up much straighter then," Terry Moore said, referring to the slap hitter who came from nowhere in 1941. "He didn't crouch nearly so much. That's something I think he picked up during the war."

Moore added, "But if you ask me, I think he'd hit over .300 on one leg with one eye closed, crouched over or standin' as straight as a barber pole. He's just a hitter, that's all."

The explanation for his power surge went beyond maturation and a shift in his technique. But Musial has suggested another reason: he saw Ralph Kiner and Johnny Mize hitting home runs and getting paid for it. Kiner came out of the service in 1946 and hit 23 homers—and then hit 271 more in the next six years, to become the highest-paid player in the National League at $90,000 in 1951, while Musial was making $75,000 plus an attendance bonus. He wanted some of that home run money, and he began circumventing the pitchers' strategy. "Pitchers generally had thrown high and tight to me, but now they were throwing low and away, a tough pitch to pull."

When he hit 4 homers in his first twenty-one games in 1948, he figured he might be good for 20 that season, one more than his highest total the year before.

Instead, he hit 39, 36, 28, 32, 21, 30, 35, 33, 27, and 29 homers in the next decade. From the age of twenty-seven to the age of thirty-six, he was a different hitter than he had been in his first five seasons, Not only that, but after the separate surgeries in the autumn of 1947, he produced batting averages of .376, .338, .346, .355, and .336, plus four batting championships in five seasons—one of the greatest spurts by any hitter ever.

Musial was also named Most Valuable Player for a third time, missing the Triple Crown by a narrow margin after he hit a home run in a game that was rained out and nullified, leaving him one behind Kiner and Mize. He also tied Ty Cobb's record by making five hits in a game four times in one season.

He still did not think of himself as a slugger and rarely intentionally swung for a home run because he said it made him overanxious, but he did drop his hands down to the knob to provide more leverage, more power. His slender body was surprisingly powerful, and he seemed to have an inner discipline and superior muscle memory. He figured out how to get more torque from an increased crouch.

After the postwar surge in 1946, Musial realized he would have to dig into his slugger's crouch in order to carry the Cardinals. Moore was just about done, Marion's back had given way, and the Cardinals could not keep pace with the Dodgers.

The cause was obvious. Former commissioner Fay Vincent said he once asked Musial about his perceptions once Jackie Robinson and the other black players joined the Dodgers.

"He said, 'Yeah, Commissioner, once the Dodgers integrated, we couldn't do it in St. Louis. We would never win again.' "

The timidity of their owners and executives doomed the Cardinals to become also-rans for the rest of the Musial generation. Management was surely affected by the racial attitudes of the border states, left over from the Civil War. St. Louis was still the gateway of the major leagues, with a loyal following to the south and west; its fans would listen on the radio and drive long distances to catch a game, but the region was not exactly petitioning the Cardinals to sign a black player.

The Browns' front office, just down the hallway in Sportsman's Park, signed a couple of black players, probably for a quick boost of attendance, which did not work out. Other teams were more committed: Cleveland signed Larry Doby, the Giants hit the jackpot with Willie Mays, the Boston Braves signed a slim kid with quick wrists named Henry Aaron, and the Reds found a man in Oakland named Frank Robinson.

Asked why the Cardinals were so slow to integrate, Musial once said: "You know, that was the decision up to the front office."

A few franchises were slow, including the Yankees, not that it hurt them much. The Phillies would win a pennant in 1950, playing the Yankees in the last all-white Series of the century. And the Red Sox became the last major-league team to bring up a black player, Pumpsie Green in 1959, twelve years after Robinson. The Sox begrudgingly gave Robinson a phony tryout in 1945 but couldn't wait to get him out of Fenway Park.

The Cardinals just bumbled along. Quincy Trouppe, scouting for the Cardinals in the spring of 1953, recommended a shortstop with the Kansas City Monarchs in the Negro League. The Cardinals dispatched another scout who sent back the word: "I don't think he is a major league prospect. He can't hit, he can't run, he has a pretty good arm but it's a scatter arm. I don't like him." And that was how the Cubs, and not the Cardinals, came to sign Ernie Banks.

Elston Howard might have loved to sign with his hometown Cardinals, but he became the first black Yankee in 1955. Watching his booming right-handed drives get caught in Yankee Stadium's Death Valley, Howard could only visualize his shots cannonading around Sportsman's Park.

Howard's widow, Arlene, has said her husband would run into Musial at the gym or sports banquets and would ask for advice about his career or contract negotiations. Musial was always kind, she said. A nice man.

In addition to losing out on potential teammates like Banks and

Howard, Musial was deprived of the tentative white-black dynamics taking place on other teams. Dixie Walker got to play with Jackie Robinson for one year and quickly came to respect him. The Cardinals finally brought up a black player in 1954, but Tom Alston, a large first baseman, was just not up to it, and that set them back even longer.

While Musial became the great player of his league, the Dodgers won pennants in 1947, 1949, 1952, 1953, 1955, and 1956. The resentments from the Durocher era remained as Robinson evolved into an intense and physical competitor.

"The only time that we would talk in a way was when we had to take a picture together," Musial said. "We both were leading the league but personally I didn't know him and I didn't get to talk to him too much."

Musial could not help chatting with Roy Campanella, the Dodgers' wise catcher, who was half Italian and half black.

"He had something to say every time I came to the plate, you know. 'I don't know how we can handle ya,' or something like that," Musial said.

As the Cardinals slipped backward, some of them still maintained a racial edge to their comments.

"We'd watch 'em in the dugout," said Don Newcombe. "Wisecracks, call names. I could see from the mound when I got there in '49. You never saw guys like Musial or Schoendienst. They never showed you up. The man went about his job and did it damn well and never had the need to sit in the dugout and call a black guy a bunch of names, because he was trying to change the game and make it what it should have been in the first place, a game for all people."

THE CARDINALS' paralysis toward black players came during a series of turnovers in ownership. Breadon bowed out in November 1947, looking to settle his estate, and would die of prostate cancer in mid-1949 at the age of seventy-two.

The new owners were Robert E. Hannegan, a former postmaster general, and Fred Saigh, a real estate investor. Hannegan lasted one year and continued Breadon's tactics of selling off players to raise cash, then became ill and sold his share to Saigh, dying on October 6, 1949.

Musial the businessman learned how to negotiate his salary from dealing with all these owners. He had committed a gaffe with Breadon early on
when he said he would have to try even harder with some of the stars away
at war; that cost him a few dollars. Breadon came to respect Musial during
the Pasquel frolics of 1946, even when Musial squawked about the raise
Breadon tried to pass off as a one-time bonus among good friends.

Musial's pose toward the owners was that he was not greedy and knew
he was living better than he ever could have imagined. But he learned to
define what was fair for him, particularly in the "adjustment" he had negotiated with Hannegan in 1948, including the attendance bonus. In 1949,
Saigh paid him $50,000 per year for two years, with a bonus of $5,000 per
year if the Cardinals went over 900,000 paid admissions. This was an astute
judgment by Musial, operating without an agent and anticipating the postwar boom in attendance. The Cardinals drew over a million each year from
1946 through 1951, when Musial was paid $75,000 plus the $5,000 attendance bonus, although he had to wait for the postwar Wage Stabilization
Board to approve his raises.

"He had always approached the subject logically and in a businesslike
manner," Saigh said in 1952. "I think the experience of operating his own
restaurant has made him conscious of some of the problems of management."

On Valentine's Day 1952, Saigh pulled a publicity stunt by calling in
whatever the media swarm was like in those days and proffering a blank
contract to Stanley, who had waited to be the last Cardinal to sign.

"I told him that anything short of his owning the St. Louis Cardinals the
next morning was all right with me," Saigh said. It is hard to imagine Tom
Yawkey coming up with a gimmick like that involving Williams, or the grim
burghers who owned the Yankees acting like that with the suspicious
DiMaggio.

Did Saigh sandbag Musial into being the polite son-husband-father figure, or was the scene prearranged, thereby making Stanley a much better
actor than anybody had realized? Musial never said. He went along with it,
either way.

"Mr. Saigh, I have been well satisfied with my contracts in the past and
I think I am going to be satisfied with my 1952 contract with the same
terms in 1951—if that is satisfactory," Musial said as flashbulbs popped.

Afterward, Harry Caray, the bumptious broadcaster, told Saigh in private, "You must be a helluva fine crap-shooter, too."

Not that good, it turned out. In January 1953, Saigh was convicted of income tax evasion and ultimately spent time in prison; he had to sell the club to the Anheuser-Busch company.

THE OWNERS came and went. Baseball remained a tight little world in the decade before expansion—eleven road games in seven parks, six cities if you combined New York and Brooklyn. Musial lived a familiar and comfortable routine. He knew the angles of the ballparks, knew the ushers, knew the fans, knew the regional accents, knew the bell captains.

As youngsters, Stan had lived on cabbage and Red had lived on squirrel. Now they knew the headwaiters; now they appreciated the menus.

"I think about that sometimes when Stan and I are ordering the biggest and freshest lobster flown in from Maine or are cutting into choice strips of sirloin steak," Schoendienst said in midcareer. "They're wonderful, the eating experiences we've had and they're part of our getting along so well together."

Other players came to think of Musial as a worldly star who knew the circuit.

"When we were on the road, we'd look for new places to eat," Hank Sauer once said. "We'd use a Diner's Club card and ask people where the best restaurants were. Musial really knows food. He can always tell the good cuts of meat from the bad ones. In New York, we'd go to the shows."

Ralph Kiner recognized Musial as a kindred soul in the big cities. "The Pirates would be in New York and the Cardinals were playing Brooklyn and we were playing a lot more day games in those days," Kiner said. He would take a few teammates to Bertolotti's, a landmark restaurant on Third Street in Greenwich Village, known for its Bohemian atmosphere and Italian restaurants.

"I'd see Musial and Red at one table, the two of them, and I'd be with some of the Pirates at another table, and we happened to meet," Kiner said. The code of the day said players did not fraternize with opponents, but Stanley and Red would salute Kiner.

Jim Brosnan, a pitcher with the Cardinals for part of 1958 and 1959, ran into Stan and Red at a midtown restaurant. They seemed impressed he knew about the place and introduced him to their dinner companion, an actor whom Brosnan does not identify but probably was Horace McMahon, a friend of Musial's. When Stan and Red left, the actor came over and sat and chatted with Brosnan.

"That was a real nice thing that Stan and Red did," Brosnan thought. "The two of them had passed along this TV star to me. It was the kind of thing you did if you were a Cardinal"—or if you were Stan and Red.

Brosnan later wrote a wry and literate book, *The Long Season,* about his view from the bullpen; he retained his impression of the kind way Stanley treated people.

WITH MUSIAL, it was a fraternity that included just about anybody putting on a uniform. At the end of the 1949 season, a wispy infielder named Wayne Terwilliger made his first start against the Cardinals.

"Early in the game, I went out to second base from our dugout and Stan was coming in from left field and as we crossed the pitcher's mound, I thought, 'There he is, Stan Musial, I watched him play,' " Terwilliger recalled. "And as I got to him, he said, 'Hi, Wayne, how's it going?' or something like that, and it really startled me. I don't think I mumbled anything really but I thought, 'Geez, Stan Musial knew my name, for cryin' out loud.' It was really a shock. I tell that every time somebody mentions him. He was a class guy from what I know and read."

Sixty years later, still slender and boyish, Terwilliger was coaching in the minor leagues, still in uniform, like Schoendienst and Johnny Pesky from his era.

"I've used that," Terwilliger said of Musial's gesture. "When I was managing in the minor leagues, I would find out their names and call 'em by name when I went by, and I knew they appreciated that."

Terwilliger wondered how Musial could hit from that crouch. "I think I did fool around with it a little because I struggled as a hitter and I was trying to find something comfortable for me. I tried the crouching, but it never felt comfortable for me. I never did find a good stance." He batted .240 in 666 games in the majors.

Catchers just up from the minors were stunned when they would squat behind home plate and Musial would introduce himself—already knowing their names. This was not fraternization; it was being human.

Musial rarely gave advice to teammates, but when he spoke it made sense to listen. When Joe Cunningham was a rookie, he was shagging flies before a game and indulging in some modest backbiting toward the manager. Musial, who had been jerked around by a manager or two by then, quickly told Cunnningham, "Joe, don't bite the hand that feeds you."

"I never forgot that," Cunningham said, long after making a good career and settling in St. Louis. He remained a friend of Musial's even though he had been moved to the outfield so Musial could play first.

"I kidded him once. I said, 'Stan, do you feel good about all the guys you sent back to the minor leagues?' He just laughed it off. You know, I've never heard Stan say a bad word about anybody."

Ed Mickelson was a pretty fair minor-league hitter who finally got called up by the Cardinals late in the 1950 season. When Musial came down with a 103-degree fever, Eddie Dyer let Mickelson start, then added that Warren Spahn was pitching that day. Given a chance, Mickelson got one of the Cardinals' two hits that day.

The following spring, Mickelson was training with the Cardinals. One day he noticed Musial sitting in the next stall in the clubhouse bathroom, separated by a partition.

"I thought, 'Okay, I got a captive audience here,' " Mickelson said, "so I asked him, 'Stan, you seem so confident and carefree, do you ever get nervous before a game?' and he said, 'Ed, I tell you what, if you don't, you might as well quit. Sure I get nervous.' "

Mickelson, who batted .081 in 18 games with the Cardinals and Browns, remembered that advice during his long career as a minor-league hitter and high school coach. "He's so calm and collected. It helped me a lot."

It was nice to be Stanley. He used to make fun of the Pirates' rudimentary batting helmets, worn on order of Branch Rickey, who had moved from Brooklyn to Pittsburgh. Joe Garagiola, who had gone on to play with the Pirates, was under orders to wear the helmet backward while catching.

"There was a half inch of rubber under the helmet," Garagiola recalled. "You hated playing on a hot day because if you caught a foul tip, the sweat would come running down your face like you needed windshield wipers.

And if you went after a foul pop, you'd throw off the mask, but the bill of the helmet would stick you in the back of the neck, like you were getting stabbed."

Stanley was having none of the helmets.

"Musial was adamant," Garagiola said. "He thought he looked funny in a helmet, so he wore a little plastic insert under his cap."

Pretty much everything was funny to Stanley.

There was a night game in St. Louis when Garagiola was catching for the Pirates and his old buddy came up to hit.

"Hey, Stan, about ten of us are coming over to the restaurant after the game. Do we need a reservation?"

Musial watched the first strike.

"Should we take taxis, or do you have enough parking?"

Musial did not answer. Strike two.

On the third pitch, Musial slugged a home run out into the humid St. Louis night. When he touched home he asked Garagiola, "How do you people like your steaks?"

Sometimes Musial even surprised himself. On May 2, 1954, he became the first major leaguer ever to hit five homers in one day.

Lil happened to stay home for the Sunday doubleheader. Stan walked the first time, then hit a homer off the left-handed Johnny Antonelli. In the fifth, Musial golfed a low inside pitch from Antonelli onto the pavilion in right field. In the sixth he singled off the right-handed Jim Hearn. In the eighth, with two men on base and the score tied, he hit a slider by Hearn onto the roof of the pavilion, the first time he had hit three homers in one game.

In the second game, with the lights on, he walked the first time up. The second time Willie Mays tracked down his drive in the deepest part of the ballpark, right-center field. Over the years both Musial and Monte Irvin would say Willie had taken away a sixth homer, but it would have had to be an inside-the-park version with a ferocious carom.

In his third at-bat in the second game, Musial hit one onto the roof of the pavilion—40 feet high, 394 feet away. The next time, Hoyt Wilhelm fluttered one of his trademark knuckleballs, and Musial hit it to right-center, on top of the roof. The last time up—one of the rare times when he actually tried to jerk one out—he popped to first. For a guy who came up as a cautious singles hitter, it was quite an afternoon.

Musial told this story on himself many times: when he got home from the ballpark that day, thirteen-year-old Dick said, "Gee, Dad, they sure must have been throwing you fat pitches today."

Then there was the 1955 All-Star Game in Milwaukee, with young Bud Selig in attendance with his mom. Musial was not voted to start that year but batted for Del Ennis in the fourth inning and was still in the lineup as the game meandered into the twelfth inning. With the players due back in uniform two days later, nobody wanted to miss the last flight or train out of town that evening. Legend says that Musial promised everybody in the dugout he was about to end the game, but Robin Roberts, who pitched the first three innings and was rooting in the dugout in the twelfth, said he did not hear any prediction.

Henry Aaron, in the same dugout at the same time, recalled Musial heading toward the bat rack and saying, "They don't pay us to play overtime."

"And he went up and hit a home run," Aaron said. "I heard that myself. I know a lot say Babe Ruth pointed"—a reference to Ruth's homer in the 1932 World Series. "I know Stan called his."

Does talking about not getting paid for overtime qualify as calling his shot? That is open to interpretation. At the very least, Musial was setting himself up for a Stanley-hits kind of moment.

Yogi Berra, Musial's St. Louis pal, had caught the entire game and was still squatting behind home plate. In one of his books, Berra and his writer put it this way: "Stash is the oldest player in the game and tells me he's getting weary. I tell him my feet are tired, too. And ain't it a shame nobody can see the ball through the shadows? Stash tells me to relax, says we're all going home soon. And he smashed the first pitch for a home run."

In a conversation in 2009, Berra recalled that All-Star Game: "It was a long game, you know. We were just talking, saying, I wish this game would get over with."

"It's been said that Stanley told you he was going to get it over with," I told Berra.

"Nah, he didn't," Berra insisted.

Then there is Frank Sullivan of the Red Sox, who delivered the pitch. Known for his wit as a player, Sullivan claimed half a century later that Musial was laughing as he got into the batter's box and that Yogi said, "For crying out loud, Stan, do something. This game has gone on far too long."

Musial promptly hit the ball into the stands (Bud Selig still waxes on about the parabola of the game-ending drive) and toured the bases, clearly quite happy with himself.

Sullivan ended his story this way: "Later, Berra came over to my locker and said, 'I should have told you he was a high fastball hitter.' "

Yogi was too much of a competitor to intentionally allow Sullivan to put the wrong pitch in the wrong place for the wrong slugger—even if it was his St. Louis pal. But that was the result: Stanley the homebody sent everybody home.

# 31

---

## STANLEY GIVES AN

## INTERVIEW

ZEV YAROSLAVSKY is not sure of the year. It was either 1958 or 1959, the first or second season the Dodgers were ensconced in Los Angeles.

Yaroslavsky would later become a supervisor of Los Angeles County, a nationally prominent politician, but back in the late fifties he had loftier goals: he wanted to be the next Vin Scully.

Scully was conducting a primer course in major-league baseball for denizens of southern California, who would bring transistor radios to the Coliseum to listen to his mellifluous yet still New York accent.

Yaroslavsky decided the best way to become the next Vin Scully was to secure an interview with the reigning grand old deity of the National League, Stan Musial.

The boy of ten or eleven did not work for a radio station. He did not even own a tape recorder. However, he did have nerve.

"I found out that the Cardinals were staying at the old Statler downtown," Yaroslavsky said. "I must have found that in a baseball media guide or something. I called the hotel and asked for Mr. Musial's room and they connected me. That wouldn't happen today, of course.

"He picked up the phone and I put on my deepest pre-puberty voice," Yaroslavsky recalled. "I said my name was Bob Price and I worked for KLAC and asked if I could have a brief interview."

Musial agreed, so Bob Price commenced.

"How's the team?"

"The Cardinals look pretty good."

"In what ways?"

"Good hitting, good fielding, good defense, good pitching."

"Let's talk about the hitting."

"We have this kid Curt Flood and he looks good, and Kenny Boyer is a good power hitter."

"What about the defense?"

"That Julian Javier is a terrific fielder."

"What about pitching?"

"Gibson and Broglio are excellent pitchers. We think we have a good staff that can win a lot of games."

Four decades later, Yaroslavsky remembered running out of questions before Stan Musial ran out of answers. Bob Price thanked Musial for his time.

Musial's last words were, "Thank you, son."


"AT THAT moment, I was very embarrassed," Yaroslavsky remembered. "My con didn't work. He could have hung up or lectured me or chewed me out, but he didn't. In his own inimitable way, he let me know that he knew, but he gave me the interview anyway.

"You know," Yaroslavsky continued, "I've been around a lot of people since then. I've seen people acting like jerks. As I got into politics, I thought about that moment. If Stan Musial could take the time for somebody, so could I. If somebody's power got cut off on a weekend, or somebody had a landslide in their backyard at night, or somebody died on a Sunday and needed a death certificate, you could never be too busy to listen to them."

Yaroslavsky never met Musial, but about a decade ago a friend arranged for Musial to autograph a ball that now sits in Yaroslavsky's living room. The inscription says: "To Zev, a great fan. Stan Musial." It does not call him "son."

The 1938 Donora baseball team included Stan Musial (fourth from left, top row) and Buddy Griffey (second from left, seated). To Griffey's right is Dr. Michael (Ki) Duda, who organized the team and was a mentor to Musial. *Donora Historical Society*

Six of Donora's most successful athletes depicted in a mural in the old high school: (Clockwise, from upper left) Ken Griffey Sr., Stan Musial, Arnold Galiffa, Ulice Payne Jr., The Honorable Reggie B. Walton, and Dan Towler. *George Vecsey*

The young Musial just wanted to make contact so he could last a few weeks or months in the majors. *The National Baseball Hall of Fame*

A very proud Lukasz Musial visited his son in New York during the 1942 World Series. Here they discuss a minor injury that did not keep Stan out of the lineup. *AP*

Musial (right) and an unidentified sailor enjoy a cup of coffee in Pearl Harbor, where Musial played baseball in 1945. *The National Baseball Hall of Fame*

Whitey Kurowski, Enos Slaughter, Marty Marion, and Musial display their uniform numbers during the 1946 World Series, the last trip to the Series for the Cardinals for eighteen years. *Getty Images*

The Donora Zinc Works sent smoke into the Monongahela River valley, contributing to the murderous 1948 smog. *Donora Historical Society*

Stan the Man went 3 for 4 in the 1949 All-Star Game at Ebbets Field, Brooklyn, where he was given his nickname. His pal from St. Louis, Yogi Berra, was the catcher. *The National Baseball Hall of Fame*

Chuck Schmidt, who coached Musial in Donora, and befriended him during his brief stay in Rochester, N.Y., in 1941, visited him at the Dodgers' training camp in Vero Beach, Florida, in 1954. *Jim Kreuz*

When the Cardinals opened a motel for all the families in spring training of 1962, Lil was front and center (white frilly blouse). She and Leila Keane, the wife of Manager Johnny Keane (standing center, dark bathing suit) set a welcome tone for the black players and their families. *Courtesy of Mildred White*

Two Stanleys: When the Cardinals returned to the Polo Grounds in 1962 to play the Mets, Musial agreed to pose with an old friend, Stan Isaacs of *Newsday,* whose column was fittingly named "Out of Left Field." *Courtesy of Stan Isaacs (photo by Luis Requeña)*

"My Buddy." With President Kennedy in the White House,
July 1962. *Courtesy of John H. Zentay*

Ted Williams always liked to claim he was the favorite player of Musial's
mother. *Dick Collins*

Musial was named an advisor on physical fitness by President Lyndon B. Johnson in 1964. *Courtesy of Gerry Ashley*

Musial and (clockwise) Waite Hoyt, Roy Campanella, and Stan Coveleski at their induction into the Hall of Fame in 1969. *Dick Collins*

Stan introduced his mother at the 1969 induction while Lil and daughters enjoyed the moment. *Dick Collins*

Musial's plaque at the National Baseball Hall of Fame. *National Baseball Hall of Fame*

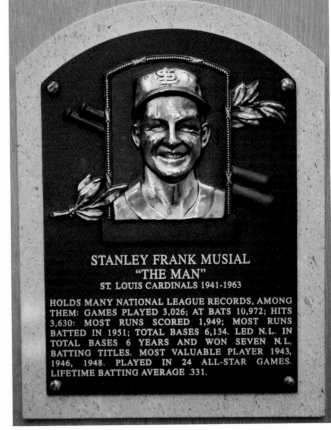

STANLEY FRANK MUSIAL
"THE MAN"
ST. LOUIS CARDINALS 1941-1963

HOLDS MANY NATIONAL LEAGUE RECORDS, AMONG
THEM: GAMES PLAYED 3,026; AT BATS 10,972; HITS
3,630: MOST RUNS SCORED 1,949; MOST RUNS
BATTED IN 1951; TOTAL BASES 6,134. LED N.L. IN
TOTAL BASES 6 YEARS AND WON SEVEN N.L.
BATTING TITLES. MOST VALUABLE PLAYER 1943,
1946, 1948. PLAYED IN 24 ALL-STAR GAMES.
LIFETIME BATTING AVERAGE .331.

Stan Musial & Biggie's was a landmark in St. Louis for decades. The food was good, too, according to Tim McCarver. *Courtesy of Mickey McTague*

Danny Kaye was a big fan of Musial and Willie Mays. *Dick Collins*

Old timers came out for a 1970 exhibition that raised funds in the name of Martin Luther King Jr. Left to right: Joe DiMaggio, Musial, John McNamara, Billy Martin, Larry Doby. *Dick Collins*

The swing that launched 3,630 hits, demonstrated once again at Cooperstown, some-time in the early 1980s. *Dick Collins*

Lil and Stan were always the life of the party at Cooperstown.
This time they were joined by son, Dick, and his wife,
Sharon. *Dick Collins*

The three amigos. Musial, Ed Piszek, and James Michener meeting in Miami, en
route to Warsaw, 1988. *Larry Christenson*

The Stance visited the Collosseum, using James Michener's cane, while Larry
Christenson observed. *Larry Christenson*

Musial and entourage with Pope John Paul II. On that same visit they had dinner
with the Pope in his apartment. *Larry Christenson*

Musial was inducted into the Brooklyn Dodger Hall of Fame in June 1990, and was greeted by former Dodgers . . . and writers and fans. *Marty Adler*

Sharing the same birth date (November 21) and the same hometown (Donora, PA), Ken Griffey Jr., dropped everything to have his photo taken with Musial at Cooperstown. Musial was a high-school teammate of Junior's grandfather, Buddy Griffey. *Dick Collins*

Growing up in Oklahoma, Mickey Mantle admired Musial. Here, Willie Mays seems dubious about Mantle's story. This photo was taken early in 1995, just months before Mantle's death. *Dick Collins*

Although not thrilled with the posture of the Carl Mose statue, Musial was nevertheless proud to have it remain a meeting point at the new ballpark in St. Louis. William O. DeWitt III stands beside him at the second unveiling. *AP*

Musial liked the energy of the smaller 1998 statue by Harry Weber and loved posing alongside it. *AP. Photographer: Tom Gannan*

Opening Day, 2009. The always-reverential Albert Pujols adjusted Musial's jacket. "It was cold," Pujols said. "I was afraid he would be cold out there." *Chris Lee*, St. Louis Post-Dispatch

The Cardinals imitated a popular
literacy project, Flat Stanley, in 2010,
mounting a Flat Stan campaign for
the Presidential Medal of Freedom.
*Courtesy of Ron Watermon, Director of*
*Public Relations & Civic Affairs, St. Louis*
*Cardinals, LLC*

In cooperation
with Dale Hubert's
Flat Stanley Project
www.flatstanley.com

STAND
FOR
STAN

In February 2011, Musial was awarded the Presidential Medal
of Freedom by President Barack Obama.
*Courtesy of Doug Mills/*The New York Times

# 32

---

## TEMPER, TEMPER

No matter who you talk to on this project, you're not going to find one person that's going to say one bad word about Stan Musial.

It's going to be very difficult. You're going to want to have somebody tell you they saw Stan kick an old grandma in the knee one time when she asked for an autograph, but you're not going to hear that. He's been gracious his entire life and he's going to be that way the rest of his life, I am sure.

—Dal Maxvill, teammate, colleague, friend

F OUND ONE.

After collecting thousands of examples of Musial's kindness and good humor, it was downright refreshing to hear of an instance when Stanley actually got angry—at a kid! Otherwise, we should be submitting his name for sainthood. Much better to think of him as a nearly but not quite perfect human being.

The eyewitness report of Stanley's Bad Moment came totally unsolicited from Steve Kaufman, a writer for trade magazines, who once was an eleven-year-old urchin on the North Side of Chicago. He heard I was doing a book on Musial and, with no malice and a wry detachment over the decades, recalled a moment in the summer of 1954 when Musial grumped at him.

On that fateful day, Kaufman recalled, he took the Kedzie bus and transferred to the Addison bus to Wrigley Field, paying 75¢ for a general-admission ticket.

"The Cubs were awful, but who cared?" Kaufman said years later. "In the opposite dugout were Jackie Robinson and Duke Snider, or Willie Mays, or Richie Ashburn and Robin Roberts, or Eddie Mathews and Henry Aaron and Warren Spahn, or Ted Kluszewski . . . or Musial."

Visiting players would leave Wrigley through a side gate, where youths would congregate, asking the ballplayers for their autograph. Kaufman spotted Musial walking with Vic Raschi, the former Yankee who had moved over to the Cardinals.

Kaufman did what kids have always done outside ballparks: he stood in Musial's path and plaintively asked, "Would you sign this, Stan?"

In those days there was no market for autographs. Children were not greedy little speculators. Cajoling a scribbled signature was a way to be in the proximity of a ballplayer for a second or two.

For whatever reason, this was not one of Musial's better days.

"Without breaking his stride, he looked down at us and hissed, through gritted teeth, I'll never forget: 'Get outta my way or I'll kick you in the shins.' "

In the shins? Stanley threatened to kick a kid in the shins?

"Not every player signed that afternoon," Kaufman said. "Most of those who didn't simply ignored us, like you try to do with beggars on Calcutta streets. But none was so openly hostile as the great Musial," Kaufman said.

"Over the years, as I'd read about his friendly nature, his grand generosity, and especially his endless patience with fans, I thought about that afternoon in Chicago. I wondered if he'd just had a bad afternoon. I'm guessing he didn't. Musial rarely had bad afternoons against the Cubs."

This outburst, which I am assuming happened just that way, is hard to understand. That summer happened to be one of the hottest ever in the Midwest. The Cardinals were not in contention. Musial was on his way to his normal .330. Who knows? All that is left for one aging fan is the memory of Stan Musial ducking down a North Side street, threatening to kick a kid in the shins.

––––––––

MUSIAL DID have a temper. People said it happened fast, a flare of anger.

Jack Buck attested to the night he and Red and Musial visited Toots Shor's oasis in New York and a group of five men from Omaha asked Musial to autograph a menu. When Musial handed it back, one of the men ostentatiously ripped it in half.

"Why would anybody do a thing like that?" Buck asked years later. "Stan flipped and started after the guy, but Toots's bartenders got there first. They jumped over the bar and had four of those people out on the street in a blink. They kept one guy inside to pay the bill and then hustled him to the sidewalk. It was a good thing Stan never got to them."

So Stanley could get riled up at a cluster of jerks who were probably, in Casey Stengel's phrase, whiskey-slick. Buck added, "By the way, I asked Musial once what he would have done if he had not been a baseball player, and he said he thought he would have been a boxer."

With those back muscles and reflexes, Musial could have been a contender, at the very least. But there is no record of him ever hitting anybody.

Musial also displayed righteous anger in New York in the mid-fifties on a cab ride up to the Polo Grounds. One of his teammates noticed a Jewish name on the cabbie's placard and starting speaking in a crude version of a Jewish accent. Musial told the teammate to cease and desist, making for a rather uncomfortable ride. When they got to the ballpark, the teammate tried to pay for the ride, as if to make amends, but Musial insisted on paying, and then he warned the teammate to never get in a cab with him. Ever. But there were no fisticuffs, and certainly no shin kicking.

That little episode outside Wrigley goes down in history as one of nature's mysteries, but affirmative in its own way. Stanley was human. Thank goodness for that.

# 33

---

# AND SOME BAD TIMES

AFTER YEARS of unstable ownership, St. Louis finally got an owner with deep pockets and civic stature. Gussie Busch, from the old brewery family, bought the Cardinals for $7.8 million on February 20, 1953.

"My ambition," Busch said, "is, whether hell or high water, to get a championship baseball team for St. Louis before I die."

Fortunately, Busch had good genes for longevity, if not for patience. His arrival was also a sign that the Cardinals had outlasted their longtime landlords, the Browns. Bill Veeck had tried to reach the large but passive segment of Browns fans by hiring icons like Rogers Hornsby and Marty Marion as managers and indulging in gimmicks like having a midget pinchhit. But Veeck was forced out after 1952 and the Browns moved to Baltimore in 1954. Meanwhile, the Cardinals and their fans could count on the deep pockets, if short fuse, of August Anheuser Busch Jr.

Known as Gussie to the public and Gus to friends, Busch was used to getting his own way; the French expression *droit de seigneur* (the right of the lord) comes to mind. He would wed four times, produce ten children, and generally demand his way in beer, baseball, and life itself. He had a lot of toys, now including a baseball team.

Joe Garagiola recalled Busch and George Vierheller, the longtime director of the St. Louis Zoo, playing pepper, with Stanley tapping the ball "so softly that if it had been an egg he wouldn't have cracked the shell," Garagiola said, and Schoendienst "playing like he was the bodyguard."

Normally, the players bet sodas when they frolicked at pepper. Tommy

Glaviano, a Cardinal infielder, watched the quartet and shouted, "Hey, Stan, what are you playing for, a keg of beer or a tiger?"

Playing pepper was the least of Busch's activities. As a young adult, to cheer up his ailing father, Busch once rode his horse right up the central stairway of the family mansion, straight into the bedroom where his pater-familias was confined.

And on the day Prohibition was repealed in 1933, the thirty-four-year-old scion drove an old-fashioned beer wagon straight down Pennsylvania Avenue to deliver a keg or two to the White House. President Roosevelt's support of repeal earned the permanent loyalty of Busch, who said, "I'll be damned if I'll bite the hand that fed me."

He had so much fun making his beer run in the nation's capital that he began hitching the ornate beer wagons to eight-horse teams of powerful Clydesdales, which were quartered in handsome stables at the family es-tate, Grant's Farm.

The stables were air-conditioned; the clubhouse at Sportsman's Park was not.

In later years, for special games, Busch would hitch up the Clydesdales and drive the wagon onto the artificial turf of the second Busch Stadium, entering the field to the jingle-jangle tune of "Here Comes the King," which sounded like an old Bavarian drinking song but was merely an ad-vertising ditty created for his product.

When Good King August waved his white cowboy hat, he gave the im-pression of a powerful landowner inspecting the serfs. Then the grounds-keepers would come out with shovels and brooms to clean up after the Clydesdales, after which Ozzie Smith would trot out and perform his styl-ized back flip at shortstop. Play ball!

From the beginning, Busch became one of the signature owners in American sport, inflicting his outsized will and corporate stamp on the Cardinals, giving them more operating capital than they'd ever had before, even in their best of years.

He tried to rename Sportsman's Park for the company's leading product—Budweiser—but that did not sit well with the commissioner, so he called it Busch Stadium, which at least was the family name.

Revamping the team itself was a bit more difficult. On April 11, 1954, the Cardinals traded Enos Slaughter to the Yankees for outfielder Bill Virdon, in an attempt to get younger and quicker. This was a wake-up call for Musial: Slaughter was only four years older than he was.

Musial hit .337 in 1953 and .330 in 1954 as the Cardinals finished sixth, twenty-five games behind Willie Mays's Giants. In 1955, the Dodgers won their first World Series and the Cardinals finished seventh. Despite his homer to win the All-Star Game and his .319 average with 33 homers, Musial would call it "The Year of the Big Minus." Mandolin-playing Doc Weaver, who had spooked the Yankees with voodoo signs during the 1942 World Series and helped create the pension plan, died of a heart attack.

After playing for Billy Southworth and Eddie Dyer in his first eight seasons, Musial began to experience a more typical turnover. Marty Marion did not work out in 1951. Eddie Stanky, Leo Durocher's intense protégé, lasted from 1952 into 1955. Harry Walker took over in the middle of 1955 but pushed the Cards with midday drills in the summer heat, and when the team finished seventh, Walker was not retained.

In 1956 the Cardinals brought in Fred Hutchinson, the burly and competitive former Detroit Tigers pitcher, who once punched out the overhead bulbs in the corridor behind the dugout after being taken out of a game. He was, in the vernacular, a ballplayer's manager.

However, the new general manager in 1956 was not a favorite of the players. Frank Lane, known as "Trader Lane," never met the man he could not dispatch somewhere.

Lane's first act was to get rid of the two cardinals (two male cardinals, to be precise, although their cheery togetherness did not seem to be the reason Lane scuttled them) that had been perched on a bat on the front of the home jersey since 1922. The fans grumbled all year, so the two birds made a comeback in 1957. But the fashion note was a warning: this man would get rid of anybody or anything.

Bob Broeg, Musial's confidant, once described Lane's need to trade people as almost lascivious, like a sexual charge. "The thrill of the trade was paramount," Broeg said. "It's ridiculous, but, you know, the guy, when he was under restraint, he was great," Broeg added.

Lane's next move was to send Virdon to the Pirates on May 17, 1956, thereby leaving a huge gap in center field for the rest of the decade. Athletes are pragmatic out of need. Their survival depends on knowing what is real, what works. If they think a manager or general manager is a wrongo, they tune him out.

Lane pronounced that Stan and Red were among the five "untouchables" on the Cardinals, but he undoubtedly sensed that the core of the team did not respect him. Schoendienst had the impression that Lane could not actually see what his players were doing on the field.

"We would be taking batting practice and he'd hear the crack of the bat and say things like, 'There's a fine ballplayer,' " Red would write in his autobiography. "He had no idea who was batting but he was able to get away with statements like that."

Lane knew only one way to make the Cardinals his team. With the trading deadline of June 15 approaching, Musial received a call from Biggie, who said the *Sporting News* was investigating a rumor that Lane was preparing to trade Musial to the Phillies for Robin Roberts.

After talking to Musial, Biggie promptly called a brewery official and said, "Well, if it's true, I've got news for you. The kid won't report. He'll quit." The "kid" always maintained that Biggie had acted on his own, but this is surely another example of Stanley's division of labor: he did the hitting, and Biggie did the phoning.

The brewery walls quivered as the news worked its way up toward Gussie Busch. Meanwhile, Musial fumed. He and Red lived a few blocks from each other, often driving together to the ballpark, which allowed Lil and Mary to drive together later.

"I'm picking up Stan this particular day, and he comes out of the house, you know, and I could see there's something wrong with him," Schoendienst recalled. "He wasn't the same old Stan. And I says, I thought maybe they had a big argument or something at home. And I says, 'What? What's wrong, Stan?' And, and he says, 'That darn Frank Lane, he wants to trade me, and I ain't going,' he said, like that."

Red tried to cheer Stan by saying Busch would never allow the trade.

"That's one time I've seen Stan upset. And he couldn't understand why he wanted to trade him," Red recalled. "He says, 'Well I'm not gonna go,' and he says, 'I'm gonna talk to Mr. Busch—to the boss.' So evidently he did."

Musial and Busch were friendly, socializing together in Florida and St.

Louis. The impulsive beer baron had not hired Trader Lane to send away the popular star who helped sell beer all over the country.

After a day or two, Lane put out a statement that said: "August A. Busch, Jr., and myself are in complete accord that Musial will not be traded."

What the statement did not say was that Lane was finished trading. He had to trade people. Otherwise, what was the point?

Red began to wonder: if Trader Lane could not get his charge by trading Musial, whom could he trade? The answer was suddenly apparent: "I guess I'll be next, because that's the way Lane was. Trader Lane. And I was. I was gone the next day."

On June 14, 1956, Lane traded Schoendienst to the Giants, theoretically to get a shortstop, Alvin Dark, who was well past his prime. Red found out about it over the radio before Lane's secretary bothered to call Red's house with the news.

Mary Schoendienst, a St. Louis girl, wrote a letter to the papers thanking the fans for their support of Red, and people from Red's hometown in southern Illinois never changed the road sign: WELCOME TO GERMANTOWN, HOME OF RED SCHOENDIENST, ST. LOUIS CARDINALS. They must have known something.

Musial's memory of that awful day: "The rest of us got the word that Red had been traded just as we were boarding a train out of St. Louis for an eastern trip. It was the saddest day of my career. I slammed the door to my train berth shut and didn't open it for a long time."

"Yeah, boy, he didn't like that at all," Red said. "I didn't either."

Long after Red was sacrificed, Broeg finally found the nerve to ask Stanley if he actually would have quit baseball rather than be traded.

"Musial just laughed," Broeg recalled. "He says, 'I wouldn't report? I got to report, you know?'" Broeg said Musial would have been "crushed" to go to another team, but as Broeg put it, "He wasn't gonna walk away from his career."

Red was pretty miserable in New York, but the trade worked out for him. A year and a day after leaving the Cardinals, he was traded to Milwaukee, and soon some of the Braves would sidle up to Musial at the batting cage and whisper that his buddy was even better than they could have imagined. Red was the missing link, the professional who helped Henry

Aaron and Eddie Mathews win pennants in 1957 and 1958. Schoendienst then contracted tuberculosis, fought his way back, and rejoined the Cardinals in 1961. By that time, Trader Lane was long gone.

One consequence of the Schoendienst trade was that Busch brought the hammer down on Lane, making him clear all trades with the brewery. But Lane was nothing if not brazen, seeking an extension of his contract. Busch clarified matters by sending Lane a telegram containing three little words: "Kiss my ass."

Lane took the hint and moved on after the 1957 season. While working in Cleveland, he would trade Rocky Colavito, one of the most popular players in the history of that franchise. He would even trade managers in 1960, swapping Joe Gordon for Jimmy Dykes, still the only time two managers have ever been traded.

Stanley was not perceived as a vengeful man, but he had his moments. In 1967, he would inherit Lane's old job as general manager, with the prodigal Red as the manager. One day the two old friends were sitting up front in the team bus that was about to leave the hotel when Trader Lane hopped on board, hoping to hitch a ride to the ballpark, a courtesy sometimes extended to baseball friends.

"I never saw Stan move so fast in my life," Red said. "He sprang up from his seat and walked to where Lane was sitting. 'Get the hell out of here,' he ordered Lane. 'Get off our bus.' "

Red added: "I wish Stan, or somebody else, had the authority to tell Lane what to do in earlier times. Then maybe I wouldn't have been headed to New York becoming a member of the Giants."

AT LEAST Red helped win two pennants. Stanley was mired in a stagnant organization, not getting any younger. Hutch was not the problem; his gruff credibility enabled him to move Musial, once again, from the outfield to first base, telling reporters that Musial did not "cover the ground that he used to. He doesn't get the ball to the infield as quickly. I thought he would be better off at first base because we do need a first baseman."

Although Musial hit .310 in 1956, Hutch dropped him from third to fifth in the lineup. True to his code, Musial did not gripe about it. He was still having his moments.

One moment came at the 1956 All-Star Game in Washington, D.C., after Williams hit a homer and the public-address announcer told the crowd that Williams had just tied Musial for All-Star home runs with his fifth. In the next inning, Musial hit a homer off Tom Brewer, prompting the revised announcement that, ladies and gentlemen, Musial has just passed Williams.

Upon turning thirty-six, Musial gave up cigarettes for the most part, although not the occasional cigar or cigarillo. His reward was his seventh and last batting championship, with a .351 average, 102 runs batted in, and 29 homers in 1957.

On June 12, he broke Gus Suhr's National League record for consecutive games with 823, after making a token appearance along the way to keep the streak going. He had also played injured a number of times, living up to the old Gashouse code that a player never took a day off.

"We were a tough bunch of guys back then," he once told Julius Hunter, a popular St. Louis commentator. "We played hurt a lot. We had a game to play, and when you hit the field you forgot a while about this or that hurting you. You get a bruise, you pour a little iodine on it and keep on playing. You get a sprain, either you or the team doctor would tape it up real tight and you'd head back out in the field. I used to think of all the fans that paid their hard earned money to come see me play. They didn't buy tickets to see me sitting on the bench."

Musial always stressed his luck in avoiding major injuries, but there was something else—his workman's pride in showing up, doing an honest job.

He had learned a lesson earlier in his career from a conversation with Al Simmons—originally Aloys Szymanski, one of the great players of Polish ancestry. Simmons, who finished his career with 2,927 hits, once told Musial he would have reached 3,000 hits if he had played a few more games every season.

The streak ended at 895 when Musial injured his left shoulder trying to pull an outside pitch to protect the runner. He wound up playing only 134 games that season, his lowest total in fifteen seasons. Athletes are always stunned at the suggestion their bodies are deserting them. The first reaction is: *Bad day.*

But at least Musial did not have to see Lane's smirking face anymore. The new general manager was Bing Devine, a local boy from Washington

University who had worked his way up in the organization. Musial's first salary negotiation with Devine involved a modest request for 1958: Kiner had reached $90,000 and Musial told Devine he wanted $91,000. Devine checked it out and came back with the news that Gussie Busch wanted Musial to become the first National League player to make $100,000, which Musial accepted gracefully.

The aura of the grand old star of the National League also carried a legend: Musial had never been thrown out of a game. He did come very close on opening day of 1958 after being called out on strikes to end the home half of the first. Musial gave a brief look to home-plate umpire Frank Dascoli, who was known to have a low tolerance for criticism, even from Stanley.

Normally, umpires began to question their call (to themselves, of course) when Stanley fixed his sad-eyed look on them. Dascoli may have taken the look as a challenge. When Musial was called out again to end the third inning, he gave Dascoli a major-league glare.

As Musial trudged away from home plate, Del Ennis, in the on-deck circle, warned him not to look back because Dascoli was glaring back at the number 6 between Musial's shoulder blades. Musial kept walking, giving Dascoli no cause to toss him.

Musial was friendly with most umpires and sometimes could even laugh at their mistakes. In return, he received just about universal respect.

"I met Al Barlick once at Cooperstown and was asking him what happened if Stan took a pitch with two strikes," Joe Torre said. "Barlick thought about it and said, 'If he didn't swing at it, it's a ball.' "

Another umpire anecdote turns out to be about seven-tenths urban myth, like alligators in the sewer system. According to legend, Stanley once had a game-winning grand-slam home run negated because time had been called as a ball rolled onto the field; thereupon Stanley promptly hit a bases-clearing triple to alleviate the home-plate umpire's guilt.

In one version, this happened off Ben Wade of Brooklyn in St. Louis in the early fifties. The only thing wrong with this version is that no box score exists for such an epic event.

Something like this did happen on April 18, 1954, off Paul Minner of the Cubs at Wrigley—a one-run double was negated when the first-base umpire blew the call and ruled Musial's ball to be foul. True story: Musial trudged home, did not complain to umpire Augie Donatelli, and promptly whacked a double to the same place, this time to be called fair. Still a nice story, however.

Stanley has even received credit for giving career-altering advice to a Hall of Fame umpire, Doug Harvey. In 1961, when Harvey was breaking in, he became so mesmerized by a curveball from Don Drysdale that he called Musial out on strikes. Musial politely told Harvey that Drysdale's excellent pitch had actually broken a few inches before home plate, and suggested Harvey slow down his procedure for making calls. Harvey listened and soon became the strict but fair presence known to the players as "God."

Musial was not playing politics with the umps; he just had a high standard.

In 1958, Musial approached another milestone—the eighth player ever to accumulate 3,000 career hits. Biggie arranged for a huge party for Musial on Sunday evening, May 11, by which time, Biggie estimated, Musial would reach that number. Accommodating soul that he was, Stanley rapped out five hits in a doubleheader that afternoon but was still two hits away when it was time for the party. Musial pulled out his harmonica and the 350 guests cheered the man with 2,998 career hits. Then the Cardinals took off for a two-day trip to Chicago.

After getting one hit on Monday, Musial mused out loud that it would be nice if he could make his 3,000th at home. Always a straight shooter, Hutchinson informed players, press, and fans that Musial would be rested on Tuesday—unless the Cards absolutely needed a hit.

On Tuesday Lil saw Stanley off to the ballpark and then made a sortie down Michigan Avenue to shop for a hat she could wear in St. Louis for the big moment a day or two later.

She found the right hat and then told her friends, "Girls, we came here to see his 3000th base hit, and even if they don't play him, we have to be at the ballpark because you never know what's going to happen."

When Lil arrived, Stanley was out in the bullpen, working on his ballplayer tan. In the sixth inning, with a runner on base and the Cardinals trailing by a run, Hutch did what any manager would do: he called on Stanley. By some odd coincidence, the pitcher was a right-hander, Moe Drabowsky, who actually had been born in Poland, Musial's ancestral home.

Drabowsky was not about to toss Musial a friendly helping of golumpki; he tried to tantalize Musial with an outside pitch. But as he had been doing since he was a kid playing on the odd-shaped field in Donora, Musial stroked the ball to the left side. Ernie Banks, one of Musial's greatest admirers, watched the ball sizzle past him at shortstop, hooking into the corner, and Banks could not help his let's-play-two smile as Musial pulled into second. Hutchinson came lumbering onto the field to congratulate Musial, apologizing for ruining the plans for St. Louis.

The ball was retrieved by the third-base umpire, none other than Frank Dascoli, who had been looking to eject Stanley back on April 15. With a big smile, Dascoli came running over to present the ball at second base. Cubs and Cardinals were applauding and laughing, and then Musial spotted Lil and kissed her as photographers clicked away. One of the photographers asked, "Who's the blonde, Stan?"

The celebration continued as the team pulled out of the Illinois Central depot, heading home. Harry Caray gave Musial a pair of cuff links with "3,000" engraved on them, and Sam Jones, the winning pitcher, delivered a magnum of Champagne. Coincidentally, with the arrival of the jet age, this was the last time the Cardinals would ever take a train on this route. Fans in Illinois waved from the side of the tracks, with fans in Springfield singing "For He's a Jolly Good Fellow."

"Now I know how Lindbergh felt," Musial told Broeg.

When the train finally reached Union Station in St. Louis around eleven that night, hundreds of people were waiting, including Gerry Musial, now a teenager.

"He told the fans, 'All you kids get a day off from school,'" Gerry recalled. "And there were a lot of kids there."

Did the Musial children follow their father's advice and become truants?

"I think Mom took us in late," Gerry said.


MUSIAL HIT .337 in 1958, with a slight drop-off in power, and Hutch was dismissed in mid-September as the Cardinals tied for fifth. Nearly thirty-eight years old, physically and mentally worn out, Musial could have used a restful off-season at home with Lil, who was pregnant with their fourth child, but the Cardinals were committed to a trip to Asia, and Musial's presence was very much part of the deal. He was allowed to miss three early stops but reported in Seoul, South Korea, before the team went to Japan.

"At first, I wasn't too keen about making the trip," Musial recalled. "I knew I'd be worn out. But I'm mighty glad that I went. That trip thirty years ago was worth it. I have lasting impressions. My wife does, too."

The trip was important because of baseball's status as the national sport of Japan. General Douglas MacArthur had encouraged the sport to be resumed quickly after World War II, and Lefty O'Doul, the great San Francisco slugger, had returned with financial and moral support. The knowledgeable and passionate fans were waiting for the Cardinals and their star player.

"They gave us a parade like we won the World Series," recalled Joe Cunningham, a younger teammate, who added: "Stan was tired. We all were tired."

Just like the American navy brass in 1945, the Japanese fans had high expectations of Musial's power.

"I tried awfully hard to please the Japanese fans. But I remember hitting only two home runs," Musial said. "Home runs were what the Japanese expected of me. I was tired, worn out after the regular season. I'm sorry they couldn't have seen me earlier."

The hosts would give a present to every player who gave an interview for radio or television, along with a gift to his wife or girlfriend. In his autobiography, Musial described "one unending whirl of parades, ball games, receptions, conducted tours, cocktail parties, dinners and entertainment. From the prime minister to the countless Japanese school kids we saw playing ball every day, the Japanese were gracious hosts, kind and courteous."

He impressed the Japanese by learning how to sign his autograph in Japanese characters. He also came up with a story he would tell for decades: "At one of the countless interviews I had with the radio and TV people, I mentioned that I was in the restaurant business. One writer asked, 'Ah, so, Musial-san. Are you then a waiter?' "

Without knowing it, Musial had a role in the career of one of Japan's greatest players—Sadaharu Oh, then seventeen, the son of a Chinese noodle-shop operator and a Japanese mother. In a country that loves its national high school tournament, the Koshien, Oh was already Japan's best known prospect.

With Musial on everybody's mind, Oh's batting coach, Tetsuharu Kawakami, strongly suggested Oh adapt Musial's coiled stance.

"Hitting is with your hip, not with your hand," said Kawakami, who had won five batting titles in Japan. "You can see the ball with your hip." But the youngster was uncomfortable twisting his body that way and, with the obstinacy of a seventeen-year-old, Oh declined.

Several years later, on the brink of failure, partially through his excesses and hardheadedness, Oh would submit to his guru and accept an even more idiosyncratic stance, with his front leg, the right one, lifted in the middle of his swing.

The flamingo stance, as the Japanese would call it, had its roots in the twisted Musial position. That barnstorming trip by the Cardinals would help produce Oh's 868 homers, the greatest total by any hitter in baseball history.

Years later, Musial and Oh would meet, shake hands, and bow to each other, left-handed sluggers from opposite shores, comrades in unorthodoxy.


PLAYING AGAINST all-star teams, the Cardinals won 14 games and lost 2. The players also had a chance to get acquainted with their new manager, Solomon Joseph Hemus, known as "Solly" or "the Mouse," one of those pepper-pot middle-infielder types out of the Durocher mold.

Hemus had come up with the Cardinals in 1949 and immediately showed an opportunistic side, slipping his shoes in Musial's locker so they would get shined on Musial's tab.

"Butch Yatkeman did a real good job," Hemus said in 2010, by which time he had long left baseball and become rich in the oil bidness. "He always took care of Stan, and I was just a rookie. I'd just slide 'em in there. One day he almost caught me. I don't think Stan cared."

His parents did not name him Solomon for nothing. Upon being traded to the Phillies in 1956, Hemus wrote a letter to Busch saying how much he loved the Cardinals and would like to come back someday.

"I thought maybe I could go back as a coach, maybe manage in the minor leagues, something," Hemus said. "I put it in the back of my mind; I don't know if I was really striving. When I had the job offered to me, naturally I took it."

Naturally. Busch never forgot the letter and told Devine that Hemus was going to be the next manager, starting with the Asian trip. Watching a tired old man trudge through a November barnstorming tour, Hemus formed his impression that Stanley had very little left.

Jeanne was born early in 1959, and Musial received permission to report late to spring training, which did not help him. He did not hit early in the season and looked awkward in left field, so Hemus moved him to first base, forcing Bill White to play the outfield. Some days Hemus did not play Musial at all. His explanation was that he was resting him, not benching him.

In August, the *Sporting News* ran a copyrighted story that Musial might be traded for Yogi Berra, who could have been a Cardinal all along if Branch Rickey had had the presence of mind to sign him. The paper also reported a "coolness" between Hemus and Musial.

This was the first time Musial had confronted the serious prospect of failure and rejection since the Trader Lane episode, yet this most stable athlete managed to not upset his entire household. Gerry Ashley could not remember any dark cloud hanging over her father as she entered her teens. Half a century later, she asked her mother about the Hemus years.

"My mom said, 'Your father was pretty inconsolable,' " Gerry reported.

Lil told her daughter, "I tried to reason with him, saying, 'You are getting older.' But looking back, I shouldn't have told him that."

It was probably not a good thing to tell a superstar who was dealing with rumors and sitting on the bench at the same time. Everybody agreed the Berra rumor was foolish, and Busch once again affirmed that Musial would never be traded. Busch also called him out to Grant's Farm to ask whether Hemus should be fired.

"I said, 'I think Solly deserves a little more chance of being the Cardinal manager,' " Musial said in the late nineties. "As I look back, I probably could have ended Solly's career at that time. He was thinking of firing him, but I gave Solly a vote of confidence. I thought maybe Solly'd let me play the next year. But I didn't play much. So he let him manage the next year, and about halfway into the next season they got rid of him."

The front office did agree that Musial would not play much the rest of the season, to give younger players a chance. Asked about reports of coolness between himself and Musial, Hemus tried to make a joke out of it: "I'd better not go to his restaurant anymore. I'll probably get nothing but tough steaks."

He was still joking about it in 2010. "His kids hated me, of course. They wouldn't talk to me," Hemus said.

"Please tell him that was not the case, at least for me," Gerry Ashley said, recalling how the Musial and Hemus women got along during that time. Marguerite Hemus and her daughter, Peggy, drove to spring training in a caravan with Lil and Gerry—a major responsibility, since Lil had not started driving until she was thirty and was still not comfortable with high speeds and long distances. Gerry remembered the drive as fun, with no sense of rancor.

"Dad never brought any problems home," Gerry said.

Hemus could joke about it years later, but he was under intense pressure to do the right thing by Stanley. Bob Broeg said he urged Hemus to give Musial more of a chance, reminding the manager how Musial had tipped him to use a lighter bat earlier in his career.

It was true, Hemus admitted in 2010. He had hit 16 homers in five years in the minor leagues, but in 1952 and 1953 he hit 15 and 14 home runs, respectively.

"He gave me a lot of good tips on hitting," Hemus admitted. "Getting out in front on the ball. He's a great baseball man. Unless you ask him, he wouldn't bother. A lot of ballplayers don't want a lot of advice. They want to go down the road themselves. I wasn't like that. I was looking for anything I could get."

Broeg told Hemus he owed Musial more patience, but Hemus used him in only 115 games and Musial wound up hitting .255 in 1959, by far the worse average of his career. Friends suggested it might be time to retire, but he shrugged them off.

He did acknowledge the miserable year by accepting the maximum pay cut allowable under union rules, twenty percent, from $100,000 to $80,000. In his Broeg-written autobiography, Musial adopts the passive voice—"I took a pretty good cut without complaint"—but in the *Sporting News* article, his quotes suggest he initiated the cut: "The Cardinals have been generous to me the past few years, so I thought I'd be kind to them." Needless to say, the Cardinals obliged his sporting gesture.

In the same winter, he worked out under the noted physical educator, Walter Eberhardt of St. Louis University, along with other players, and when Musial reported to spring training in 1960 he looked five years younger.

He still did not hit. This time Hemus did not deny that Musial was being benched rather than merely rested. That fall, while campaigning for John F. Kennedy, Musial told his new friend James A. Michener that the Cardinals had tested his eyesight.

"Stan Musial, who functioned longer than most, told me a bittersweet story," Michener wrote. " 'One of the saddest days of my life was when I found out about my eyes. Before age forty I hadn't felt the slightest loss in seeing. Then my eyes started to go bad. The ball looked so much smaller than it used to. First base seemed to be actually farther away. So the Cards sent me to the top eye doctors, and they examined me for a while with the latest machines, and at the end they gave me the bad news. "There's absolutely nothing wrong with your eyes." I was just getting older, like everybody else.' "

Hemus made the benching worse by misleading Musial. On May 14, he told Musial he would play in the second game, but when he made out the lineup card, Musial was not on it. Musial questioned Hemus about it in the clubhouse, maybe the first time he had ever been heard to openly challenge a manager.

Things got worse. On May 16, Hemus used Musial as a pawn, sending him up to pinch-hit with first base open, an obvious invitation to the opposing manager to walk Musial on purpose. By that strategy, Hemus bestowed the responsibility on Carl Sawatski, a backup catcher who would hit .229 that season. Sawatski promptly made Hemus look like a genius by stroking a game-winning sacrifice fly—no surprise to Solomon.

Hemus did make two good moves that season, sending Curt Flood to center field and restoring Bill White to first base, the natural positions for both. However, for much of the season left field was patrolled by a cast of thousands. As the fans fretted, Busch summoned Musial, Hemus, Bing Devine, and the brewery official Richard A. Meyer to Busch's estate, and the Cardinals publicly confirmed that Musial was being benched indefinitely.

While Musial was observing the open tryout in left field, he came as close to leaving the Cardinals as he ever would. When the Pirates were in St. Louis in June, Les Biederman of the *Pittsburgh Press* quoted a "friend" of Musial's as saying: "You don't take a player who has starred for nineteen years and stick him in the corner of the dugout and let him die."

The "friend" continued: "You know, I believe there's only one team Stan would play for aside from the Cardinals. I mean, the Pirates. I sort of think he's going to say his farewell going down the stretch with a pennant contender from his old home town."

Biederman, as beat reporters do, promptly asked Danny Murtaugh, the manager of the Pirates, about the possibility of acquiring Musial, and Murtaugh was quoted as saying, "You know, I do believe we might be able to find a place for a fellow like Stan Musial." Murtaugh was also quoted as saying, "But heck, Stan never would leave the Cardinals."

Many years later, Broeg confirmed he was indeed the friend, but said Joe L. Brown, the general manager of the Pirates, had told him, "As much as we'd like to have Musial, we won't make an offer for him. I just can't do it to Bing Devine, a fine man. Sure, if Musial were released, we would grab him in a minute." Busch was not about to give Musial away, and the Pirates could not afford him. But for a few days, the option was there.

In late June, Bob Nieman, who had played very well in Musial's absence, was injured, and Musial was back in the lineup, quietly seething, going on a 20-for-41 tear. Totally by statistical accident, he happened to murder the Pirates the rest of the year, as they won the pennant.

"By then, when I'd go home to Donora to visit my mother, even friends and neighbors were giving me a hard look. They were happy I was hitting, but not when I beat their Bucs."

In 1964, Musial and Broeg would come out with Musial's autobiography, which mildly criticized Hemus for benching him. Hemus, by then the third-base coach in Cleveland, put out a statement:

> I benched Musial because he was in a batting slump in 1960 after the Cardinals had finished seventh in 1959. I'd bench my own brother under similar circumstances.
>
> The newspapers in St. Louis published editorials when I benched Musial but nobody said anything when we climbed up to third place. Bob Nieman, who replaced Musial, saved my job for me. He carried the whole team on his back until he injured his leg. If Nieman hadn't been hurt, Musial would have stayed out much longer than the month and a half he was benched.
>
> Musial and I are friends. He's good for the team on and off the field. He's the easiest player I ever managed. But there's no room for sentiment in baseball.

Musial got through 1960 the same way he had outlasted Trader Lane. He hit .275 in 116 games with slightly more power, and the Pirates wound up winning the World Series without him.

It probably worked out for everybody. Moving to his home region might have smacked of a mercy move, and Stanley had a good thing going in St. Louis. His basic instinct was, *Do not disturb.*

# 34

## ON THE HUSTINGS

STANLEY RAN with a different crowd in the fall of 1960. Instead of traveling with Red and the other Cardinals, he was part of a merry band that romped around the middle of the country, campaigning for John F. Kennedy for president.

By now, Musial had been out and about, had met a lot of celebrities, and was not in awe of much. In his own Stanley way he fit right in with temporary teammates like Byron (Whizzer) White, a former professional football player and later a Supreme Court justice; James A. Michener, the Pulitzer Prize–winning author; Arthur M. Schlesinger Jr., the writer; Ethel Kennedy and Joan Kennedy; and Hollywood stars Jeff Chandler and Angie Dickinson.

"Oh, my God, he was always funny," Dickinson said about Musial in 2010. "Of course, he wasn't funny when we were giving speeches but funny when we hung out together. We all ate dinner together after our rallies and he was the life of the party. Such a dear guy."

They all bonded quickly, like an all-star team thrown together for a short time, eager to hear one another's shop talk. They were united in support of the young senator from Massachusetts, who was forty-two at the time, three and a half years older than Musial.

Musial often told how he had been recruited after meeting Kennedy on a street corner in Milwaukee in September 1959. The senator sought out the ballplayer while he was touring Wisconsin, preparing for his presidential run, and was told the Cardinals were outside their hotel, waiting for the team bus.

"They tell me you're too old to play ball and I'm too young to be president, but maybe we'll fool them," Kennedy said.

Musial, who had favored Dwight D. Eisenhower, the Republican moderate, in the 1952 and 1956 elections, was already kindly disposed toward the energetic young senator, through Musial's partnership with Biggie, who was active in Democratic politics.

The Kennedy "vigah"—as people pronounced it in those days, imitating the family Boston accent—also won Musial over. The Kennedys were Roman Catholic as well, which undoubtedly touched a nerve in Musial.

The young senator was having a hard time in many midwestern and western states, facing questions about whether he would be loyal to his religion, to a foreign pope, rather than to the United States. The Kennedy people wanted to flood some Republican states with familiar names and faces, and apparently White suggested Musial, who had never been politically active. Musial agreed to go along for the last week of the campaign in Michigan, Illinois, Nebraska, Utah, Idaho, Colorado, Indiana, and Kentucky.

The group was flown from rally to rally in the private plane of Jerold Hoffberger, the president of the National Brewing Company and principal owner of the Baltimore Orioles, who was between Musial and Kennedy in age. It was summer camp.

"No time was designated for meals or washing up. There were speeches, short plane hops, more speeches, long plane hops, more speeches, and a distant hotel in which to flop," wrote Michener, who had been active in Democratic politics in the Philadelphia area.

"Each day saw four or five meetings, interviews with press and television, impromptu talks to clubs or boys' houses or supermarkets, and an endless procession of local political aspirants who hoped that we would say something to further their candidacies. It was as grueling a tour as could have been devised."

All the campaigners turned out to be troupers, already used to the rigors of the road. Musial, who had slept in the bunks of trains, seemed energized by the campaign, fitting in with academics and actors. Michener called him "one of the most hilarious characters I have ever met," and he added: "I was constantly astonished at how the men in the cities we stopped at would crowd the airports to see Stan Musial. He seemed about fifteen years younger than he was, and men who were now quite old remembered him as a beginner in the big leagues."

Musial's campaign style was straight and simple: see ball, hit ball. He would make a brief baseball allusion and then a quick plug for Kennedy. Michener described his talk in Denver: "I played in Denver once about ten years ago. I struck out three times." When the laughter subsided, Musial said, "Tonight I'm not here to play baseball. I'm here to ask you to vote for Senator John F. Kennedy."

A lifelong friendship was developing from this first meeting between Michener and Musial. Everybody saw the outgoing side of Musial, but in this long road trip through America, Michener saw the serious side, too, as Musial expressed his remorse about the declined (and perhaps mythical) basketball scholarship to Pitt.

On one ride, Musial told his new friend why he was campaigning for the young Democrat who talked of a more just society. "All that I have I got because older men helped me. That's why I'm for Kennedy." It was an acknowledgment of the Barbaos and Russells, the Dudas and Pizzicas, who had directed him toward this time, when he could stand in front of crowds and ask them to vote for a Roman Catholic from back East.

Michener also praised two Kennedy wives—Ethel, the wife of Robert F. Kennedy, and Joan, then the wife of Ted Kennedy—as good speakers with strong and impeccable political instincts.

And Michener was totally taken with Angie Dickinson. What man would not be? He described her as "a strikingly beautiful young woman with golden blond hair, dark eyes and a truly gamin manner." (That description matches the very same breathtaking young actress I spotted in a box seat on my first visit to Dodger Stadium in 1962. *So this is Los Angeles*, I thought.)

Born in North Dakota, Dickinson had grown up in Los Angeles, had just appeared in a movie with Frank Sinatra, and ran with him and his Rat Pack friends. Michener described her as "a delightful girl to have aboard an airplane," and he added, "She had a low raucous laugh that quite demoralized serious discussion." He marveled at her talent for "looking gorgeous despite the primitive conditions."

Dickinson declined to go by formalities, even toward the august Schlesinger, whom Michener describes as "not a man who unbends easily."

Dickinson addressed Schlesinger as "Artie"—probably the only person in history who did.

"Artie, you were a sensation tonight. Nobody could understand a damned word you said, but you said it so impressively!"

Dickinson was the baseball fan in the group. Like many Angelenos, native or imported, she had been attracted to the sport when the Dodgers came to town in 1958. Suddenly the dulcet voice of Vin Scully could be heard, describing major-league baseball to southern California.

"We had no ball club and they won their second year here and went to the World Series," Dickinson said. She remembered going out to dinner one night, seeing a waiter with a plug in his ear, and blurting, "Oh, isn't that a shame, he's hard of hearing." Her companion said, "No, Angie, he's listening to the ball game."

Her good friend Johnny Grant, a prominent man about town, escorted her to the Dodgers' temporary home in the football stadium, the Los Angeles Coliseum. Grant had worked for Gene Autry, the singing movie cowboy who would buy the new Los Angeles Angels in 1961, and Grant knew everybody in baseball.

"Johnny had the great seats in the Coliseum, if there was such a thing," Dickinson said, recalling how Grant would catch the attention of somebody on the field during batting practice. She once was introduced to Musial from a distance, with Dickinson waving and mouthing an exaggerated "Hi, I think you're great."

The next time they met was in Oklahoma. Dickinson had been recruited to the Kennedy campaign by Jeff Chandler, who was suave and handsome and gray-haired, like an earlier George Clooney.

"Jeff and I had dated, and he called me up and said, 'How would you like to go out and campaign for the Kennedys?' I said I'd love it. He said we would leave Monday and go to Tulsa, and travel through seven states. You give your spiel at every stop. I was one of those liberal Democrats and I was single and free. I said, 'I'm on.' "

Now, instead of watching from a seat in the sprawling Coliseum, Dickinson got to meet Musial up close, and vice versa. There were no secrets on the plane.

"These were the days before hot curlers," Dickinson recalled. "You started from scratch every day. I remember getting on the plane one day, bandana on, wet curlers underneath, and Stan saying, 'Oh, do we have to look at you all day?' "

Wherever the plane touched down, they would talk up John F. Kennedy to crowds of Republican Protestants. In between, they would pick each other's brains. Dickinson recalled: "They all want to know, 'What's John Wayne like?' and we all want to know, 'How do you hit like that?' "

Dickinson remembered a Stanley tale about a teammate who was feeling so good one day that he blurted, "I feel like going four for four today." Musial quickly told him: "Hell, I feel like that every day."

Dickinson recalled: "Mostly, when we gathered at the end of the day, we let our hair down. You know, after Senator Kennedy became president, he came out to his sister's house, there were only ten of us, he said, 'You all want to talk politics, I want to talk movies.' "

It was the same thing during the campaign, Dickinson said. "When you got through the day, you were ready to relax and not talk about things that upset you, have a good meal and a drink and start out the next day."

The way the tour worked, the plane would land somewhere, and they would face the crowds. They had all experienced public adulation. Whizzer White had scored touchdowns in giant stadiums. Dickinson had entertained troops at Christmastime, heard thousands of wolf whistles. Chandler had heard female shrieks at movie premieres.

One day at a windswept airport, Chandler heard a roar from the crowd and wondered why Republicans were being so enthusiastic. Then he realized they were cheering for Stan the Man, as if it were Sportsman's Park.

"We were well aware they were against us," Dickinson said. "That's why they booed us and threw things at us. That's why we went to those states."

This was red-state/blue-state tension in an earlier time. Michener described one country club in Boise, Idaho, where the well-turned-out "bridge-playing women" would not even acknowledge the Democratic celebrities.

In Bloomington, Indiana, home of the University of Indiana, the Kennedy supporters were trailed by Republican fraternity and sorority members who were determined to shout them down. It got pretty nasty, Dickinson recalled.

"Boise, Salt Lake City, Denver," she remembered. "They were all tough states."

In Indianapolis, Shelley Winters showed up and so did Ernie Banks, who was a friend of Musial's. Then the entourage moved on to Lexington, Kentucky.

"We all had people driving us around to our hotels," Dickinson said. "I remember quite a tall guy drove me. About fifteen years later, I met Governor John Y. Brown and he said, 'I was your driver.' " It was an experience a man would tend to remember.

Musial left after Lexington because he wanted to be home for the weekend, even though it meant missing the wrap-up rally at the New York Coliseum.

"He said, 'Will you tell Senator Kennedy how sorry I am that I didn't get to finish the trip?' " said Dickinson, who would be one of the speakers at the finale.

"My big claim to fame is that I was making my speech, I heard a hush, and they wheeled in Mrs. Roosevelt, Eleanor Roosevelt, and I got to say, 'What I have to say isn't important.' I almost was finished. 'Ladies and gentlemen, the great Eleanor Roosevelt.' "

Dickinson said she conveyed Musial's regrets to Senator Kennedy. From a distance of all those years, all the gossip, her name linked to both Sinatra and Kennedy, Dickinson, with great warmth and dignity, recalled that short, heady era of John Fitzgerald Kennedy: "We got to be in the in crowd, the Sinatra crowd, and I got to meet him again. All the passion of wanting him to win."

John F. Kennedy did win—"by a hundred thousand votes," Dickinson said, still exuberant half a century later. "I take a lot of credit for those hundred thousand."

Kennedy received 34,220,984 popular votes and Richard M. Nixon received 34,108,156, but the total that really mattered was the electoral votes. Kennedy gained 303 of them and Nixon had 219.

This result became a punch line for Musial over the years.

"We went to nine Western states," he often said. "And would you believe Kennedy lost every one? Kennedy's people said, 'It's a good thing we didn't send this group to New York. We'd have lost the election.' "

After Kennedy squeaked through, Michener signed a photo of himself and wrote "Nixon 9, Kennedy 0" on it—just the kind of clubhouse humor Musial appreciated.

It was a good joke, although not quite accurate. Michener mentions visiting Michigan, Illinois, Nebraska, Utah, Idaho, Colorado, Indiana, and Kentucky. And Dickinson recalls Tulsa, Oklahoma. Nixon did win seven of them, but Kennedy won Michigan handily and Illinois by less than seven thousand votes. Every vote counted. And Stan the Man, at the very least, had charmed many Republican fans.

For his reward, Musial was included on the A-list at the inauguration, where Dickinson got to observe his sense of loyalty up close.

A well-connected Washingtonian, Jane E. Wheeler, who had helped during the campaign, organized a dinner party for one hundred Kennedy supporters at her home the night after the inauguration. Stan and Lil were included.

"You can imagine what a hard ticket that was," Dickinson said.

However, there was a complication. Biggie and Teresa Garagnani had accompanied the Musials to Washington to celebrate the election of the Democrat. Musial asked that the Garagnanis be included, but Wheeler politely said she could not find two more places.

At the gala on inauguration night, Dickinson told Stan and Lil, "I'll see you tomorrow," but they said they would not be there.

"I said, 'Oh, my God, why?' and they said, 'We couldn't bring Biggie, so we won't abandon our friend,' so they did not attend one of the most memorable dinner parties ever. Everybody who made a difference was there."

Dickinson thought about how loyal Stan and Lil were to their friends.

"If that was me? 'See you later,' " she said.

Dickinson would always feel close to her friends from summer camp. Although she never met Michener again, she said, "We were all bound emotionally as well as physically."

A few years later, she received a photograph from Spain, where Michener was working on his book *Iberia*. The photo was of a marquee of a movie theater where Dickinson's film, *The Poppy Is Also a Flower,* was playing. She had a major role, along with E. G. Marshall and Trevor Howard, with supporting roles from stars like Rita Hayworth, Yul Brynner, Jean-Paul Belmondo, and Marcello Mastroianni. On that marquee, Angie Dickinson's name was in the biggest letters.

"He knew I'd like that," Dickinson said, noting that transmitting a photograph was not as simple as in today's digital age. "What a gracious man."

Dickinson kept up with the Musials, once sharing girl talk with Lil at a Cardinals game in the Coliseum. "She was adorable," Dickinson said.

When the Dodgers and Angels both moved to the new Dodger Stadium, she and Johnny Grant would sit in Sinatra's box seats between home and first ("Frank was smart, he knew there was more action between home and first").

Over the years, Dickinson would meet the Musials at the home of Gene and Jackie Autry. "Stan played his harmonica, Tommy Lasorda was there. Gene was a wonderful host."

Lil could sizzle a bit when women fussed over her husband, so there was the question of what she thought of Stan's week on the road in such gorgeous company. However, when Tom Ashley, her son-in-law, was making a documentary about Stan years later, Lil told him, "You ought to talk to Angie Dickinson." Ashley never got to California to meet Dickinson, but Lil's reaction indicated she felt friendship toward the actress.

Musial and John F. Kennedy would meet only once again, during the All-Star Game in Washington in 1962. Musial always referred to him as "my buddy"—a generational thing between two gregarious warriors who knew the roar of the crowd.

# 35

---

# BETTER PANTS

RUBEN AMARO was called up in the summer of 1958, a slender shortstop from Mexico, the son of a famous Cuban-born slugger named Santos Amaro, who never got a chance in the majors because of his dark skin.

Worldly beyond his twenty-two years, Amaro knew a rookie's place in the clubhouse—the far end. He observed that Musial was given two lockers, close to the tunnel, where a breeze blew in from the field.

In his own locker, Amaro found a pair of game pants at least two sizes too big. He knew better than to complain. He put on the baggy uniform and was heading toward the field when Musial turned and introduced himself.

"Everybody tells me your father was a great player in Cuba," Musial said.

"Yes, sir," Amaro said.

Musial said he had gone barnstorming in Cuba years earlier with the Cardinals' coach, Mike Gonzalez.

"I believe I played against your father," Musial said.

Then Musial called over the diminutive clubhouse man, Butch Yatkeman, who had been there forever, and said, "Butch, would you get this young man a pair of pants so he can play like a major leaguer." Butch quickly came up with better pants.

That wasn't the end of the kindness.

The Cardinals still had a pecking order during batting practice—older players first, younger players later, maybe. Amaro stayed back with the irregulars until Musial noticed it and told his teammates, "Hey, he's playing today—let him have some swings."

Amaro would have a long career as shortstop, coach, and scout; his son, Ruben Amaro Jr., would play in the majors and become general manager of the Phillies.

Santos Amaro's son never forgot the man who made it easier for him in a major-league clubhouse.

# 36

---

## WHEN THE TIMES CHANGED

AFTER SO many years of spring training, the Musials had a routine:
They would rent a house in Passe-a-Grille, near the lapping waters
of the Gulf of Mexico. Yogi and Carmen Berra would rent a house nearby,
and the couples would often go out for dinner, following the aroma of
grilled shrimp or steaks in the warm evening air.

Dick was at Notre Dame; the two older girls would board at their
Catholic school in St. Louis. It was only six weeks or so, Gerry said, but her
stint in boarding school felt like six months. Jeannie was little, so Lil would
take her along, a nice break from late winter in St. Louis. The Cardinals
did not make Stan take many bus trips to other towns in Florida, so sometimes he would be home in midafternoon, with time to go to the beach.

The privileged life came under scrutiny in 1961, when some of the
African American players began to protest the segregated living conditions
of spring training.

By dragging their feet on race, the Cardinals had performed a disser-
vice to everybody. Seven years after Jackie Robinson's debut, the Cardinals' first successful black player, Brooks Lawrence, a rookie pitcher with a
15–6 record, still had to sit in the "colored" waiting room in Union Station
in St. Louis while the Cardinals were waiting for their train.

Bob Dylan was preparing to write "Blowin' in the Wind" in 1963 and
Sam Cooke was about to write his prophetic "A Change Is Gonna Come,"
but the Cardinals were still back in the era of "Pass the Biscuits, Mirandy."

Trader Lane and Bing Devine had accumulated black talent but Bob
Gibson, a pitcher and former basketball star out of Creighton University,

became alienated when Hemus confused Gibson with Julio Gotay, a Latino shortstop. Even when Hemus learned to tell them apart, he made it clear that he did not think Gibson could be a major-league star.

Ruben Amaro, who got along with almost everyone, was left with the impression that Hemus did not like black players. It did not help that Hemus kept himself on the active list as a shortstop. One day Hemus put himself into the game as a pinch hitter and called Bennie Daniels, a pitcher with the Pirates, a "black son of a bitch." Gibson, standing a few feet away, never forgot it.

Amaro did not see Musial as having any racial issues. He admired Musial's style: the man kept an extra suit or two in every clubhouse on the road, which meant he could travel light but always wear a jacket and tie. *Imagine that*, Amaro thought. *Stash has an entire league full of suits.*

After one season, Amaro was shuttled to the Phillies. "I cried when they traded me," he said.

In 1959, the Cardinals acquired the type of player they had never had before—an older black leader, George Crowe, thirty-eight years old, a legendary basketball player from Indiana, who had been confined to Negro League baseball before finally making it to the majors in 1952.

By the time he reached the Cardinals, Crowe was a wise old presence—at least for the black players. "He was more like a dad and a teacher than teammate, and most of what he counseled me on had nothing to do with playing the game," Bob Gibson said. Crowe also lent out his Jeep to some of the younger players, which earned him the nickname of "Jeep."

Crowe would hit fourteen pinch homers in the majors, a record for the time. With the Cardinals, he would pad up and down in the dugout, quietly spreading wisdom but not asserting himself because he knew this was not his town and not his team.

Musial seemed to respect Crowe's professionalism. "I watched George punish himself in practice and asked him about it," Musial said through Bob Broeg in a *Sport* magazine piece. Musial quoted Crowe as saying, "The more time you spend on the bench the harder you've got to work to be ready when you're called."

Broeg made it sound as if Musial and Crowe were kindred old souls, working together to help the Cardinals, but half a century later Crowe did not profess the same memories. He had never been able to get a job in the majors after his playing career ended in 1961 and had become something of a curmudgeon and recluse in the woods.

In 2009, Crowe was living in a nursing home in California, about to turn eighty-eight. He was not the presence he had been decades earlier, but he seemed alert, not interested in diplomacy.

Crowe praised Musial as a hitter—"right up there with them"—but insisted he never got to know him in his two-plus seasons with the Cardinals. He also suggested Musial was encouraged to keep playing "whether he was producing or not, because of the past. He'd been there so long."

"He was kind of quiet . . . he didn't say much," Crowe said. "I stayed away from him pretty much. I was a newcomer and I was black so I just stayed away."

They didn't get to know each other?

"No, no," Crowe replied.

Crowe and Musial were from the same generation, from opposite sides of the racial divide. The younger African American players showed a double disconnect, mimicking Musial's whaddayasay-whaddayasay persona.

Curt Flood wrote about Musial in his autobiography:

We played side by side for eight years, occupied space in the same locker room, negotiated with the same employer and, within those limits, had experiences in common. But he had other things going for him.

Stan was one of the outstanding players of all time. He was so exceptionally talented, popular and durable that he played for twenty-one seasons, amassed substantial wealth and became a member of the Cardinal management. As an authentic superstar, he lived remote from the difficulties encountered by lesser athletes. Like Mays, he saw the world entirely in terms of his own good fortune. He was convinced that it was the best of all possible worlds. He not only accepted baseball mythology but propounded it. Whereas the typical player all but choked while reciting the traditional gibberish of gratitude to the industry, and whereas Bob Gibson, superstar of another hue, would simply change the subject, Musial was a true believer. Gibson and I once clocked eight "wunnerfuls" in a Musial speech that could not have been longer than a hundred words.

"My biggest thrill is just wearing this major-league uniform," Stan used to say. "It's wunnerful being here with all these wunnerful fellas.'"

At this point Flood described Gibson reciting a litany of profanity, sotto voce. Then he continued:

We admired Musial as an athlete. We liked him as a man. There was no conscious harm to him. He was just unfathomably naive. After twenty years of baseball, his critical faculties were those of a schoolboy. After twenty years, he was still wagging his tail for the front office—not because he felt it politic to do so but because he believed every word he spoke.

Raised in Oakland, California, Flood was wary in St. Louis. He told of taking a date to Musial's restaurant and being refused service, and when Flood mentioned it, Musial "turned livid. He said he'd look into it. I never raised the topic with him again, nor did he with me." Flood later confirmed that Musial had checked and been told the kitchen was already closed when Flood arrived. Either way, Flood admitted, he never had a problem at Musial's restaurant after that.

Musial was upset by Flood's comments, one of the few times he had ever been publicly criticized in St. Louis, or anywhere.

The sixties were beginning; the younger players were speaking up. In 1961, Bill White, born in Florida and educated at Hiram College in Ohio, told Joe Reichler, a well-connected baseball writer with the Associated Press, that he was tired of watching the white Cardinals being invited to the annual Salute to Baseball breakfast by the St. Pete Chamber of Commerce.

"They invited all but the colored players," White said. "Even the kids who never have come to bat once in the big leagues received invitations—that is, if they were white. . . . How much longer must we accept this without saying a word? This thing keeps gnawing away my heart. I think about this every minute of the day."

The Cardinals insisted they had invited only players living downtown and that Musial had not been expected to attend, since he lived out by the beach. The burghers of St. Pete hastily issued an invitation to White, who promptly informed them he did not like getting up early for a public appearance.

White also complained to Reichler about the way the Cardinals housed their white players in the Vinoy Hotel, alongside Tampa Bay, but the black players were forced to stay in private homes in the black neighborhood.

"When will we be made to feel like humans?" White asked.

This had been going on since the Yankees and Cardinals first signed black players a decade earlier. The black players stayed with Dr. Ralph Wimbish, the head of the St. Petersburg chapter of the NAACP, and a dentist, Robert J. Swain, who built the Rosa Apartments next to his office and sometimes rented rooms in his home to black players.

In 1961, the two doctors said they felt "degraded" at having to provide housing for major leaguers, in the words of Rosalie Peck, the former wife of Dr. Swain. "They said, 'Damn it, we're not going to do this anymore,'" Peck said in 2008.

Curt Flood, who had access to Gussie Busch, took up the issue of housing with the owner. Flood quoted Busch as saying, "Do you mean to tell me, that you're not staying here at the hotel with the rest of the fellas?"

"Mr. Busch, don't you know that we're staying about five miles outside of town in the Negro section?" Flood asked. Busch said he would do something about it the next year.

"Busch was just worried about profits," Bill White said in 2009.

The Cardinals teetered into the 1961 season, winning only thirty-three of their first seventy-four games, and Hemus was fired. Gibson still refers to 1961 as "the year I got out of prison."

The new manager was Johnny Keane, a former seminarian whose major-league hopes had been set back by a fractured skull in 1935. Keane had the wrinkled look of Colonel Potter, the avuncular officer in the television series $M^*A^*S^*H$, but could occasionally stun umpires with language distinctly secular. His first move as manager was to hand the ball to Gibson and say, "You're pitching, Hoot."

The Cardinals could not catch the Reds in 1961, as Musial hit .288 in 123 games, but they began to repair the clubhouse.

For the spring of 1962, Gussie Busch followed through on his promise to Flood. He arranged to rent two motels on the south end of town, near the skyway to Bradenton and Sarasota, and let it be known that all players and their families would be welcome. The announcement stopped just short of an order, and was something of an inconvenience to families used to living out by the beach, with space for visitors, cookouts, and privacy.

Mildred White, who was married to Bill White at the time, was not sure the Musials and Boyers would be supportive. "All those years, they had a place by the beach and a lot of them put their kids in school or got themselves a tutor," she said.

On her first day at the motel, Mildred White noticed Stan and Lil and Jeanne staying in one room. The players went off to work every morning, leaving the wives and children behind.

"There was really nothing for the kids to do," recalled White, who had taken education courses in college. "I had two daughters. I said, why don't I get all the kids together from nine to twelve, listen to records, play games, keep the kids busy." The motel came up with a small building in the back and cleaned it out for her.

"Every morning at nine o'clock, the little kids would come out of their hotel rooms and we would walk down and play ring-around-the-rosey, London Bridge, little dance games, or we would color, just do anything that a kindergarten kid would be doing, keep them busy. Then they would go back to their little rooms, and they would have lunch and in the afternoon they would go to the swimming pool, and the fathers would come home and have dinner or do whatever they were going to do. But at least we kept them out of their moms' hair for a while. It gave them something to do, just to let them sit around and talk."

White has an enduring memory of that spring: "Little Jeannie Musial would come and sit at the table because she and my girls were the same age. The kids all stuck together and played together."

Stan and Lil have never talked much about that spring in the motel. Did they contemplate asking Busch for a dispensation? Did they see living in the motel as noblesse oblige, a gesture for those times—or a total pain in the neck?

Jeanne Edmonds, their youngest child, now a wife and mother, has told her sister Gerry she did not remember much about that spring or that motel. This suggests that whatever the Musials did, it was no big deal. They were with the team.

When Walter Eberhardt, the physical educator who helped the Cardinals with their training, came down from St. Louis, he would meet the wives and girlfriends alongside the pool and lead them in calisthenics. Unobtrusive, in the middle of the pack, was Lela Keane, the wife of the manager. Front and center, big smile on her face, was Lil Musial.

"Lil was great," Mildred White recalled. "She had this attitude that everybody is here."

The *Sporting News* carried a short article with the headline "Bill's Wife Solved Problem, Led Romper-Room Classes." The article added, "Owner Gussie Busch expressed pleasure with her work." Years later, White spoke of those weeks in Florida as a lovely time in her life.

Even hard-shelled Gibson was impressed: "Musial and Boyer were living in beachfront bungalows, but they gave them up to come stay with the rest of us."

The players entered into the spirit, with White and Gibson cooking, coach Howie Pollet making the salad, and Boyer and Larry Jackson buying and grilling the meat.

"People would drive by just to see all these black and white guys swimming and grilling steaks together," Gibson said.

The motel was their home. A championship team was being built, every morning in the Romper Room, every evening at the grille.

"If you were driving by and wanted to stay there, you couldn't," Mildred White said. "We had the dining room, nobody could come in. We had the whole place. He leased the whole thing so he would have control of it. He said to us, 'As long as you stay in any place I own, I will back you but if you go to a department store or anything, I can't vouch for you because this is their town, their place. What I own, I can back it up.'"

The Cardinals took the families to Weeki Wachee Springs to watch the pseudo-mermaids, and one day there was an outing to Busch Gardens.

"Charlene Gibson and I had two girls about the same age," Mildred White recalled. They took their girls to the bathroom, and one white woman made a comment. "I said, 'Ma'am, Augie Busch owns Busch Gardens, and he is my husband's boss, and if you don't watch out, I will have you put out of here.' And she looked at me like, 'Oh.' That's what the South was like."

Mildred White said once in a while she would hear a wife say, "Last year, we stayed at the beach," but in general "the wives were good, the wives got along very nicely, we did things together."

She recalled how friendly Lil Musial was in the organization of baseball wives, known as the Pinch Hitters, but that the wife of a prominent journalist used to back away from White and Beverly Flood.

"She must have thought it would rub off or something," White said. So she would be extra friendly to the woman, introduce herself every time, and shake her hand. "The older ones, we had to break in."

The same thing was happening with the players. The sly Gibson once spotted McCarver sipping from a soda bottle on the team bus and Gibson asked for a sip. McCarver said he would save some—a tip-off he did not want the bottle back after Gibson had used it. Gotcha, Gibson said. It was an early step in the education of James Timothy McCarver.

With all this testing going on, the younger players tried to get a measure of Stan the Man.

"Best hitter I ever saw," White said in 2009. "Nice guy, I guess. I don't know Stan. He was a great player, but I don't know him. I don't think any white guys knew him, either."

White had many careers: he helped the Cardinals win the 1964 World Series, tried to straighten out the syntax of Phil Rizzuto as a broadcaster with the Yankees, and served as president of the National League. He had mixed feelings about Musial but knew he was not one of the athletes who talked about striking when Jackie Robinson arrived in 1947.

"The Pittsburgh area has a lot of great athletes," White said. "I don't think he had any prejudice toward blacks. I think Stan didn't want to get involved either way."

When I suggested Musial had set an example to southern teammates like Harry Walker, White was defensive about the man who had been his hitting coach.

"Walker was instrumental in my career," White said, citing Walker's advice to drop a few bunts early in the season, when nobody was on guard, just to get a few surprise hits in the ledger. They had also talked openly about race.

"We'd yell and scream and get it out into the open," White said, suggesting Musial was more opaque—even about hitting.

"I think Stan was Stan," White added. "He was serious about hitting. Nobody could hit like that. He couldn't tell you how to hit.

"In batting practice, he hit the ball to left field, left center, center field, and then he'd say, 'Hey, hey, how do you like that hitting? Tee-hee, tee-hee.' And then he'd get the hell out of there."

Late into the conversation, White remembered one time he and Musial indulged in shop talk: "He did tell me he cut his eyelashes so he could see the ball better, so after that I cut my eyelashes, too."

The way things happen in life, some black players softened their views over the decades. Gibson was much too complicated to go on perceiving Musial as merely a man who spouted "wunnerful" all the time. They also wound up having the same business agent in Dick Zitzmann. By 2010, Gibson had nice things to say about Musial.

"The Cardinals were different. A group of us would go out to eat after a game on the road, and there'd be a dozen guys or so, black and white. Some of the white players—Stan Musial and Ken Boyer, to start with—were as adamant against segregation as the black players were."

Flood had found Musial saccharine in the early sixties and probably was not thrilled when Musial did not openly support his challenge to the reserve clause, but toward the end of Flood's short and turbulent life, he ran into Musial at the ballpark during the making of a documentary about Stan the Man. In the sweetest way, Flood told Musial that everybody on the Cardinals had tried to win one more pennant for him in his final season.

# 37

## OLD FOLKS

IN THE final weeks of the 1961 season, Johnny Keane called Musial into his office. Probably even the most loyal Musial fans would have understood if Keane had shuffled his extra lineup cards, looked up at the ceiling, and said, "Stan, a man's got to do what a man's got to do."

Musial was getting the feeling that nobody thought he had much left, maybe even the owner, maybe even Bing Devine, a supportive presence but also a general manager rebuilding a ball club. Stanley could catch the drift.

Only eighty games into his long-delayed chance to manage the Cardinals, Keane was about to show his independence. He had been admiring Musial from his days as a minor-league manager, when Keane was a perpetual candidate to take over the big club but was bypassed in favor of Walker, Hutchinson, and then Hemus. The front office finally brought Keane to the Cardinals in 1959 as a coach, maybe part of the master plan or maybe just a reward for a forty-seven-year-old lifer, to get him on the pension plan. Whatever the reason, Keane became a sane and unobtrusive buffer for the players, the way coaches can be. Then, probably to his own surprise, he replaced Hemus.

Keane immediately established himself as his own man, abolishing the poker games in the back of the plane because he did not like the idea of players losing money to teammates, with resentments carrying from plane to clubhouse. Now Keane had to make up his mind about Musial.

"Stan was on the bench," Keane said a few years later. "And as far as the Cardinals' organization was concerned, he was through as a player. He'd had it. I went over to him, and I said, 'Stan, I want you to play. What are you resting for? You haven't got far to go. Let's run the string out, but let's run it out on the ball field.'

"Stan Musial is the greatest guy in the world, and he reacted right away. He said, 'That's just exactly what I want to do, Johnny.' "

It is not enough to believe in oneself. Self-motivation and self-delusion are mirror images. What Musial wanted to hear was: "We need you, big guy."

Keane was not threatened by Musial, as managers are often threatened by fading superstars. He did not have the insecurity of Trader Lane or Solly Hemus, who had to shake up the team on a daily basis, to make the team over in their images. Keane and Musial seemed comfortable with each other, both of them disciplined men who understood they were not perfect.

The manager could blister the ears of an umpire with language that would have gotten him tossed out of Kenrick Seminary (where he cut class to moonlight as a high school quarterback). Musial could drop a bawdy line. They both smoked cigars. Musial drank a bit more than Keane, who sipped only out of politeness. It takes a great deal of inner security to say, "I want the old guy back." And toward the end of the 1961 season, that was what Keane said.

With Keane's encouragement, Musial went back to the gym in the winter of 1961–62, performed some of the old Falcons agility exercises, and came back more slender and lithe than he had been in a while. He had weighed 175 as a rookie and had gone up as far as 187—imagine: a slugger who weighed only 187 pounds—but in 1962 he was back down to 180, "and I could tell the difference," Musial said.

He had another reason to feel rejuvenated. In 1962 the National League expanded, after political pressure from the ubiquitous Branch Rickey for a third league. The league added teams in Houston and New York, the latter managed by Casey Stengel, who had taken one look at Musial in the tail end of 1941 and pronounced him one for the ages. Stanley openly adored Stengel—stood around and listened with a wide smile, called him "Case."

The hideous Mets—everybody could tell how awful they were after a few days in spring training—opened the season in St. Louis in what turned out to be typical fashion: a few of them got stuck in the elevator of the Chase-Park Plaza Hotel. How was that for an omen?

Just in case anybody had forgotten him back in Gotham, Stanley sent a little calling card, best described in the box score: Musial . . . 3-1-3-2.

From that perfect opening night, Musial just kept hitting. There is a theory that hitters benefited from expansion because each league suddenly had twenty pitchers who might not have been in the majors otherwise. When the American League expanded in 1961, Roger Maris hit 61 homers. More likely, Musial's renaissance was a credit to his winter workouts, Johnny Keane's faith in him, and Musial's own talent.

Musial enjoyed his visit to the Mets' temporary home in the rusting old Polo Grounds in uptown Manhattan. As dreadful as they were, the Mets had made possible a number of joyous returns by players not seen in those parts since 1957. Willie Mays came back with the Giants. Duke Snider came back with the Dodgers. And Stanley came back with the Cardinals.

Just the sight of Musial in the Polo Grounds raised instinctive respect in Alvin Jackson, out of the Pittsburgh organization, a decent left-hander good enough to lose twenty games in 1962.

"We've got a one-run lead with two outs and he comes up to pinch-hit," Jackson recalled in 2010. "My momma didn't raise no fool. He's not beating Mrs. Jackson's son. Not this day. No. So I walked him. And people are going, 'You put the tying run on base,' and I said, 'Don't even go there.' And Curt Flood came up and grounded out and people said, 'You walked a left-handed hitter,' and I said, 'That was no left-handed hitter. That was Stan Musial.'"

In early July 1962, Musial had himself quite a weekend with the extremely short porch in right field in the Polo Grounds. On Saturday he hit a homer in his last at-bat, just to get warmed up. Keane put him back in the lineup on Sunday.

Lil had missed his two other big home-run days. The time he hit three homers in Springfield in 1941, she was diapering their son. The time he hit five homers in a doubleheader in 1954, she was staying home after a late Saturday night. This time she was present as Stanley drilled three homers.

Immediately after that splurge, Musial went down to Washington, D.C., for the All-Star Game and a reunion with President John F. Kennedy, who openly cheered as Musial pinch-hit a single in the sixth inning.

The next day Senator Stuart Symington of Missouri arranged a tour for Stan and Lil and Janet, starting with meeting Robert F. Kennedy, the attorney general and brother of the president, who showed them around the Department of Justice. Then the Musials visited FBI headquarters, including the firing range.

"We came back to Bob Kennedy's office and he said, 'How would you like to visit my brother at the White House?' " recalled John H. Zentay, then a young staff aide to Senator Symington, who was escorting the Musials. "Stan, being Stan, said, 'No, we wouldn't want to bother him.' " Zentay assured him that if the Kennedys invited Musial to the White House, they meant it.

"I started driving Stan around for a few hours," recalled Zentay, who was thrilled to be handed Symington's Oldsmobile convertible with senatorial license plates. "The Jefferson Memorial, the Lincoln Memorial, all the sights around Washington. I noticed how often he was recognized and how much he loved it."

Musial insisted upon returning to the hotel to change into more formal clothing, and the small group arrived at the White House at three o'clock. Dave Powers, one of JFK's closest friends, traded baseball talk with Musial in a small room off the Oval Office.

"The photographer came in and took pictures of us while Janet sat in the president's chair," Zentay recalled. "I looked down at her and she went bug-eyed as in walked the president."

In his autobiography, Musial recalled: "Sure enough, President Kennedy greeted us personally and spent about fifteen minutes with us. He gave my wife a pen with his name on it. Janet received a paperweight medal and I got a PT Boat tie clasp."

Zentay, who had known Kennedy as a Senator from Massachusetts, noted that Musial and the president seemed to get along beyond the natural bonhomie of politician and athlete.

"It was clear there was affection," recalled Zentay, later a prominent lawyer in Washington.

When the president had to get back to work, he asked if they would like a tour of the living quarters.

"We found out later very few visitors are accorded this privilege," Musial said.

A White House aide escorted them to the kitchen and the solarium upstairs and then to the bedrooms. Zentay would remember the president's bedroom, with a four-poster bed and small table alongside it, containing perhaps twenty-five pillboxes. Nobody mentioned them. Then they visited Jackie Kennedy's bedroom and saw the extensive wardrobe in her closet.

"My mom was impressed by how Mrs. Kennedy's shoes were lined up to match her dresses," Gerry Ashley said.

After the unexpected hour in the White House, Zentay drove the Musials around Georgetown, where they sat on his landlord's porch and had a drink in the late-afternoon sun.

A few days later, Musial told a reporter: "Everything I have I owe to baseball. Can you imagine the son of a poor steel worker from Donora being invited to visit the President of the United States in the White House?"

KEANE MADE sure Musial took a day off here and there for important days like Dick's graduation from Notre Dame and Gerry's graduation from high school. Stanley wound up playing in 135 games in 1962 and batting .330, third in the league behind Tommy Davis and Frank Robinson.

"From the day he took over the Cardinals, Johnny Keane let me know that I was not only wanted but needed. He instilled enthusiasm and inspiration in me, and helped me find myself again," Musial said after the season.

However, as the season came to a close, Musial saw a familiar shadow over his shoulder: Gussie Busch, tired of waiting for a pennant, summoned Branch Rickey to be his advisor.

Rickey insisted publicly he was not there to subvert Devine, but Devine knew better and walked out of Rickey's first press conference. Rickey then moved into Devine's neighborhood and asked for a ride to the ballpark, which meant Devine not only had to feel Rickey's stiletto poised at his shoulder blades but also got to sample the blue fumes from Rickey's cigars and the verbiage on the run downtown.

One of Rickey's first acts was to force George Silvey, a prominent member of the front office, to return from a postseason vacation that Devine had authorized. The Cardinals quickly resented Rickey's meddlesome ways. Decades later, Tim McCarver would say: "I despised the guy."

Obviously Rickey had not been paying attention to the Trader Lane frolics of 1959, because he sent out hints that it was time for Musial to retire.

"Since when do you ask a .330 hitter to retire until you've got his equal to replace him?" Busch said, following with this declaration: "I told Frank Lane five years ago that Musial wouldn't be traded and I'm repeating now that Stan will finish his playing career in the Cardinals' uniform and that no one will wear his number 6 again."

One of Rickey's strengths was that he was not easily embarrassed.

"I'm afraid that I was under the impression, gained earlier, that Stanley intended to retire after this year. This was a misunderstanding," he said.

Broeg, in his complicated role as friend of Stan and *Post-Dispatch* sports editor, printed Musial's response to Rickey's not-so-subtle hints that he retire.

"This is hard to believe because both Bing and Johnny said they were counting on me. I won't retire, not in the good shape I'm in and hitting the way the way I did this year. If the Cardinals don't want me, I know some others that do."

Early in the 1963 season, Rickey sent a memo to Busch blaming two losses on Musial's slowness, once in left field, once in running out a double play. "He is still a grand hitter but not at all the hitter of former days," the memo said.

Musial was the first to admit he was no longer the Donora Greyhound, but he still had his moments, even at forty-two. Early in the 1963 season, Musial made quite an impression on his old pal Warren Spahn, thirty-nine and going strong.

Stanley would hit seventeen home runs off Spahn, more than off any other pitcher, which was mostly a tribute to the longevity of both great players. One of Spahn's best pitches was a screwball, which broke in on a left-handed hitter, acting like an ordinary curve from a right-hander.

Over the years, Spahn had tried everything against Musial.

"I tried to pitch in, out, up, down," Spahn once said, adding, "Stan was able to get over the top. He can hit the good curveball and the good high fastball."

So Spahn came up with an idea: maybe he could disarm his old adversary by throwing a curve so mediocre it might lull Musial into submission.

"It was a theory," Spahn said a few years later, wincing from remembered pain.

On May 14, 1963, in County Stadium, Spahnie tried out his mediocre-curveball theory. Del Crandall was behind the plate that night, but Joe Torre, a young catcher, was in uniform, observing how the two old hands pitched to Stanley.

"Normally, a guy would go like this," Torre said, mimicking a left-handed hitter dropping down, anticipating a left-handed screwball breaking in on his knees.

"But Stan never moved," Torre recalled. "Hit a line drive."

The St. Louis paper the next day said Spahnie was hit in the stomach; he only wished.

"Spahnie didn't wear a cup," Torre recalled, referring to the protective cup players wear over their groin. "He couldn't, because of that high leg kick.

"Spahnie went down, got up, picked up the ball and threw it and got Stan out at first base, and then he lay down again," Torre recalled.

While the trainer elevated Spahn's legs and Spahn waited for the initial wave of pain to subside, Stanley trotted across the infield toward the dugout, right past his ancient opponent.

"So Stan said to Spahnie, 'You all right, Old Folks?' "

What did Spahnie have to say about that?

"Groaned for a while," Torre recalled.


STANLEY WAS hitting .213 after that game. The sport was still fun—between the lines—but he was growing tired of the second coming of Branch Rickey, who was agitating to replace Keane with Leo Durocher. One thing Stanley knew: he did not want to play for Leo the Lip, ever.

On August 12, 1963, at a team picnic at Grant's Farm, Musial broke the news that he would retire at season's end. There were tears all around. Johnny Keane said, "One of the biggest honors and privileges of my life has been to put on a Cardinal uniform the same as Stan's, dress in the same clubhouse as Stan and be on the same field and club as Stan. Think of all the good words in the English language, and they all fit Stan."

The Cardinals chased the Dodgers into the final month. On September 10, Dick Musial and his wife, Sharon, had their first child, Jeffrey Stanton Musial, while Dick was on military duty in Kansas. The family stayed up much of the night celebrating—Gerry remembered drinking White Russians—and a few hours later Grandpa whacked a home run.

The Cardinals came close, finishing with a 93–69 record and a percentage of .574, the best by the team since Eddie Dyer, Keane's mentor, had a percentage of .623 in 1949. But just as in 1949, the Dodgers outlasted the Cardinals.

On the last Friday night of the season, Musial took Gerry to the Veiled Prophet's Ball, one of the major society events in town. He was tired on Saturday and saved his strength for his final game, September 29.

Despite the legend that Musial did not get attention from the national media, several New York–based magazines had requested permission to follow him step by step on his final day. This was a national hero winding up his career. Attention most definitely was paid.

That final Sunday morning, Musial attended Mass and then had breakfast with his actor friend Horace McMahon. Then he headed for the ballpark in his blue Cadillac, smoking a cigarillo along the way, with a photographer from *Look* magazine, Arnold Hano from *Sport,* and W. C. Heinz from *Life* all squeezed into the backseat.

At the ballpark, Musial politely obeyed requests from the squadron of photographers waiting for him at the cramped old clubhouse. *Hey, Stan, walk through that door again?* they asked. *Sure, fellas.* He signed autographs for teammates collecting instant memorabilia.

Before the game, the Cardinals staged a one-hour ceremony of gifts and tears and speeches, the most memorable coming from Commissioner Ford C. Frick.

Once a writer, Frick said he hoped Musial would be remembered for not just all the hits but for the joy he brought to the game. Then Frick proposed that Musial be remembered this way: "Here stands baseball's perfect warrior. Here stands baseball's perfect knight."

It was almost as if Frick were chiseling the words in stone—and soon enough they would be. How many commissioners write their own words and have them become immortal while they are still echoing around the ballpark?

Musial's final game, on a dank early autumn day, was a relief. In the fourth inning, Musial smacked a single past Pete Rose, the Reds' second baseman with the Prince Valiant haircut, who would eventually break Musial's league record for hits.

In the sixth inning, against Jim Maloney, Musial slapped a single between first and second for his 3,630th hit and his 1,950th run batted in. Then Keane sent out Gary Kolb to run for him, invoking automatic boos from fans who never wanted it to end.

Musial went to the clubhouse, where he had a beer, and then another beer, chatting amiably with photographers, reporters, friends, and interlopers as the game meandered anticlimactically into extra innings.

Far too many people reminded Musial that he had made two hits in his first game and two hits in his last game.

No improvement, he kept saying, armed with a wunnerful new punch line.

That evening, there was a party for three hundred people at Stan Musial and Biggie's. Old friends like Frank Pizzica came in from Donora to talk about his basketball prowess. Ki Duda, now the president of the state college in California, Pennsylvania, told how Musial had struck out eighteen batters in seven innings.

"I don't wear dark glasses," Duda said, "but I have them today because tears came to my eyes."

Normally the life of the party, Stanley seemed subdued that evening.

"What's a fellow do when you're out of a job?" he asked, more than once. He had been working since he was a teenager; he did not know the meaning of leisure time. He thought out loud. Maybe he would take his family to the Kentucky Derby, the Indy 500, a picnic on the Fourth of July.

"What else do they do in the summer? I don't know."

# 38

---

# FENDER BENDER

**J**UST BECAUSE Stanley was retired did not mean he had run out of good fortune.

The next spring, he was back in St. Pete, pretty much living the same life, except for playing baseball.

One day he whipped out into traffic and grazed the side of another car.

"Stan always drove fast, and he always drove a Caddy," Tom Ashley said.

Ashley loved just about everything about his father-in-law, but he had to admit, the man drove fast.

"Stan got out, all apologetic, and the guy recognized him," Ashley said.

There were scrapes on both cars, plenty of reason for the man to be annoyed, but Stanley Luck kicked in.

"The guy said, 'I've got to tell my friends Stan Musial hit my car,'" Ashley recalled.

Meanwhile, Stanley was shuffling around in his pockets, looking for his wallet, a pen, a piece of paper, an insurance card, all the things we do when we have just scraped somebody's vehicle—flustered and embarrassed and hoping the insurance policy would cover this.

"Stan was offering to pay for it," Ashley said, "but the guy said, 'No, no, that's all right, would you just sign my car?' So Stan signed the crease in the car. The guy was thrilled."

# 39

## RETIREMENT

REALITY STRUCK home within two months of Musial's last game. John F. Kennedy—"my buddy"—was assassinated on November 22, 1963, a day after Musial's forty-third birthday. The charming, entitled young president, who had shared some laughs with Musial, was gone.

Gerry, now a student at Marymount College in Arlington, Virginia, went to the funeral procession as it approached Arlington National Cemetery. She knew how much her father admired Kennedy, and she felt she was representing her family.

With the nation, and pretty much the whole world, in mourning, one young man in St. Louis could not face sitting around, so he and his girlfriend went out for a quiet dinner at Stan and Biggie's. Knowing Musial to be an admirer of the president, the young man figured he would be secluded, grieving, not working at the restaurant.

"Stan was there, and he graciously went around to each of the tables in the room and asked how the dinners were, how the food was, and just generally acted like a perfect gentleman and host," the man said in an anonymous Internet posting many years later. "The mood in the room, as all over America, was subdued, numb; but Stan added a bit of humanity and life to it all.

"Stan was right there, in public, helping strangers cope with the national tragedy."

In that terrible week, Musial seemed to understand his role: his buddy had been gunned down, and the world needed to see Stanley. And if that was not how he was thinking, it was how he came off.

The restaurant became even more important to Musial upon his retirement. Greeting strangers was part of his persona. Besides, the family was spread out. Dick and Sharon were new parents, and Gerry was in college back East.

In her first few months away from home in the fall of 1962, Gerry had been living across the Potomac from Washington, D.C., as President Kennedy stared down the Soviet Union in a nuclear confrontation after the failed invasion of the Bay of Pigs in Cuba.

"Washington would have been the first place bombed," she recalled. "I called my mom and asked what I was going to do. She said, 'Well, we're going to be with Mr. Busch. He has a bomb shelter and we'll be there. Try to get there as best you can.'"

Gerry said she felt "deserted and grown-up—all at once," but it was nice to know that her parents were on Gussie's ultimate A-list.

The missile crisis was averted, but soon the nation had to cope with the assassination. While the grief was still raw, the new president, Lyndon Baines Johnson, asked Musial to become the special consultant to the president on physical fitness, replacing Bud Wilkinson, the former Oklahoma football coach. The job was partially a showcase for a celebrity like Musial, but it could have been an opportunity to influence policy.

The Musials flew into Washington on February 27, 1964, for the ceremony. Stan alluded to the gymnastics programs of the Polish Falcons, and he also tried to sketch out a broader vision.

"Calisthenics are fine but they are not the entire basis of physical fitness," he said in spring training in March. "Exercise is only one phase. Games and other means of recreation are important, too." He said he would concentrate on adults as well as children.

Because the job paid a per diem of seventy-five dollars, Musial sometimes had to choose between making real money at his business and doing something more or less for the public good. He asked his friend Bob Stewart, the athletic director at St. Louis University, to be his liaison with the government, but Stewart did not have the Washington contacts needed for that role. Without an insider guiding him, Musial turned down most invitations for personal appearances all over the country.

There was also more politics than Musial would have liked. Once he was told not to make a public appearance with a baseball official from Rochester, New York, because the man happened to be a Republican.

"LBJ had Stan lobbying a Polish congressman for one thing or another," recalled Tom Ashley. "Stan would call and say, 'I'm doing this because the president asked.' After a while he got word to the president that he didn't want to do that."

Johnson was busy expanding the war in Vietnam, lobbying for civil rights, and waging a so-called war on poverty, all at the same time. He had his priorities, and physical fitness was not among them. He was a dominant personality who tended to put his hands on senators to manipulate them into doing his will. There is no indication he and Musial ever meshed.

"But didn't you find Johnson vulgar?" somebody asked Musial in 1976.

"No," Musial said politely, "because we only talked politics."

MUSIAL STILL gravitated to the ballpark, spending more time than was healthy in the press box, which in St. Louis pretty much meant hot dogs and beer. One night he found himself in the hospital, being treated for indigestion and exhaustion.

Feeling better, Musial had a front-row seat for the bizarre doings of 1964. In June, Devine engineered a trade for an outfielder named Lou Brock, who was underperforming with the Cubs, and Keane installed Brock in left field and let him run. However, with the Cardinals still eight games out of first place in mid-August, Busch fired Devine and replaced him with Bob Howsam, a baseball man but not a Cardinal—a very big thing in that insular town.

Keane went around during the late season with a tight smile on his face, knowing that Rickey planned to bring in his old pal Leo Durocher after the season. With Durocher warming up his lungs in the managers' bullpen, Brock ignited the Cardinals while the Phillies staged one of the epic collapses in pennant race history, losing 10 straight games and blowing a 6½ game lead with 12 games to play.

On the final Wednesday night, the Cardinals surged into first place by beating the Phillies in chilly St. Louis.

As reporters crowded into Keane's tiny office—and I was there—a door opened and in popped Branch Rickey, rumpled suit, whiff of cigar, thick eyeglasses, pulpit timber: "Johnny Keane, you're a gosh-danged good manager," Rickey enunciated.

Rickey's praise reverberated during the next two weeks as the Cardinals won the pennant and then beat the Yankees in the World Series.

"They finally got a good left-fielder," Musial would tell everybody, laughing and displaying not the slightest bit of remorse about his retirement. His team won. That was what counted.

The Cardinals' victory surely could be dated back to Devine's hiring of Keane in 1961 and Keane's handing the ball to Gibson. Asked why he kept going to the weary Gibson in those final days, Keane said one of the finest things I ever heard from a manager. It still brings chills when I type it: "Because I had a commitment to his heart," Keane said.

Immediately after the Series, Busch told Keane he would be back in 1965, upon which Keane informed Busch that he most certainly would not. The next day Keane turned up in New York to take the Yankees job, after Yogi Berra had been pushed out.

Somewhat in shock, Busch consulted his advisors for candidates to be manager. Howsam was pushing Charlie Metro, a baseball man but not a Cardinal, while Musial recommended—who else?—his car-pool buddy, Red.

"I knew Red needed experience—we all did—but we felt he was the best man for the job," Musial said a few years later.

The Cardinals did not win pennants in Red's first two seasons, but the team remained near the top. Musial enjoyed schmoozing in the clubhouse now that Red was manager, but he also found time to concentrate on retirement. He had always talked about doing things other Americans did, so he visited the Indy 500 once and became something of a regular at the Kentucky Derby.

He also spent time on business. The boy who had turned crimson when he had to speak in school, the teammate who dreaded making a clubhouse speech, now used his familiar crouch as a way of being himself—Stan the Man in a suit and tie, Stanley the entrepreneur.

Rather than spending more than half a year in clubhouses and dugouts, Musial suddenly had more time to socialize. Somebody who was around him in those years described Musial at a gathering: quiet, reserved, off in a corner. Asked if he was going to play the harmonica, Musial would insist no, not tonight. But later in the evening there would be a shift of mood.

"There were times I would see this wonderful explosion of energy and laughter in Stan," the acquaintance said. "You'd see it when he played harmonica, or really got into a story or enjoyed a good laugh with a Ted Williams or someone.

"He had this explosive energy, this spirit that I believe must have been key to his brilliant batting—coiled up and then explode on the ball. And what I am trying to say is that when I got to see him a bit, it looked like much of that may have become muted or submerged as he would kind of withdraw or sit silently saying little until someone came up to him and ask questions or want an autograph."

Musial was a man of moderation but also a man of the times—the age of the social drink, the patter that it must be five o'clock somewhere in the world so let's have a martini, or a bourbon, or a beer.

By all accounts, Stanley liked a drink now and then. Some of his best days had come after a drink or two. The five home runs in a doubleheader in 1954 came after a fun night with neighbors. In 1960 he went out in Manhattan on the eve of the All-Star Game in Yankee Stadium and would have been perfectly happy sitting out the game, but he pinch-hit a single in the late innings. In 1963 only a few hours after celebrating his first grandchild by sipping White Russians, Grandpa hit a homer.

Throughout his retirement, Musial would often discover that spare harmonica in his pocket later in the evening. In the early nineties, while recovering from prostate cancer, he traveled to a golf outing for Mickey Mantle's charity and played "The Wabash Cannonball" onstage—much too long, as far as Mantle was concerned. The Mick lurched onstage and essentially hauled Musial off, both of them giggling as they departed.

A COUPLE of years after his retirement, Stan and Lil moved up, buying a house farther out in the county, in tony Ladue, near the Old Warson Country Club. This was a huge step for a couple from Donora, but they could afford the space, the privacy, and the feel of having made it.

The new house was hidden from the road, essentially a ranch but a very large one, much more formal than the suburban ranch on Westway. There was even a service entrance for deliveries and help. In one wing was a living room with a piano, and over the fireplace was a portrait of the six family members, a photograph painted over in oils. There was a large pantry off the kitchen, a formal dining room, and a den. In another wing were four bedrooms, more than enough for a family whose children were moving away. And in the back was a porch where Stan liked to watch the birds and smoke his cigar, and beyond that a swimming pool.

The house was something of a shock to Gerry, who was used to walking around the old neighborhood and waving at friends across the modest lawns. Now the Musial family was secluded.

"When you're in that house, somebody can come in the driveway," Gerry said. "You can be in the bedroom and not really know."

The kids decided the house was haunted by the builder, a man of French origin who had died before he could move in. Strange things happened there. Gerry had an old music box with a dancing ballerina on top who had been dormant for a decade or more. One time she was visiting her parents and was all alone in the new house when the music box started up and the ballerina began twirling in place.

"I'm a scaredy-cat," Gerry said. "I don't like being alone; it's so isolated. One time I left the TV on and when I went back it was off. People have heard cabinets opening and closing. We've all heard something. We think he's benign. A benign ghost."

While Stan and Lil's new house had a formal design to it, they were not formal people.

"Their house is like anybody else's house—not ostentatious, but beautiful," said Helen P. Nelson, a friend who visited several times. "When you walk in, you feel very comfortable, you don't feel, 'Oh, geez, I can't sit on that chair.' No. A real warm home. And a lovely swimming pool. A finished basement where he's put a picture of every person he's ever met. And that was neat. In the kitchen, a few seats from the old Busch Stadium."

Some men retire and decide they will show the little lady how to run a household. That was definitely not the case with Stanley. This was Lil's house, and she made it work for her husband.

"Lil is one of a kind," Nelson said. "She's protective of Stan."

"Lil is one of the finest ladies you ever been around," said Danny Litwhiler, Stan's former teammate, who became a renowned coach at Florida State and Michigan State.

"Lil is very thoughtful," said Pat Litwhiler, who married Litwhiler after his first wife, Dorothy, died in 1971. "Lil continually sends things to Danny. I don't think Stan ever answers the phone."

Without a clubhouse or neighbors a few steps away, the gregarious Stanley needed an outlet.

"Dad loved to go out in the yard," Gerry said. "Lord knows what he was doing. Drive the tractor, pick up a couple of fallen tree branches."

Gerry did not think her father actually cut his own grass. She was surprised to learn, years later, that Stanley had been cutting the lawn of his closest neighbor, Robert R. Hermann, at one point the president of the National Professional Soccer League. Stanley started out mowing his own expanse—and kept going.

One day Hermann entertained Pelé, the great Brazilian soccer player, who was finishing up his career with the New York Cosmos.

"He came to my house and said I had a beautiful lawn, and asked in pretty good English who cut my grass," Hermann said. "I told him it was Stan Musial and was surprised that he actually knew who he was. Charming fellow."

Hermann had a paddle tennis court, with high screens on four sides creating a 360-degree game. There was action every Sunday. One day only two other players showed up, so Hermann called Musial and told him to come over.

"He said, 'Bob, I've never played tennis in my life,'" Hermann recalled, "and I told him to come over anyway and I showed him how to hold the racquet. We had some pretty good players. One of our regulars was the sixteenth-best college player and second-best doubles player.

"In thirty minutes, Stan was the best player on the court. Just a natural. He was pretty darn good. Which made sense, when you think of it."

Until Hermann moved in 1974, Musial was a regular in the game, and the wives would come around and have a drink afterward. Once in a while a neighbor would throw a party for fifty or a hundred people, and Stan and Lil fit right in, Hermann said.

Musial's grandson Tom Ashley Jr. had never heard about Stanley's mowing the neighbor's lawn, but he said, "I'm sure it happened. My grandfather loved tinkering on his mower and tractor. I think it was a great way for him to relax. He showed all the grandkids how to drive it, with him next to us."

Ashley thought about his active grandfather for a moment and added, "It took me years to realize that he is just a country boy at heart, without the accent."


NOT PARTICULARLY caught up in the national turmoil over Vietnam and civil rights, Musial received a blast of reality in 1966 when he was invited to tour Vietnam with Brooks Robinson, Joe Torre, Henry Aaron, Harmon Killebrew, and the great Yankee broadcaster Mel Allen. This was no meet-and-greet opportunity in a secured camp.

"He was up near the front lines with bullets flying," his son-in-law said.

"It was pretty dangerous over there," said Colonel James Hackett, the chief of detectives in St. Louis and one of Musial's best friends. When he got home, Musial told Hackett about flying in a helicopter with no doors and asking himself, "What the hell am I doing over here?"

The other players on the trip confirmed this was no armchair experience.

Brooks Robinson had idolized Musial while growing up in Little Rock, listening to games over KMOX and catching the Cardinals' annual exhibition with the White Sox on their way north. In many ways, Robinson was the Stan Musial of Baltimore. Now Robinson got to see his role model in the middle of a war.

"We would split up each day and go to different places," Robinson said. "I got to meet the Montagnards. I remember climbing up in a tree hut and drinking whatever they drank, like sake. We flew in helicopters and C-130s.

"I got to fire a howitzer into North Vietnam. We went all the way from the Delta to Da Nang. We visited a lot of hospitals. It was very inspirational. Those guys were heroes to me."

Robinson told of visiting a hospital with Musial and chatting with an American soldier who had lost both legs to a bomb.

"Stan went over to him and said, 'Hi, I'm Stan Musial of the St. Louis Cardinals,' and the soldier said, 'Oh, Mr. Musial, I'm sorry I didn't recognize you.'

"And that's where I lost it," Robinson admitted.

In Da Nang, the players had lunch with General William Westmoreland, the commander of the U.S. operation in Vietnam, and dinner with Lieutenant General Lewis Walt, the commanding general of the III Marine Amphibious Force. Shortly after that, the general's quarters were bombed by the Vietcong. Musial was still talking about that bombing when he got home a few weeks later.

Torre, who later became very close to Musial when he managed the Cardinals, remembered that he was not particularly frightened in Vietnam.

"I was just young and stupid," Torre explained. But Aaron, Allen, and Musial had the good sense to be, as Torre put it, "uncomfortable."

"You saw tracer bullets every night," Torre said. "We were in that outpost and every night you could hear that harassment fire going off."

When Musial got home, a reporter described him "shaking like a leaf" as he talked about his adventures. Musial called it a "rewarding experience," saying, "We were up every day at six o'clock, taking pictures, signing autographs, shaking hands all day and then at night, showing films of the All-Star Game," but he was graphic about the dangers. "We flew over areas held by the Charlie," Musial added, noting that without helicopters, "we couldn't have got around," but also well aware that the open helicopters would not necessarily shield anybody from a bullet coming up from the jungle.

"I'll tell you," his son-in-law said, "he was a pacifist"—not necessarily in his politics but in his innards.

Musial had great respect for the troops he met in Vietnam, but he did not lead cheers for the mission. He had seen the war that LBJ expanded, and had enough sense to be scared.

# 40

STANLEY RUNS THE TEAM

MUSIAL TURNED his Vietnam experience into a punch line. Asked about his duties as an "advisor" to the front office, he said: "The Cardinals have been sending men to look over our players in Florida, Puerto Rico, and the Dominican Republic."

But where did they send Stanley?

"To Vietnam," he said.

Within a few months, he was back in baseball. Bob Howsam, tired of the tight control by the brewery, left the Cardinals early in 1967 to go work for the Reds. Ever loyal, Musial agreed when Busch asked him to take over. He may have underestimated the job, since he said he would try to remain as the presidential physical fitness advisor while running the Cardinals, but he soon realized the need to concentrate on his club.

When he resigned the fitness post, Musial had applied for only 114 days of his stipend in nearly three years in the position, compared to 203 days by Wilkinson in his first three years.

AT LEAST one former teammate was dubious about Musial as an executive.

"As the reader already knows, Stan's administrative gifts were not exactly apparent while he was knocking the shit out of the ball," Curt Flood wrote a few years later. "But no matter. He was Stan the Man and Busch could bolster him with whatever assistance was needed."

Stanley Luck held again. Howsam had left the Cardinals in good shape, having traded for Roger Maris to play right field. Red was already drilling Mike Shannon—Dick Musial's football teammate from high school—to move to third base, and first baseman Orlando Cepeda was now healthy.

"I can put myself back on the active list," Stanley said, more than once. "After all, I've been resting for three years."

His first chore was to round up a few unsigned players, including Dal Maxvill, the shortstop, one of the new breed, with a major in electrical engineering at Washington University. Maxvill had grown up in Illinois, across the river, and spent part of his childhood in Sportsman's Park. On his first time in the Cardinal clubhouse in the spring of 1962, Maxvill was welcomed by Musial, and as soon as he could, Maxvill slipped over to the pay phone and relayed this news to his wife: Stan Musial had said hello to him!

A regular by 1967, Maxvill had declined Howsam's first contract. The night before his meeting with Musial, Maxvill visited a troop of Boy Scouts, who gave him a baseball bat with an axe attached to it—"a real nice gift," Maxvill recalled.

Maxvill decided to carry the souvenir into negotiations with Stanley. A few players might have made a general manager nervous by carrying a sharp object into negotiations, but the slender college graduate was not one of them.

"Stan said, 'Hey, how you doing, what you got there?' " Maxvill recalled. "I said, 'Stan, this is what I'm going to use on you; the Boy Scouts gave it to me last night, if we can't reach agreement on a contract.' Well, he laughed like hell, took a couple of swings with the bat with the hatchet head on it, and we sat down and after about fifteen or twenty minutes, I had gotten a nice increase over what I'd been sent in the mail, and he was his usual self."

Years after his own ten-year stint as general manager of the Cardinals, Maxvill remembered the nice way Musial had handled the negotiations.

"He said, 'I think you deserve more than you're getting. You're our regular shortstop and are going to be our shortstop for a number of years and I think you deserve more money.' I said, 'Good, I'm glad you feel that way.' "

Stanley also had a nice touch with Maris, who had grown grouchy after his life-changing 61 homers in 1961. Although he and Mickey Mantle were friendly, Maris resented having to play center field while Mantle was hurt, feeling the Yankees had not recognized his own injuries.

"Maris was very temperamental," said Bill Bergesch, a veteran baseball man who was working with Bing Devine for the Mets in those years. "Stan could quiet him down," Bergesch added.

Musial chatted up Maris and revived the sardonic team player Maris had been in his earlier days. Maris began to enjoy life in a clubhouse with the sarcastic Gibson and the exuberant Cepeda, and would help win two pennants before retiring.

But could Stanley run a team? Reporters raised that question with Devine in spring training.

"Tell me one thing Musial has ever done wrong," Devine said.

Musial showed his diplomatic side at a banquet in St. Louis on the eve of the 1967 season, with the Cardinals and their opponents, the San Francisco Giants, in attendance. "Gentlemen, I have a feeling the National League's 1967 pennant-winning ball club is one of the two in this room," he said.

Stanley had a soft spot for the Giants. Many years earlier, Horace Stoneham, the convivial owner of the Giants, had learned that he and Musial had the same shoe size. Every time the two teams met, Stoneham would have a gift pair of shoes for lucky Stanley.

The Cardinals won their first six games in 1967, and Musial established his style early—one of the boys.

"It was so cold, around twenty degrees," recalled Alvin Jackson, who had come over from the Mets that season. "Everybody was complaining it was cold. He comes over and does this"—Jackson imitated the Musial crouch—"and says, 'Today, I'd go four for four.' " Of course, Musial was likely to go four for four any day, but his point was clear: play ball.

As general manager, Musial was a benign presence, showing no inclination to tinker. Trader Lane he was not.

"When the club was in St. Louis, he'd come down to the clubhouse and schmooze when the club was going good," Maxvill recalled. "But when the club wasn't going good, he knew nobody really wanted to sit around and talk about things. I think he was smart enough to know. That didn't happen much in '67 because we had a pretty good ball club, but on the road he'd show up—team plane to the West Coast, New York, maybe some of the places that he and Red liked to go to have dinner.

"It wasn't like he was an absentee GM. I don't think Mr. Busch would have put up with him not putting his finger on the pulse of the team.

"We were very lucky that year," Maxvill continued. "We avoided injury. Our roster was pretty much set. We didn't really need a lot, and nobody really got hurt for a great length of time. Stan did his job as GM. We didn't make too many moves because you make moves when guys are playing poorly or you have injuries. And we were fortunate."

Red remembered how he would visit his old buddy in his office while Musial was going over the waiver list.

"He says, 'Well I got some more telegrams, this guy's on waivers, we can pick him up,' " Red recalled, "and we'd look at him and throw him right in the waste paper basket." The two of them agreed: "We got a ball-player like him, so why go through the paper work and get him?"

For a time, Musial relied on Bob Stewart, who had been his adminis-trator in the physical fitness post, but Stewart was not familiar with the rudimentary baseball finances of the time.

When Stanley really needed advice, he would place a call to Bing Devine, who was living out of a suitcase in New York, working for the Mets, his wife and three daughters not about to leave St. Louis and move to somebody else's city.

"Graciously, Der Bingle would straighten out the fine points for me," Musial once wrote in Broeg-speak.

General managers normally chat with friends in other organizations; neither man was giving away industrial secrets. Maxvill never heard that Musial and Devine talked on occasion but said he would not be surprised if they did.

"Obviously, he and Bing had known each other a long, long time. He would be one guy that Stan would call and say, 'Hey, explain this to me. I'm doing this or I'm doing that. Is there anything I need to check with the commissioner's office?' Something that simple."

Nowadays, despite rules forbidding "fraternization," ballplayers talk, laugh, hug, pray, exchange useful telephone numbers, and trade agent gos-sip around the batting cage, in full view of the fans. In Musial's time as general manager, Gibson would have thrown at any opponent who made the gaffe of speaking to him or digging in at the plate. ("Gibby, you're crazy, man," Bill White said when his pal drilled him after White was traded to the Phillies.)

But there was no anti-fraternization code stopping a couple of St. Louis guys from chatting on the phone. Devine probably explained the mysteries of the waiver rule to his friend, not that Stanley was doing much waiving.

"If ever a general manager under–general managed, I guess it was me," Musial said.

Tim McCarver said Musial "had no true skills to be a general manager because he was an ex-player, so they helped him along. He was more a figurehead in '67." McCarver meant it in the nicest way.

The Cardinals shuffled a few fringe players in 1967 but went out of their organization only once—when Roberto Clemente hit a shot off Gibson's leg in mid-July. Gibson told everybody to get the heck away from him and pitched to three more batters before leaving the game. Turned out he had a broken leg.

Musial needed a pitcher, so he turned to Devine, who sent over Jack Lamabe, a durable veteran who took some of the workload until Gibson came back in September.

The Cardinals virtually ran themselves under Stan and Red.

"He has actually shown more patience than I thought he'd have," Musial said about Schoendienst, "and he didn't panic or press when things didn't go well his first two years."

Musial added, "Red doesn't try to over-manage, doesn't try to fancy up too much a basically simple game. . . . It was tough on Red, having to start managing in the majors but he has learned how to handle men, when to give them a rest and when to take out his pitchers."

As might be expected, Red had nothing but good things to say about his buddy, calling him "a manager's general manager." He said Musial added to the confidence of the Cardinals just by visiting the clubhouse.

"He calls, though, often before a game and always afterward. Stan has patience, knows the game and we talk about it. He might see something and tell me what he's seen or ask me about something. He believes in paying ballplayers well but he shares my views that it's wise to get rid of discontented or unhappy ballplayers and not to take on any who are apt to disrupt harmony.

"Above all, he let me keep the players I wanted."

MUSIAL WAS gliding between his business and the front office until June 19, 1967, when Biggie Garagnani died suddenly of a heart attack at fifty-three. He had been under a doctor's care for heart and blood pressure problems but had not slowed his hectic pace, including raising more than $80,000 for Governor Warren E. Hearnes's reelection campaign of 1964. Musial had relied on Biggie for his business acumen and psychic muscle. Now at a shockingly early age, Biggie was gone.

THE CARDINALS won the 1967 pennant with a 101–60 record and then beat the Red Sox in the World Series, with its echoes of 1946. Musial enjoyed the triumph but soon grew tired of details he kept discovering were in his domain. A mix-up in distributing tickets at the first home World Series game forced ushers to bring out chairs and seat people in the aisles, which temporarily inconvenienced guests and might have been an issue for fire marshals. Presumably the Cardinals could have hired somebody to dole out World Series tickets next time around, but Musial was not long for that job.

"Stan twiddled his thumbs in the front office for less than a year till, he told me, he 'couldn't stand being cooped up not knowing what I was doing in there,'" wrote Julius Hunter, a St. Louis television personality who knew Musial.

Shortly after the Series, Musial told Red he was getting out. "You can't do that," Schoendienst blurted, but Musial said he certainly could.

"If you want to do the right job, the good job, you have to be here twenty-four hours a day. And I just can't handle that, with all the other business that I have," Stan told Red.

On December 5, Busch announced that Devine was coming back to run the Cardinals and that Musial was going back to being a businessman, goodwill ambassador, and team vice president. Musial was not around to comment. After the winter meetings in Mexico City, he and Lil took off for a vacation in Acapulco.

Clearly, Biggie's death forced Musial to change his priorities. The two partners had invested in several hotels in Florida as well as the Redbird Lanes in St. Louis with Joe Garagiola. Musial and Teresa Garagnani delegated responsibility to their respective sons, Richard Musial and Jack Garagnani, and Stan relied on Pat Anthony, his longtime assistant, but there was only one Biggie. Somebody had to watch the store.

IT WAS Christmas Eve 1967, getting late at the Redbird Lanes. The last group bowled its final frame and was changing shoes, about to head home for the holidays, except for John Kopchak, a Cardinal farmhand who had been called up late in the season but had not gotten into a game. He was still in St. Louis, two and a half months later.

Kopchak was nursing his beer when he noticed the last worker at Redbird Lanes hovering near him.

"I sure would like to clean up," Stan Musial said, recognizing the young player. "Why don't you go home to your family?"

Kopchak said his family lived east of Los Angeles. Musial thought about this for a moment and promptly invited the young man home for dinner. Forty-three years later Kopchak could still describe the feast Lil had prepared for her family: ham, fried chicken, polish sausages, sweet potatoes, mashed potatoes, the works.

Lil fussed over the nineteen-year-old. "A lady, very sweet," Kopchak recalled in 2010. "A mother figure."

After dinner, Musial said he had to make a run to the airport and asked Kopchak to keep him company. Stanley parked the car and said he had to go inside to pick up a package. Twenty minutes later he came back bearing an airplane ticket, round-trip, to Los Angeles.

"You've got thirty minutes to catch your plane," Musial said.

Kopchak does not remember how much the ticket cost—"More than I had, I can tell you that." He called his folks, flew home for the holidays, and when he returned to St. Louis he tried to return the money, but Musial would not hear of it.

"It was my Christmas present to you," he said.

Before long, Kopchak was drafted during the Vietnam War, and when he got back it was too late for the majors. In recent years he has worked as chief of security for the Memphis Redbirds, a Cardinal farm team. He occasionally gives talks to baseball fans, who want to know what Stan Musial is really like.

Musial worked harder than many retired players know how to do, spending regular hours in his office, dressing in a suit, reading the *Wall Street Journal,* making investment decisions about his money.

"Are you a millionaire like Hank Greenberg?" Roger Kahn asked Musial in 1976.

"Just write that I'm not hanging for my pension," Musial told Kahn, sounding justifiably proud of his own disciplined life. "A long time ago I knew I couldn't hit forever, and I knew that I didn't want to be a coach or manager. So Biggie Garagnani, who died young, and I started the restaurant in 1949. Biggie knew the business, and I knew that just my name wasn't enough. I put in time. I like mixing with people up to a point, and my being here was good for business. I still walk around in the place six nights a week when I'm in town. So while I was playing, I was building a permanent restaurant business, and that just led naturally into the hotels. What's my title? President of Stan Musial & Biggie's, Inc."

Without Musial, the Cardinals reached the World Series again in 1968, losing the final three games to Detroit, with Flood misjudging a drive off the magnificent Gibson.

The following spring, Gussie Busch thought he detected complacency in the Cardinals, who had merely won two World Series and another pennant in the previous five seasons. The beer baron had the players herded into the clubhouse, along with Dick Meyer, Bing Devine, Red Schoendienst, and Musial. Gussie also thoughtfully invited the press, who rarely get to witness an owner chewing out his players.

"Gentlemen, I don't think there is any secret about the fact that I am not a very good loser," Gussie began, expanding on the theme that his hirelings seemed more interested in salary negotiations than in winning another World Series.

Gussie noted the growing power of the union and said, "I am saying, though, we are beginning to lose sight of who really has to pay the ultimate bill for your salary and your pension . . . namely the fan."

During what the Associated Press called "an unusual forty-minute clubhouse meeting," Busch told the players, "I plead with you not to kill the enthusiasm of the fans and the kids for whom you have become such idols."

The Cardinals did not even win the division title in 1969, the year of the Miracle Mets. Curt Flood was convinced Busch had destroyed the club's unity with his sclerotic outburst in St. Pete. The pride that had made the Cardinals one of the best teams—and one of the best clubhouses—was gone.

And soon Flood was gone. Shortly after the 1969 season, the Cardinals included him in a trade to the Phillies, in return for the legendary slugger Dick Allen.

Flood decided he did not want to be traded, not right then, and not to Philadelphia, so he refused to go—thereby touching off an eventual Supreme Court case he would lose but which would lead to unimaginable free-agency salaries decades down the line.

At the Supreme Court session, very few baseball people showed up in support of Flood: Hank Greenberg, Jackie Robinson, the pitcher-turned-writer Jim Brosnan, and Bill Veeck, the maverick who seemed to exist only to make other owners look even more ossified.

There was no reason to expect Musial to join them as they paid public tribute to Flood's stand. Musial had been supportive of the union's formation back in 1946, but he seemed to believe the owners could not retain fiscal sanity without a reserve clause. As a businessman, Musial was management, not labor, and he seemed to favor the reserve clause. So did most players, at least until free agency fell into their laps.

Mostly Musial was also a loyal baseball man who enjoyed dispensing cryptic hitting tips in his Stanley fashion.

"Spring of 1972," recalled Keith Hernandez. "I'm eighteen years old and Stan and Gibson came down from the big club, all of us in the outfield. Six, seven hundred players. Gibson talked about pitching.

"Musial got a bat in his hand and started talking about hitting and for a minute and a half he was all stops and starts and stutters," Hernandez recalled. "Getting frustrated, he threw the bat down and he said, 'Oh, hell, look for the ball, see it, and hit it.'

"Great for you, Stan, with your hand-to-eye coordination," Hernandez muttered fondly.

In January 1969, Musial was voted into the National Baseball Hall of Fame, along with Roy Campanella and old-timers Waite Hoyt and Stan Coveleski.

Twenty-three eligible writers did not vote for Musial on his first attempt, but then again there has never been a unanimous selection. As of 2010, the number of eligible baseball writers who voted for him, 93.24 percent, was the nineteenth-highest among the 106 players who were voted in via mass balloting. Inexplicably, twenty writers did not vote for Ted Williams in 1966; twenty-eight did not vote for DiMaggio in 1955, after he had been turned down on his three previous tries for the Hall, if you can imagine. Apparently some writers thought Joe D. would come out of retirement, and wanted to make sure he was really done.

Just before Musial was inducted in Cooperstown, a drizzle was falling on the open-air ceremony outside the Hall. But as Commissioner Bowie Kuhn introduced Musial, the sun came out.

"With Musial, it figured," said Pat Dean, the wife of Dizzy Dean.

Stanley turned the induction into a Musial reunion.

"I invited my old coaches from high school," he recalled, laughing about the way his friends and family were looking for hotel rooms "all the way to Syracuse."

Years later, Musial's strongest memory of the day was of the induction of Coveleski, an old-time pitcher who had been honored by the veterans committee at the age of eighty—"and he was Polish," Musial said proudly. Musial, never a comfortable public speaker, was touched by the kindness of Kuhn when Coveleski could not get a word out. Kuhn walked over, put his arm around Coveleski, and said, "This is your day. Take as much time as you need."

And then, Musial said tenderly, the old player "made the most beautiful speech."

Small-town boy, man of the establishment, harmonica player to the world, Musial fell in love with the annual induction weekend in the picturesque little town in upstate New York, where baseball most emphatically was not invented. He became a regular at the midsummer ceremonies, with Lil at his side for many years, and pals like Joe Medwick and Red Schoendienst accompanying him.

On Sunday mornings Musial would attend Mass at the pretty little Roman Catholic church.

"The church was jammed and a priest from Brooklyn recognized a lot of people, and then he recognized Musial, who was there with Schoendienst," said Fay Vincent, who became commissioner in 1989. "As they got to the front door, about a hundred people crowded around them, pulling out little scraps of paper, church bulletins, and they both signed.

"The modern player would breeze right through," Vincent said, "but they must have stood there, it must have been half an hour, and just right on the step of the church. A few people asked me to sign. A little later I went up to Stan and I said, 'That was so nice of you to stand there,' and he said, 'If those people want my autograph, I'm always delighted to help.' And I thought that was so nice. They were of a different generation. They would never have been rude."

Late into the night, Musial could be found at the bar facing the lake in the Otesaga Hotel, playing his harmonica with the jazz combo.

He could show up anywhere. In 1994, eighty-one-year-old Dom Corio of New York attended the induction of Phil Rizzuto, whom Corio knew from sandlot ball many decades earlier. That night, at the Pepper Mill restaurant, Dom and his newspaperman son, Ray, were introduced to Musial by a mutual friend, who told Stanley that Dom played a mean harmonica. Later, when Dom took a long time getting back from the men's room, his son went off to search for him. In the next room, his dad and Musial were playing a duet of "Take Me Out to the Ballgame" for the patrons.

"My father died eight years later," Ray Corio said, "but for one night in Cooperstown, he tasted heaven."

# 41

## HOMETOWN

WHENEVER STAN was honored, his mother was there—for the dedication of the bulky statue outside the ballpark in August 1968, for his induction into the Baseball Hall of Fame in 1969. As soon as her son was introduced, Mary Musial would start crying out in the audience, and Stan would see her and he would start crying, too.

And when Stan was honored on *This Is Your Life,* Mary flew out to Los Angeles, accompanied by Verna Duda, their old friend from Donora.

"Stan included her in things," Verna said with obvious fondness. "I drove to Cooperstown with her. She was a home-loving mother and never capitalized on him."

Mary had gone to St. Louis when Lukasz took sick in the fall of 1948, but she was too young and had too much energy to be a guest of her daughter-in-law for long, so she went home to Donora.

While Stan was still playing, Roger Kahn showed up in Pittsburgh to do a cover story on him for *Newsweek.* A cover story was a big deal, and Musial was comfortable with Kahn, who had covered the Dodgers back in Brooklyn, but he could cooperate only so much. Musial said he was driving down to Donora on a day off, but certain subjects would have to be off-limits.

"I promised someone I'd visit sick kids in the hospital," Musial told Kahn. "If you write that, it'll look like I'm doing it for publicity."

That was fine, Kahn said, but the magazine really wanted him to write about Musial's mother, what her life was like, what she thought of his success. Musial said he was sorry but his mom was off-limits, too.

"My mother lives above a store there," Musial told Kahn. "That's where she wants to live. We had her in St. Louis, but she missed her old friends, so we found a place she liked. And no matter how you write it, it will come out, 'Stan Musial Makes $100,000 a Year and His Mother Lives Above a Store.' "

So Kahn did not go down to Donora but instead got Musial to make some unusually coherent comments about hitting. Kahn would have preferred something more personal but was running into the barricade, high and powerful, that Musial was erecting around his family and his childhood.

It was too bad Kahn did not get to visit Donora because he would have found a tasteful way to describe how Mary Musial was very much her own person. By some accounts, she continued to clean houses for a while, with no sense of embarrassment, because that was who she was, that was what she did.

"She had a hard life," Tom Ashley said with evident sympathy. "She was ill at ease with the fame. She was uneducated. When anybody would talk to her about Stan, she would start crying. Her life was changed. She would burst into tears, after that enormous poverty. She didn't fit into the limelight, ever. Even in Donora, she was ill at ease."

Ashley visited Donora a few times with his father-in-law and could see how Musial began to change as they drove south from Pittsburgh.

"He was really affected by being as poor as he was. Something he hated. When he saw it, he would do what he could."

Whenever the Cardinals played in Pittsburgh, all family members were welcome. Broeg described watching the Pirate broadcasters, Bob Prince and Rosey Rowswell, a couple of characters, hang out of the booth and "holler down to her, and she was cheerful as heck."

Broeg said his pal had gotten his "liveliness" from his mother's side. "She was a statuesque woman, kinda cute, a handsome woman," Broeg said.

Stan's nephew Edward S. Musial remembered his first trips to Forbes Field with his grandmother, sitting behind the dugout, and how his dad would lift him onto the field, where his uncle would introduce him to some of the Cardinals. All four of Stan's sisters had moved with their husbands closer to Pittsburgh and were often at the Cardinals games. Pirates-

Cardinals games at Forbes Field were one of the rare occasions when the Musial family could move closer together again, if only for a few hours.

"We would see him with the Cardinals, but other than that, he didn't come back at Christmas," the nephew said, adding that Stan would usually appear when Donora invited him for one celebration or another. He was helping to support his mother, but the five other children saw her more often than he did. Lil would come home occasionally to visit her own family, which meant her children knew her family better.

In 1965, Musial had a ranch house built for his mother at 21 Second Street Extension, up on the hill in a nice section of town. Broeg accompanied his friend to Donora one week when the old football Cardinals were playing in Pittsburgh, and described Mary Musial at home as "a real strong, bare-legged woman, you know, a great hostess."

To balance things out, Broeg quickly added, "He really loved his father. He really worshipped his dad."

The grandchildren in Pennsylvania got to see Mary regularly at birthdays and holidays. Edward S. Musial, Stan's nephew, recalled: "She made these beautiful Easter eggs, paisley-style. Put them in some kind of oil. They were just beautiful. She would never tell us how she did them. And she would crochet things, too."

In later years, Mary Musial was sometimes seen walking around outside her home, not at all unusual for the elderly.

Some people have suggested she displayed erratic behavior, but other old-timers in Donora say nothing serious ever crossed their radar.

"In a small town, you know a lot of things about people," one pillar of the community said, citing a longtime resident who was known to lift things from downtown stores and whose affluent relatives would quietly make restitution.

"I never heard a thing about Mrs. Musial," the man added.

Her grandson Edward said, "I was young. I don't know much about my grandmother. You look back, you wish you did. She might have had some kind of Alzheimer's deal. She'd ask you a lot of questions. It's hard to remember. I was a little kid."

Mary Musial died early in 1975 at the age of seventy-eight and was buried in the finest cemetery in town.

STAN WOULD also return for family reunions, where relatives would tell the same old stories, as families will do, bringing everybody back to some earlier time. His brother, Ed, would express wonderment at Stan's success in business. "It's hard to figure out, because he barely got through high school," Ed said with a laugh during an interview years later. "He was a bad student, so I don't know—let's put it this way."

Ed lived with a famous name and the memories of his own career. Just like his brother, he had signed as a pitcher, with Oshkosh in the Wisconsin State League in 1941, but he wound up spending the entire war in Europe, losing four full years from his career. After the war he was converted to the outfield with Fayetteville in the Coastal Plain League in 1946, when he hit .334. Then he shuttled around the low minors, finishing up in 1950 with a career total of 469 games, 23 home runs, 188 runs batted in, 67 stolen bases, and an average of around .300. In later years, Ed admitted he had let himself get distracted by life on the road, but then he came home and settled down, working for the Westinghouse Electric Company near Pittsburgh as a machinist and boilermaker.

"I wasn't that good in school, but when I worked for Westinghouse, I got the opportunity to work different machines," Ed said, proud of having become a good operator.

Stan had a sanguine understanding of what it took to be a major leaguer, the same respect that led him to welcome rookies to the big time. He would sometimes say, apparently casually, that he had played three games a day back in Donora, but Ed had played fewer. Was he saying he had wanted it more?

The nephew said there was no jealousy between his father and uncle. "There was nothing like, 'You made it, I didn't make it, I don't like you.'" If there was any jealousy in his father, Edward added, "he never let on."

The younger brother seemed aware of all the time that had passed, all the changes in their lives. "When we were younger, we were close," Ed once said, but after the war, he added, "We separated."

Ed did work with Stan and Dick in a short-lived baseball equipment business, but as he said in 1990, "I went the other way, because I says, 'You have your following, and I have my following, what little I have. And that's it, that's the way we worked it, but we always knew that if we needed help, where I can get it." Ed acknowledged they had moved apart over the years, but added, "Lately now it's real good."

A heavy smoker, Edward J. Musial developed lung cancer and died on December 10, 2003, at the age of eighty-one. Stan, two years older, put himself on a small regional flight and made it to the funeral.

Ed's son, Edward, a retired steelworker, spoke well of his uncle and said he was proud to have the same last name.

"Certainly—all the time," he said. "He's one of the greatest baseball players of all time, right up there with Ruth and DiMaggio."

From a few trips to St. Louis, Edward understood how much the people loved his uncle. "Can't say enough good things about him. When he came to town, every kid in town wanted his glove signed. He'd sign every glove I could carry."

From living in the Mon Valley all his life, Edward certainly heard the complaints that Stan did not come back often enough, did not do enough for the valley.

"People expect a lot," the nephew said. "Same thing with Joe Montana. These people moved on. I don't know how much you are supposed to give. Are you supposed to build roads? Libraries?

"He wasn't making that much money in those years, not the millions they do today. He made more as a businessman. If you look at it, baseball was an avenue for him. He did very well. They liked him. He was an ordinary kind of guy, a nice house but I wouldn't say a mansion.

"I know a lot of people say, 'They don't give back.' But this isn't your home. You don't live here. It's your hometown, but my uncle has lived in St. Louis for almost seventy years."

Stan remained loyal to old friends like Dr. William Rongaus, one of the heroes of the 1948 smog, who often bragged: "I delivered Stan Musial, and I delivered Ken Griffey Sr."

When Donora named ball fields for both players, Griffey Senior could not be there for the dedication because he was managing a minor-league team, but Musial sat in a small tent in the heat for three hours, signing autographs. Other times when Musial came back for reunions, he would often pay for the entertainment.

Still, while visiting Donora in 2009, I heard somebody tell me Musial had set too steep a price for memorabilia for a display case at his old high school. Nobody could verify it, but somebody told it to me as gospel.

"Maybe it is characteristic of athletes from western Pennsylvania," said Charles Stacey, the retired superintendent of schools, but some people were always looking to see "if you got too big for your britches."

Musial's old school, Donora High, and Joe Montana's old school, Monongahela High, had been folded into Ringgold High School, leaving both great athletes more or less without an alma mater. People told me that residents of Monongahela were annoyed when Montana chose to watch his son play in a high school game in California rather than come back for a sporting function. Hometowns can be rough.

IN MARCH 2009, I got a guided tour of Donora from Bimbo Cecconi, the great Pitt tailback. He took me up to the old high school, where Musial had hit his epic grand slam into the trees, and he showed me the gym, where he used to watch Musial work out during the baseball off-season.

We drove past all the ethnic clubs that were still open for a beer and a shot. Bimbo showed me where some of the old athletes had lived, and then we visited the library, whose staff was extremely helpful. A few older female patrons of the library fluttered around Cecconi, still handsome at eighty. He still lived near Pittsburgh, which apparently did not qualify as moving "away."

Somebody mentioned recent shootings involving youths from Donora and Monessen, just across the river. One version was that the shootings were over girls, but another version was that the shootings were over drugs.

Charles Stacey, now the head of the historical society, showed us the new headquarters in a former Chinese restaurant. Then the three of us took a walk down McKean, the main drag, virtually silent at midday, like a scene out of *High Noon*. One young man, waiting in a doorway, greeted Stacey, who recognized him as a former student. My reporter instincts told me the young man was a lookout.

As Stacey walked along, he suddenly had a memory of Lukasz Musial shortly after the Cardinals beat the Yankees in the 1942 World Series: "He was walking down the street and he had a baseball in his hand and he was tossing it up in the air and catching it and singing."

We stopped in front of Costas Restaurant, where Donorans used to go for lunch or to celebrate a sports victory. It was shuttered now.

"It seemed bigger," Cecconi said, peering in.

The two men recalled a state basketball tournament in Philadelphia in the mid-forties, when Donora got screwed by the big-city timekeeper.

"I passed to Pope and he missed and that was it," Cecconi said, reverently mentioning his late friend Arnold Galiffa, who went on to play quarterback for Army.

Just about everything was shuttered on McKean. Most commerce now took place in a graceless mall on what looked like a reclaimed strip mine on the hill across the river. I did not see where anybody could buy a sandwich in Stan Musial's hometown.

"It's bad because I remember the good times," Cecconi said. "We'd walk from the top of the hill, walk down Main Street, we walked everywhere, we knew everybody, it was so personal. So many churches. So many small groups. So many people."

Cecconi and Stacey heard some people say that Musial did not support his hometown. They shook their heads mournfully, recalling him sitting under an awning on a hot day, shaking hands, signing autographs, chatting with people. He cared about his town, they said. And they paid him the highest compliment they could give to a man: he took care of his mother.

# 42

## STANLEY GOES
## TO A REUNION

"I NEED to stop at a bank," Musial told Tom Ashley.

Ashley had been a key executive in the early days of Ted Turner's network, and later he made a documentary about his father-in-law—a labor of love, really.

This was sometime in the eighties, when Ashley was accompanying Musial to a reunion of the Cardinals, ranging back to the old days, the forties. Stanley popped into a bank and came out pocketing a thick roll of hundreds.

At the reunion, Stan hoisted a glass, played the harmonica, went into his crouch. Wouldn't be Stanley without the crouch. He also huddled with this old teammate or that old teammate—names from old bubble-gum cards, names from World Series box scores. Sometimes they would hug, sometimes they would shake hands.

Stanley did not go into detail, but Ashley guessed that on this one evening Musial had given, only to those who needed it, around $10,000.

# 43

## THE POLISH CONNECTION

As a player, Musial got to meet public figures on his circuit around the league, but in retirement he expanded his circle to a philanthropist, a Polish labor leader, and, if one is really dropping titles, the pope.

This new path in Musial's life began in 1960 when he campaigned for John F. Kennedy along with James A. Michener. The writer and the slugger became the odd couple on their sojourn through Middle America.

Whatever the chemistry, Michener and Musial liked each other's company and remained in touch after those autumn days on the road. The question immediately comes up: what did they have in common?

From Musial's perspective, Michener was responsible for one of the most popular musicals in American history—*South Pacific*, which opened on Broadway in 1949 and was the hottest ticket when Stan and Red would take in the occasional show.

Michener had used his navy experience to write *Tales of the South Pacific*, a series of short stories that won the 1948 Pulitzer Prize and was turned by Joshua Logan into a Rodgers and Hammerstein musical, which still touches hearts today.

*South Pacific* was revived in 2008 at New York's Lincoln Center, reminding people of the America that helped end World War II—a country of strong ideals that was beginning to encounter its racial prejudices.

Without Michener, young and alive and observant in the middle of a war, there would have been no French planter singing "Some Enchanted Evening," no nurse from Little Rock singing "I'm in Love with a Wonderful Guy," no lieutenant singing "You've Got to Be Carefully Taught," a biting condemnation of intolerance. The revival made some old-timers (me, for one) weep in honor of the country of the late forties. Michener touched a nerve, caught a time and place.

Just the aura of this great postwar musical might have been enough to make Musial—who had played ball at Pearl Harbor during the war and later in postwar Japan—glad he met Michener.

It is also possible that the values Michener could express were the same ones that ran within Musial, whether or not he could articulate them. They found each other; they formed a sweet friendship.

Musial, who said he read nonfiction, particularly histories and biographies, once said, "Jim knew I read his books, but we never talked about the books. He was a great sports fan. And he was a nice, low-key guy."

Plus, celebrities often tend to relate to one another as kindred souls who understand public scrutiny and expectation, who have come through under pressure. Each was in awe of what the other did; both understood discipline and hard work; both were shy, in their own ways.

"They liked being out somewhere and somebody would recognize one of them but not the other," said Tom Ashley. "Michener was not a lot of laughs. He got a kick out of Stan."

Both came from rather bleak childhoods. Michener was born in New York City in 1907 and was raised around Doylestown, Pennsylvania, by a widow, Mabel Michener, who sometimes had to farm him out to an orphanage when she ran low on money and space. He grew up understanding he would have to make his own way in the world, and was constantly on the move, writing about other people's lives, other people's homes.

"As a boy I had nothing," Michener said before his eighty-ninth birthday. "No toys. No baseball gloves. No wagon. No skates. Nothing. But I did have people who loved me and looked after my education."

Musial appeared to be a more gregarious soul than Michener. As it is with writers, Michener recognized some quality in the other person that he admired, maybe even needed to tap into, to get his work done.

It took an army or a village to help Michener, who always spent a few years researching his next subject, usually rooted in geography and history. Michener's quartermaster was his wife, Mari, but he also depended on friends like Herman Silverman, a builder of pools and a real estate developer in Bucks County, Pennsylvania. (In his bachelor days, Michener had scored a lot of points with Silverman by showing up as a weekend guest with his girlfriend of the time, Janis Paige, the actress.)

Silverman was glad to serve as a Sancho Panza who could read maps, settle bills, and jolly tour guides and desk clerks; his wife, Ann, tended to think Michener was a bit on the rude side.

Musial was always a welcome addition to the party—the seemingly secure athlete who could charm people. Through Michener, Musial met John Wayne for an impromptu lunch that would forever make Musial's life easier. While the three of them were chatting, fans kept coming over to seek autographs.

"Jim and I were signing napkins and pieces of paper," Musial recalled. "John Wayne was handing out these picture cards that he'd already signed. I went home and said, 'That's a good idea. People could lose a napkin.' But you know what happened? I forgot to get the Duke's autograph."

Soon Musial was carrying signed cards for fans, enabling him to smile and make small talk rather than sign his name.

The slugger and the author had politics in common. Michener once noted that Musial was the only superstar he knew who was a Democrat. Musial apparently remained a Democrat despite his exposure to LBJ, although some people who knew him said he was more conservative than many liberal Democrats. Musial not only supported George McGovern for president in 1972 but still admitted it four years after the Nixon landslide.

"I'm a Democrat," he told a friend in 1976. "Tom Eagleton, the Senator, says he remembers sitting in my lap when he was a kid visiting our spring-training camp years ago."

Soon Michener and Musial had something else in common: Lukasz Musial's homeland, Poland.

One of Michener's friends was Edward Piszek, a self-made millionaire, son of Polish immigrants who ran a grocery store in Philadelphia. While operating a bar as a young man, Piszek cooked too many crabcakes and decided to freeze the leftovers. The process worked so well that he and a partner, John Paul, began a company called Mrs. Paul's Kitchens, whose major product was fish sticks.

Piszek eventually bought out his partner, and also graduated from the Wharton School of Business at the University of Pennsylvania after attending night classes. He began using his money to benefit his ancestral homeland, sending generator-powered X-ray units to help eradicate tuberculosis, organizing a group called Project Pole to abolish Polish jokes.

Piszek also became friendly with Philadelphia's John Cardinal Krol, who was of Polish extraction. In 1980, Piszek sent forty million fish cakes to Poland, whose people were hungry under Communism.

Musial first met Piszek in 1962 when Michener made a losing campaign for Congress.

"The relationship between Dad and Stan Musial was more of a brother relationship," said Piszek's daughter, Helen P. Nelson. "My father was a driven man, very autocratic, he had a quick temper, which you never saw in Stan Musial. Of all the people I've ever met through my father, and I've met a lot of famous people, he's probably my number one person. Just his honesty, his integrity, he's just one simple, nice human being.

"When the three of them were together, I recall Stan was something of a conservative," Nelson said. "Dad was a pick-and-choose, and Michener was very liberal."

Nelson added, "The relationship with Dad and James Michener was more of a business relationship. Jimmy Michener was a different person. He was always nice to me and my husband. You didn't get the warm and fuzzies from him that you got from Stan." Nelson felt a reserve in Michener, perhaps because he relied on his wife for logistics and security. "His wife was extra protective," Nelson said. "When she was around, forget it."

Mari Michener was formidable. On one early trip to Poland, Michener, a Quaker, and his wife, who was of Japanese ancestry, met a young prelate who innocently noted that he did not meet many Japanese ladies in Poland.

"She corrected him, as she does all people who use that term, by saying proudly, 'Japanese-American. I was born in the United States,' and he accepted the correction," Michener wrote.

And that was how the Micheners got to meet Karol Jozef Wojtyla, the archbishop of Krakow and a cardinal.

At first Michener did not gauge the potential of Wojtyla, but Piszek advised him, "Keep your eye on that one. He could go far." When Michener asked why, Piszek said, "That one has guts of steel. He's been in the frontline battles since the age of six."

Piszek accompanied Stan and Lil to Poland in 1970, upon the invitation of the Polish Olympic Committee. Musial carried letters from John Cardinal Carberry of St. Louis to the archbishop of Warsaw plus the energetic young archbishop of Krakow.

In 1976, Stan and Lil returned to Poland in the company of Tom Fox of the *Philadelphia Daily News* and his wife, Karen Wessel Fox.

"Mr. P. was relentless in getting the media to go along on his trip with Cardinal Krol to Poland," Karen Fox said years later. At first, the Foxes were put off by Piszek's aggressive manners, but they upgraded their impression the more they saw of him.

"When I first met Mr. P.—before the first trip to Poland with Cardinal Krol—I asked him what his compulsion was," Karen Fox said. "Why was it that he was going to all the trouble and expense of the travel? And he said that it was important for him, to 'travel back up the river, and find from whence I came.' That I remember clear as yesterday. He was sitting in his humble office of Mrs. Paul's on Henry Avenue, and at the time was making multimillions with his products."

Tom Fox called Piszek's journeys "the Papal Primaries," a suggestion that Piszek was looking ahead to the next conclave, on the theory that Pope Paul VI was probably not going to live forever.

Musial's 1976 trip to Poland (Michener was not on this one) was in Piszek's Learjet, starting with a stop in Norway for a look at the fjords.

"We were in Oslo on National Day and had a lot of fun watching the parades—beautiful families in colorful regional dress," Karen Fox recalled. "Musial never had a bad day—he always greeted the day early, with a song in his heart, and a litany of teases for his beloved Lil. I recall he was delighted with the Norwegian breakfast—what a spread—breads, warm rolls and spiced loaves, fishes, pickles, jams, an assortment of eggs from baked to deviled, oatmeal and other hot cereals. I think he and Lil tasted every dish.

"On flying out of Oslo on a beautiful day we all remarked how patriotic and moving that every farm was flying the national flag. The flags punctuated the well-manicured patchwork below."

Having fallen in love with Norway, the Musials now explored Poland.

"I think the revelation for Musial was that he could be proud to be Polish," Karen Fox said years later. "I am not sure if he ever previously concentrated on the fact that he was Polish, and that it was important.

"From my observations, it was Mr. P. who wakened Musial's Polish roots," she added. "It was amazing to Musial, like a movie, sort of, that his genes were from this wonderful, beautiful country, with its lovely people, who had been so torn by war—and yet, survived in fine style, and great determined spirit, despite living under the boot of Communism at the time we visited.

"He and Mr. P. spent a lot of time together, away from the rest of us, like brothers really, absorbing from whence they came. There were times when Musial was like a schoolkid—he couldn't believe he was on this trip. He is a great ambassador. His personality is so winning. I don't think most Poles even knew who he was. That didn't matter; he went his merry way, winning over everyone with his impish, happy-go-lucky self."

Musial was also observing and learning. In a conversation with Roger Kahn in 1976, Musial noted how he once had made Polish jokes and laughed at Polish jokes but no longer could.

"I don't think Polish jokes or Jewish jokes or black jokes are really funny," Musial said. "My dad came out of Poland and worked like hell all his life. What was funny about that? Pulaski came out of Poland and helped out in the American Revolution. Was that a joke?"


ALWAYS LOOKING for his next project, Piszek began working on Michener to write a book about Poland, introducing him to Lech Walesa, the leader of the Solidarity movement, and talking up Cardinal Wojtyla from Krakow.

"Wojtyla wanted to know, what is this guy doing?" Nelson recalled, adding: "They believed in the same things."

Piszek traveled with large amounts of American dollars on his person, to distribute to clerics in Poland or the Vatican, to keep the Polish church solvent under Communism. His persistence in Polish politics and religion may have had more influence in the selection of Wojtyla as pope than has ever been understood.

Nelson added that her father "was very tight with Krol. They spent a lot of time together. I would assume that was a conversation they had."

Perhaps not even knowing it, Musial was on the fringe of a dynamic that probably impacted church and world politics for decades.

As it happened, I was covering religion in 1978 and was at the first conclave in Rome after Pope Paul VI died in August. The cardinal from Venice, Albino Luciani, was elected and chose the name John Paul I. (The housekeeper at our borrowed flat in the Piazza Navona, a Sardinian named Grazia, was the only person in all of Rome who had predicted the Venetian would win, citing the cardinal's family's socialist views.)

A day or two later, at a press conference of the North American cardinals at the Vatican, I heard Cardinal Krol say how delighted he was that the Holy Spirit had chosen the new pope, which is what all cardinals say after a conclave. Then Krol volunteered—and I paraphrase—that he had also been highly impressed with the cardinal from Krakow, that is to say, Karol Wojtyla. These were unusual words, since a conclave is not a presidential primary, in which a promising contender who falls short may immediately be set up to run four years hence. However, the Polish American cardinal from Philadelphia put out an unusual tribute to the Polish cardinal from Krakow. A month later Luciani died suddenly, forcing a second conclave, while memories of the first conclave were still vivid.

Ed Piszek went to the second conclave of 1978, carrying $25,000 in a briefcase to finance the unexpected expenses of the Polish cardinals. When he arrived at Fiumicino Airport, in haste and jet-lagged, Piszek forgot his briefcase. He discovered the absence when he arrived at the Vatican and quickly retraced his steps to the airport. To everyone's shock, he retrieved the briefcase intact.

Everybody in the streets and coffee bars of Rome knew that only an Italian could become pope. However, on October 16, 1978, Michener was at his desk in Maryland when he heard that a Polish cardinal had been elected pope. Michener assumed it was Stefan Wyszynski, the archbishop of Warsaw. It was not. It was the cardinal from Krakow.

AS SOON as Wojtyla was elected, Piszek went back to work on Michener.

"He drove Michener insane," Helen Nelson said. "I was there when Michener agreed, and my dad was on cloud nine."

Nelson insisted her father did not pay Michener for writing the book. "What my dad did was provide all the support," she said.

Well aware that Michener was in the habit of hunkering down for years on a project, Piszek made sure Michener was introduced to every Polish scholar he wanted. Sometimes Piszek even rented helicopters and hired researchers to make Michener's work go faster.

"The clock was ticking," Nelson said.

Under Piszek's prodding, Michener finished his novel, *Poland,* in one year rather than his more typical three to five years. His depiction of Communism and religion in Poland immediately made Michener persona non grata for many years, but Piszek kept working on the government to relax its ban.

In 1988, because of Piszek's lobbying, Michener was invited back to Poland to give a talk and was allowed to bring friends.

Piszek, Musial, and Michener met at the Miami airport, joined by Larry Christenson, a pitcher with the Phillies from 1973 to 1983 who had done well in finance in Philadelphia and was close to the Piszek family.

Ed Piszek expected formality from his own children, demanding they call him "sir," but Christenson, who had a distant relationship with his own father, bonded with older men like Musial and Piszek. Years later, Christenson would grow tender as he referred to Piszek as "my best buddy."

Christenson had met Walesa when the leader of Solidarity stayed at the Piszek home; Christenson was very much part of the team on the road trip to Europe.

The party landed in Warsaw in November, and Michener was delighted by the friendly reception.

"But that was explained by the fact that with me when we met was Stan Musial, the Hall of Fame baseball player whose amazing feats and hilarious nature made him a favorite everywhere," Michener wrote. "Stan's mission to Poland was an amusing one, as explained by Piszek: 'Baseball is to be a sport in the 1992 Olympics at Barcelona, and Cuban experts are training the Russians. Musial is twice as smart as any Cuban, and he'll train the Poles to beat the Russians.' Stan said he doubted that any one man could make that much difference, but he was entering the competition joyously, so our joint mission was off to a flying start."

Michener was given a medal and asked to make a speech, as government officials did their best to mend the rift, surely a tribute to Piszek's diplomacy (or his briefcase filled with dollars).

Musial met some Polish relatives and spent an evening comparing notes and laughing and singing. He and Michener also made a side trip to the Majdanek concentration camp near Lublin, where an estimated 79,000 people, including 59,000 Polish Jews, had died during World War II. That excursion put the jolly trip in sober perspective for them.

On the night of November 30, Musial was present for an epic event in Polish history. Walesa, by then the winner of the Nobel Peace Prize, was debating Alfred Miodowicz, the head of the government trade union, on television, as part of the Communist regime's professed openness to dialogue. Because Miodowicz was seen as a smooth politician and Walesa was viewed as a gruff electrician, out of his element, Miodowicz was expected to score points for state competence.

A staggering portion of the Polish citizens—78 percent of adults—was estimated to be watching on television that night as Walesa stood up to Miodowicz. The public immediately judged that Walesa had won the debate.

Musial and the rest of the American party watched in the home of the archbishop of Warsaw. Within minutes after the debate ended, an exuberant Walesa came bounding into the room. As Michener described the moment, the Pole seemed like "some notable opera star who had come into Sardi's theatrical restaurant on Broadway at the end of the grand performance to receive the applause and adulation of the crowd awaiting him there."

Two years later, Walesa would be elected president of Poland, and would serve for five years. Musial had been there the night Walesa won over the Polish nation.

ON DECEMBER 3, the tour continued to Rome, where the three amigos were invited to dinner at the pope's quarters in the Vatican, a rare honor. Michener greeted the pope by saying, "I am so glad to see you, my dear friend," a Quaker touch that seemed to boggle the Polish pope. Twice during dinner, Michener duly reported, John Paul II "looked across the table at me and said: 'So you are the man who called me his friend.' "

Michener added, "I could not tell whether this was a rejection of what he had deemed an unwarranted familiarity or simply a reflection of an unusual greeting. But I did get the feeling that at his second repetition there was a sharp edge to his voice." Given that Wojtyla was an actor, writer, and linguist as well as a prelate, the odds are essentially 99–1 that he knew exactly what he was saying and what inflection he intended.

A master of detail, Michener also recorded the meal. "Three courses served by a nun: some of the best cannelloni I have ever had; an excellent chicken dish, and, I feel sure, some kind of dessert; but I was so busy listening that I took no specific notice of it. The pope ate none of this: he had soup with crackers and a plate of fruit."

There is no record of how closely Musial followed the byplay between the pope and the author. By all recollections the pope knew Musial as a famous retired American athlete and a Roman Catholic of Polish ancestry, and the two robust, secure men were physically and psychically comfortable with each other.

At five-thirty the next morning, the amigos were summoned to the Vatican for a private Mass said by the pope. As they prepared to climb six or seven flights of stairs to his personal chapel, Musial was recognized by some young American priests.

"I'm entitled to be here because I'm also a Cardinal," he said, delighting the priests.

The American group had expanded to include Jim Murray, the former general manager of the Philadelphia Eagles and a friend of Piszek's.

"I watched Stan interact with the pope," Murray said, adding that Musial's demeanor was that of an altar boy in awe of the pontiff.

The participants at the Mass included four nuns from Vietnam and an Irish tenor who would sing the Ave Maria. Michener also observed that the pope celebrated Mass old-style, with his back to his guests.

As the guests left, the pope gave each celebrant rosary beads he had blessed. Michener noted that the pope "joked and exchanged pleasantries as if he were a parish priest at the close of prayer."

Larry Christenson, a Lutheran, would always treasure his rosary, as well as the way the athletic pope—a linebacker, by body type—looked up at Christenson's six feet four inches and 215 pounds.

Like many people who heard John Paul II speak English (and speak it quite well), Christenson would forevermore imitate the Polish inflections as the pope told him: "You are a big dude."

Then it was time for the pope's nuanced farewell to Michener.

"Grasping my hand in both of his, he said: 'Keep writing those long books,' " Michener dutifully recorded.

These words constitute perhaps the most trenchant literary criticism ever uttered by a pope. To his credit, Michener repeated the line in his subsequent book.

The Americans were invited to the residence of the American ambassador to Italy, Maxwell M. Rabb. Among the guests was Richard L. Thornburgh, the former governor of Pennsylvania who had been appointed attorney general by President Reagan that summer and was visiting Europe to investigate the links between drugs and terrorism.

"When I saw Musial there, I was blown away. I was going back to my early teens," said Thornburgh, who had grown up near Pittsburgh and had mastered the art of copying Musial's signature as a kid.

Thornburgh spotted a recent signature ostensibly by Musial, and although he had never met him before, he bluntly told Musial: "That is not your autograph."

Thornburgh recalled: "He looked at me kind of askance and I said, 'Here's your autograph,' and I remembered well enough how to fake his autograph in grade school. He was just completely blown away. He said, 'That used to be my autograph but I guarantee what I have given you is the real McCoy.' "

Twenty years later, Thornburgh still glowed at the memories of "a very, very pleasant evening. Crowd of people, highly impressed with Musial and Michener, the whole idea of their mission, just about at the end of the Soviet empire. Unforgettable evening." (When he got back to Washington, Thornburgh would receive a ball, definitely autographed by Musial.)

Stanley was in rare form that night at the embassy, performing his famous banana trick—somehow slicing it within the skin after sprinkling it with his own special "woofer dust."

At the same time, intrigue was taking place beyond the hilarity. It turned out that the three amigos had also been invited to the residence of the American ambassador to the Vatican, Frank J. Shakespeare. Two dinners at the same time, a mile or so apart—a difficult trick, even for those guys.

While Stanley was performing, the Vatican embassy was calling the Rome embassy to say that Ambassador Shakespeare was expecting Michener and Musial and Piszek. Not wanting to offend anybody, the first team jumped in a waiting limousine and sped across Rome to the next party. Christenson, Murray, and some other friends—who called themselves "the turd team"—stayed behind.

Reunited with all his friends the next day, Stan posed for a photo wearing three championship sports rings—his own from the Cardinals, Christenson's ring from the 1980 Phillies World Series, and Murray's National Football Conference ring from the 1980 Eagles. They also made a trip to the Colosseum, where Musial posed in his familiar crouch, using Michener's aluminum cane for a bat.

Later, Musial spotted a wedding and somehow or other crashed it, knowing no Italian or, for that matter, anybody in the wedding party.

"Stan could have been the bride's father," Murray said. "We had so much fun, we were like little kids."

There was another side venture when Musial noticed there was an Italian baseball league in Anzio, where Allied troops had landed early in 1944.

"We got to Anzio and the cemetery was closed, so we broke in and did our thing and then we found the ball game," Murray said. "All of a sudden, the announcer stops the game and says, 'Stan Musial is here' and everybody came around to talk to him, and even the people who ran the club, they asked if he could get them a pitcher, and Stan was like a general manager, taking down notes: 'Let me see if I can help.' "

Murray—a generous man and a pioneer in the Ronald McDonald houses for children with cancer—enjoyed seeing Musial and Michener together.

"A perfect marriage," he called it. "Both had total ability and total confidence. You would never recognize their status, seeing them. On that Poland trip, Michener was the star, and Stan loved seeing Michener get the award. Total respect. Some guys are just pros. Some guys have that aura. And both of them were like that. They had what I call a tangible intangible. Big leaguers."

Murray continued: "Stan would take out his harmonica and you could see a little sparkle between them. It wasn't them telling war stories or anything. It was just total awe of each other."

Musial was so identified as a prominent Polish American that he became something of a touchstone for Polish contacts. Pat Henry, a professor in Washington State (from Brooklyn!), advised Musial he had a counterpart in Krakow—Father Stanislaw Musial, who was honored for his long support of the Jewish community in Poland. Father Musial's family had shielded a Jew early in the war, and was nearly executed until the four-year-old pleaded with a Nazi soldier, who granted them mercy. Stan Musial was delighted to know of the priest and sent autographed photos of himself to Henry in Brooklyn and Father Musial in Krakow.


MUSIAL RETAINED his bond with Poland and its fledgling baseball program.

On July 7, 1989, President George H. W. Bush invited Musial to the White House lawn for a Little League celebration. A few days later, on a trip to Poland, the president referred to Musial's frequent trips to Poland and also mentioned other stars of Polish ancestry.

In 1990, Stan and Lil and Piszek traveled to Wroclaw, three hours from Warsaw, to bring 486 bats, 250 gloves, 925 Cardinals caps, and uncounted baseball cards. Wroclaw dedicated a six-foot granite marker in Musial's honor.

On July 23, the Stan Musial Little League Field in Jaslo was dedicated, through donations by Polish Americans. Musial cried as the field was opened, saying, "It's my father's homeland. And it's quite an honor to be honored like that for something you loved doing all those years—baseball."

Murray said Musial was still something of an innocent about life in Poland. One day Musial rented a car and went off by himself to visit distant relatives in another corner of Poland, carrying a video camera to record the meeting.

That evening, Musial was late for a reception with the American ambassador, John R. Davis Jr. When he finally arrived, he told Murray he had been taking pictures of the beautiful Polish countryside when suddenly the police swooped in and arrested him.

"What he doesn't know is there's a Russian tank farm in the forest," Murray explained. "We found out later. This is pure Stan Musial. He's going to help somebody he hasn't even met before, some relative. He didn't know the tanks were there. He was talking into a camera.

"The point of the story is," Murray continued, "he didn't pull rank. He didn't say, 'Hey, I'm a great American baseball player looking for a poor relative.' He had no idea of the security."

Murray then told Stanley that the arresting officer was probably on his way to Siberia for disturbing a state guest. That made Musial feel even worse, Murray said. "That's the kind of humility he has."

THE FRIENDSHIP between Michener and Musial endured on domestic soil, a sort of movable feast. Julius Hunter, a television personality and writer in St. Louis, got a glimpse of the friendship when he was invited to join the Musials and Micheners for dinner. Totally by coincidence, Hunter's wife, Barbara, was reading Michener's book *Iberia,* because the couple was planning a trip there.

Michener, Hunter recalled, was not feeling well and let his wife answer some of the questions. "It took only a couple minutes to realize that she was the more articulate, and perhaps deeper of the two," Hunter wrote.

Hunter did ask Michener how he came to be so prolific, and Mari replied that he often worked with three secretaries and three typewriters at once.

During the lunch, Hunter observed that Michener's drink of choice was bourbon, whereas Musial stuck with beer. The two buddies clearly shared memories of all-guy rambles around Florida. As Hunter noted, "A listener would also pick up that wives need not know all the details of the boys' boozing, card-playing and cigar-smoking."

One outing by Michener and Musial was described by Tom McEwen, the longtime sports columnist and power broker with the *Tampa Tribune.*

McEwen wrote he had received a phone call from Art Pepin, the powerful Busch distributor in the Tampa area, saying he was in a recreational vehicle with Musial, Michener, and Red Schoendienst. Apparently, Michener was thinking of writing a book about aging in America, and wanted to scout the area as a possible locale.

I waited at the door when the great man got out, jacket and hat with a brim, cane. He came to the door and I introduced myself. Said he knew me. Said he often read me. Didn't matter that he did or did not, he said it, and looked to the right to my pretty comfortable office and he said it was much like his. Sure. And then, the great James Michener lifted his cane a bit in gesture, and asked: "May I ask you a question, Tom?"

Well, sir, of course, sir, I think I stammered. Him, Mr. Michener, asking me a question? I knew something he did not?

"What is the matter with Vinny Testaverde?"

Michener was, of course, referring to the Tampa Bay Buccaneers' quarterback, who was prone to interceptions.

"He's colorblind," McEwen told Michener—inside sportswriter stuff.

McEwen joined the lads on the RV during their trek around Tampa. Many years later he recalled how Musial turned to Pepin and said, "Art, I have been on this bus an hour and a half and you have not offered me a beer. Not feeling well?"

Michener echoed Musial, asking: "Got any bourbon, Art?"

So that may have been the extra ingredient in the friendship: the Pulitzer Prize–winning writer and the Hall of Fame ballplayer were drinking buddies.

McEwen also recalled a birthday dinner that Stan and Lil held for Michener with guests like Gussie Busch, Art Pepin, and Jack Lake, the publisher of the *St. Petersburg Times,* as well as Al Lopez, Ted Williams, and Robin Roberts.

To McEwen's chagrin, Musial introduced him as a "member of Mr. Michener's profession" and suggested McEwen might like to say a few words. McEwen was horrified that a self-styled "klutz" like himself would be compared to the source of *South Pacific,* but he would indeed say a few words.

I took the bouquet off my table, took it to Mr. Michener and said something numbskullish like he was his craft's flagship, how we all saluted him for his skill and speed, thanked him for his work and so would he accept this bouquet on our behalf, which, I noted, was an aphrodisiac. I took a bite of a flower in the bundle and so did he, then offering his lady a bite as well. Even Ted Williams laughed.

Michener was wearing down. He was honored on February 3, 1992, for his eighty-fifth birthday, at a black-tie dinner in New York at the Pierpont Morgan Library. Walter Cronkite and Musial were the only two of the 130 guests to be singled out by name in the *New York Times*.

Mari Michener, who was younger than her husband, died first, on September 25, 1994. Michener developed severe kidney problems, and Musial visited him several times in Austin, Texas, and sometimes phoned him.

"He's on a dialysis machine three days a week," Musial said in 1996. "It was his eighty-ninth birthday. So I got my harmonica out and played 'Happy Birthday' for him, and Lil was singing."

After turning ninety on February 3, 1997, Michener began talking of stopping dialysis, which he knew would end his life. In his final days, Michener alternated between sleep and taking calls from old friends like Merv Griffin, Cronkite, and Musial. He died on October 16, 1997, at his home in Austin. Musial went down for the funeral.

Musial described him as a "down-to-earth guy" who liked sports and knew a great deal about the world. "Jim was an outstanding guy," Musial said. "We are all saddened by the passing of a dear friend."

FIFTEEN MONTHS later, a weary Pope John Paul II stopped off for a thirty-one-hour visit to St. Louis on his way home from Mexico. Musial greeted the pope at several receptions, one at the cathedral and another at a luncheon at the archbishop's residence. Musial also attended the evening Mass at the domed arena downtown. Colonel James Hackett, one of Musial's closest friends, recalled Musial's generosity in making sure that Musial's business manager, Dick Zitzmann, Zitzmann's mother, and another friend, Bill Suntrup, a prominent Ford dealer, had tickets for the papal Mass.

Edward Piszek later went through some turbulent financial times and finally sold Mrs. Paul's in 1982, but he still lived comfortably, and was still a philanthropist when he died of bone cancer on March 27, 2004. Musial flew to Philadelphia to attend the Mass, and the pope sent a note that he was "deeply saddened" by Piszek's death.

After years of visibly growing weaker, Pope John Paul II died on April 2, 2005, at the age of eighty-four.

"They remained friends until Dad died," Helen Piszek said. "I'm glad Dad died first because I think he would have been devastated."

For Musial, the long friendships, the international and domestic rambles, were also coming to a close.

# 44

## THE FACE IN THE CROWD

B OB COSTAS had dreaded Mickey Mantle's funeral, although he had known it was coming. Mantle was his boyhood hero; Costas carried the 1958 Mantle bubble gum card in his wallet as a statement of devotion.

A longtime resident of St. Louis, Costas had entertained Mantle in his home, along with Stan Musial and other baseball people. He'd seen the good side of Mantle and, on occasion, the bad.

Now Costas had been asked to speak at Mantle's funeral on a hot August day in 1995 at the Lovers Lane Methodist Church in Dallas. He would not try to hide his adulation of the flawed, golden star.

Afraid he would lose his composure, Costas avoided even a glance at the Mantle family in the front row. They had gone through many tortured years in public, through Mantle's drinking and his escapades, until, in his final years, he had willed himself into sobriety. Then he had been brought down by liver cancer a few months short of sixty-four. Costas could feel the sadness in the church. Just when the Mick had gotten control of his life, it was all over.

Adept at public speaking, Costas could deliver his address while shifting his gaze around the room, the journalist, the observer.

"I had come in through the back, and I hadn't seen everybody who was there," Costas recalled years later. "I was looking over the audience, making an inventory, to see who is here."

Even as he spoke about his hero, Costas made a discovery that touched him.

"Against the wall, to my left, sitting by himself, about halfway back, against one of the windows with the light streaming in, there sits Stan Musial," Costas recalled.

"In that split second, it became clear: Here's what happened today. A man, what, seventy-four years old, who has had prostate cancer, got up this morning in St. Louis and said, 'It's the right thing to do.'"

For some reason, the sight of Musial—the church man, the family man, the disciplined man, the polar opposite of Mantle—distracted Costas, almost made him lose his composure.

"Think of all the people who were more directly associated with Mickey," Costas continued. "Nobody would have marked Stan as absent. He didn't stay overnight. He got on a plane. He showed up. Then he flew back to St. Louis. There is some old-school code in that, or maybe it's the decency that not many people have in their nature, but Stan Musial does."

Costas knew the respect Mantle had for the greatest players, for Williams and DiMaggio and Musial, and knew that Mantle was honest enough with himself to recognize they had marshaled their talents better than he had.

In their presence, Costas had seen Mantle restrain his surly side, his Rabelaisian excesses, out of respect for who they were.

Williams and DiMaggio, both getting on, were not present in this church in Dallas, and nobody expected them to be. But one of the lodge brothers from the forties had flown a long way to pay his respects.

"I don't think Stan is overly sitting around ruminating about this stuff," Costas said later, "but I think he understood what it would mean to Mickey's family, to Mickey himself while he's lying there in a casket, that it would have meant something for Stan to be there, that he hauled his ass out of bed and went to Dallas."

Somebody as fundamentally Catholic as Musial would also see his journey as a way to bring a tangible blessing to the Mantle family. Prayers might mean more in person. Normally private and lighthearted, Musial made himself available to reporters who wanted to talk about Mantle.

"He was a lovable guy," Musial told them. "Everybody loved Mickey." He added, "He hit more long home runs than anybody I ever saw. He could really powder that ball, you know?"

Musial recalled how, after the Cardinals beat the Yankees in the 1964

World Series, Mantle had come to Musial's restaurant to congratulate the winners, a classy thing to do.

Few people in the church knew that Musial had been Mantle's favorite player back in Oklahoma, when he listened to Cardinal games on the radio like everybody else in the southwest.

When Mantle was fourteen his father drove them up to St. Louis to see a game. Mickey happened to spot Musial in a hotel, but Mutt would not allow his son to ask Musial for an autograph.

The two players had something else in common—zinc. Mutt Mantle had died of Hodgkin's disease at thirty-nine after working in the mines. Lukasz Musial had ruined his body inhaling the poisonous air of Donora. It is not clear if the two players had ever discussed this bond, but there Musial was, an outpatient himself, in a church in Dallas.

They had seen each other for the last time in the spring of 1995. "He came to town and wanted me to have breakfast with him," Musial said, "which we did. We had a real nice chat, a nice talk, just he and I. We talked a lot about baseball and a lot of other things.

"He told me that one of his sons just passed away shortly before. And he told me at that time he wasn't drinking anymore, and that he went to the Betty Ford Center. And I told him how proud we are of him. And I told him one other thing. I said, 'Mickey, we love you.' You know, he was a great idol."

Years later, Costas was still touched by Musial's gesture.

Musial's presence in his field of vision, Costas decided, was a gift from "one of the better angels of our nature."

"We're all messed up in one way or another," Costas added, "but this was just a moment of grace, what a decent thing for a person to do."

Costas thought about Musial for a moment, and added, "And he probably knew it at some level."

# 45

## STANLEY'S STATUES

O N LABOR Day 1998, giddy baseball pilgrims gathered in St. Louis to root for home runs by the two modern sluggers, the Cardinal and the Cub. How innocent it all seemed that summer.

Before the game, the fans clustered at the statue of Stan the Man, the one with the big beam, the one he hated. I was covering the McGwire-Sosa frolics, heard some commotion by the statue, and wandered over.

At the base of the statue, an elderly gent was wearing a tomato-can-red jacket, a garment only a highly secure individual could wear.

Above him were Ford Frick's words: "Here stands baseball's perfect warrior. Here stands baseball's perfect knight."

The perfect knight himself was noodling away on a harmonica, playing "Take Me Out to the Ball Game."

Unprotected, without phalanxes of security guards, Musial looked as comfortable as an old bluesman playing for his buddies in front of a Delta country store. There was a merry twinkle in those gimlet eyes that had once launched 3,630 hits.

Grandfathers smiled to themselves, entertaining memories of the lithe young man springing out of his corkscrew stance. Keepers of the flame, they nudged their grandchildren, as if to say, *You should have seen him back then.*

The bronze statue loomed over them, suggesting the brute power of the old Soviet Union, its oversized locomotives, its massive parades, as if honoring the People's Hero of the Autumn Harvest, who wielded a bat instead of a scythe.

Musial had disliked the statue from the beginning. The legs were too thick, for one thing, making him look like one of those Clydesdales out at the Busch estate rather than the limber youth who had been labeled the "Donora Greyhound."

The statue was originally supposed to have been based upon a painting by Amadee Wohlschlaeger, himself a St. Louis icon known by his first name. The original was titled "The Boy and the Man . . . Baseball's Bond," but the boy in the painting never made it to the statue, and the man became bunchy, inflexible. The mayor of St. Louis, Raymond Tucker, chose the sculptor, Carl Mose, a highly reputable artist based at Washington University in St. Louis, and the statue emerged from the artistic vision of Mose, which, come to think of it, is how art happens. But statues of hero-athletes fall into a different category. At least, people have been arguing about reality versus impression ever since. How bad is that?

Ten feet five inches tall, on a marble pedestal eight and a half feet high, the People's Hero looked awkward, off balance, not coiled like a gymnast, which the perfect knight had been in his childhood. It was almost as if Mose did not believe anybody would really twist himself into a human corkscrew, so he had brought the body back toward middle ground, with thicker muscles, as if to justify all those home runs in Stan Musial's resumé.

"I saw the sculptor when he was working on it," Musial said in 1976. "I told him I never looked that broad. He said it had to be that broad because it was going to be against the backdrop of a big ballpark. He missed the stance, but what kind of man would I have been if I'd complained. The writers were generous to put it up. The sculptor did his best. Look, there's a statue of me in St. Louis while I'm still alive."

Thirty years after the statue was unveiled, Musial would call the statue "a great, great honor"—a message to young people.

"This is sort of an example," he once said. "They can excel in school, in business, in anything. It can happen to them."

However, Musial reserved the right to critique the statue. In the revised version of his autobiography, he addressed his youngest child, who had come along too late to remember seeing him play.

"I'll say this, Jeannie. I didn't hit the way that guy in the statue does," Musial wrote.

Everybody in St. Louis used the statue as a meeting point; so did

Musial, sometimes. He was the life of the party, the unpaid greeter, playing his harmonica for love, but on another level—never underestimate Stanley—he deftly understood it was to his advantage to put himself out in public, the man of the people.

His legs were going, but he would hobble out in front of the fans and say: "If I had known what it would do to my legs, I wouldn't have hit so many triples."

They loved to laugh at his old lines, the way listeners back in the days of radio loved to hear Jack Benny wheedle nickels from his friends, the way people laughed at Lucille Ball's wide-mouthed terror when Ricky said she had some 'splainin' to do. Musial fans knew all of Stanley's lines, knew his batting stance, and wanted to hear them and see it all over again.

On this humid Labor Day in 1998, Musial had cared enough to come out and greet the fans, who were celebrating a new age, a new body type— the beefy boys. Mark McGwire and Sammy Sosa had muscles unimagined back in Stan the Man's day, when men did not lift weights because, everybody knew, it might render them musclebound.

In old age, dwarfed by his statue, the man was still whippet-lean, with no trace of bulk under the tomato-can-red jacket, no bulge from the weight room, no muscles from some laboratory.

It was getting to be game time. Musial coiled his aging body into that iconic stance, peered over his right shoulder at a phantom pitcher, and unleashed a double into a mythical corner, inspecting his imaginary hit as the crowd responded with pitty-pat applause. He liked it so much he did it again, giggling, proud of himself. The fans parted lovingly.

STARTING IN 1998, there were two statues of Stanley at the Cardinals' ballpark, as the Cardinals unveiled ten statues by Harry Weber, two-thirds human size, capturing the essence of ten great St. Louis ballplayers— George Sisler of the Browns; Cool Papa Bell, the old Negro League star; and eight Cardinals: Rogers Hornsby, Dizzy Dean, Ozzie Smith, Red Schoendienst, Bob Gibson, Enos Slaughter, Lou Brock, and Musial. (McGwire was in storage, indefinitely; Pujols was a statue waiting to be commissioned.)

On sweet summer nights, people congregated at Eighth and Clark, milling around these vital statues, which I likened to ancient Xian terra-cotta warriors, guarding the Chinese emperor forever. Smacking a double into the corner, pouncing from the batter's box, Stanley was forever young, and heartland America had made his statues a gathering point.

# 46

## MORE FUNERALS

OLD AGE is not a lot of laughs, particularly in public.

It is particularly difficult for athletes who are remembered—who remember themselves—as magical creatures who can run and jump and perform prodigious acts with their bodies.

For the fans, a random meeting with a favorite old athlete produces a mixture of joy and despair: *Hey, didn't you used to be . . . ?* says one. *Daddy, why is he limping?* murmurs another. The millions who loved Stan Musial now saw him need a subtle hand from friends, then a cane, eventually a wheelchair.

His first illness was a gastric ulcer in 1983. Then in 1989, after ignoring symptoms for a year, he needed surgery for prostate cancer. With the ensuing pain and inconvenience and weight loss, Musial became depressed and stayed away from the public for many months.

He had always seemed so effortless in swinging his way through life, but now he was working hard at being Stan the Man, as if aware he might not go on forever.

He had enjoyed better second and third and fourth acts than most great athletes ever do, but once in a while he could voice regret.

"I wish I could have gotten a college education," Musial said in 1996. "There's something about a college education that gives you a broad look at things, to kind of make you complete."

Musial was beloved in his chosen hometown, but in his later years he probably shortchanged himself: Aside from the dueling Musial statues outside the ballpark, there was no secular place where one could worship

Musial. He never got around to creating a Musial foundation, never established a Musial collection at a prestigious university or library. Asked where any possible Musial archives might be displayed, friends and associates would say, *Well, Lil saved a lot of stuff in the house.*

He did have a business, Stan the Man, Inc., which sold memorabilia and booked him for autograph shows. He was certainly civic-minded about showing up for good causes, was generous in many ways. But DiMaggio had his name on a children's hospital in Florida, and Williams was identified with the Jimmy Fund in Boston. Yogi had an active museum in his name on a college campus in Montclair, New Jersey. Musial was mostly identified with the Cardinals, with his crouch, which was more than fine for fans of a certain age.

In his own whaddayasay manner, Musial presented his version of Stan the Man. This was the impression of Fay Vincent, the business executive who became an accidental commissioner when his friend Bart Giamatti died suddenly in 1989. Vincent had worked in Hollywood, understood the power of image, and sensed that Musial did, too. Vincent felt the man was more complicated than he appeared, had an agenda, a perfectly fine one, behind the smile and the harmonica.

"You have a feeling, he's been a public figure for so long, there is a public figure that he wants you to see," Vincent said, adding, "I saw a little glimpse of it."

Vincent continued: "If you opened the door of the public Musial and went to the next level, there are a fair number of other dimensions to him. I think he works very hard, as DiMaggio did, to keep you and other people from ever getting to any of those other rooms or dimensions. DiMaggio was world-class at it."

Each member of The Big Three had his own style in old age.

Musial was as close to a normal retired guy as a superstar can become, a frequent sight in the normal life of St. Louis. One friend of mine recalls Stan and Lil testing mattresses in a St. Louis department store by bouncing around on them.

Ted Williams mellowed, became accessible—goddam right he did— talked hitting endlessly.

Joe DiMaggio was more of a hermit, trusting himself with a few close friends, hoarding freebie golf bags he had cadged at celebrity outings.

For many years, the Clipper would visit the Super Bowl with Nick Nicolosi, a businessman from New Jersey, who organized the annual Super Bowl golf party. Nicolosi, who referred to himself as "The Ringmaster," would rent a suite with two bedrooms connected by a parlor and install the Clipper in the other room.

DiMaggio had a few demands, including a supply of fresh bananas. When visitors came to the suite to pick up tickets or to schmooze, DiMaggio was not shy about letting them know the bananas were his and his alone.

In return for the bananas, DiMaggio would answer calls for his buddy.

One afternoon DiMaggio picked up the phone and said, "Yes, Nick is here, may I tell him who's calling?"

"My name is Stan Musial," the voice said.

"Musial, Musial, how do I know that name?" DiMaggio asked.

The voice at the other end said, well, he had played a little ball.

"I played a little ball too. My name is DiMaggio. Joe DiMaggio."

At that, DiMaggio held out the phone for Nicolosi, who could hear Musial sputtering on the other end.

When Musial finally regained his speech, he said: "Boy, Nick, you must pay pretty good to have the great DiMaggio answering your phone."


SOMEHOW, VINCENT felt, he did not get to know Musial as well as the other two sluggers.

"There were many, many sides for him," Vincent said. "The kid from Donora. The prodigy, if you will. He never forgot that. The religious side of him, very, very Catholic," said Vincent, who often saw Musial at Mass.

Musial sometimes sent Vincent an itinerary or folder or Michener memento from his trips to Poland—"something he wanted me to see," Vincent said. But that was not so unusual, either, because Musial was a generous writer of notes, a spontaneous giver of gifts.

"He was very aggressive in making me see the celebratory side of him, a little like DiMaggio," Vincent continued. "Here was this legend, this great figure. It was almost like he was making me see that he was a great man and a great ballplayer. He didn't have to persuade me at all, but he worked pretty hard at it."

Well, don't we all. Sportswriters spend decades speaking the patois of the locker room, as if that makes athletes out of us. Everybody wants street cred. It would be a shock if the greatest of ballplayers, the ultimate self-made men, did not privately ponder what civilians really thought of them.

Williams hid his complexities behind his bluster. DiMaggio held people off with a hauteur that could only have been intentional.

"There was a fundamental insecurity in him, as there was in DiMaggio," Vincent said of Musial. "I don't know if it was ethnic. There is in all of us, I guess," mused Vincent, whose own nickname is a diminutive, among the Irish, of his given name of Francis.

Vincent loved his job, loved spending part of his life around such a man. He could totally understand that Musial might have "sort of a compulsion to convince you how good he was."

There was little ambiguity to Musial. He had almost never been criticized in public, encountered no pressure to push up his draft call during the war. When Bob Burnes criticized him in a column for endorsing cigarettes in his smoking days, Musial gave up the few dollars of income long before he gave up the habit, and he always told children never to touch tobacco. He had never held himself up as a model of anything, just lived his life.

THE BIGGEST public blowup in Musial's life came after the death of Biggie in 1967. Without his partner to rely on, Musial turned over more of the business to his oldest child, Richard.

From the start, Stan seemed to understand he could not take his son into that exalted level of the family business, that is to say, hitting. Stan also recognized that the road trips and the hours at the restaurant had taken him away from his oldest child during his formative years.

"I wasn't able to give Dick the close relationship many fathers and sons enjoy, and, in an old-fashioned way, I expected more of him than I did his sisters. I guess girls do wrap their fathers around their little fingers," Musial said in his autobiography.

Coming through the ubiquitous Broeg filter, this comment suggests a distance between father and son. By the time Musial retired in 1963, Dick was already a father, who continued to work with—or for—his father for many decades. Dick managed hotels in St. Louis, Florida, and the Ozarks, along with the bowling alley in St. Louis, a dealing that ultimately became toxic.

Musial and Joe Garagiola had become business partners in 1958 with the Red Bird Lanes on Gravois in South St. Louis. This was a logical extension of the psychic partnership they had formed back in Springfield in 1941, when Garagiola had been salted away by Branch Rickey. Although he was five years younger than Musial, the kid from the Hill showed far more public assurance than the slender young man from the Mon Valley.

When Garagiola arrived to help win the 1946 World Series, Musial recognized that Garagiola possessed what is called the gift of gab, and they developed a tandem, an act. Musial would be invited to sports functions and would bring along his pal, the talking catcher. Stan would chatter for as long as he could, then he would ask Garagiola to say a few words, or more than a few words.

"You know, Joe and I both have mike fright," Musial would say. "I'm afraid to get the mike, and he's afraid he's not going to get it."

Their friendship grew as they drove the highways of Missouri and Illinois to their speaking engagements. When Musial retired in 1963, Garagiola served as master of ceremonies at the huge celebration.

In 1986, St. Louis residents were stunned to learn that two of their greatest civic heroes were involved in litigation.

"The headline in the newspaper, 'Garagiola Sues Musial,' made Cardinal fans wince. It was a dagger in Stan's heart. Who the hell could sue Stan Musial?" said Jack Buck.

Actually, headlines in the *Post-Dispatch* included: "Musial Cries 'Foul' on Garagiolas' Suit" and "Stan and Joe: Business Splits Old Friends," but give Buck credit for poetic license.

The suit was filed in April 1986 in the U.S. District Court, Eastern District Court of Missouri. Garagiola and his wife, Audrie, claimed that Dick Musial, Theresa Garagnani, Biggie's widow, and Jack Garagnani—as management of Red Bird Lanes—had lent approximately $130,000 to the restaurant Stan Musial and Biggie's, which was now going through hard times. The two sons had tried switching the menu from steak to French, producing a loss of around $3 million.

The suit also claimed that Dick Musial and Jack Garagnani had received approximately $54,000 in management fees from the partnership over three years without the knowledge of the Garagiolas.

The Musial lawyers said the loans from the bowling alley to the restaurant, and other businesses, had been paid back, but the Garagiolas claimed this happened only after the suit was filed. Lawyers for the Musials said the Garagiolas had moved from St. Louis long ago and had not taken an active part in the business, and that the two sons had taken a more active role in 1982 out of necessity.

It is hard to imagine Stan Musial kiting money or approving of it. Whether the two sons consciously hid their management fees from Garagiola is not easy to determine. A confidante of Musial said years later that when Garagiola raised the issue, "Stan's position with Joe was, 'Give me a number.' "

The suit was settled just before a court appearance, with both sides pledged to confidentiality and sharing the court costs. Like a messy divorce that haunts weddings, funerals, and birthdays, the Musial-Garagiola feud complicated St. Louis gatherings both public and private for decades, catching loyal friends in the middle.

Garagiola rarely spoke about the rift, once telling somebody he had come to realize Musial was not a nice person. There were suggestions that Musial, prior to settling, had shown a heretofore unseen brusque side, in effect saying, *Who are they going to believe, you or me?* Having known Garagiola since the 1960s, I thought he might talk about the rift, but he declined, graciously. His pain came through the phone.

"It was no coincidence that the only year Musial did not go to Cooperstown for the Hall of Fame ceremonies was the year Garagiola was inducted into the broadcaster's wing of the Hall," wrote Jack Buck (with the assistance of, you guessed it, Bob Broeg).

Buck/Broeg added: "If I want to get a rise out of Musial even today, I'll say, 'Heard from Joe lately?' Stan will answer, 'You mean DiMaggio?' Then I'll respond, 'No, Garagiola' and he will become airborne. It's a shame, but they'll never patch it up. I know Joe feels badly about it and when Stan was ill a few years ago, Joe was really hoping they could get back together, but it never happened."

The Cardinals' staff learned to separate Musial and Garagiola when they absolutely had to be at the ballpark at the same time, but sometimes there was the occasional gaffe. When the Cardinals played in the 2006 World Series, somebody on the promotion staff arranged for Musial and Garagiola to throw out the ceremonial first ball together. On the morning of the game, Musial called in sick and Ozzie Smith was hastily recruited to replace him. As soon as Garagiola was out of St. Louis airspace, Musial recovered sufficiently to toss out the ball the next day.

The ruined friendship hung over Musial, exposed a melancholy side, a trace of vindictiveness. Or maybe it was old age coming on.

"Stan hated confrontation. He could get down, to where you didn't want to approach him. He wasn't a lot of fun for a year or so after that," somebody close to him said.

IN JULY 1996, James N. Giglio published an article in the *Missouri Historical Review* about Musial's few months in Springfield in 1941. While depicting Stan and Lil as doting young parents, Giglio quoted an elderly bartender recalling the young wife saying she did not like baseball.

If it happened at all, it was a fairly innocuous and understandable remark from a young wife with a child, far from home, who had seen her husband play four years in the minors for minimal pay. When the article appeared, Musial was apparently infuriated by the sentence. Ultimately, Giglio did not use the bartender's comment in his very thorough biography, *Musial: From Stash to Stan the Man,* but the damage was done: Musial proactively closed many doors to Giglio, a professor from what is now known as Missouri State University.

One shunned acquaintance was William Bottonari, a high school classmate from Donora who had gone away to college and settled in a suburb of Harrisburg, Pennsylvania. Occasionally he and Musial would get together in St. Louis when Bottonari came to town on shoe business.

Bottonari said Musial once told him: "You can hold the meeting in my hotel, you can meet at my restaurant and you can bowl at my bowling alley. The only thing you can't have is the shirt off my back." Musial often sent gifts to Bottonari, a Musial bat or a Musial poster, addressing them himself with his elegant cursive script, signing them to his good friend Bill.

Sometimes they would meet at reunions in Donora, where Musial would greet everybody, pass out autographed cards, and even slip money to one cause or another, although never enough to satisfy everybody.

"Heroes are not appreciated," Bottonari said in 2008. "I suggested to one of the businessmen there ought to be a Stan Musial museum and he just made a face."

Bottonari was a civic gadfly who attended public hearings in his town to complain about school taxes, who fought for public gardens. He also went back home and gave Giglio a walking tour of Donora.

Shortly thereafter, Musial called Bottonari at home, "which he had not done in many years, or ever," Bottonari said. Musial fished around—*Hey, Bill, what are you up to?*—until Bottonari finally got his drift and said, "Aw, heck, Stan, I was over at Donora." Musial probably already knew this, since he had his eyes and ears in his hometown. He did not confront Bottonari about the tour but chatted a few more seconds and then said goodbye. Bottonari never heard from him again.

STAN AND Lil hunkered down for the long haul, loving grandparents by all accounts. Bob Costas, watching his daughter play soccer in the park, would spot Musial rooting for a granddaughter.

"Stan would sit on a lawn chair and he would bring with him, not out of any sense of entitlement but because he had learned that people would ask, autographed cards for everyone. I never, ever, saw him say no."

Costas said he learned a Musial family lesson on the soccer sidelines.

"It's natural for the children of very famous persons to be asked, 'How's your dad?' " Costas said. "But whenever you ask one of his kids, his daughter, Jeanne Edmonds, who's roughly my age, would say, 'He's well . . . and my mom is doing well, too.' A small act of decency. And I never again did not ask about both of them."

Stan and Lil were a couple for the ages, but with vastly different roles. She was the queen of the house. He was the king of the road. This comes through in the documentary *The Legend of Stan the Man Musial*, produced in 1990 by Tom Ashley, along with Mark Durand.

In one outdoor scene, Stan and Lil are sitting on a bench on a nice sunny day, talking about their lives. Clearly, giving interviews is Stanley's job, keeping things going with his *wunnerfuls*.

When Lil is asked about their lives, she begins to talk, and Stan begins to fidget, as if batting against some wild rookie. His eyes dart; his admirable short-twitch muscles seem to be contracting inside his bright sport jacket. Lil does not say anything controversial, but Stan's nervousness is tangible. It seems as though, in his mind-set, it is still the forties, when the little woman stayed home.

"We've learned a lot and done a lot in our lives, and travelled all over," Lil says. "Everybody just loves us here in St. Louis. Everywhere we go, people call me Lil. It's nice to be known like that. Everything is God-given to us, and we know it. We have such a wonderful life, with a lot of wonderful children, and everything is so perfect in our lives. What kind of story would that be?"

Stan dutifully responds: "A fairy tale."

Fairy tales usually end with the words "lived happily ever after," but fairy tales are not real life. Lil began to suffer from arthritis and eventually began using a wheelchair, still running the household with the help of valued housekeepers.

Lil was protective of her family, particularly her oldest child. One family friend has said that Lil did not like to hear the Garagiola matter discussed, period. After many jobs and many moves, Dick and Sharon moved to Houston, where he had a leg amputated because of cancer. When his health improved, Dick and his family were able to drive to St. Louis for Christmas in 2009. He and Sharon have a son, Jeffrey, and two daughters, Laura and Natalie.

Gerry and Tom Ashley lived in New York when Tom worked for Ted Turner's network, TBS. Stan and Lil would visit them in their summer hideaway in the Rockaways, near the ocean; the Musials fit in with the police officers, teachers, and other working people of Queens. The couple later divorced, with Tom staying in New York and Gerry moving to San Francisco, both speaking well of the other. They have three children—Tom Junior, and twins, Camille and Christopher, known as Kit.

The two younger Musial daughters stayed in town and remained a daily presence in their parents' lives. Janet, five years younger than Gerry, married Dr. Martin Schwarze, and has two children, Julie and Brian, the athletic young man who escorted his grandfather to the office, to lunch, to Cardinals' games, and referred to Stanley as his best friend.

Jeanne is married to Dave Edmonds, a lawyer, and they have three children, Andrew, Lindsay and Allison.

IT TOOK Stan a while to bounce back from prostate cancer, but by June 1990 he was able to get back on the circuit, including an induction into the Brooklyn Dodgers Baseball Hall of Fame, in the category of "Outstanding Opponent."

The celebration had its own bizarre Stanley twist. He was forty minutes late in arriving at the hall in the Flatbush section, and when he arrived, a worried Roger Kahn blurted out, "Stan, where the heck have you been?"

Musial then told about his odyssey through modern Brooklyn. His cabbie had dropped him off at the wrong place, over a mile away, he said, and, because he was recovering from surgery, he could not walk that far. He was standing on the corner, wondering what to do next, when an old car pulled up to the curb and a man in black Hasidic garb, including black hat and flowing white beard, rolled down the window.

In a lush accent that Musial tried to imitate, the man had gushed, "Stan! Stan Musial! Vot are you doing here in Brooklyn?" When Musial showed him the address, the man told him to get in, and drove him to the hall.

On another return to Brooklyn, Tom Ashley accompanied him to dinner at Gage and Tollner, the classic steakhouse, with nineteenth-century gaslight decor and waiters also of ancient vintage. As soon as Stanley materialized, old-time waiters, many of them African American, with chevrons on their sleeves denoting decades of service at the restaurant, clustered around his table, chattering about the time Stanley went five for five and other glory days.

Gage and Tollner closed in 2004, but in Brooklyn he would always be Stan the Man.

HE CONTINUED to explore corners of the world he had never seen before.

"I quit while I still enjoyed it, but I put in my time," he told Roger Kahn. "I like to travel now, but not with a ball club. Have you ever seen Ireland? Do you know how beautiful it is?"

In 1990, on the way back from a Little League excursion to Poland, Lil and Stan stopped off in Dublin for the Irish Derby. Jim Hackett recalled Musial playing the harmonica at a castle in the presence of Tony Bennett, or maybe it was Donald O'Connor, or maybe both. On the same trip, Stan and Lil took in the tennis at Wimbledon.

No longer due at the ballpark every day, Musial still cared about the Cardinals. When Joe Torre managed the club from 1990 to 1995, the Musials sometimes invited Torre and his wife, Ali, out to dinner, but not to talk baseball. Stan and Lil understood: the Torres needed a family, needed a night out.

Torre also went on a cruise to South America with Musial, Willie Stargell, Bob Gibson, and their wives. "He's always onstage for everybody," Torre said. "One little gem every night. He would pull out a dollar bill and make something out of it. And his jokes were always terrible."

Musial still went on the road to the collector shows, too lucrative to pass up, but he increasingly stayed close to home, a regular at lunches in pubs and taverns. Mickey McTague, who has long roots in town, recalled seeing Stan, Red, Broeg, Tom Eagleton, and dozens of other aging St. Louis guys who now had time for camaraderie. Stanley would almost always show up at banquets and luncheons. After one trip to Poland, he was roasted in St. Louis, with Jack Buck noting that Poland now had "the only baseball field with goalposts." Musial laughed, overlooking his acquired aversion to Polish jokes.

When he was in town, Musial would pop into his office, Stan the Man, Inc., in suburban Des Peres, to see what Dick Zitzmann had lined up for him.

"Stan would sign all the pictures and all the baseballs and tell stories," Larry Christenson recalled of one visit. "And Zitzmann would roll his eyes because he's heard them over and over again."

Another constant in Stan's life was Pat Anthony, his loyal secretary for decades—"like a member of the family," Gerry Ashley said. "If you need anything, you go to Pat. She's devoted to Dad." She was still in the office as of 2010, still indispensable.

For a very long time, Musial remained the same old Stanley. John McGuire, a pixielike reporter, respected by police and gangsters alike, once made the mistake of showing up for an interview with Stanley while wearing his old straw boater plus a designer tie depicting several baseballs. McGuire's outfit put Stanley in a playful mood, so he grabbed a felt pen and signed his autograph—right across McGuire's tie. McGuire kept it to the day he died.

Most days, Stanley and Zitzmann would go out for lunch, sometimes to the Charcoal Lounge, sometimes to the Missouri Athletic Club out in the suburbs. If the ladies who lunch did not wave at him quickly enough, Stanley would walk over and serenade them.

"Put his arm around you, laugh, such an outgoing friendly smile," Christenson said. "And after lunch he would say, 'I'm tired,' and go home and take a nap."

IMPORTANT PEOPLE continued to die.

On September 29, 1989, Gussie Busch died at ninety, after driving his Clydesdales and his carriage around the ballpark almost to the end. Julius Hunter, the television personality who had shared the literary dinner with Musial and Michener, dropped by the house for a comment. Lil was in her wheelchair—"pleasant, always gracious, she, too, extended us a warm welcome," Hunter said—and Musial recalled how Busch had voluntarily made him the first $100,000 player in the National League. "Stan told me, with a very sad look in his eyes, that he would really miss his boss and his pal," Hunter recalled.

The year 2002 was brutal. Jack Buck died on June 18, Ted Williams died on July 5, and Enos Slaughter died on August 12.

"Well, I'm hanging in there," Musial told a reporter. "You know, when you get to be eighty-one, every day is a blessing and every year is a blessing. I'm feeling pretty good."

The Big Three had kept in touch in their later years. "Williams, DiMaggio and Stan were real close. They corresponded. When a statue was dedicated to DiMaggio in Chicago's Italian section, he wanted Stan there. And Ted only spoke at a dinner in St. Louis because Stan wanted him to," Pat Anthony said in 2004.

Musial and Williams served on the Hall of Fame Veterans Committee, empowered to add deserving old-timers to the Hall. One year Williams showed up in a wheelchair, and the committee members, hearing he had been named an honorary colonel by the Marines, honored him with "The Marines' Hymn," with Musial on the harmonica. The old jet pilot forced himself up from his wheelchair and saluted during the anthem.

The two great rivals from the 1946 World Series were kindred souls, dedicated to correcting inequities of the past. Williams had previously used his induction to the Hall to make a plea for the inclusion of Negro League players. He and Musial became activists on the committee, according to Monte Irvin, the Negro League and New York Giant veteran who later worked for the commissioner.

"I've always liked him," Irvin said, calling Musial a positive figure from the Jackie Robinson days to his time on the committee. "Never had one cross word with him. Never saw him say anything bad about anybody. Just because he didn't think somebody didn't belong, he didn't make it personal. Just voicing his opinion.

"Stan was fair," Irvin said. "If somebody's name was mentioned and he didn't believe they belonged, he'd say, 'I think they're a little short,' or 'What about this guy?' and he'd say, 'I liked him. I think he belonged.' He'd say something like that."

From the time Musial joined the committee in 1973, some of the veterans voted into the Hall included Sunny Jim Bottomley, Billy Herman, Earl Averill, Hack Wilson, and in 1981 Johnny Mize, whose trade had weakened the Cardinals for a generation. In 1984, the Cardinals' respected rival, Pee Wee Reese, got in, and in 1985, Enos Slaughter.

"I do know that Bob Broeg told Slaughter to issue a statement stating his intentions and so on," Irvin said, referring to the strike rumors in 1947, "and he apologized for some of the stories that were told, some of them true, some of them not." Irvin believed Slaughter was "a great ballplayer, raised in the South," who had learned, who had grown.

In 1986, Williams joined the committee, which promptly voted in his old teammate, Bobby Doerr. In 1987, Ray Dandridge ("same country you did") was voted into the Hall, although that could not make up for his never getting to play a single game in the majors. In 1989, Musial and Williams made sure that good old Red made it. In 1989, it was Al Barlick, Musial's favorite ump; 1991, Bill Veeck and Tony Lazzeri; 1994, Phil Rizzuto and Musial's old buddy, Leo Durocher; 1995, Richie Ashburn; 1998, Lee MacPhail and Larry Doby; 1999, Orlando Cepeda, the jolly first baseman who coined the name "El Birdos" for Musial's championship season as general manager in 1967; and in 2001, Bill Mazeroski from Musial's hometown team, the Pirates.

The Big Three got together in rural Florida on February 9, 1994, for the opening of the Ted Williams Museum, devoted to hitters. Muhammad Ali was there, and so was the Marine Corps Band. DiMaggio's lawyer tried to get his client to time his arrival in his rented limousine fashionably late, for maximum effect, but DiMaggio understood the pecking order that day: "No, this is Ted's day; I've got to go in before him."

Later that evening, the Big Three huddled at Williams's home and "talked into the night," according to Leigh Montville, Williams's biographer.

"It might have been the longest single stretch of conversation between Williams and DiMaggio in their entire lives. It definitely was the first time one had visited the other's house." Soon afterward, Williams had a stroke.


THE CLIPPER went first, at the age of eighty-four, on March 8, 1999. The funeral in his home neighborhood in San Francisco came after a power struggle between Joe's brother, Dominic, and his lawyer, Morris Engelberg. Dominic, a successful businessman in Boston and Florida, ultimately had the legal power to bring his brother home to North Beach.

The funeral was held in the neighborhood at Saints Peter and Paul Roman Catholic Church, with its white Gothic Revival façade and a quotation from Dante's *Paradiso*, in Italian, on the façade. The English translation is: "The glory of Him who moves all things penetrates and glows throughout the universe."

The neighborhood, settled by Italians, was now considerably Asian. As the cortege arrived, more than a hundred Chinese elders were conducting their daily regimen of the robust motions and tonal chants of tai chi.

The funeral was private, attended by approximately forty members of the DiMaggio family along with a few remaining old friends and baseball officials, including Commissioner Bud Selig. As the mourners left the church, we could spot a graying man with a ponytail, wearing "a new suit, and a new set of teeth, that a cousin had bought him for the occasion," in the words of Richard Ben Cramer, DiMaggio's biographer. That was Joe junior, the Clipper's only child. Six months later, Joe junior would die "from an overdose of crank, heroin mixed with crack cocaine," according to Ben Cramer. In the days after the funeral, details emerged about the tension between brother Dom and lawyer Engelberg, who flashed a ring he claimed DiMaggio had given him on his deathbed.

The Kid died on July 5, 2002, after years of suffering. I had one of the last interviews with him, when he came to New York to plug a documentary on his old friend Hank Greenberg. Williams did not know me very well, but I pushed the right buttons to loosen him up, reminding him of an ankle-high catch he had made in his first old-timers' game in Fenway in the early eighties. "Goddam right I did," he roared. He was a rip, but he was suffering. "You sound like a nice guy," he told me from a few feet away, which told me the man with the fighter pilot's eyesight could now barely see.

Williams passed at the age of eighty-three, and the Red Sox put together a highly secular celebration. He had always wanted people to say of him, "There goes the greatest hitter who ever lived." The Sox displayed those words in huge letters on the message board.

In shimmering midsummer Fenway, more than ten thousand fans filed around the warning track to pay their respects to Williams. Young boys right out of a Norman Rockwell painting made leaping catches in front of the Green Monster in left field. Old-timer fans reminisced about Williams's 521st and last home run, into an autumn gale, in September 1960. A black Marine sergeant stood on guard in front of Williams artifacts. The Kid's old feuds with fans and reporters were long gone.

That night, with no regular game scheduled, the Sox held a memorial for Williams, with Dommie and Pesky arrayed near home plate. Williams's old wing squadron leader from Korea, the former senator and former astronaut John Glenn, who once said the Kid was the greatest pilot he had ever seen, was there. And in huge limestone numbers on the dirt near third base was his batting average in 1941—the awesome figure of .406.

IN HIS mid-eighties, Musial was diagnosed with Alzheimer's disease. The family pitched in, learned about the illness, tried to keep him as active as possible, to reinforce his contact with the world. From Musial's rare public appearances, people figured out that this merry and decent force in their lives was fading away.

No longer able to tool around on his tractor, Stan enjoyed sitting outdoors, smoking a cigar, and watching the birds, even in the coldest weather.

When the children came home, they hoped to catch him on a good day. At Christmas 2009, Gerry drove in from Colorado with her daughter, Camille, and her family for a large dinner at Lester's Sports Bar and Grill in Ladue, with its slightly larger-than-life statue of Stanley outside.

At the family Christmas gathering, Gerry watched her father, hoping to see traces of the jovial man who used to clown around with the children.

"Back in the day, when Dad was his old self, and would shake the hand of a little kid, he would all of a sudden get a painful expression on his face and say 'Ow!' like the little one was so strong that he was hurting him," Gerry said.

At that Christmas party in 2009, Gerry noticed her dad holding hands with her grandson, Clifford. "It was so touching," she said. "Dad has gotten so quiet lately, not quite his old self. At one point though, he took his right hand and shook Clifford's hand and did the old 'Ow!' to Clifford. Some of the old spark is left. It made us feel good."

Having covered the deaths of DiMaggio and Williams, I knew that Musial's funeral, whenever it happened, would be far more religious, far more civic, far more loving. Stan Musial might finally surpass the Clipper and the Kid. Posthumously.

## 47

---

# UPSTAGED AGAIN

THERE WAS still a chance to get it right.

The 2009 All-Star Game was coming to the third Busch Stadium, and Musial's fans were hoping for a Stanleyfest to match the emotional reception for Ted Williams in Boston ten years earlier.

By now, baseball had long since merged with show biz. The fans were connoisseurs of reality shows and makers of home videos, fancying themselves as potential Spielbergs. They remembered how Henry Aaron and Junior from Donora had physically and psychologically lifted the old pilot, giving him one more glory day in Fenway.

The Musial support system began to envision the worldwide television audience paying homage to Musial. They could imagine him responding to the crowd, feeling the love from all over the world, and willing himself back into The Stance, one more time. Or more likely, a few more times.

The Cardinal organization was always so nice to Musial, acknowledging him as the greatest Cardinal of all, introducing him on special occasions, giving him a motorized ride around the ballpark, the way Gussie Busch used to tour the premises behind his Clydesdales. Time was running out.

ON OPENING day of 2009, Musial was driven onto the field for another ovation. Albert Pujols, sitting next to Musial on a golf cart, adjusted his red Cardinals jacket, while Musial's left hand was braced on Pujols, the way an old man will lean on a younger man, for strength. The body language was clear: Musial knew he was in the company of an equal, who had the strength and stature Stan had once enjoyed.

The next day there was a beautiful color photo in the *St. Louis Post-Dispatch* of Pujols caring for Musial, deferring to him, not because time was on his side but because grace was in his soul.

Pujols was already a civic treasure—born in the Dominican Republic, moved to Kansas City in his teens, thoughtful and talented. With every Most Valuable Player Award, with every home run, with every charitable deed and gracious gesture, he became acknowledged as the greatest Cardinal hitter since Musial.

A few weeks after opening day in 2009, I asked Pujols about the moment captured in the photo. Pujols is a proud man, a solid citizen, and he does not chat idly with reporters, particularly strangers. He seemed a trifle mystified by my question, as if saying, *Look, this is what anybody would do*—treat an older man, particularly Stan Musial, with love and respect.

"It was cold," Pujols said. "His jacket wasn't buttoned. I was afraid he would be cold out there."

Musial and Pujols seemed almost mystically linked. Totally by accident, Musial happened to be in Denver at an autograph show when Pujols made his major-league debut on opening day in 2001 and thereby witnessed Pujols's first hit.

Their mutual admiration cut through the mists of time. Whenever they were in the same place, Musial would perk up, as if somebody had injected him with youth serum.

Rick Hummel, the longtime baseball sage of St. Louis, witnessed this in July 2009 when Musial and Pujols were brought together for a photo shoot to prepare for the All-Star Game. At first they were polite, doing their job and looking at the camera, but to Hummel's delight they soon began talking baseball: their stances, their bat sizes, their playing weights (175 to 240, to mutual amazement).

Sample:

PUJOLS: Do you have anything to help me out?
MUSIAL: Know the strike zone.

PUJOLS: What if you have a bad umpire?

MUSIAL: If they called a bad strike on me, I would give him a mean look.

Pujols left that photo shoot about six feet off the ground. Hit two homers that night. After that, Pujols put out the word around town. People had begun calling him "El Hombre," but Pujols politely rejected that nickname. Never has a young superstar been so gracious to an old superstar. *There is only one Man in this town,* he said.

ALL OF St. Louis began anticipating the 2009 All-Star Game, and the Cardinal front office began planning for an extravaganza, a night of nights.

Except for one detail beyond their control. Major League Baseball had invited the new American president, Barack Obama, to the game. It would be his first major baseball function since the inauguration in January. There was no political or social statement in the president's invitation; given baseball's vestigial status as national pastime, there is a standing invitation to any president to any baseball event.

The new president accepted. And nothing was ever the same. Whatever videos had been planned to depict the glory of Musial's career were now downsized. A parade around the warning track? An honor guard of old teammates encircling him? His own harmonica rendition of "Take Me Out to the Ball Game"? Albert Pujols helping him take one more swing?

Whatever was in the hearts and minds of St. Louis impresarios, official and unofficial, was now obliterated by the hard reality of the White House and the Secret Service and the need for Major League Baseball to make the president the center of attention.

Nearly half a century earlier, Musial had been charmed by a charismatic young candidate named John F. Kennedy. Now he was overshadowed by protocol, by fate, by time, by another magnetic young president.

"The whole dynamic changed," said Dick Zitzmann, Musial's business associate.

The Musial family could see it happening. There was nothing to do but show up.

"Mom and I were worried because we had to go so early because of the security," said Gerry Ashley, who understood that even Hall of Fame ball-players must go into lockdown when a president is expected. Doors and corridors and rooms that are normally available are suddenly unavailable.

The Musials were legitimately concerned that the weary man might get upset and ask to go home, but something wonderful happened: in the company of fellow Hall of Famers—Lou Brock, Bob Gibson, Bruce Sutter, Ozzie Smith, and, of course, Red—a version of the old Stanley emerged. He passed the time chatting with them, being one of the boys, until it was time to go on the field.

Musial was the last player to be introduced. Wearing a red jacket, riding in from center field in a cart, his grandson Brian Schwarze at his side, he carried the ceremonial first ball, as cameras flashed and people cheered.

Then President Obama was introduced. The athletic basketball player bounced up the dugout steps, wearing blue jeans and a Chicago White Sox jacket, striding over to Musial's cart, taking the ball from Musial. The president then made the ceremonial first pitch to Pujols, bouncing the ball in the dirt.

The moment passed quickly—nothing like the swarm of love for Williams in 1999—and the Musials reconvened in a suite high above the field.

To their delight, the president arrived later, chatting with everybody. Stan was pretty low-key, but Lil, ever the social director, took charge.

"My mom, knowing that Obama likes basketball, told him, 'Stan was offered a scholarship to the University of Pittsburgh but he turned it down to play baseball,' " Gerry Ashley reported.

With his winning smile, Obama told Lil: "I guess he made the right decision."

Already an Obama fan, Gerry was totally charmed.

"Obama's so cute," she said.

Not everybody was charmed. Part of the annoyance might have been political, but most of it stemmed from the civic hero's rule having been minimized once again.

"For the next three days, all of St. Louis was on the talk radio," Gerry said. "They kept saying that Major League Baseball had promised the same thing it did for Ted Williams."

Reflecting the mood of her hometown, Gerry concluded: "Same old, same old."


FEELING THE rush of time, in 2010 the Cardinals picked up on a suggestion five years earlier by the *Post-Dispatch* columnist Bernie Miklasz that Musial deserved the Presidential Medal of Freedom, which had been given to other prominent athletes including, yes, DiMaggio and Williams.

William O. DeWitt Jr., the owner of the club, approved a sophisticated electronic campaign called "Stand for Stan." DeWitt formally nominated Musial for the medal, and fans seconded the motion through the Cardinal website. Often they were photographed in ballparks or more exotic settings with a flat cartoon likeness of Musial, adapted from the Flat Stanley series, used in literary programs.

"The day we started, the team was in San Diego, and there were fans in the stands with Flat Stanley posters," said Ron Watermon, the Cardinal official who led the project. The campaign was backed up by two Missouri senators and one Illinois senator and the White House staff presented a list to President Obama, including the aging gentleman the president had met at the 2009 All-Star Game.

On November 17, 2010, the White House announced that Musial was to receive the medal, along with Bill Russell, the great center of the Boston Celtics, and former President George H. W. Bush and other prominent Americans as well as German chancellor Angela Merkel. DeWitt and everybody else who congratulated Musial reported that he felt honored and humbled by the news.

Stan and Lil were flown to Washington for the ceremony on February 15, 2011, on a plane provided by Bill DeWitt. All four children were there, Dick and Gerry, Janet and Jeanne, bubbling to be with their parents on this day. In the East Room of the White House, wearing his Cardinal red jacket, Musial sat quietly as President Obama raved about his playing career and then recalled how Musial once requested a cut in pay when he had a bad year.

"You can imagine that happening today," the president said drily.

Then Obama reminded the guests that there was so much more to this man: "Stan remains, to this day, an icon, untarnished; a beloved pillar of the community; a gentleman you'd want your kids to emulate."

In the presence of two presidents, poets and cellists, philanthropists and activists, Musial was being honored as a good citizen, a role model, the American success story. Somehow, through all the hairstyles and music styles, the wars and the booms and the recessions, he had played by the rules, had done things right, had met the ball squarely.

The medal just might help new fans discover Stan the Man. They may look at all the records he set, may see a grainy film of him taking off for second base, may see his lopsided smile, may even say, *Wow, that Stan Musial, he was good.*

The guests applauded Stan the Man as he faced them, a trace of a smile on his face. He knew they were applauding for him; he had heard this sound before. And then he put his hands together and he applauded the applause. It was his day. People were rediscovering the old master.

# Epilogue

## HERE HE COMES NOW

I WAS told I would not get to meet Musial while I was working on this book. For one thing, he was smoldering over an earlier biography about him by another writer, and for another, he was not up to being interviewed.

Old players shook their heads and lowered their voices as they told me Stan was, um, not doing well. After seeing the lovely photo of Musial's trusting face as he leaned on Pujols on opening day, I was convinced I would never meet him.

Oh, we had met in 1962 and 1963, when the Mets writers would go out with Casey on a Saturday night to Stan and Biggie's. The Old Man would have a scotch or three and laugh it up with Stanley, but I had never really connected with the hero of my first year as a child fan, and now I realized I never would.

The day after my brief conversation with Albert Pujols in the clubhouse in 2009, I was the guest of a dear friend of Musial's, Colonel James Hackett, once the deputy police chief of St. Louis. They went way back, to when Hackett did odd jobs at the ballpark as a kid. A Gene Hackman look-alike (in one of Hackman's more sympathetic roles), Hackett was clearly saddened by his friend's diminishment.

Hackett invited me and John McGuire, the legendary St. Louis reporter, to the grille at the Missouri Athletic Club. The general manager, Larry Thompson, has accumulated Musial memorabilia—photos and jackets and autographed balls—in the area called the Musial Room.

"This is Stan's table," Hackett said, nodding toward the number 6 Cardinals jersey hanging on the wall over our table. "He eats here when he comes around."

Then Hackett looked past me.

"Here he comes now," he said.

Stan the Man was in a wheelchair, being pushed by his grandson Brian Schwarze.

"You set it up," I told Hackett, jokingly.

The man, after all, was a detective. He could do anything.

"Not at all," Hackett said. "Total coincidence."

Musial smiled warily at Hackett, as if from a great distance. McGuire, who had met him often, and I were introduced briefly, and of course, I did not mention my book project. Musial extended his hand and I shook it. It was soft and warm and supple, and I realized it was true, as Bob Gibson had said: for a .331 hitter, he had small hands.

Musial was taken to a back table while we continued with our lunch at the Musial Table. Stan was not having one of his good days. Tough to see. Jim Hackett grew quiet.

In the months ahead, I would talk to several hundred people, almost all of whom love Stan Musial, who think he is one of the most special people they ever met. I am grateful for the memory of the warmth of his hand.

# ACKNOWLEDGMENTS

Not every writer gets to look into the life of somebody he has admired since he was a child; even fewer writers retain the same admiration when they are finished. So I am doubly privileged.

I am grateful to many people, starting with Steve Wulf at ESPN Books and Paul Taunton, Kelly Chian, Cindy Murray, and Mark Tavani at Ballantine Books, who sensed my long respect for Stan Musial. I appreciate their giving me time and leeway to do the book my way, and for their insights and suggestions.

Also, I thank Esther Newberg of International Creative Management, for always being on my side.

My editors at the *New York Times,* Tom Jolly, Sandy Keenan, and Jay Schreiber, were more than considerate with my vacations and days owed, and I thank them.

So many kind people explained Stan Musial when he could not do it for himself. John McGuire, a journalism legend in St. Louis, opened doors and got me going with his enthusiasm. Then he went to sleep one night and did not wake up. Corporal McGuire, you were supposed to celebrate with me.

William Bottonari wanted to make one Donora run with me. I regret that he did not have the time.

And I also honor Robin Roberts, who loved Musial—despite the 10 home runs.

My insights into the Musial family are graced by Gerry ("not Geraldine") Ashley, who opened her abundant heart and memory.

Tom Ashley shared his filmmaker's memory and his love of the Musial family.

All the other good people I will place in alphabetical order.

Marty Adler. Ruben Amaro Sr. Craig Anderson. Marty Appel. Tom Ashley Jr. Brian Bartow. Fred Bear. Jack Bell. Bill Bergesch. Howard Berk. Jack Berke. Ira Berkow. Yogi Berra. Dick Bily. Dr. Mieczyslaw B. B. Biskupski. Curt Block. Doug Boyd, Ph.D., director, Louie B. Nunn Center for Oral History, University of Kentucky Libraries. Ralph Branca. Eddie Brash. David Brokaw. Howard Bryant.

Lou (Bimbo) Cecconi, for the memorable tour of Donora. Brian Charlton. Julia Cheiffetz. Larry Christenson, for his love of Stan Musial and Ed Piszek, and his generosity. Adam Clymer. Dick Collins. Ray Corio. Bob Costas. George Crowe. The Hon. Bill Cunningham, Supreme Court of Kentucky. Angie Dickinson. William O. DeWitt Jr. Scott Dine. All the staff at the Donora Public Library: director Beth Vaccaro, archivist Donnis Headley, and Mary Olivieri, Dennis Lomax, and Judy Thomas. Joseph Dorinson, Long Island University.

Mark Durand, senior director, ESPN Films, who found transcripts, videos, and contacts for me. Gerald Early. Mark and Marisa Fasciano. Karen Wessel Fox. Jim Frey. Roman Gackowski. Joe Garagiola. Ned Garver. James N. Giglio, whose research and writing blazed the trail. Jeff Gold (Tapeman), Creative Seminars, West Hurley, New York. Victor Gold.

Col. James J. Hackett. John Hall. Fran Healy. Solly Hemus. Pat Henry. Brian Herman, *Valley Independent,* Monessen, Pennsylvania. Robert R. Hermann. Keith Hernandez. Mark R. Hornak. Sam Hornak. Jay Horwitz. Arlene Howard. Col. Frank Hungerford. Chris Ilardi. Monte Irvin. Stan Isaacs. Alvin Jackson. Roger Kahn. David Kaplan, director, Yogi Berra Museum, Montclair, New Jersey. Steve Kaufman. Michael Kimmelman, European cultural correspondent for the *New York Times.* Ralph Kiner. John Kopchak. Ed Kranepool. Jim Kreuz. Laurel Laidlaw, Stan Musial Society, Washington, D.C.

Jane Leavy, my pal, who did such a great job with Mickey Mantle while I worked on Stanley. Richard Levin. Danny and Pat Litwhiler. Evan Makovsky. Frank Mankiewicz. Boris "Babe" Martin. Dal Maxvill. Tim McCarver. John McDermott. Joe McDonald. Tom McEwen. Mickey McTague, who volunteered for duty when Corporal McGuire went down and gave me great insight into his beloved St. Louis. Ed Mickelson. McGraw Milhaven. George Mitrovich. The Monessen Public Library, for the microfilm of Musial's high school basketball games in 1938. Irvin Muchnick. Edward S. Musial.

All my friends at the National Baseball Hall of Fame and Museum: Jeff Idelson, president; Tim Wiles, director, research; James Lloyd Gates Jr., librarian; Bill Francis, who always gets back to me; Freddie Berowski, library associate; John Horne, photo department. Helen Piszek Nelson. Jack Nelson, the legendary Scoop. Don Newcombe. Nick Nicolosi. Paul Nuzzolese. Carroll O'Connor. Jim O'Leary of the Sports Gallery, Toronto, for the introduction to the *Sport* magazine collection and photographs. Gene Orza. Robbie Oswald. Mark Pawelec. Ulice Payne Jr. Neal Pease, associate professor and chair, Department of History, University of Wisconsin–Milwaukee. Rosalie Peck. Nicholas J. C. Pistor. Dean Plocher. Joe Pollack. James H. Prime. Joe Ravasio, Ringgold High, Pennsylvania. Josh Rawitch. Kit Reath. Joshua Robinson.

Ray Robinson, for the great lunches and the advice on writing biographies. Abe Schear. Betty Jane Schmidt. Freddy Schmidt. Alan Schwarz, for the technology tips. Bob Schwarz. Tom Schwarz. Charles Selden. Bud Selig. Stephen Shepard, General Research Division, New York Public Library, and also David Smith, his predecessor and a beacon to researchers for a generation. George Shuba. Mike Shuba. My colleague Michael B. Sisak III. Brad Smith. Claire Smith. Curt Smith.

Dr. Charles E. Stacey, Donora Historical Society, a wise and friendly presence. Jim Swire. Alan Taxerman. Wayne Terwilliger. Larry L. Thompson, general manager, Missouri Athletic Club. John Thorn. Richard L. Thornburgh, who gave me a primer on jury selection in 1971 and insight into Musial in 2009. Joe Torre. Ed Van, St. Petersburg, Florida, NAACP. Dr. Ben Vanek. Fay Vincent. Bill Wakefield. The Hon. Reggie B. Walton. Ron Watermon, Director of Public Relations & Civic Affairs, St. Louis Cardinals. Willie Weinbaum, producer, ESPN, for some amazing introductions. Ron Weiss. Bill White, Allentown *Call-Chronicle*. Bill White, former Cardinal. Mildred White. Mike Whiteford. Rick Wilber. Ethan Wilson. Ralph Wimbish. Jim Woodcock, Fleishman-Hilliard Sports Business. Zev Yaroslavsky. John H. Zentay. Jason Zillo. Dick Zitzmann, vice president, Stan the Man, Inc.

Our children, Laura Vecsey, Corinna V. Wilson, and David Vecsey, encouraged me and at the same time explained to their children where Pop was during the past two years.

My wife, Marianne Graham Vecsey, could have been painting, but instead she kept me going with sound advice and comfort when I was miserable or absent, somewhere back in 1946. I keep saying I will make up for all the distractions.

To everybody who got me through, thank you.

# Notes

## 1 | THE DO-OVER

6  **"Ughhhh," Selig groaned:**   Bud Selig, interview, Nov. 20, 2008.

7  **Fortunately, Bud Selig's oversight committee:**   Email messages from Richard Levin, John Thorn, and Gene Orza.

7  **"The first thing we said was":**   Bob Costas, interview, Nov. 18, 2008.

10  **"St. Louis thinks of itself":**   Rick Wilber, interview, Mar. 25, 2010.

10  **The statue is just about:**   Roger Kahn, "Of Galahad and Quests That Failed," *Sports Illustrated,* Aug. 23, 1976.

11  **"May I tell you":**   Marty Marion, interview on ESPN *SportsCentury,* Nov. 29, 2000.

12  **"Oh, it wasn't unanimous":**   Jim Murray, "Let's Hear It for the Guy in the White Hat, Stan the Man," *Los Angeles Times,* Jan. 23, 1969.

12  **"If they'd traded uniforms":**   Dave Kindred, quoted in Kevin Cowherd, "Baseball: The 'All-Century Team' from Some Serious Fans," *Baltimore Sun,* Oct. 25, 1999.

## 2 | LUCKY STANLEY

14  **Tim McCarver was called up:**   Chapter is derived from an interview with Tim McCarver on Nov. 13, 2008. Also from the video by ESPN, *SportsCentury,* 2000.

## 3 | THE OLD MASTER

16  **"The image of Musial":**   Bill James, *The Bill James Historical Baseball Abstract* (New York: Villard, 1986), 633.

17  **One was the Black Ink test:**   http://www.baseball-reference.com/about/leader _glossary.shtml.

17  **so-called Gray Ink test:**   http://www.baseball-reference.com/leaders/gray_ink .shtml.

17 **In 2001, James ranked:**   Bill James, *The New Bill James Historical Baseball Abstract* (New York: Free Press, 2001).

18 **"Serene dependability":**   Ira Berkow, "In the Editing Room With: Woody Allen; From Defense to Offense," *New York Times,* Nov. 2, 1995.

18 **Many other odes to Musial:**   Articles from *Sport* magazine, courtesy of Jim O'Leary, the Sports Gallery, Toronto.

19 **Almost by accident, I postulated:**   George Vecsey, *Baseball: A History of America's Favorite Game* (New York: Modern Library Chronicles, 2006).

19 Frank Mankiewicz, interview, Nov. 25, 2008; Victor Gold, interview, Nov. 25, 2008.

20 **"It has taken a while":**   Michael Kimmelman, "Pierre Bonnard Retrospective at the Musée d'Art Moderne in Paris," *New York Times,* Mar. 30, 2006.

20 **Asked to name:**   Emails from Michael Kimmelman, 2009.

21 **"I'm happy to be":**   Mike Sullivan, "Musial Didn't Find Oversight Unusual; Stan the Man Has Fond Memories," *Columbus Dispatch.* Oct. 25, 1969.

22 **"It's what the fans wanted":**   Rick Hummel, "In Return to Park, Rose Makes an Impact," *St. Louis Post-Dispatch,* Oct. 25, 1999.

## 4 | STANLEY HITS

23 **Frey thought he might:**   Jim Frey, interview, Feb. 22, 2009.

24 **Frey would never play:**   George Vecsey, "The Race by Numbers," *New York Times,* Sep. 10, 1984.

## 5 | THE STANCE

26 **Perhaps he used the whaddayasay:**   *Stan Musial: "The Man's" Own Story, as Told to Bob Broeg* (Garden City, N.Y.: Doubleday, 1964), 12.

27 **"I said,'My question is this' ":**   Fay Vincent, interview, Dec. 30, 2008.

27 **the Strangest Batting Stance:**   Bill James, *The Bill James Historical Baseball Abstract* (New York: Villard, 1986), 202.

27 **Ted Lyons, an older pitcher:**   James N. Giglio, *Musial: From Stash to Stan the Man* (Columbia, Mo.: University of Missouri Press, 2001), xi.

28 **"Musial reminds me of a housewife":**   *Stan Musial: "The Man's" Own Story,* 252.

28 **"The only real good hitter":**   Bob Gibson and Reggie Jackson, with Lonnie Wheeler, *Sixty Feet, Six Inches: A Hall of Fame Pitcher and a Hall of Fame Hitter Talk About How the Game Is Played* (New York: Doubleday, 2009), 38.

28 **"Stan Musial will twist around":**   Gibson and Jackson, *Sixty Feet, Six Inches,* 48.

29 **"I never thought":**   Ralph Kiner, interview, Aug. 24, 2009.

29 **"Every time I see Stan":**   Don Newcombe, interview, Jan. 7, 2009.

29 **"The preliminary movement":**   Branch Rickey, interviewed in *The Legend of Stan the Man Musial,* 1990, produced by Mark Durand and Thomas J. Ashley.

29 **"Stance is not so important":**   *Halls of Fame: Stan Musial,* MSG Network.

30 "I said, 'Stan' ": Ed Kranepool, interview, Apr. 21, 2010.

30 "I have a theory": Ed Mickelson, letter 2009.

31 "Curt, all you can do": Joe Garagiola, *Just Play Ball* (Flagstaff, Ariz.: Northland Publishing, 2007), 142–43.

31 "Do you guess?": Roger Kahn, "Of Galahad and Quests That Failed," *Sports Illustrated,* Aug. 23, 1976.

32 Roberts said he had exactly one: Robin Roberts, interview, Jan. 27, 2009.


### 6 | A HAND ON THE SHOULDER

33 John Hall's father died: John Hall, interview, Feb. 2, 2009.


### 7 | LUKASZ AND MARY

35 In the afternoon: *Stan Musial: "The Man's" Own Story,* 6.

35 Lukasz Musial was not much more: Wayne Stewart, *Stan the Man: The Life and Times of Stan Musial* (Chicago: Triumph Books, 2010), 7.

35 "They didn't even have enough money": Gerry Ashley, interviews, Mar. 1, 2009, and Jul. 2010.

35 When the boy was seven: Stewart, *Stan the Man,* 7.

36 "As far as drinking": Mark Pawelec, interview, Apr. 2, 2009.

36 "I think he struggled with alcohol": Gerry Ashley, interview, Nov. 2009.

37 Family members told Broeg: *Stan Musial: "The Man's" Own Story,* 7.

37 according to immigration records: Giglio, *Musial,* 4.

37 The family's name was pronounced: *Stan Musial, "The Man's" Own Story,* 46.

38 although the marriage certificate: Giglio, *Musial,* 5.

38 There was a pecking order: Bimbo Cecconi, interview, Mar. 24, 2009.

38 "Mommy did a lot of housework": Ed Musial, interview on ESPN *SportsCentury,* Dec. 18, 2000.

38 carrying homemade bread: Bill Bottonari, interview, Nov. 12, 2008.

38 "My grandmother would tell me": Gerry Ashley, interview, Nov. 2009.

39 "I'll never forget the 'hunky' dishes": *Stan Musial, "The Man's" Own Story,* 8.

39 He liked being called Stash: Ruben Amaro Sr., interview, Mar. 2010.

39 "She did not care": Ray Robinson, interview, 2009.

39 "Mr. Musial never had": Ray Robinson, *Stan Musial: Baseball's Durable "Man"* (New York: G. P. Putnam's Sons, 1963), 12.

39 "We had a shaft": Ed Musial, interview on ESPN *SportsCentury.*

40 "He was always the nice boy": Roger Kahn, "The Man: Stan Musial Is Baseball's No. 1 Citizen," *Sport,* Feb. 1958.

40 in a classic study: Bryng Bryngelson and Thomas J. Clark, "Left-Handedness and Stuttering," *Journal of Heredity,* 24 (1933): 10.

41 "I saw a group of women":   Kahn, "The Man."

41 Stan was alert, observant:   Betty Jane Schmidt, interview, 2008.

41 "Three times a week":   *Stan Musial, "The Man's" Own Story*, 11.

42 Upon Frank's death:   Pawelec, interview, Apr. 2, 2009.

42 "One thing the children of alcoholics":   Roger Rosenblatt, "Person of the Year," *Time*, Jan. 2, 1981.

43 "Addicted parents often lack":   National Association of Children of Alcoholics, "Children of Addicted Parents: Important Facts," http://www.nacoa.net/pdfs/addicted.pdf.

## 8 | INVITATION TO LUNCH

44 They had never met:   Ulice Payne Jr., interview, Apr. 7, 2009.

## 9 | HOW DONORA GOT ITS NAME

47 In 1753, working for the British:   Borough of Donora, Pa., *Donora Diamond Jubilee*, 1901–1976.

47 The Iroquois who fished and hunted:   William Keyes, ed., *Historic Site Survey of the Greater Monongahela River Valley* (Pittsburgh: Historical Society of Western Pennsylvania, 1991).

47 the Carnegies and Fricks:   William Serrin, *Homestead: The Glory and Tragedy of an American Steel Town* (New York: Times Books, 1992).

47 In May 1899:   Keyes, ed., *Historic Site Survey*, 113.

47 West Columbia:   Charles E. Stacey, Brian Charlton, and David Lonich, *Images of America: Donora* (Charleston, S.C.: Arcadia Publishing, 2010), 9.

47 While on a European vacation:   David Cannadine, *Mellon: An American Life* (New York: Knopf, 2006).

48 There is no record:   Charles E. Stacey, interview, Mar. 24, 2009.

49 Belgians settled farther:   Keyes, ed., *Historic Site Survey*, 112.

49 At its peak:   Borough of Donora, Pa., *Donora Diamond Jubilee*, 1901–1976.

49 "The monstrous crucibles of molten iron":   Serrin, *Homestead*, 62.

49 Sometimes death happened fast:   Devra Davis, *When Smoke Ran Like Water* (New York: Basic Books, 2002).

50 During World War II:   Stacey, interview, March 24, 2009.

50 Working in the steel mills:   Serrin, *Homestead*, 62.

50 "That's why I appreciate the unions":   Cecconi, interview, March 24, 2009.

51 "the strong smell of sulphur":   *Stan Musial, "The Man's" Own Story*, 6.

51 "Fumes from the mills":   Davis, *When Smoke Ran Like Water*, 11–15.

52 "There was always a store":   Ulice Payne, interview, Apr. 7, 2009.

52 Davis also recalls:   Davis, *When Smoke Ran Like Water*, 6.

52 **Old photographs suggest:** Cassandra Vivian, *The Mid-Mon Valley* (Charleston, S.C.: Arcadia Publishing, 2004).

53 **"On the southern end":** Stacey, interview, Mar. 24, 2009.

53 **In the winter, the children:** Cecconi, interview, Mar. 24, 2009.

54 **Some of the Italian families:** Bill Bottonari, interview, Nov. 12, 2008.

55 **In 2007, Judge Walton presided:** Neil A. Lewis, "Libby Guilty of Lying in C.I.A. Leak Case," *New York Times*, Mar. 6, 2007.

55 **Judge Walton is proud:** Judge Reggie Walton, interview Jun. 22, 2009.

55 **After law school:** Fascinating profile of Judge Walton: http://www.dcd.uscourts.gov/dcd/walton.

## 10 | MENTORS

57 **"We were standing":** Email from Scott Dine, May 2009.

58 **"We all had 'relations' ":** Ed Musial, interview, Dec. 18, 2000, *The Legend of Stan the Man Musial.*

58 **The boys played at Weed Field:** Charles Stacey, interview, Dec. 4, 2010.

59 **"You had to wait five minutes":** Stan Musial, interview, *Halls of Fame: Stan Musial.*

59 **Joe Barbao, who had played:** *Stan Musial: "The Man's" Own Story,* 11–13.

60 **"When I came in":** Ed Musial, interview, *The Legend of Stan the Man Musial.*

60 **The head coach was:** *Stan Musial: "The Man's" Own Story,* 16–22.

60 **Another adult:** Verna Duda, telephone interview, Jan. 23, 2009.

60 **In the summer, Duda:** Jim Kreuz, "Musial and Griffey," Ragtyme Sports, Oct. 1995, 80.

61 **The business manager at Monessen:** *Stan Musial: "The Man's" Own Story,* 15–19.

61 **"It was deep in the Depression":** Neal Russo, "Vanek's Decision 25 Years Ago Made Stan Musial a Cardinal," *St. Louis Post-Dispatch,* Jan. 7, 1962.

61 **"He looked, as Ollie described him":** Jack Sher, "The Stan Musial Nobody Knows," *Sport,* March 1949.

62 **Musial was a very ordinary student:** *Stan Musial: "The Man's" Own Story,* 18–19.

62 **"His father wanted him":** Verna Duda, interview, Mar. 25, 2009.

62 **One constant in the telling:** *Stan Musial, "The Man's" Own Story,* 21–22.

62 **"She's a big woman":** *Stan Musial, "The Man's" Own Story,* 20.

63 **the Donora Dragons surprised:** Clippings courtesy of the Monessen Public Library, Monessen, Pa.

63 **The team was also tested:** *Stan Musial: "The Man's" Own Story,* 17.

63 **Through his basketball ability:** Tom Ashley, interview, Feb. 2009.

64 **When Pizzica was quite old:** Tom Ashley Jr., interview, Aug. 13, 2009.

64 In the spring of 1938: Mary Jane Schmidt, interview, Nov. 14, 2008.

64 "We played baseball": Cecconi, interviews, 2008, Mar. 2009.

65 Jerry Wunderlich, a gym teacher: Mark Pawelec, interview, Apr. 2, 2009.

65 But Ki Duda recommended: Norma Miller, interview by Roger Kahn, 1957.

65 "hypocritical Protestant bastard": Lee Lowenfish, *Branch Rickey: Baseball's Ferocious Gentleman* (Lincoln: University of Nebraska Press, 2007), 280.

65 "I honestly hoped": Peter Golenbock, *The Spirit of St. Louis: A History of the St. Louis Cardinals and Browns* (New York: Avon, 2000), 237.

65 In the spring of 1938: Lester J. Biederman, "Modest Stan Musial Still Embarrassed by Hero Worship," *Pittsburgh Press*, Dec. 22, 1957.

65 There are several reasons: Sher, "The Stan Musial Nobody Knows."

65 "Even though Donora": *Stan Musial: "The Man's" Own Story*, 23.

66 There was another trip: Ibid., 24.

## 11 | LIL

67 He was a familiar sight: Bill Bottonari, interview, Nov. 12, 2008.

67 "My grandparents married so young": Gerry Ashley, interview, 2009.

68 thereby nicknamed "Shrimp": *Stan Musial: "The Man's" Own Story*, 16.

68 "Always neat as a pin": Mrs. Stan Musial, "My Life with Stan," *Parade*, Jul. 13, 1958.

68 "Stan was never idle": Jim Kreuz, "Musial and Griffey," Ragtyme Sports, Oct. 1995, 83.

68 "It's tough to be the wife": Tom Ashley, interview, Jun. 25, 2009.

69 Anna Mikula: 1920 census, courtesy of Gerry Ashley.

69 "I've been in that house": Gerry Ashley, interview, 2009.

69 Long after they were married: Robinson, *Stan Musial*, 21,

70 "I wasn't sure": Kahn, "The Man."

70 Perhaps he sensed: Giglio, *Musial*, 29.

71 Very much an outsider: Mike Whiteford, "Musial's Lowly Beginning: A Bus Ride to Williamson," *The Charleston Gazette*, Jul. 22, 1988, 1B.

71 "I didn't have confidence": *Halls of Fame: Stan Musial*.

71 He also caused a stir: Email message from Randolph Fiery, Feb. 17, 2011.

71 "She wanted him to get a job": Verna Duda, interview, Mar. 25, 2009.

72 On May 25, 1940: Giglio, *Musial*, 37.

73 Far away: *Stan Musial: "The Man's" Own Story*, 33.

73 "I didn't even see a doctor": *Halls of Fame: Stan Musial*.

73 "He called me one day": *The Legend of Stan the Man Musial*.

73 "You won't make it": Sher, "The Stan Musial Nobody Knows."

73 **Skip ahead:** "Kerr Family Happy in New Home, a Gift From Musials," *St. Louis Post-Dispatch,* May 21, 1958.

74 **Over the years:** Giglio, *Musial,* 37.

## 12 | TAKEOFF

75 **"And he is sitting":** Bob Broeg, interview, ESPN *SportsCentury,* Nov. 29, 2000.

76 **Shotton watched Musial:** *Stan Musial: "The Man's" Own Story,* 37–38.

76 **Years later:** Ibid., 57–58.

76 **"He was signed":** *The Legend of Stan the Man Musial.*

77 **"I told Clay":** *Halls of Fame: Stan Musial.*

77 **Vanek, who had praised Musial:** Sher, "The Stan Musial Nobody Knows."

77 **"Oh, sure, I remember":** *Stan Musial: "The Man's" Own Story,* 39.

78 **Who was Ollie Vanek?:** Dr. Ben Vanek, interview, Dec. 1, 2008.

78 **"Mr. Rickey, in a fairly loud":** Jim Kreuz, "Stan's Rise to the Majors," *Mound City Memories,* Summer 2007, 26.

79 **"Vanek spoke up":** Bob Broeg, "Vanek Provided an Early Assist in Musial's Career," *St. Louis Post-Dispatch,* Jul. 9, 2000.

79 **Springfield's White City Park:** John Hall, interview, Feb. 2, 2009.

80 **"I would pat him":** Frank Hungerford, interview, Sep. 19, 2009.

80 **"She was the one":** *Halls of Fame: Stan Musial.*

80 **Stan and Lil and Dickie:** Tom Fox, "Killed by Greed: The Baseball Season Ended Early This Year," *Philadelphia Inquirer,* Aug. 30, 1981.

80 **Lil also told Fox:** Karen Wessel Fox, interview, 2009.

81 **"Goodbye, Stan":** Sher, "The Stan Musial Nobody Knows."

81 **The next morning:** John Hall, interview, Feb. 2, 2009.

81 **"I'll let you in":** Sher, "The Stan Musial Nobody Knows."

81 **Stan and Lil took the train:** Mrs. Stan Musial, "My Life with Stan."

82 **As luck would have it:** Giglio, *Musial,* 53–54.

82 **Lil and Dick joined:** Betty Jane Schmidt, interview, Nov. 14, 2008.

82 **Manager Tony Kaufman immediately:** Giglio, *Musial,* 54.

82 **"Well, guess I'll be seeing you":** Jim Kreuz, "Musial and Griffey," Ragtyme Sports, Oct. 1995, 81.

83 **Lil met him in Pittsburgh:** *Stan Musial: "The Man's" Own Story,* 44.

## 13 | PENNANT RACE

84 **he missed the train:** *Stan Musial: "The Man's" Own Story,* 45.

84 **"Get your ass out of there":** Dave Anderson, *Pennant Races: Baseball at Its Best* (New York: Doubleday, 1994), 144.

85 "This is strange": *Halls of Fame: Stan Musial.*

85 Stengel watched the kid: W. C. Heinz, "Stan Musial's Last Day," *Life,* Oct. 11, 1963.

85 "Your club has got a guy": Bob Broeg, interview, ESPN *SportsCentury,* Nov. 29, 2000.

86 Not everybody was impressed: Boris "Babe" Martin, interview, Jan. 30, 2009.

86 On September 20: Martin J. Haley, sports editor, *St. Louis Globe-Democrat.*

86 In a doubleheader: James P. Dawson, "St. Louis Defeats Cubs, 6–5, 7–0; Daring Dash Decides First," *New York Times,* Sep. 22, 1941.

87 "Musial is really the answer": Robert L. Burnes, *St. Louis Globe-Democrat,* Sep. 1941.

87 As the team embarked by train: *Stan Musial: "The Man's" Own Story,* 46.

87 Looking back at Musial's debut: Sher, "The Stan Musial Nobody Knows."

87 "Pop and I": *Stan Musial: "The Man's" Own Story,* 51.

88 "A group of unidentified citizens": Robert L. Burnes, *St. Louis Globe-Democrat,* Sep. 29, 1941.

## 14 | MEET ME AT THE FAIR

89 "It's where he played": William O. DeWitt Jr., interview, May 5, 2010.

90 "I was able": *Halls of Fame: Stan Musial.*

90 At the start of the twentieth: U.S. Census, http://www.census.gov/population/www/documentation/twps0027/tab13.txt.

90 by 2010 its population: Malcolm Gay and Campbell Robertson, "Population Off Sharply in St. Louis and Birmingham," *New York Times,* Feb. 24, 2011, A19.

90 *Meet Me in St. Louis*: Music and lyrics by Hugh Martin and Ralph Blane, 1944.

92 "Monkus," he said quietly: Thomas Wolfe, *You Can't Go Home Again* (Garden City, N.Y.: Sun Dial Press, 1934), 65–66.

93 Other writers took their measure: Kate Shaw, "St. Louis Writers Who Fled, and the City That Loves Them," *Current on Line,* University of Missouri at St. Louis, Jan. 24, 2005.

## 15 | THE MAHATMA OF THE MIDWEST

95 "I went down to see him": *The Legend of Stan the Man Musial.*

96 "He was very diplomatic": Stan Musial, St. Louis, May 17, 1978, A. B. Chandler Oral History Project, University of Kentucky Library, Lexington.

96 Wesley Branch Rickey: Lowenfish, *Branch Rickey,* 19–25.

97 After serving: Henry D. Fetter, *Taking on the Yankees* (New York: W. W. Norton, 2003), 122.

97 "You know": William O. DeWitt Sr., Cincinnati, Sep. 29 and Oct. 1, 1980, A. B. Chandler Oral History Project.

98 "Pepper played the banjo-guitar": Robert Creamer, "Mudcats in the Gashouse," *Sports Illustrated,* Apr. 22, 1957.

99   "That one really got to him":   Tom Ashley, interview, Feb. 2009.

100   "I didn't do well":   *Halls of Fame: Stan Musial.*

100   "He was big":   Garagiola, *Just Play Ball,* 171–73.

100   "I'm tearing it up, my boy":   *Stan Musial: "The Man's" Own Story,* 55.

101   "Don Padgett told me":   John J. Archibald, "Musial . . . Musial . . . Musial . . . Name and Fame Here to Stay, All Agree," *St. Louis Post-Dispatch,* Jan. 25, 1957.

101   "Everybody started laughing":   Marty Marion, interview, ESPN *SportsCentury,* Nov. 29, 2000.

101   "I didn't have my good arm":   *Halls of Fame: Stan Musial.*

101   "Whenever the center fielder":   Enos Slaughter, interview, ESPN *SportsCentury,* Dec. 13, 2000.

101   Leo would put one foot:   John Heidenry and Brett Topel, *The Boys Who Were Left Behind: The 1944 World Series Between the Hapless St. Louis Browns and the Legendary St. Louis Cardinals* (Lincoln: University of Nebraska Press, 2006), 57.

102   This was the only time:   Broeg, *The Man Stan,* 75.

102   "Pass the Biscuits, Mirandy":   *Stan Musial: "The Man's" Own Story,* 238.

102   double whammy:   Ibid., 70–71.

103   The Yankees were not used to:   Lowenfish, *Branch Rickey,* 317.

103   "Stan was having a terrible time":   Sher, "The Stan Musial Nobody Knows," 66–67.

103   Now that Rickey was gone:   Bob Broeg, "Baseball Vastly Different from Breadon's Day," *St. Louis Post-Dispatch,* May 11, 1997.

103   "They were entirely opposites":   William O. DeWitt Sr., Cincinnati, Sep. 29 and Oct. 1, 1980, A. B. Chandler Oral History Project.

104   Marty Marion has talked about cliques:   Golenbock, *The Spirit of St. Louis,* 256.

105   "We'd cook corn":   Danny Litwhiler, interview, Apr. 13, 2010.

105   Most of the Cardinals rented rooms:   Freddy Schmidt, interview, Apr. 14, 2010.

105   "We had a young club":   Danny Litwhiler, interview, Apr. 13, 2010.

106   "Musial came up next time":   Mickey Owen, Springfield, Mo., May 27, 1989, A. B. Chandler Oral History Project.

106   Players had their own ways:   Tim Cohane, "Cards' Walker Cooper Draws $850 Penalty," *New York World-Telegram and Sun,* Aug. 2, 1943.

107   The Yankees were so decimated:   Heidenry and Topel, *The Boys Who Were Left Behind,* 44.

107   "Brownie town":   Ibid., 81.

**16  |  OLD NAVY BUDDIES**

Keith Hernandez, interview, Nov. 10, 2008.

## 17 | THE WAR

110 **"I was fortunate":**    Musial, St. Louis, May 17, 1978, A. B. Chandler Oral History Project.

110 **The people of Donora:**    "Donora Honors Musial," *Sporting News,* Oct. 21, 1943.

110 **"They were called into service":**    Bimbo Cecconi, interview, Mar. 24, 2009.

110 **Musial was playing:**    Heidenry and Topel, *The Boys Who Were Left Behind,* 116–17.

111 **"A storm came out":**    Richard Goldstein, *Spartan Seasons: How Baseball Survived the Second World War* (New York: Macmillan, 1980), 81–82.

111 **As Litwhiler told it:**    Danny Litwhiler, with Jim Sargent, *Danny Litwhiler: Living the Baseball Dream* (Philadelphia: Temple University Press, 2006), 86–87.

111 **"The pilot gave me a seat":**    Danny Litwhiler, interview, Apr. 2010.

112 **"If I hadn't done it":**    Ed Linn, *Hitter: The Life and Turmoils of Ted Williams* (New York: Harcourt Brace, 1993), 127.

113 **"Doesn't he know":**    Richard Ben Cramer, *Joe DiMaggio: The Hero's Life* (New York: Simon and Schuster, 2000), 198.

113 **"People just don't like":**    Ibid., 200.

113 **Joe D. had other trouble:**    Ibid., 207.

114 **"I remember that very well":**    Stan Musial, St. Louis, May 17, 1978, A. B. Chandler Oral History Project.

114 **In January 1945:**    "Musial of Cards Accepted by Navy," *New York Times,* Jan. 20, 1945.

114 **"Why didn't you tell me":**    *Stan Musial: "The Man's" Own Story,* 83.

115 **Bill Dickey, the old Yankee catcher:**    Leigh Montville, *Ted Williams: The Biography of an American Hero* (New York: Doubleday, 2004), 118.

115 **"After bouncing around":**    Frederick W. Turner, *When the Boys Came Back: Baseball and 1946* (New York: Henry Holt, 1996).

115 **Eager to please the brass:**    Goldstein, *Spartan Seasons,* 236.

115 **He was also persuaded:**    Stewart, *Stan the Man,* 78.

116 **"My five-year-old":**    *Stan Musial: "The Man's" Own Story,* 84.

116 **Late in October:**    Montville, *Ted Williams,* 118.

116 **"The day before I was scheduled":**    *Stan Musial: "The Man's" Own Story,* 84–85.

117 **he did pitch in the minors:**    Letter from George Shuba, 2009. Shuba would recall bunting on Shepard and being secretly happy when the one-legged pitcher fielded the ball and threw him out.

117 **"They sent the whole unit":**    Turner, *When the Boys Came Back,* xiii.

117 **"It happened right near the end":**    Goldstein, *Spartan Seasons,* 252.

118 **"All the guys":**    George Vecsey, ed., *The Way It Was: Great Sports Events from the Past* (New York: McGraw-Hill, 1974), 48.

118   Other Cardinals came back wounded:    Turner, *When the Boys Came Back,* 6.

118   "Some of the guys":    Vecsey, ed., *The Way It Was,* 49.

118   "He stands in awe":    Tom Ashley, interview, 2009.

## 18 | CHECKS ALL OVER THE BED

120   Stan and Lil stared:    *Stan Musial: "The Man's" Own Story,* 90.

120   "Assassins of careers!":    Lowenfish, *Branch Rickey,* 393.

120   Willie Wells, an African American:    Wendell Smith, *Pittsburgh Courier,* May 6, 1944.

121   "Same country you did":    George Vecsey, "Ray Dandridge, The Hall of Fame and 'Fences,' " *New York Times,* May 10, 1987.

121   An American advance man:    Mickey Owen, Springfield, Mo., May 27, 1989, A. B. Chandler Oral History Project.

121   "I don't think I will go":    Giglio, *Musial,* 129.

121   "Stan, you've got two children":    *Stan Musial: "The Man's" Own Story,* 91.

122   "Musial was smoking":    Mickey Owen, Springfield, Mo., May 27, 1989, A. B. Chandler Oral History Project. UK.

122   "As I recall":    *Stan Musial: "The Man's" Own Story,* 90.

122   "Packing":    Ibid.

123   "I told 'em that I wasn't":    Stan Musial, St. Louis, May 17, 1978, A. B. Chandler Oral History Project.

123   "Breadon said, 'I want to see' ":    Bob Broeg, interview, ESPN *SportsCentury,* Nov. 29, 2000.

123   Gardella, a fringe outfielder:    Danny Gardella, Yonkers, N.Y., Aug. 27, 1980, A. B. Chandler Oral History Project.

124   "A little later on":    Stan Musial, St. Louis, May 17, 1978, A. B. Chandler Oral History Project.

124   "And Stan made a great decision":    Marty Marion, St. Louis, May 19, 1978, A. B. Chandler Oral History Project.

124   "I'm sure that he had signed":    Mickey Owen, Springfield, Mo., May 27, 1989, A. B. Chandler Oral History Project.

## 19 | JUBILEE

Much of this chapter and also Chapter Twenty-one is informed by conversations over the years with Joe Garagiola, Dominic DiMaggio, Johnny Pesky, and Harry Walker, and also by a book I edited: *The Way It Was: Great Sports Events from the Past,* 33–51.

126   "He'd shake hands solemnly":    Red Schoendienst with Rob Rains: *Red: A Baseball Life* (Champaign, Ill.: Sports Publishing, 1998), 24.

128   "So you're the little SOB":    Vecsey, ed., *The Way It Was,* 34.

128   "He had a bad knee":    Stan Musial, St. Louis, May 17, 1978, A. B. Chandler Oral History Project.

128 "I didn't like first base":    *Stan Musial: "The Man's" Own Story,* 104.

128 cornball music returned:    Broeg, *The Man Stan,* 105.

129 "Terry would chew you out":    Vecsey, ed., *The Way It Was,* 35.

130 "Oh, man, we were fearless":    Ibid., 34.

130 Garagiola was outwardly brash:    Broeg, *The Man Stan,* 164.

130 "Durocher would say anything":    William Marshall, *Baseball's Pivotal Era 1945–1951* (Lexington: University Press of Kentucky, 1999), 102.

131 "I remember one time":    Marty Marion, St. Louis, May 19, 1978, A. B. Chandler Oral History Project.

131 On October 1:    John McGuire, "Safe at Home: When War Veterans Returned to Baseball 50 Years Ago, They Staged a Season Like No Other," *St. Louis Post-Dispatch,* May 26, 1996.

131 Once the Cardinals' farm director:    Turner, *When the Boys Came Back,* 221.

## 20 | A VISITOR ON THE TRAIN

Bimbo Cecconi, interview, Nov. 24, 2008.

## 21 | BEST SERIES EVER

136 "The big individual duel":    *Stan Musial: "The Man's" Own Story,* 95.

136 Williams had taken his first look:    "Ted Williams Gets Eyeful of Stan Musial," *World-Telegram and Sun,* Sep. 20, 1946.

136 The Red Sox came into the Series:    Turner, *When the Boys Came Back,* 226.

137 Another difference:    Vecsey, ed., *The Way It Was,* 39.

137 A note of defiance:    Turner, *When the Boys Came Back,* 227.

137 "Me, I'd have hit a ton":    *Stan Musial: "The Man's" Own Story,* 109.

138 Once Williams had shot out:    George Sullivan, "The Kid and I," www.bu.edu/bostonia/fall02/kid.

138 "Ted! Ted! They're up there":    Freddy Schmidt, interview, Apr. 14, 2010.

138 "Twenty years old":    Joe Garagiola, interview, Apr. 16, 2010.

138 "Once he missed":    *Stan Musial: "The Man's" Own Story,* 96.

139 "If I'm breathing":    Vecsey, ed., *The Way It Was,* 42.

139 Before the sixth game:    Turner, *When the Boys Came Back,* 241.

140 "Gonzalez couldn't have stopped Enos":    Vecsey, ed., *The Way It Was,* 51.

140 "I've looked at those films":    Ibid., 50.

141 "I'm out for the season!":    Ibid., 43.

141 Less than two hours later:    McGuire, "Safe at Home."

141 When the Sox arrived:    Vecsey, ed., *The Way It Was,* 43.

## 22 | BOAT-ROCKER

143 **It was not the first time:**   Giglio, *Musial,* 59–60.

143 **Musial said he loved barnstorming:**   Marshall, *Baseball's Pivotal Era,* 343.

144 **The Court had declined:**   Fetter, *Taking on the Yankees,* 67.

144 **"I think a lot":**   Stan Musial, St. Louis, May 17, 1978, A. B. Chandler Oral History Project.

144 **Murphy's efforts were blocked:**   Lowenfish, *Branch Rickey,* 430.

145 **On June 7:**   Turner, *When the Boys Came Back,* 142.

145 **Ralph Kiner, later a Hall:**   Ralph Kiner, interview, Aug. 24, 2009.

145 **After the game, Brown was roughed:**   William O. DeWitt Sr., Cincinnati, Sep. 29 and Oct. 1, 1980, A. B. Chandler Oral History Project.

145 **"Murphy money":**   Turner, *When the Boys Came Back,* 192.

145 **"If it hadn't been":**   Marty Marion, St. Louis, May 19, 1978. A. B. Chandler Oral History Project.

145 **"Marty was kinda our leader":**   Stan Musial, St. Louis, May 17, 1978, A. B. Chandler Oral History Project.

145 **"I had to go":**   Marty Marion, St. Louis, May 19, 1978, A. B. Chandler Oral History Project.

146 **One of the leaders:**   Turner, *When the Boys Came Back,* 194.

146 **On October 13:**   Associated Press, "$175,000 in Radio Fee to Pension Fund," *New York Times,* Oct. 14, 1946.

146 **"We wanted some representation":**   Stan Musial, St. Louis, May 17, 1978, A. B. Chandler Oral History Project.

146 **"Mr. Breadon, I don't care":**   *Stan Musial: "The Man's" Own Story,* 101.


## 23 | STANLEY THE SCOUT

Musial, Feller, and Slaughter, from a tape at the conference "Jackie Robinson: Race, Sports and the American Dream," Long Island University, Brooklyn, New York, Apr. 3–5, 1997; Marty Adler, interview, Jun. 24, 2009.


## 24 | THE STRIKE THAT NEVER HAPPENED

151 **All the attention to Robinson:**   Timothy M. Gay, *Satch, Dizzy and Rapid Robert: The Wild Saga of Interracial Baseball Before Jackie Robinson* (New York: Simon and Schuster, 2010), 222.

151 **"He didn't impress me":**   Stan Musial, St. Louis, May 17, 1978, A. B. Chandler Oral History Project.

152 **For those who wondered:**   Lowenfish, *Branch Rickey,* 23–24.

152 **"You know, he wasn't":**   Stan Musial, St. Louis, May 17, 1978, A. B. Chandler Oral History Project.

152 **"Well, that was probably true":**   Ibid.

153 "I wasn't in that meeting":    Ralph Branca, interview, Nov. 14, 2008.

153 "I'll play an elephant":    Lowenfish, *Branch Rickey,* 418–19.

154 Rumors of a strike:    Jonathan Eig, *Opening Day: The Story of Jackie Robinson's First Season* (New York: Simon and Schuster, 2007), 97.

154 The strike rumors:    "Cards' Strike Plan Against Negro Dropped," *New York Times,* May 9, 1947; "Robinson Reveals Written Threats," *New York Times,* May 10, 1947.

154 "Sam was one of their own":    Bob Broeg, interview, ESPN *SportsCentury,* Nov. 29, 2000.

154 Frick quoted Breadon:    Eig, *Opening Day,* 97.

155 "The National League will go down":    Harold Rosenthal, "The Story Behind the Story," *New York Times,* May 4, 1997.

155 Breadon later told Jerome Holtzman:    Eig, *Opening Day,* 94.

155 Most of the Cardinals:    Dom Amore, "Freddy Schmidt, 92, Came Out of Hartford, Won Two World Series Rings and Saw Jackie Robinson Break In, But Let Him Tell You," *Hartford Courant,* Jun. 29, 2008.

155 "Nothing was ever concrete":    Harry Walker, Leeds, Alabama, May 11, 1988, A. B. Chandler Oral History Project.

156 Breadon labeled Woodward's:    *New York Herald Tribune,* May 10, 1947.

156 calling them "carpetbaggers":    Amore, "Freddy Schmidt."

157 "I think they felt":    Stan Musial, St. Louis, May 17, 1978, A. B. Chandler Oral History Project.

157 "I heard talk":    Roger Kahn, *The Era: 1947–1957: When the Yankees, the Giants, and the Dodgers Ruled the World* (New York: Ticknor and Fields, 1993).

157 In 1997, Musial told:    Robert Dvorchak, "Donora's Stan Musial Is Still 'The Man,'" *Pittsburgh Post-Gazette,* Mar. 12, 1997.

157 Besides, Musial was dealing:    *Stan Musial: "The Man's" Own Story,* 104.

158 Dr. Hyland proposed:    Sher, "The Stan Musial Nobody Knows."

158 "Dyer says, 'Hiya, pal' ":    Bob Broeg, interview, ESPN *SportsCentury,* Nov. 29, 2000.

158 The Cardinals were on:    Arnold Rampersad, *Jackie Robinson, a Biography* (New York: Knopf, 1997), 182.

159 The spiking happened:    Eig, *Opening Day,* 222; Roscoe McGowen, "Kurowski's Homer Stops Brooks, 3–2," *New York Times,* Aug. 21, 1947.

159 "How he didn't go tumbling":    Ralph Branca, interview, Nov. 14, 2008.

159 "I see it developing":    Joe McDonald, interview, Nov. 25, 2008.

160 "He said something to me":    Stan Musial, St. Louis, May 17, 1978, A. B. Chandler Oral History Project.

160 In another version:    Kahn, *The Era,* 87.

161 "I'm glad you asked that question":    Enos Slaughter, at the conference "Jackie Robinson: Race, Sports and the American Dream," Long Island University, Brooklyn, New York, Apr. 3–5, 1997.

161 "You have to admire":   Stan Musial, St. Louis, May 17, 1978, A. B. Chandler Oral History Project.

162 "They were making such a big deal":   Marty Marion, St. Louis, May 19, 1978, A. B. Chandler Oral History Project.

163 "Robinson had said":   Julius Hunter, *TV One-on-One* (St. Louis: Gashouse Books, 2008).

163 "He was like Gil Hodges":   Roger Kahn, interview, 2010; Kahn, "Of Galahad and Quests That Failed."

164 And then there was the story:   David Falkner, *Great Time Coming: The Life of Jackie Robinson, from Baseball to Birmingham* (New York: Simon and Schuster, 1995), 225.

164 "After I warmed up":   Joe Black, at the conference "Jackie Robinson: Race, Sports and the American Dream," Long Island University, Brooklyn, Apr. 3–5, 1997.

## 25  |  STANLEY AND THE KID

165 The way Ted Williams told it:   Ted Williams with John Underwood, *My Turn at Bat: The Story of My Life* (New York: Simon and Schuster, 1969), 243–44.

165 In Musial's version:   *Stan Musial: "The Man's" Own Story*, 208.

## 26  |  THE BIG THREE

168 Giuseppe DiMaggio came to the States:   Cramer, *Joe DiMaggio*, 16–17.

168 The family spoke a Sicilian dialect:   Ibid., 214.

169 "I never wore a uniform":   Williams, *My Turn at Bat*.

171 "For some reason, Ted Williams":   Ned Garver, interview, Jun. 30, 2009.

172 "Just don't let John Henry know":   Curt Block, friend of Ned Garver, interview, May 6, 2010.

172 "When he was taking batting practice":   Ned Garver, interview, Jun. 30, 2009.

173 "I don't want to say":   Joe Williams, "Musial Rates DiMaggio over Ted Williams," *New York World-Telegram and Sun,* Mar. 23, 1949.

174 Musial met Cobb once:   Tom Ashley, interview, 2009.

174 Bill White, a teammate:   Bill White, interview.

174 "I only faced him":   Dom Amore, "The World According to Freddy," *Hartford Courant,* Jun. 29, 2008.

175 in April 1947, Tom Yawkey:   Cramer, *Joe DiMaggio*, 228.

175 "If we had traded Williams":   Linn, *Hitter,* 21.

175 "Sure, he can hit":   Cramer, *Joe DiMaggio*, 188.

175 DiMaggio thought of Williams:   Ibid., 164.

176 Williams's brother, Danny:   Linn, *Hitter,* 325.

176 "He once told me":    Letter from Jim Prime, 2009.

177 "All he ever wants":    Cramer, *Joe DiMaggio,* 179.

177 "When I get asked":    Warren Mayes, "Stan the Man Still a St. Louis Icon at 81," Associated Press, Aug. 17, 2002.

177 Cronin did not vote:    Linn, *Hitter,* 21.

### 27 | BAD AIR

178 Miss Halloween:    Verna Duda, interview, Mar. 25, 2009.

178 In the middle:    Dr. Charles Stacey, interview, Mar. 24, 2009.

179 "My *zadie* said":    Dr. Devra Davis, interview, Apr. 17, 2009.

180 Killer smogs in cities:    Davis, *When Smoke Ran Like Water,* 11–29.

181 "Our grandfather Musial":    Gerry Ashley, interview, 2009.

### 28 | FAMILY LIFE

182 "Every time my dad":    Sher, "The Stan Musial Nobody Knows."

184 "Frankly, I would just as soon":    *Stan Musial: "The Man's" Own Story,* 120.

185 Ed Carson had recognized:    Sher, "The Stan Musial Nobody Knows."

186 Biggie was the son:    Giglio, *Musial,* 170.

186 Later he moved into patronage:    "Julius (Biggie) Garagnani Dies," *St. Louis Post-Dispatch,* June 20, 1967.

186 "larger than life":    Tom Ashley, interview, 2009.

187 "A bit rough around the edges":    Gerry Ashley, interview, Mar. 2009.

187 "I had a moderate amount":    *Stan Musial: "The Man's" Own Story,* 121.

187 Carmen would always remember:    Christopher Hann, "It Ain't Over," *New Jersey Monthly,* Feb. 1, 2008.

188 "I had my first sour cream":    Tim McCarver, interview, Nov. 13, 2008.

188 Another view of Biggie:    Biggie Garagnani, as told to J. Roy Stockton, "My Partner Stan Musial," *Sport,* July 1950.

189 "Say, Big, have you been over":    Mickey McTague, email, Dec. 8, 2010.

189 "He and my mom":    Gerry Ashley, interview, 2009.

189 Musial insisted:    *Stan Musial: "The Man's" Own Story,* 121.

190 "Sometimes if they do something":    Mrs. Stan Musial, "My Life with Stan."

191 The Musials were friendly:    Gerry Ashley, interview, 2010.

193 "He'd always be holding":    Roger Kahn, "The Man."

194 "My dad was interested":    Dr. Ben Vanek, interview, Dec. 1, 2008.

196 "Dick isn't interested in baseball":    Hugh Brown, "Young and Old Flock to 'The Man,' " *Philadelphia Evening Bulletin,* May 21, 1958.

196 "Those kids used to try":    Mike Shannon, interview, *The Legend of Stan the Man.*

## 29 | DAY OFF IN CHICAGO

198 "The kids were all thrilled":   Prof. M. B. B. Biskupski, Ph.D., S. A. Blejwas Endowed Chair in Polish History, Central Connecticut State University, interview, Nov. 4, 2008.

## 30 | PRIME TIME

200 after Dr. Hyland removed:   Associated Press, "Stan Musial Doing Well," *New York Times,* Oct. 16, 1947.

200 "Stash seemed to stand up":   Sher, "The Stan Musial Nobody Knows."

200 But Musial has suggested another reason:   *Halls of Fame: Stan Musial.*

201 "Pitchers generally had thrown":   *The Legend of Stan the Man Musial.*

201 "He said, 'Yeah, Commissioner' ":   Fay Vincent, interview, Dec. 30, 2008.

202 "You know, that was the decision":   Stan Musial, St. Louis, May 17, 1978, A. B. Chandler Oral History Project.

202 Quincy Trouppe, scouting:   James, *The New Bill James Historical Baseball Abstract,* 228.

202 Howard's widow, Arlene:   Arlene Howard and Ralph Wimbish, *Elston and Me: The Story of the First Black Yankee* (Columbia: University of Missouri Press, 2001); Arlene Howard, interview, 2008.

203 "The only time":   Stan Musial, St. Louis, May 17, 1978, A. B. Chandler Oral History Project.

203 "He had something to say":   Marshall, *Baseball's Pivotal Era.*

203 "We'd watch 'em":   Don Newcombe, interview, Jan. 7, 2009.

204 Musial the businessman:   Sher, "The Stan Musial Nobody Knows."

204 Musial's pose toward the owners:   *Stan Musial: "The Man's" Own Story,* 114–20.

204 "He had always approached":   Fred Saigh, "What Musial Means to the Cards," *Sport,* Jul. 1952.

204 "Mr. Saigh, I have been well":   Ibid.

205 "I think about that sometimes":   Red Schoendienst, as told to Bob Broeg, "Me and My Roomie," *Sport,* Jun. 1955.

205 "When we were on the road":   Kahn, "Of Galahad and Quests That Failed."

205 "The Pirates would be":   Ralph Kiner, interview, Aug. 24, 2009.

206 "That was a real nice thing":   Golenbock, *The Spirit of St. Louis,* 424–25.

206 "Early in the game":   Wayne Terwilliger, interview, Feb. 27, 2009.

207 Musial rarely gave advice:   Joe Cunningham, interview, Jan. 16, 2009.

207 "I thought, 'Okay' ":   Ed Mickelson, interview, Feb. 3, 2009.

207 "There was a half inch":   Joe Garagiola, interview, Aug. 2009.

208 "Hey, Stan, about ten of us":   Garagiola, interview, 2009. Yogi version: Yogi Berra, with Dave Kaplan, *You Can Observe a Lot by Watching* (New York: John Wiley and Sons, 2008), 20.

208 **Lil happened to stay home:** *Stan Musial: "The Man's" Own Story*, 165.

209 **Legend says that Musial promised everybody:** Robin Roberts, interview, Jan. 27, 2009.

209 **Henry Aaron, in the same dugout:** Wayne Stewart, *Stan the Man: The Life and Times of Stan Musial* (Chicago: Triumph Books, 2010), 145.

209 **"Stash is the oldest player":** Berra, *You Can Observe a Lot by Watching*, 162.

209 **"It was a long game":** Yogi Berra, interview, Dec. 9, 2008.

210 **Then there is Frank Sullivan:** Frank Sullivan, *Life Is More Than 9 Innings: Memories of a Boston Red Sox Pitcher* (Honolulu: Editions Limited, 2008), 58.

## 31 | STANLEY GIVES AN INTERVIEW

Interview with Zev Yaroslavsky, Dec. 30, 2008.

## 32 | TEMPER, TEMPER

213 **"No matter who you talk to":** Dal Maxvill, interview, Jan. 14, 2009.

214 **"The Cubs were awful":** Email message from Steve Kaufman, 2009.

215 **"Why would anybody":** Jack Buck, with Bob Broeg and Bob Rains, *"That's a Winner!"* (Champaign, Ill.: Sports Publishing, 2002).

215 **Musial also displayed righteous anger:** Giglio, *Musial*, 233.

## 33 | AND SOME BAD TIMES

216 **"My ambition," Busch said:** "The Barons of Beer," *Time*, Jul. 11, 1955.

216 **Known as Gussie:** Robert McG. Thomas Jr., "August A. Busch Jr. Dies at 90; Built Largest Brewing Company," *New York Times*, Sep. 30, 1989.

216 **Normally, the players bet sodas:** Garagiola, *Just Play Ball*, 82–83.

218 **"The Year of the Big Minus":** *Stan Musial: "The Man's" Own Story*, 172.

218 **Bob Broeg, Musial's confidant:** *The Legend of Stan the Man Musial*.

219 **Lane pronounced:** Associated Press, "Only Five Cards 'Untouchables,' " May 21, 1956.

219 **"We would be taking":** Schoendienst, *Red: A Baseball Life*, 81–82.

219 **investigating a rumor:** Robin Roberts, interview, Feb. 1, 2010; "Phils Are Not Talking Trade for Roberts," *St. Louis Post-Dispatch*, Jun. 13, 1956; Bob Broeg, "Lane Tones Down Trade Talk After 3-Way Meeting," *St. Louis Post-Dispatch*, Jun. 13, 1956.

219 **Biggie promptly called:** *Stan Musial: "The Man's" Own Story*, 178.

219 **"I'm picking up Stan":** *The Legend of Stan the Man Musial*.

220 **After a day or two:** Associated Press, "Musial Deal Not in Cards, Lane Insists," Jun. 11, 1956.

220  Red began to wonder:   Schoendienst, *Red: A Baseball Life*, 83.

220  Musial's memory of that awful day:   Ibid., vii.

220  "Yeah, boy, he didn't like that":   *The Legend of Stan the Man Musial.*

220  "Musial just laughed":   Ibid.

220  Red was pretty miserable:   Louis Effrat, "Schoendienst Misses His Room-Mate Most of All," *New York Times*, Aug. 7, 1956.

221  One consequence:   Roger D. Launius, *Seasons in the Sun: The Story of Big League Baseball in Missouri* (Columbia: University of Missouri Press, 2002).

221  "I never saw Stan":   Schoendienst, *Red: A Baseball Life*, 83.

222  One moment came:   Giglio, *Musial*, 200.

222  Upon turning thirty-six:   *Stan Musial: "The Man's" Own Story*, 183.

222  "We were a tough bunch":   Hunter, *TV One-on-One.*

223  Musial gave a brief look:   Giglio, *Musial*, 222.

223  "I met Al Barlick":   Joe Torre, interview, Jul. 9, 2009.

223  Another umpire anecdote:   Joe Posnanski, "Where Are They Now?" *Sports Illustrated*, Aug. 2, 2010.

224  Stanley has even received credit:   Craig Mulder, "The Right Call: Widely Respect, Harvey Earns an Umpire's Highest Honor," *Memories and Dreams* (National Baseball Hall of Fame), Spring 2010.

224  After getting one hit on Monday:   *Stan Musial: "The Man's" Own Story*, 202.

224  On Tuesday Lil:   *The Legend of Stan the Man Musial.*

225  "He told the fans":   Gerry Ashley, interview, 2009.

226  "At first, I wasn't too keen":   Lee Kavetski, "Stan 'The Man' Musial—A Class Guy," *Stars and Stripes*, Pacific edition, Jan. 24, 1988.

226  The hosts would give:   Ruben Amaro Sr., interview, Mar. 22, 2010.

226  Without knowing it:   Sadaharu Oh, with David Falkner, *A Zen Way of Baseball* (New York: Times Books, 1984), 82.

227  "Butch Yatkeman":   Solly Hemus, interview, Apr. 14, 2010.

227  His parents did not name him:   Curt Flood, with Richard Carter, *The Way It Is* (New York: Pocket Books, 1972), 67.

228  "My mom said":   Gerry Ashley, interview, Jul. 14, 2010.

228  "I said, 'I think Solly deserves' ":   Golenbock, *The Spirit of St. Louis*, 432–33.

229  "His kids hated me":   Solly Hemus, interview, Apr. 14, 2010.

229  "Please tell him":   Email from Gerry Ashley, Apr. 2010.

229  "He gave me a lot":   Solly Hemus, interview, Apr. 14, 2010.

230  "I took a pretty good cut":   *Stan Musial: "The Man's" Own Story*, 211.

230  "The Cardinals have been generous":   *Sporting News*, Jan. 27, 1960.

230  "Stan Musial, who functioned":   James A. Michener, *Sports in America* (New York: Random House, 1976), 271.

231  Hemus did make two good moves:   *Stan Musial: "The Man's" Own Story*, 214.

231 While Musial was observing: Lester J. Biederman, "Musial Deeply Hurt by Card Treatment, His Friends Claim," *Pittsburgh Press*, Jun. 14, 1960.

231 Many years later: Broeg, *The Man Stan*, 31.

231 "By then, when I'd go home": Bob Broeg, "Stan Musial's Fight to Keep Playing," *Sport*, Apr. 1963.

### 34 | ON THE HUSTINGS

233 "Oh, my God": Angie Dickinson, interview, Mar. 10, 2010.

233 Musial often told: *Stan Musial: "The Man's" Own Story*, 3.

234 apparently White suggested Musial: James A. Michener, *Report of the County Chairman* (New York: Random House, 1961), 155.

234 "No time was designated": Ibid.

234 Michener called him: Ibid., 158.

235 "I played in Denver": Ibid., 159.

235 "a strikingly beautiful young woman": Ibid., 155.

236 "Artie, you were a sensation": Ibid., 163.

236 "We had no ball club": Angie Dickinson, interview, Mar. 10, 2010.

236 "Jeff and I had dated": Ibid.

237 This was red-state: Michener, *Report of the County Chairman*, 179.

239 "I said, 'Oh, my God, why?'": Angie Dickinson, interview, Mar. 10, 2010.

240 "You ought to talk to Angie": Tom Ashley, interview, Mar. 22, 2010.

### 35 | BETTER PANTS

241 In his own locker: Ruben Amaro Sr., interview, Mar. 22, 2010.

### 36 | WHEN THE TIMES CHANGED

243 Brooks Lawrence, a rookie pitcher: Golenbock, *The Spirit of St. Louis*, 414.

244 Hemus confused Gibson: Gibson and Jackson, *Sixty Feet, Six Inches*, 235.

244 "He was more like a dad": Gibson and Jackson, *Sixty Feet, Six Inches*, 214.

244 "I watched George punish himself": Broeg, "Stan Musial's Fight to Keep Playing," *Sport*.

244 "The more time you spend": *Stan Musial: "The Man's" Own Story*, 216.

245 Crowe praised Musial: George Crowe, interview, Jan. 7, 2009.

245 "We played side by side": Flood, *The Way It Is*, 52–53.

246 Musial was upset: Ibid., 77.

246 "They invited all but the colored": Ibid., 56.

247 In 1961, the two doctors: Rosalie Peck, interview, Oct. 2008.

247 "Do you mean to tell me": Flood, *The Way It Is*, 57.

247 "Busch was just worried": Bill White, interview, 2009.

247 "the year I got out": Bob Gibson interview, Sep. 29, 2009.

248 "All those years": Mildred White, interview, Dec. 5, 2008.

248 Stan and Lil have never talked: Gerry Ashley, interview.

249 "Bill's Wife Solved Problem": *Sporting News*, spring 1962, undated clip courtesy of Mildred White.

249 "People would drive by": Brad Snyder, *A Well-Paid Slave: Curt Flood's Fight for Free Agency in Professional Sports* (New York: Viking Press, 2006), 180.

250 "Best hitter I ever saw": Bill White, interview, 2009.

251 "The Cardinals were different": Gibson and Jackson, *Sixty Feet, Six Inches*, 189.

This chapter is informed by: Howard and Wimbish, *Elston and Me*, and interviews with both. Also, Brian Carroll, "Wendell Smith's Last Crusade: The Desegregation of Spring Training, 1961," *The 13th Annual Cooperstown Symposium on Baseball and American Culture*, ed. William Simons (Jefferson City, N.C.: McFarland Press, 2002).

## 37 | OLD FOLKS

252 "Stan was on the bench": Jack Olsen, "That Johnny Keane Is a Fine Manager Is What He Sure Is," *Sports Illustrated*, Apr. 13, 1964.

253 With Keane's encouragement: *Stan Musial: "The Man's" Own Story*, 84.

254 "We've got a one-run lead": Alvin Jackson, interview, Feb. 13, 2009.

254 Lil had missed: *Stan Musial: "The Man's" Own Story*, 227.

255 "We came back": John H. Zentay, interview, Nov. 29, 2010.

255 "It was clear there was affection": Ibid.

256 "Zentay would remember: Ibid.

256 "My mom was impressed": Gerry Ashley, email message, Nov. 29, 2010.

256 "Everything I have I owe": Les Biederman, "Musial's Storied Career Opposite of Reckless Cobb's," *Pittsburgh Press*, July 17, 1962.

257 Decades later, Tim McCarver: Tim McCarver, interview, Nov. 13, 2008.

257 "I'm afraid": Bob Broeg, "Devine, Busch Say No; Cards to Make Stan Veep When He Quits," *St. Louis Post-Dispatch*, Nov. 6, 1962.

257 "I tried to pitch": *The Legend of Stan the Man Musial*.

258 "Normally, a guy": Joe Torre, interview, Jul. 9, 2009.

258 Musial broke the news: Olsen, "That Johnny Keane Is a Fine Manager."

259 The family stayed up: Gerry Ashley, interview.

260 "I don't wear dark glasses": W. C. Heinz, "Stan Musial's Last Day," *Life*, Oct. 11, 1963; Hano, "Stan Musial's Last Game," *Sport*.

## 38 | FENDER BENDER

Thomas Ashley, interview.

## 39 | RETIREMENT

262 "Stan was there":   Anonymous posting on St. Louis Memories, 2009, http:// genealogyinstlouis.accessgenealogy.com.

263 "Washington would have been":   Gerry Ashley, interview.

263 "Calisthenics are fine":   Associated Press, "Cardinals Give Musial Free Hand to Encourage Physical Fitness," Mar. 22, 1964.

263 Because the job paid:   Giglio, *Musial*, 277–78.

264 "LBJ had Stan lobbying":   Tom Ashley, interview, 2009.

264 "But didn't you find":   Kahn, "Of Galahad and Quests That Failed."

264 Musial still gravitated:   *Stan Musial: "The Man's" Own Story*, 230.

265 "I knew Red needed experience":   Bob Broeg, "Red and Stan—Spirit of St. Louis," *St. Louis Post-Dispatch*, Oct. 7, 1967.

265 He had always talked:   Bob Broeg, "Honored in Brooklyn and Poland, Stan Remains the Man in Motion," *St. Louis Post-Dispatch*, Jun. 21, 1990.

267 "When you're in that house":   Gerry Ashley, interview, 2009.

267 "Their house is like anybody else's":   Helen P. Nelson, interview, Jun. 29, 2009.

267 "Lil is one of the finest":   Danny and Pat Litwhiler, interview, Apr. 2010.

268 "He came to my house":   Robert Hermann, interview, 2009.

268 "I'm sure it happened":   Tom Ashley Jr., interview, Aug. 13, 2009.

269 "It was pretty dangerous over there":   Col. James Hackett, interview, May 12, 2009.

269 "We would split up":   Brooks Robinson, interview, Oct. 5, 2009.

270 "I was just young and stupid":   Joe Torre, interview, July 9, 2009.

270 When Musial got home:   Jack Herman, "War Zone Trip Warms Musial," St. Louis *Globe-Democrat*, Nov. 21, 1966.

## 40 | STANLEY RUNS THE TEAM

271 Musial agreed:   Neal Russo, "Musial Replaces Howsam as GM," *St. Louis Post-Dispatch*, Jan. 23, 1967.

271 "As the reader already knows":   Flood, *The Way It Is*, 66.

272 "Stan said, 'Hey' ":   Dal Maxvill, interview, Jan. 14, 2009.

273 "Maris was very temperamental":   Bill Bergesch, interview, 2008.

273 "Tell me one thing":   Bob Broeg, "Gussie Scores on Devine's Home Run," *St. Louis Post-Dispatch*, Dec. 6, 1967.

273 "Gentlemen, I have a feeling":   Broeg, *The Man, Stan*, 234.

273 "It was so cold":   Alvin Jackson, interview, Feb. 13, 2009.

273 "When the club":   Dal Maxvill, interview, Jan. 14, 2009.

274 "He says, 'Well' ":   Red Schoendienst, interview for ESPN Century 2000, Nov. 29, 2000.

274 When Stanley really needed:   Broeg, *The Man, Stan,* 234–35.

275 Tim McCarver said:   Tim McCarver, interview, Nov. 13, 2008.

275 "He has actually shown":   Broeg, "Red and Stan."

276 "Stan twiddled his thumbs":   Hunter, *TV One-on-One.*

276 "If you want to do":   Red Schoendienst, interview for ESPN, Nov. 29, 2000.

276 On December 5:   Stan Isle, "A Big Rumble in Cardinals' Executive Suite," *Sporting News,* Dec. 1967; John J. Archibold, "Bing's Return," *St. Louis Post-Dispatch,* Dec. 5, 1967.

277 It was Christmas Eve 1967:   John Kopchak, interview, Nov. 29, 2010.

278 "Are you a millionaire?":   Kahn, "Of Galahad and Quests That Failed."

278 "Gentlemen, I don't think":   "Busch Lectures on Fan Alienation," *New York Times,* March 23, 1969.

279 At the Supreme Court:   Snyder, *A Well-Paid Slave.*

279 There was no reason to expect:   Flood, *The Way It Is.*

279 "Spring of 1972":   Keith Hernandez, interview, Nov. 10, 2008.

280 "I invited my old coaches":   *Halls of Fame: Stan Musial.*

281 "The church was jammed":   Fay Vincent, interview, Dec. 30, 2008.

281 Late into the night, Musial:   Paul Nuzzolese, interview, 2008.

281 He could show up anywhere:   Ray Corio, interview, 2008.

## 41 | HOMETOWN

282 "Stan included her in things":   Verna Duda, interview, Mar. 2009.

282 While Stan was still playing:   Roger Kahn, interview, Mar. 4, 2010.

283 "She had a hard life":   Tom Ashley, interview, Feb. 2009.

283 Whenever the Cardinals played:   Bob Broeg, interview, ESPN, Nov. 29, 2000.

284 "We would see him":   Edward S. Musial, interview, Jun. 2, 2009.

284 In 1965, Musial had a ranch:   Stewart, *Stan the Man,* 165.

284 erratic behavior:   Giglio, *Musial,* 296.

285 Stan would also return:   Ed Musial, interview, ESPN, Dec. 18, 2000.

285 Then he shuttled around:   Statistics courtesy of John Hall.

285 Ed did work with Stan:   Giglio, *Musial,* 289–90.

285 "I went the other way":   Ed Musial, interview, ESPN, Dec. 18, 2000.

286 Stan remained loyal:   Stewart, *Stan the Man,* 212.

287 "Maybe it is characteristic":   Dr. Charles Stacey, interview, May 12, 2009.

288 "I passed to Pope":   Bimbo Cecconi, tour of Donora, Mar. 2009.

**42 | STANLEY GOES TO A REUNION**

Tom Ashley, interview.

**43 | THE POLISH CONNECTION**

291 "They liked being out somewhere":  Tom Ashley, interview, 2009.

291 "As a boy I had nothing":  Anne Morris, "Passing of a Man of Letters," *Austin American-Statesman,* Oct. 17, 1997.

291 It took an army:  Herman Silverman, *Michener and Me* (Philadelphia: Running Press, 1999), 29, 32.

292 "Jim and I were signing":  Tom Wheatley, "Musial Admired," *St. Louis Post-Dispatch,* Feb. 13, 1996.

292 "I'm a Democrat":  Kahn, "Of Galahad and Quests That Failed."

293 "The relationship between Dad and Stan":  Helen P. Nelson, interview, Jun. 29, 2009.

293 "She corrected him":  James A. Michener, *Pilgrimage: A Memoir of Poland and Rome* (Emmaus, Penn.: Rodale, 1990), 71–72.

294 "Mr. P. was relentless":  Email from Karen Wessel Fox, Oct. 7, 2009.

295 "I don't think Polish jokes":  Kahn, "Of Galahad and Quests That Failed."

296 Ed Piszek went:  Michener, *Pilgrimage,* 76.

297 "The clock was ticking":  Christine Schiavo, "Personal Words Mark Funeral for Mrs. Paul's Mogul," *Philadelphia Inquirer,* Apr. 4, 2004.

297 Christenson had met:  Larry Christenson, interview, Jan. 6, 2009.

297 "But that was explained":  Michener, *Pilgrimage,* 17.

298 Musial met some Polish relatives:  Ibid., 32.

298 A staggering portion:  Lech Walesa, "Excerpts from Debate Between Lech Walesa and Alfred Miodowicz, Nov. 30, 1988," *Making the History of 1989,* http://chnm.gmu.edu/1989/items/show/540.

298 Musial and the rest:  Michener, *Pilgrimage,* 35.

298 Michener greeted the pope:  Ibid., 85.

299 "Three courses served by a nun":  Ibid., 86.

299 "I'm entitled to be here":  Ibid., 89.

299 "I watched Stan interact":  Jim Murray, interview, Jan. 20, 2009.

299 Like many people:  Larry Christenson, interview, Jun. 26, 2009.

300 "Grasping my hand":  Michener, *Pilgrimage,* 93.

300 "When I saw Musial":  Richard L. Thornburgh, interview, Jan. 7, 2009.

300 intrigue was taking place:  Christenson, Murray, Thornburgh interviews.

301 "Stan could have been":  Jim Murray, interview, Jan. 20, 2009.

302 Musial was so identified:  Pat Henry, interview, Dec. 3, 2010.

302 Musial retained his bond:  Maureen Dowd, "For Bush, a Polish Welcome Without Fervor," *New York Times,* Jul. 11, 1989.

302 In 1990, Stan and Lil:  Giglio, *Musial,* 300.

303  **The friendship between Musial and Michener:**  Hunter, *TV One-on-One.*

303  **McEwen wrote he had received:**  Tom McEwen, "Mr. Michener's Tour of Tampa," *Tampa Tribune,* Feb. 9, 2008.

304  **"I took the bouquet":**  Tom McEwen, "A Sports Night to Remember with Stan the Man," *Tampa Tribune,* Jul. 25, 2009.

305  **After turning ninety:**  Frank Eltman, "James Michener Remembered by Friends, Colleagues at Manhattan Memorial," Associated Press, Nov. 18, 1997.

305  **Musial described him:**  Stephanie Simon, "Famous Novelist James A. Michener Dies at Age 90," *Los Angeles Times,* Oct. 17, 1997.

305  **Fifteen months later:**  Patricia Rice, "Area Basked in Pope's Visit," *St. Louis Post-Dispatch,* Apr. 3, 2005.

305  **Edward Piszek later went through:**  Schiavo, "Personal Words Mark Funeral."

306  **"They remained friends":**  Helen P. Nelson, interview, Jun. 29, 2009.


### 44 | THE FACE IN THE CROWD

George Vecsey, "Mantle's Teammates Say Goodbye," *New York Times,* Aug. 16, 1995; Bob Costas, interview, Nov. 18, 2008; Tom Wheatley, "Farewell to the Mick; Mantle Dead at 63: 'A Yankee Forever,' " *St. Louis Post-Dispatch,* Aug. 14, 1995.

309  **Few people in the church knew:**  Jane Leavy, *The Last Boy: Mickey Mantle and the End of America's Childhood* (New York: HarperCollins, 2010), 56.

309  **The two players had something else:**  Leavy, *The Last Boy,* 38.


### 45 | STANLEY'S STATUES

311  **Ten feet five inches tall:**  Neal Russo, "Smiles, Kisses and Tears at Musial Statue Unveiling," *Sporting News,* Aug. 17, 1968.

311  **"I saw the sculptor":**  Kahn, "Of Galahad and Quests That Failed."

311  **"great, great honor":**  *Halls of Fame: Stan Musial.*

311  **"I'll say this, Jeannie":**  Broeg, *The Man, Stan,* 240.


### 46 | MORE FUNERALS

314  **"I wish I could have gotten":**  Tom Wheatley, "Musial Admired by Those Whom Musial Admires," *St. Louis Post-Dispatch,* Feb. 13, 1996.

315  **"You have a feeling":**  Fay Vincent, interview, Dec. 30, 2008.

316  **For many years, the Clipper:**  Nick Nicolosi, interview, 2008.

318  **"You know, Joe and I":**  Garagiola, *It's Anybody's Ballgame,* 94.

318  **"The headline in the newspaper":**  Buck, *"That's a Winner,"* 82.

318  **Actually, headlines in the *Post-Dispatch*:**  Bill Smith, "Musial Cries 'Foul' on Garagiolas' Suit," *St. Louis Post-Dispatch,* Apr. 19, 1986; Joe Mannies, "Business Splits Old Friends," *St. Louis Post-Dispatch,* Apr. 27, 1986.

318  The suit was filed:   Giglio, *Musial*, 292–95.

319  "It was no coincidence":   Buck, *"That's a Winner,"* 82.

319  The Cardinals' staff learned:   Bill Madden, "Musial Tosses Gutter Ball Over Garagiola Split," *Daily News*, Oct. 26, 2006.

320  In July 1996:   James N. Giglio, "Prelude to Greatness: Stanley Musial and the Springfield Cardinals of 1941," *Missouri Historical Review*, July 1996, 429–52.

320  If it happened:   Email from James N. Giglio to Scott Lehotsky, Mar. 5, 2004.

320  One shunned acquaintance:   William Bottonari, interview, Nov. 12, 2008.

321  "Stan would sit":   Bob Costas, interview, Nov. 18, 2008.

322  "We've learned a lot":   *The Legend of Stan the Man Musial.*

322  Gerry and Tom Ashley:   Tom Ashley, interviews.

323  Musial then told:   Roger Kahn, interview, Mar. 4, 2010.

323  "I quit while I still":   Kahn, "Of Galahad and Quests That Failed."

324  Dublin for the Irish Derby:   James Hackett, interview, May 12, 2009.

324  Torre also went:   Joe Torre, interview, Jul. 9, 2009.

324  Stanley would almost always show up:   Mickey McTague, interview, 2010; Bob Broeg, "The One-Man Band Played On and On," *St. Louis Post-Dispatch*, Apr. 14, 1996.

324  "Stan would sign":   Larry Christenson, interview, Jan. 6, 2009.

324  Another constant in Stan's life:   Gerry Ashley, interview.

324  For a very long time:   John McGuire, interview, 2009.

325  Most days, Stanley and Zitzmann:   Dick Zitzmann, interview, Dec. 17, 2008.

325  "Stan told me":   Hunter, *TV One-on-One.*

325  "Well, I'm hanging in there":   Warren Mayes, "Stan the Man Still a St. Louis Icon at 81," Associated Press, Aug. 17, 2002.

325  Williams, DiMaggio and Stan:   Dave Newhouse, "Musial's Secretary: Stan's Still the Man in Baseball," *Oakland Tribune*, Apr. 4, 2004.

326  "I've always liked him":   Monte Irvin, interview, Dec. 5, 2008.

327  "No, this is Ted's day":   Montville, *Ted Williams*, 372–73.

327  As the mourners left the church:   Ben Cramer, *Joe DiMaggio*, 511.

328  In his mid-eighties:   Gerry Ashley, interview.

329  "Back in the day":   Gerry Ashley, email, Dec. 28, 2009.

## 47 | UPSTAGED AGAIN

331  "It was cold":   Albert Pujols, interview, 2009.

331  Musial and Pujols seemed:   Bernie Miklasz, "It's Hard to Find Words to Describe Cards Star," *St. Louis Post-Dispatch*, Apr. 12, 2009.

331  Their mutual admiration cut:   Rick Hummel, "Albert and the Man," *St. Louis Post-Dispatch*, Jul. 15, 2009.

332  "The whole dynamic changed":   Dick Zitzmann, interview, 2010.

333 **"Mom and I were worried":**   Gerry Ashley, interview, 2009.

334 **Feeling the rush of time:**   Derrick Goold, "Meet the Man: La Russa Spread the Word of Musial," *St. Louis Post-Dispatch,* Mar. 20, 2010.

334 **Often they were photographed:**   George Vecsey, "For Musial, a Birthday and a Medal," *New York Times,* Nov. 20, 2010.

334 **"The day we started":**   Ron Watermon, interview, Nov. 18, 2010.

334 **DeWitt and everybody else:**   William O. DeWitt Jr., interview, Nov. 18, 2010.

## EPILOGUE | HERE HE COMES NOW

Lunch with Jim Hackett, John McGuire, Larry L. Thompson, Missouri Athletic Club, 2009.

# Bibliography

## BOOKS

Allen, Maury, with Susan Walker. *Dixie Walker of the Dodgers: The People's Choice.* Tuscaloosa: University of Alabama Press, 2010.

Anderson, Dave. *Pennant Races: Baseball at Its Best.* New York: Doubleday, 1994.

Asinof, Eliot. *Eight Men Out.* New York: Holt, Rinehart and Winston, 1963.

Barrett, James R. *William Z. Foster and the Tragedy of American Radicalism.* Champaign: University of Illinois Press, 2002.

Ben Cramer, Richard. *Joe DiMaggio: The Hero's Life.* New York: Simon and Schuster, 2000.

Berra, Yogi, with Dave Kaplan. *You Can Observe a Lot by Watching.* New York: John Wiley and Sons, 2008.

Borough of Donora, Pa. *Donora Diamond Jubilee, 1901–1976.*

Broeg, Bob. *The Man, Stan: Musial, Then and Now.* St. Louis: Bethany Press, 1977.

Buck, Jack, with Bob Broeg and Bob Rains. *"That's a Winner!"* Champaign, Ill.: Sports Publishing, 2002.

Bukowczyk, John J. *And My Children Did Not Know Me: A History of Polish-Americans.* Bloomington: Indiana University Press, 1987.

Cannadine, David. *Mellon: An American Life.* New York: Knopf, 2006.

Davis, Devra. *When Smoke Ran Like Water.* New York: Basic Books, 2002.

Eig, Jonathan. *Opening Day: The Story of Jackie Robinson's First Season.* New York: Simon and Schuster, 2007.

Falkner, David. *Great Time Coming: The Life of Jackie Robinson, from Baseball to Birmingham.* New York: Simon and Schuster, 1995.

Fetter, Henry D. *Taking on the Yankees.* New York: W. W. Norton, 2003.

Flood, Curt, with Richard Carter. *The Way It Is.* New York: Pocket Books, 1972.

Frick, Ford C. *Games, Asterisks, and People: Memoirs of a Lucky Fan.* New York: Crown, 1973.

Garagiola, Joe. *Just Play Ball.* Flagstaff, Ariz.: Northland, 2007.

Gay, Timothy M. *Satch, Dizzy and Rapid Robert: The Wild Saga of Interracial Baseball Before Jackie Robinson.* New York: Simon and Schuster, 2010.

Gibson, Bob, with Lonnie Wheeler. *Stranger to the Game.* New York: Viking Penguin, 1994.

Gibson, Bob, and Jackson, Reggie, with Lonnie Wheeler. *Sixty Feet, Six Inches: A Hall of Fame Pitcher and a Hall of Fame Hitter Talk About How the Game Is Played.* New York: Doubleday, 2009.

Giglio, James N. *Musial: From Stash to Stan the Man.* Columbia: University of Missouri Press, 2001.

Goldstein, Richard. *Spartan Seasons: How Baseball Survived the Second World War.* New York: Macmillan, 1980.

Golenbock, Peter. *The Spirit of St. Louis: A History of the St. Louis Cardinals and Browns.* New York: Avon, 2000.

Halberstam, David. *October 1964.* New York: Villard, 1994.

Heidenry, John. *The Gashouse Gang.* New York: Public Affairs, 2007.

Heidenry, John, and Topel, Brett. *The Boys Who Were Left Behind: The 1944 World Series Between the Hapless St. Lous Browns and the Legendary St. Louis Cardinals.* Lincoln: University of Nebraska Press.

Howard, Arlene, and Wimbish, Ralph. *Elston and Me: The Story of the First Black Yankee.* Columbia: University of Missouri Press, 2001.

Hunter, Julius. *TV One-on-One.* St. Louis: Gashouse Books, 2008.

James, Bill. *The New Bill James Historical Baseball Abstract.* New York: Free Press, 2001.

———. *The Bill James Historical Baseball Abstract.* New York: Villard, 1986.

Kahn, Roger. *Beyond the Boys of Summer: The Very Best of Roger Kahn.* New York: McGraw-Hill, 1999.

———. *The Era: 1947–1957: When the Yankees, the Giants, and the Dodgers Ruled the World.* New York: Ticknor and Fields, 1993.

Keyes, William, ed. *Historic Site Survey of the Greater Monongahela River Valley.* Pittsburgh: Historical Society of Western Pennsylvania, 1991.

Lansche, Jerry. *Stan the Man Musial: Born to Be a Ballplayer.* Dallas: Taylor, 1994.

Launius, Roger D. *Seasons in the Sun: The Story of Big League Baseball in Missouri.* Columbia: University of Missouri Press, 2002.

Leavy, Jane. *The Last Boy: Mickey Mantle and the End of America's Childhood.* New York: HarperCollins, 2010.

Linn, Ed. *Hitter: The Life and Turmoils of Ted Williams.* New York: Harcourt Brace, 1993.

Lowenfish, Lee. *Branch Rickey: Baseball's Ferocious Gentleman.* Lincoln: University of Nebraska Press, 2007.

Marshall, William. *Baseball's Pivotal Era, 1945–1951.* Lexington: University Press of Kentucky, 1999.

Meyer, Philipp. *American Rust.* New York: Spiegel and Grau, 2009.

Michener, James A. *Pilgrimage: A Memoir of Poland and Rome.* Emmaus, Penn.: Rodale Press, 1990.

———. *Report of the County Chairman.* New York: Random House, 1961.

———. *Sports in America.* New York: Random House, 1976.

Montville, Leigh. *Ted Williams: The Biography of an American Hero.* New York: Doubleday, 2004.

Musial, Stan. *Stan "The Man's" Own Story, as Told to Bob Broeg.* Garden City, N.Y.: Doubleday, 1964.

Oh, Sadaharu, with David Falkner. *A Zen Way of Baseball.* New York: Times Books, 1984.

Piszek, Edward J., with Jake Morgan. *Some Good in the World: A Life of Purpose.* Boulder: University Press of Colorado, 2001.

Rampersad, Arnold. *Jackie Robinson, a Biography.* New York: Knopf, 1997.

Robinson, Ray. *Stan Musial: Baseball's Durable "Man."* New York: G. P. Putnam's Sons, 1963.

*St. Louis Post-Dispatch. Stan Musial: Baseball's Perfect Knight.* St. Louis: St. Louis Post-Dispatch Books, 2010.

Schoendienst, Red, with Rob Rains. *Red: A Baseball Life.* Champaign, Ill.: Sports Publishing, 1998.

Selzer, Steven Michael. *Meet the Real Joe Black: An Inspiring Life, Baseball, Teaching, Baseball.* Giving New York and Bloomington: iUniverse, Inc. 2010.

Serrin, William. *Homestead: The Glory and Tragedy of an American Steel Town.* New York: Times Books, 1992.

Shuba, George, as told to Greg Gulas. *My Memories as a Brooklyn Dodger.* Youngstown, Ohio: George Shuba Family Enterprises, 2007.

Silverman, Herman. *Michener and Me.* Philadelphia: Running Press, 1999.

Smith, Curt. *Voices of Summer: Ranking Baseball's 101 All-Time Best Announcers.* New York: Carroll and Graf, 2005.

———. *Voices of the Games.* New York: Simon and Schuster, 1987.

Snyder, Brad. *A Well-Paid Slave: Curt Flood's Fight for Free Agency in Professional Sports.* New York: Viking Press, 2006.

Stacey, Charles E.; Charlton, Brian; and Lonich, David. *Images of America: Donora.* Charleston, S.C.: Arcadia Publishing, 2010.

Stewart, Wayne. *Stan the Man: The Life and Times of Stan Musial.* Chicago: Triumph Books, 2010.

Sullivan, Frank. *Life Is More Than 9 Innings: Memories of a Boston Red Sox Pitcher.* Honolulu: Editions Limited, 2008.

Toor, Rachel. *The Polish Americans.* New York: Chelsea House, 1988.

Turner, Frederick. *When the Boys Came Back: Baseball and 1946.* New York: Henry Holt, 1996.

Vecsey, George. *Baseball: A History of America's Favorite Game.* New York: Modern Library Chronicles, 2006.

———. *One Sunset a Week: The Story of a Coal Miner.* New York: Saturday Review Press, 1974.

———, ed. *The Way It Was: Great Sports Events from the Past.* New York: McGraw-Hill, 1974.

Vincent, Fay. *The Only Game in Town: Baseball Stars of the 1930s and 1940s Talk About the Game They Loved.* New York: Simon and Schuster, 2006.

————. *We Would Have Played for Nothing: Baseball Stars of the 1950s and 1960s Talk About the Game They Loved.* New York: Simon and Schuster, 2008.

Vivian, Cassandra. *The Mid-Mon Valley.* Charleston, S.C.: Arcadia, 2004.

Wilber, Rick. *My Father's Game.* Jefferson, N.C.: McFarland, 2008.

Williams, Ted, with John Underwood. *My Turn at Bat: The Story of My Life.* New York: Simon and Schuster, 1969.

Wolfe, Thomas. *You Can't Go Home Again.* Garden City, N.Y.: Sun Dial Press, 1934.

## TRANSCRIPTS

A. B. Chandler Oral History Project. University of Kentucky Library, Lexington, Kentucky, 1978. All interviews conducted by William Marshall.

## VIDEOS

Durand, Mark, and Ashley, Thomas, producers. *The Legend of Stan the Man Musial.* 1990.

ESPN. *SportsCentury,* 2000.

MSG Network. *Halls of Fame: Stan Musial.* A Fran Healy Production, 1998.

# Index

Dixie Walker and, 203
Mexican League and, 120
Musial and, 19, 25, 32, 45, 148–49,
150–64, 201
New York and attention paid to, 10
St. Louis Cardinals and, 158, 250
strike by players rumors (1947) and, 45
Shotton and, 76
spiking by Slaughter, 159–61
Robinson, Ray, 39
Rochester, New York, 81
Rochester Red Wings, 81–82
Rockne, Knute, 60
Roe, Preacher, 31
Rongaus, William, 286
Roosevelt, Franklin Delano, 110, 217
Rose, Pete, 5–6, 7, 8, 21, 260
Rosenblatt, Roger, 42
Ross, Roscoe, 45
Rowswell, Rosey, 283
Rush, Bob, 31
Russell, Bill, 334
Russell, James K. "Jimmy," 60, 61, 65,
67, 178
Ruth, Babe, 10, 11, 13, 17, 65, 82, 170,
209

Saigh, Fred, 203–5
blank check stunt with Musial
contract, 204–5
St. Louis, Missouri, 10–11, 89–94. *See
also* Stan Musial and Biggie's
restaurant
1944 (all–St. Louis) World Series, 107
all-girls, all-boys schools in, 195
as baseball town, 10, 11, 89
Browns favored by, 107
Catholic churches in, 194
Forest Park, 127, 189
the Hill, 127, 130, 131, 187
as home of Stan Musial, 12, 90–94,
122, 182–95, 322
literary references and authors from,
92–94
love for Stan Musial in, 7, 89, 111, 286
Oldani's restaurant, 187
Olympic Games in, 91
population, 90
racial issues, 243, 246
Ruggeri's restaurant, 131, 187
song, 90
statues of Stan Musial, 10, 282,
310–13

Union Station, 141, 225, 243
Veiled Prophet's Ball, 259
World's Fair, 1904, 90–91
St. Louis Browns, 30, 95, 97, 104, 107,
116, 145, 202, 216
St. Louis Cardinals, 201. *See also* Musial,
Stan; Rickey, Branch; Sportsman's
Park
1926–1934 pennants and world
championships, 97, 98
1926 pennant, 97
1934 pennant, 86
1941 pennant race, 82, 84–88
1941 season, 11
1942 World Series, 102–3, 287
1943–1944 season, 105
1943 pennant, 106
1943 World Series, 107
1944 pennant, 107
1944 World Series, 107
1946 pennant, 131
1946 playoff with Brooklyn, 3,
131
1946 season, 129–32
1946 World Series, 8, 118, 135–42,
146, 326
1947 strike rumors, over integration,
153–57, 250
1958 Asian trip, 226–27
1961 season, 247, 252–53
1962 season, 253–54, 256
1963 season, 256–60
1964 pennant, 265
1964 season, 264–65
1964 World Series, 265, 308–9
1967 pennant, 276
1967 season, 271–76, 327
1967 World Series, 276
1968 World Series, 278
2002 opening day, 46
2006 World Series, 320
Branch Rickey as advisor, 256–57
Branch Rickey as manager, 95–99,
103, 130, 131
Breadon as owner, 81, 97, 103–4, 123,
124–25, 127–28, 131, 137, 146–47,
183, 203, 204
Britton as owner, 97
Busch as owner, 79, 205, 216–21, 223,
228, 231, 247–48, 249, 256–57, 263,
271, 276–79, 304, 325
cliques on team, 104
decline of, 1950s, 218

## ABOUT THE AUTHOR

GEORGE VECSEY has been a sports columnist for *The New York Times* since 1982. He specializes in international sports, such as the World Cup of soccer, the Tour de France, the Olympics, and Wimbledon, but considers baseball his favorite sport to cover because of the daily soap opera and opportunity to interview players and managers. Vecsey has written a dozen books, including *Coal Miner's Daughter* for Loretta Lynn, later made into an Academy Award–winning movie. A graduate of Jamaica High and Hofstra College, he considers himself a New York boy who has lived in Kentucky and traveled extensively in Europe. He is married to Marianne Graham, an artist, and their three children have all worked in journalism.

## ABOUT THE TYPE

This book was set in Caledonia, a typeface designed in 1939 by William Addison Dwiggins for the Merganthaler Linotype Company. Its name is the ancient Roman term for Scotland, because the face was intended to have a Scotch-Roman flavor. Caledonia is considered to be a well-proportioned, businesslike face with little contrast between its thick and thin lines.